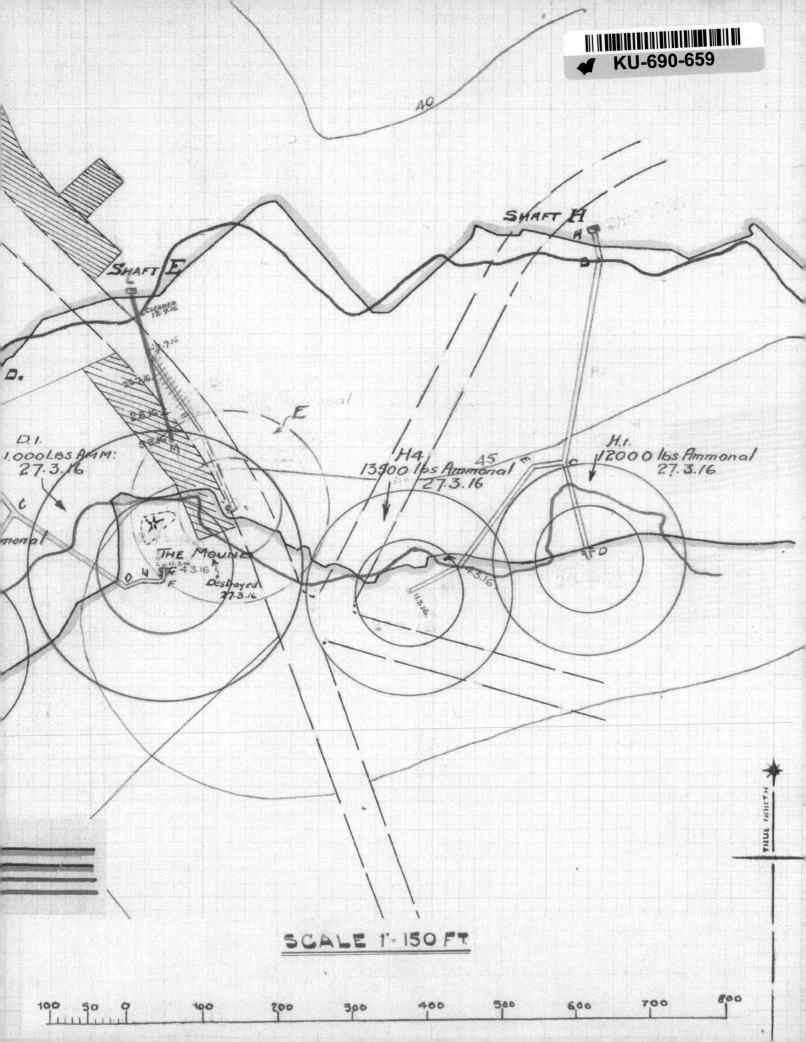

SHAFT H

SHAFT E

D.1.
1,000 LBS AMM:
27.3.16

H4
13500 lbs Ammonal
27.3.16

H.1.
12000 lbs Ammonal
27.3.16

THE MOUND

Destroyed
27.3.16

TRUE NORTH

SCALE 1"- 150 FT.

100   50   0   100   200   300   400   500   600   700   800

BENEATH FLANDERS FIELDS

THE TUNNELLERS'
WAR 1914-1918

BENEATH FLANDERS FIELDS

THE TUNNELLERS' WAR 1914-1918

Peter Barton, Peter Doyle and Johan Vandewalle

SPELLMOUNT

Staplehurst

ENDPAPERS

Front Endpaper:
Map showing the five St Eloi mines blown on 27 March 1916 by 172 Tunnelling Company officers (inset), a seminal date for mine warfare in the Ypres Salient. 'Shaft E' is the origin for the great mine blown on 7 June 1917; the progress of the offensive gallery up to 9 August 1916 can be seen

Rear Endpapers: 1
Plan of the chamber of the St Eloi mine blown on 7 June 1917; 5,800 linear feet of 9"x 3" timber was required to build this structure alone

REAR ENDPAPERS: 2
A segment of a Messines sector trench map showing completed mine schemes, plus others which were progressing. Additional targets are also marked: in Wytschaete Wood, east of Maedelstede (N 24 d 32.61) and at Rag Point, Hop Point and Bone Point. The mine charge which was lost to difficult ground in the Peckham scheme is marked at N 30a 88.93. All three offensive galleries at Peckham are illustrated in Chapter IX. The working marked as 'Van Tunnel' was a deep subway scheme

British Library Cataloguing in Publication Data:
A catalogue record for this book is available
from the British Library

Copyright © Peter Barton, Peter Doyle and Johan Vandewalle 2004
Colour photographs © Johan Vandewalle
Line drawings copyright © Andy Gammon
Maps copyright © Peter Doyle
Design: www.mousematdesign.com

ISBN 1-86227-237-9

Published in the UK in 2004 by
Spellmount Limited
The Village Centre
Staplehurst
Kent TN12 0BJ

Tel: 01580 893730
Fax: 01580 893731
E-mail: enquiries@spellmount.com
Website: www.spellmount.com

1 3 5 7 9 8 6 4 2

Printed and bound in Great Britain

CONTENTS

In memory of Bert Fearns (1898–1997)
Volunteer, tunneller, husband, father,
friend and storyteller
. . . but never Cabinet Minister

Bert Fearns at 18 and 99

PREFACE

THE TUNNELLER
a sketch at Chatham

Everybody damns the Tunneller; GHQ because he invariably has his job finished months before the rest of the Army are ready for the 'Great Push'; Army troops because he invariably upsets all their preconceived notions as to the safety of trenches and dugouts; Divisional troops damn him because he is outside their sphere of influence; Brigade troops because he refuses to move when they do and because he knows by heart that part of the line to which they come as strangers; Brass hats because they dislike his underground habits; Regimental officers because he refuses to allow them to use his deep and snug dugouts; Subalterns because of his superior knowledge; Tommy because he is the direct cause of numerous extra fatigues and – alas that it should be so – because of his extra pay; and last and loudest, the Boche damn him because of his earnest and unceasing attempts at uplifting and converting them into surprised angels. It is also owing to his success in this noble work of the missionary that the Tunneller is highly respected by all branches of the forces.

E Synton, 1918

For over eighty-five years, and despite the passing of a second global war, the battlefields of the Great War of 1914–1918 have remained tranquil. Millions of mourners, tourists, casual visitors, pilgrims even, have visited Ypres and its arc of trenches since the guns fell silent on Armistice Day, 11 November 1918. From the immediate end of the conflict, unemployed officers with memories of battle indelibly locked into their consciousness led parties over the old front lines and rear areas of the Salient, unwittingly contributing to the development of the first burst of mass tourism in history. Over the past twenty-five years, battlefield tourism has become big business in Ypres and its satellite villages, and the First World War has reverted to its original title – the Great War.

Unbeknown to most visitors to the Salient is the vast network of tunnels, subways and dugouts that everywhere lie hidden beneath their feet. They are making their presence felt in a limited way through collapse, a crack in a wall here, a dip in the road there, and apparently benign holes in the middle of fields – clues to an unimagined underground world in which tens of thousands of young men relaxed, laughed, wrote letters home to sweethearts and families, ate and slept, cowered, and fought and died. Some still lie in the ever silent tunnels today.

The war beneath the fields was not reported in the same way as the great battles, Loos, Somme, Arras, Verdun, Passchendaele, but nevertheless it was a crucially important conflict, and contributed materially to the struggle on the surface. It was a peculiar secret war which triggered extraordinary feats of initiative, inventive engineering, creativity, human endeavour, and courage – often by men who were too old to take part in the trench war above. Theirs was a different form of heroism and sacrifice, their war one which was almost divorced from the conflict on the surface, indeed, from the army itself. It has always been deserving of more attention.

This book is a result of many years' labour on the battlefield, underground, and in the archives. Its purpose is simple; to recount the story of the tunnellers in Flanders from 1914–18, and tell it in such a way that the nebulous third dimension of the battlefront – that which lies beneath the battlefields – becomes clear. It examines the development of mine warfare, and its logical re-invention and new expression during the unparalleled siege conditions of the Western Front; through illustration and the words of the participants, it describes why this secret war was fought, what it was like to fight it, and tellingly, of the legacy it has left for future generations.

We alone are responsible for the contents of this book, and for any error and omission. We are, however, grateful to the following individuals who have helped us in our quest for information, and in providing other assistance, both above ground and beneath: Phillipe Acke; Gary Andrews; Donna Baldey; Jeremy Banning; Tom and Bex Barton; Matthew Bennett; Craig Bowen; Martin Brown; Nico Broukaert; Colin Butler; Andre and Simonne Callens; Jane Carmichael; D A Cassels; Rebecca Cheney; Peter and Carolyn Chasseaud; Stefaan Coopman; C H Cowan; Marc Dejocheere; Del De Lorme; Mathieu De Meyer; Marc Dewilde; Julie and James Doyle; Nick Fear; Mick Forsyth; Chris Fowke; Mike and Kate Fox; Mary Freeman; Andy Gammon; Joyce Gillard; Nicholette Goff; Giles Guthrie; Peter Hart; Karen Harvey; Patience Hilton; Andre Hooreweghe; John Howard; Kristof and Anne Jacobs; Alain Jacques; Angela John; Simon Jones; Chris and Liz Lane; Stephen Lee; Didier Lenglaert; Guy Lucas; Roy Macleod; Laurie Milner; Alan Moore; Anne Morgan; Gerald Napier; Steve O'Grady; Neil Oliver; Phillippe Oosterlynck; David Parry; Ian Passingham; Paul Peppiate; Tony Pollard; Hilary Roberts; Andy Robertshaw; Simon Robbins; Phillip Robinson; Ted Rose; Mike Rosenbaum; Rik Ryon; Luc Salomez; Nick Saunders; Guido Scharre; Roni Schnable; Wilf Schofield; Geoffrey Smith; William Spencer; Nigel Steel; Ross Thomas; Brian Todd; Joris Van Acker; Jan Vancoillie; Paul Van Damme; Richard Van Emden; Patrick Van Wanzeele; Diederik Vyncke; Kate Wade; Beverley Williams; Jamie and Bev Wilson; Barbara Woodward; and the staff of The Anchor, Faversham for the foaming ale and excellent lunches. We also thank the Imperial War Museum, the Royal Engineers' Museum and Library, and the Manchester Museum, for permission to reproduce certain photographs, maps and plans; Marc Dewilde, Mathieu de Meyer and Pedro Pype of the Instituut voor het Archeologisch Patrimonium (IAP) for their assistance with archaeological investigations; BACTEC International, Rochester, for geophysical support; and the staff of the Public Record Office (now National Archives) for their help with our research. Extracts from the diaries of Frank Hurley are by kind permission of the Australian War Memorial, which holds the original documents in its collection. We would like to thank the following landowners for permission to work on their property: Frans Aernoudt, Eric Boussery, Maurice Cappoen, Andre Dejonckheere, Gerard Devos, Bernard de Tavernier, Itienne van Cayseele, Willy Vermeulen. However, this book could not have been contemplated without the support, experience, knowledge and patience of Maggie Lindsay Roxburgh, curator of the wonderful Royal Engineers' Library – our eternal gratitude goes to her. New (non-map) line illustrations are copyright Andy Gammon, 2003; all colour photographs are copyright Johan Vandewalle. We have attempted to obtain permission to reproduce illustrations and where necessary, text quotations. Where this has not been possible, we would be happy to hear from the copyright holder.

Peter Barton
Peter Doyle
Johan Vandewalle

Vlaanderen,
January 2004

Authors' note

Throughout the pages of this book we have retained the convention of using the French spelling of towns, villages and geographical features; these are now more properly signposted in Flemish, but to most of the armies fighting in Flanders Ypres – 'Y', 'Yeepree' or 'Wipers' to the British – would be more easily recognisable than its more correct modern equivalent of Ieper. Punctuation in diary and letter extracts is as seen in the original documents.

We have used metric measurements in our own descriptions and discussions; imperial measurements, the standard of the day in 1914, are retained without translation in original quotes. For reference, one yard is equivalent to 0.91 metres and one inch, 2.54 centimetres. British tunnels and dugouts were built to standard imperial measurements; where given in our own text the appropriate metric equivalent is provided.

Abbreviations

AEMMBC – Australian Electrical, Mechanical, Mining and Boring Company
Bde – Brigade
BEF – British Expeditionary Force
Btn – Battalion
Cpl – Corporal
CO – Commanding Officer
Coy – Company
CRE – Commander, Royal Engineers
CQMS – Company Quartermaster Sergeant
CSM – Company Sergeant Major
DCM – Distinguished Conduct Medal
DSO – Distinguished Service Order
E in C – Engineer in Chief
GHQ – General Headquarters
HQ – Headquarters
HLI – Highland Light Infantry
Lt – Lieutenant
2 Lt – Second Lieutenant
MC – Military Cross

MEBU – Mannschafts Eisenbeton Unterstände
MG – Machine gun
MM – Military Medal
MO – Medical Officer
NCO – Non Commissioned Officer
OC – Officer Commanding
OP – Observation Post
Pte – Private
QM – Quartermaster
RA – Royal Artillery
RAMC – Royal Army Medical Corps
RE – Royal Engineers
RFC – Royal Flying Corps
SAA – Small arms ammunition
Sgt – Sergeant
SME – School of Military Engineering
TC – Tunnelling Company
TM – Trench mortar
VC – Victoria Cross

INTRODUCTION

It is interesting to think what a section of one of these trenches will look like when dug up in years to come by some research party. Dead British, German and French soldiers, rifles, equipment, bully beef, biscuits, Tickler's jam – all mixed up with wood, straw and mud, and forming various strata.

Lieutenant W Congreve,
3rd Battalion, Rifle Brigade,
Ypres, 19 December 1914

These words describe the British trenches at Petit Bois below the village of Wytschaete, near Ypres, in Belgium. They are prophetic, recognising before the first Christmas of the war that the confrontation was to be a long and bitter struggle; a struggle that would leave a lasting legacy, inscribed in both the strata of Flanders and so deeply in human memory. Congreve's concept of an indelible record which would be pored over by future research teams in an attempt to decipher the events and conditions of his battles betrays how symbolic the landscape of Flanders had already become to those serving there, after only four months of fighting.

Ypres, a small but attractive mediaeval city now more commonly known by its Flemish name of Ieper, was to become the hub of action in Belgian Flanders. To the armies of the Great War, Belgian, French, British, German, and many others from the continents of North America, Australasia, Asia and Africa, it represented a precious jewel or a coveted prize, and was contested passionately during almost five years of bitter conflict. Never lost by the Allies, it was the centrepiece of four major battles and many more minor actions. Overlooked on three sides by the Passchendaele Ridge, the city was almost permanently shell swept; British names such as 'Hellfire Corner' give an indication of life during daylight hours. Outside the city walls, elaborate trench systems were developed that followed the arcuate form of the higher ground to the north, east and south, on a trace which almost embraced the town. These trenches formed what became known as the Ypres Salient; a huge, curving, forward bulge in the British lines which allowed the Germans to direct a semi-circle of fire down on the defenders within its arc.

The Salient – 'the Immortal Salient' as it became known after the war – was to the British what Verdun was to become for the French nation – a symbol of freedom, and the most symbolic battlefield of the Western Front. Winston Churchill was even to suggest that Ypres be left in ruins as a testament to commitment and sacrifice. With a resurgence of interest in the Great War in recent decades, 'the Salient' has once again become a site of mass 'pilgrimage'. The Menin Gate, the primary memorial to the missing with its portal looking towards a road along which millions of men had to pass to reach the front, is its focal point.

In the decades since 1918, the battlefields of the Salient have been reclaimed. The plough and bulldozer have together groomed away most of the evident scars of warfare that Billy Congreve saw. Of the colossal number of earthworks which once disfigured the fields of Flanders, only a handful now remain – a sad situation for the ever-growing numbers of visitors anxious to experience a taste of authentic battleground. In today's Salient new roads, factories, and agricultural buildings arrest and distract the eye, and with yet more new highways planned to slice through the old battlefields in the coming years, the region is becoming more and more like parts of southeast England, where the throbbing resonance of the internal combustion engine is ever present. To the eyes of the uninformed the landscape of battle has long since become unrecognisable.

Underground, however, it is a different tale. Here, just beneath the rich Flemish soil, history is still very tangible; go deeper still and in many places it is complete in every detail, precisely as the soldiers left it at the beginning of the Advance to Victory in late 1918, and in such a state of preservation as to allow the reconstruction of the 'social history' of the war beneath the surface in such fine detail that the old workings can almost be repopulated. Tunnels and subways, dugouts and galleries have been left untouched, forgotten as the war swept on from Ypres towards its conclusion. These are eerie, dangerous places to dwell, and in many cases their existence is being revealed through decay and collapse. All the armies which laboured in Ypres and the Flanders plains were involved; indeed tunnels were dug wherever trench systems developed during the Great War. But this book is about Flanders, and particularly the work of British, Australian and Canadian military miners and engineers – often collectively and proudly known as the Corps of Royal Engineers, RE, or just sappers – and the *Pioniere* of the German armies that opposed them. We have tried to tell the story as far as possible in their own words. They were indeed the most versatile of soldiers.

Recounting the story of tunnels and dugouts is fraught with other less obvious dangers. The conflict was so secret, and the personnel involved so secretive that personal reminiscences and diaries are rare. Official accounts of actions were, apart from technical detail, often brief and lacking the dash and 'colour' of infantry escapades. Britain's official military historian, Brigadier-General Sir James Edmonds (an RE officer himself), struggled at times to gather definitive information even of renowned tunnelling actions, his preferred solution being to appeal to ex-sappers through the correspondence columns of the *Royal Engineers Journal* and *The Sapper*, hoping to benefit from direct personal memories rather than official documents to fill in missing data. His 'begging' letters were usually headed 'Troubles of an Official Historian'.

The engineers effectively dictated the way the whole war was conducted, and their contribution was so vast and varied that it would take a lifetime to recount in full. This is illustrated by a conspicuous omission from the series of British publications entitled *The Work of the RE in the European War 1914–1919*, a set of volumes produced in the 1920s. So great was the task of compilation that no one could be found who was willing to write a 'Fieldworks' volume to complement those on *Military Mining*, *Geological Work*, *Water Supply*, *Supply of Stores and Equipment*, and so on. It has often been surmised that had Edmonds not been engaged on the mammoth task of writing the official history – a sign outside his office in Whitehall stated 'Visitors are warned that any time wasted in frivolous conversation may delay the completion of the Official History' – he might well have been tempted by *Fieldworks*. Fortunately, two volumes of the Royal Engineer Series, *Military Mining* and *Geological Work*, exist to provide a basis for the RE's war beneath Flanders' fields, the rest of the mountain of data is distributed throughout myriad official war diaries and reports and notes.

Fewer than one percent of the front line forces were employed in underground work during the war. The conflict was far too secret for anything but the scantest details to be known during hostilities, and in the initial flood of reminiscences published soon after the Armistice it is therefore unsurprising that so few were by tunnellers. Books, essays, articles and papers on underground work remain relatively rare, although a slow drip of precious material continues to emanate from family archives as books and films illuminate the story. As for books there are two recognised British classics in the field: *Tunnellers* by W Grant Grieve and Bernard Newman, and *War Underground* by Alexander Barrie. Neither could be written today as the testimonies of the men who served beneath the battlefields of the Western Front are no longer available to detail and colour what was one of the most veiled conflicts in the history of warfare.

Published in 1936, *Tunnellers* was produced in honour of Grieve's tunnelling comrades, with the poignant dedication 'To Those Who Stayed Underground'. Grieve wrote from personal experience, and his book pays particular attention to technical detail, and is consequently not really for those without an elementary grasp of mining methods and terminology. It is, however, essential reading if a deeper understanding of the work of the military tunneller is required. Sandy Barrie's *War Underground* on the other hand, first published in 1962, is much more of the modern mould and aimed at a general audience. Barrie was not versed in mining ways, and therefore made sure to provide accessible descriptions relying heavily upon his many interviews with tunnellers – which, in a different way, we too have done. His eminently readable work rattles along, skilfully managing to avoid repetitive episodes, which is not an easy task when most of the activity takes place in almost exactly the same environment. Blending these two books produces an excellent text history. However, despite Barrie's vivid descriptions, many readers might find that it is still difficult to conjure an image of the environment of this bizarre conflict in the mind's eye, and the true nature of the tunnelling war consequently remains hard to fully understand. The keys, we believe, are illustrations combined with direct personal testimony.

In producing this book we have relied on four principal sources: the tunnels and dugouts we have seen and documented with our own eyes; published accounts such as those of Grieve and Barrie, Edmonds' official works, and many other war, unit and formation histories; war diaries, official documents and original maps and plans; unpublished accounts, and direct personal reminiscences – contributions, wherever possible, from the words of the sappers and tunnellers themselves. For those who wish to delve further, a great deal more detailed information can be gleaned from the list of references at the back of the book. As far as possible we have set out to cover the most important aspects of the tunnellers' work, animating everyday lives and revealing the sheer scale of their achievements beneath the fields of Flanders in their own words, and in previously unpublished maps, plans, photographs and sketches. Sandy Barrie's priceless interview transcripts for *War Underground*, preserved in the archives of the Royal Engineers' Museum, have formed a textual 'core' alongside diaries and accounts from the RE Library at Chatham; Johan Vandewalle's astonishing photographs, taken during fifteen years of underground investigations, are the heart of the book.

The book commences with the outbreak of war in Flanders and the development of the Salient, and the tactical imperative of returning to the ancient arts of sapping and mining, practices which have been employed in every century except perhaps the present. The history of military mining is concisely set out, before the underground war in its most modern incarnation is explained and recounted.

Chapter I

FLANDERS FIELDS: THE YPRES SALIENT

Do you know the terrain of Flanders? The trench lines weaved their way over long and gently rolling ridges, through shallow depressions and across wide expanses of almost flat countryside. In the rich alluvial and sedimentary deposits forming the upper strata of earth and clay, water collected in the trenches, especially in the winter, and even more so in the mine galleries, initially only one or two metres below the surface and later four metres deep, progressively transforming them into quagmires.

Oberstleutnant Otto Füsslein,
Kommandeur des Mineure,
4th German Army

Flanders is a region of Europe that has been fought over for centuries. Predominantly a low-lying plain, it stretches from the chalk uplands of Artois and Picardy in northern France to the coastal strip of sand dunes between Dunkirk and Ostend. French Flanders incorporates the coal-fields of Loos and Lens, also to be bludgeoned by the Great War, whilst Belgian Flanders, running from the French border to the North Sea, is a centre of hop production giving the country its fame for beer, its coastal estuaries their fame for mussels. Squeezed between the rugged Ardennes mountains and the North Sea, Flanders has throughout history been the main route for countless invading and retreating armies intent on east-west movement, and vice versa.

The region is divisible into belts of simple geology. From a military viewpoint these are critical. For millennia, the extensive dune belt has protected the flat and very low lying terrain

inland of the dunes – the Polders – from flooding, a fact that military engineers have taken full advantage of in the past. From the twelfth century the town of Nieuport situated on the edge of the Polders, had been successfully defended by inundation – deliberate flooding – five times between 1488 and 1677, on one occasion holding out against Louis XIV for no less than five years.

Inland from the Polders, the ground slowly begins to rise. Gently and almost imperceptibly the zone of potential inundation gives way to the 'wet Flanders plain', a region which is founded on the *Argile dc Flandres*, Flanders clay. Of exactly the same composition as the clay beneath London, both were formed in a geolog-

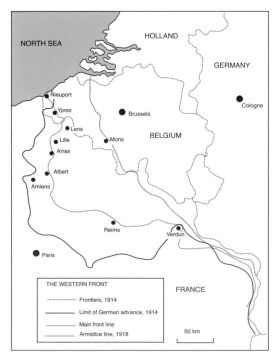

The trench lines of the Western Front as they lay between 1914-1918

13

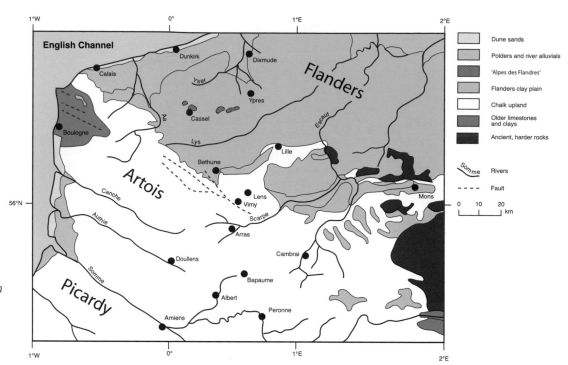

The basic geology of the British sectors of the Western Front showing the delineation between clay and chalk areas

ical age named after the town of Ypres – the Ypresian. Both are also naturally impervious, confining all rainwater close to the surface. Consequently, drainage from the flat and fertile fields of Flanders is slow, and to describe the soils during wet periods as 'heavy going' is more than an understatement. Canals, culverts, ponds and moated farms abound, and the local population has derived water from these natural and man-made features for centuries. Ironically beneath the bed of Flanders clay is a deep, untapped layer of fine sands filled with pure water prevented from moving upwards to the surface by the same clay barrier that blocks percolation downwards. It is an often ignored fact that during the Great War some of the swamp-like conditions for which the battlefields became renowned were created not only by the destruction of drains and streams on the surface, but also by the piercing of the deeper clay layer by huge ground-penetrating shells, allowing water under pressure to be forced upwards from depth, adding to surface flooding and the nightmare conditions of battle. To farmer and soldier alike, water has been a bugbear in Flanders for millennia: how to shelter from it, how to supply it for man, beast and machine, and how to get rid of it.

Situated upon the clay plain close to the Yser river, and nestling against the low slopes of the Passchendaele Ridge, lies the town of Ypres. As the wealthy centre of the European cloth trade until the end of the sixteenth century,

Ypres had played shuttlecock to forces from across Europe and beyond for many centuries, each invader keen to annex her great wealth. The British had been regular visitors, sometimes in defence, sometimes in attack. In the fourteenth century the Bishop of Norwich besieged the town, almost starving the inhabitants to death; in 1658 the forces of Oliver Cromwell captured Ypres whilst fighting alongside the French against Spain; in 1793 the Duke of York passed through during yet another struggle in

The Passchendaele Ridge system: the controlling topographical feature of the Ypres Salient

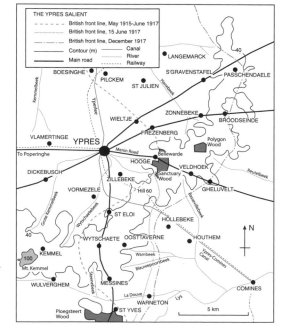

Flanders – nearby Mont Kemmel was the hill which the 'Grand Old Duke' marched his men up and down. In a more benign visitation during the Hundred Days War which culminated at Waterloo, British military engineers surveyed and strengthened dozens of existing fortifications throughout the Low Countries, and Ypres and many other fortified settlements benefited from a limited reconstruction of their defences.

The evenness of the clay plain around the city is broken by a complex of low lying hills of clay and sand that have been sculpted over millennia by the action of lazy streams draining down to major waterways such as the Yser and Lys rivers. Forming part of a chain known euphemistically as *Les Alpes de Flandres*, few are more than fifty metres high, while others reach a breathtaking altitude of around a hundred metres. They are composed of strata collectively known as the Paniselian, named after Mont Panisel near Mons. Importantly, the subtle but complex geological make-up of the ridges includes a substantial percentage of sand – a naturally more free draining material than the heavy soil of the clay plain below. Particularly important among *Les Alpes* is the Passchendaele Ridge. Its numerous streams – *beeks* – break its profile into distinctive spurs such as the Messines, Pilckem, Westhoek and Broodseinde ridges – names which would become indelibly engraved into the bloody history of not only the Flanders region but the whole world by 1918. The ridges provide a range of panoramic viewpoints over what is otherwise a relatively featureless landscape – a landscape perfect for manoeuvring large bodies of troops. Since before Roman times the apparently quiet, timeless, rural Flemish idyll has been a battleground; not for nothing did it earn the nineteenth century title of the 'Cockpit of Europe'.

THE COMING OF WORLD WAR

Belgium was not even a hundred years old when war came in 1914. The peoples of West Flanders however, were used to change, and although peace had reigned since the birth of their nation there was no reason to believe that this new European war would be any different from all the others which had come and gone over many centuries: the Flemish peoples and culture would continue to survive somehow. One thing was certain: it was sure to be a mobile affair, everybody said so, and if the invader did happen to come their way, as history indicated, he would pass swiftly through *en route* for the coast.

As the war burst onto the world stage, the Germans enacted a variation of the Schlieffen Plan, a scheme planned some years before which envisaged action against France in the west before tackling Russia in the east. Like so many armies before them, Germany had read the terrain carefully and chosen to follow the northern route through Belgium into France to avoid more inhospitable locations farther south: the wooded uplands of the Ardennes, a string of fortresses from Belfort to Epinal and Toul to Verdun, the Vosges mountains and, practically on the Swiss border, the great fortress of Belfort itself. For the opening offensive in August 1914 it was established that a small German force would defend and if necessary retire in these well-protected southern sectors, whilst in the north an army six times as strong would seek a lightning envelopment of the enemy, employing a great anti-clockwise wheeling movement revolving around the hub of Metz. Their target was Paris, and a swift French capitulation. After France had fallen Germany would turn her full attention upon Russia, a nation with almost unlimited manpower, but one, it was assumed, that would take a long time to mobilise. Indeed, Flanders was looked upon as a theatre of secondary importance, and protestations from young Belgium were to be brushed aside.

In July 1914 the Belgians were well aware of the growing danger and had mobilised their army – totalling 150,000 men – accordingly. In pursuance of the Schlieffen Plan, in just thirteen days the Germans had mobilised 1.6 million troops to fight in the Western Theatre. They concentrated four formidable armies on the Belgian frontier, and on the night of 3 August 1914 intelligence reports suggested that an attack was about to take place. They advanced on 4 August with two cavalry divisions crossing the border, effectively signalling the commencement of hostilities on what was to become known as the Western Front – and at the same time guaranteeing a British Imperial involvement.

THE OPENING MOVES

Until Allied assistance arrived to drive the invader out, the Belgians felt quite confident and able to depend upon her well-developed system of fortified towns with many outlying 'detached' forts, to hold back, or at least hold up, the enemy advance. The immense fortress systems were carefully designed and comprehensive, and had been updated in recent decades by the addition

An 'outwork' at Liège. A typical example of modern Belgian home defence in 1914

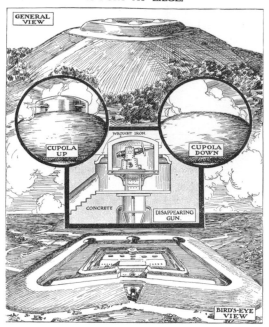

A FORT AT LIÉGE.

GENERAL VIEW

CUPOLA UP

WROUGHT IRON.

CUPOLA DOWN

CONCRETE

DISAPPEARING GUN.

BIRD'S-EYE VIEW

of ferro-concrete to the ancient stone-built defences. But they were simply no match for Germany's modern artillery. On 17 August, having come under intense and heavy shellfire from massive howitzers, the Liège forts were the first to fall. The next day King Albert of Belgium ordered his army into its first retirement, hoping to reach the relative safety of the vast Antwerp fort system. In less than three weeks after the first German soldier had set foot over the border, Brussels had fallen and half of Belgium was under enemy occupation. On 24 August the Germans crossed the French border, thrusting into the Champagne region, and on the same day the Belgians were forced to evacuate Namur, another great fortress town upon which high hopes had been placed. Its garrison too fell back on Antwerp.

The British Expeditionary Force (BEF) – then a small army of highly trained regular troops – went into action near Mons on Saturday 22 August and pushed forward counter-attacks. Encouraged by the stiff fighting both there and on the Sambre river, the Belgian General Staff ordered localised sorties in the form of counter-attacks outside Antwerp, but the actions were short-lived. When news of the beginnings of an Allied retreat at Mons arrived, the Belgian cavalry once more slipped back to the dubious shelter of the ancient city. By the end of August the French had also been forced to abandon Lille

and Soissons, Laon, Craonne, Maubeuge and Reims, and on 3 September German cavalry were within thirteen kilometres of Paris.

The situation looked bleak for Belgium, France and Britain, but farther south a spectacular reversal in fortune was about to take place. Between 5 and 10 September at the Battle of the Marne, the Germans were unexpectedly forced into retreat, with the battlefront eventually coming to a standstill along the line of the Aisne river. To great rejoicing, Reims was retaken by the French. Then the sector deadlocked. The seeds of the Western Front were fast being sown as both sides began extending their lines northwards in a series of unsuccessful attempts to outflank each other. As the line inexorably lengthened, doors of tactical opportunity began to close; soon there would be no flanks left to turn. To achieve their final ambitions the Germans were forced to look as far north as was physically possible – to the Belgian coast.

By 17 September the entire Belgian Army lay within Antwerp's ring of magnificent forts. The Germans brought up super-heavy artillery and mortars, planning a traditional old fashioned siege, and knowing full well after the victories at Namur and Liège that the fortifications would not survive the pounding of their guns – at Antwerp, with any luck, the Belgian army could be eliminated from the war altogether. The great German howitzers roared into action on 28 September. Inside the city walls the authorities, both civil and military, having already witnessed the destruction wreaked elsewhere by the massive weapons, were left in little doubt of their fate: if even a remnant of their army was to be saved, the forts and the city would have to be abandoned. The decision to retire was swiftly made, and the coastal town of Ostend was chosen as the next refuge. By 10 October the whole of the Belgian Army had crept away bit by bit, night by night, until Antwerp was left undefended. The Mayor had no choice but to capitulate; the city had fallen to a force one-third the size of its defending garrison.

The war was now but nine weeks old, three-quarters of Belgium had fallen, and its army had been reduced from 150,000 to 82,000 men. By falling back on Ostend it was hoped that with Allied assistance another stand could be made to secure western Flanders, but at this time British reinforcements were only just disembarking at St Omer, and the left wing of the French force was still over ninety kilometres away at Arras. Without assistance, Ostend too was seen to be untenable; there was no choice but to retreat yet farther to the Yser river – and wait.

By 15 October, with the fighting in the south dying down, the French were drawing closer. They had pushed their front north to La Bassée, not far from the Belgian border, and the British 7th Infantry Division and 3rd Cavalry Division had arrived at last to take up positions in front of Ypres, on the right of the Belgians. The front lines now stretched from the Argonne to the North Sea, but nowhere were they strong enough to withstand piercing by a concerted attack. All the signs were that a massive German effort would shortly be made to crash through the ever deteriorating northernmost coastal sector to capture the Channel ports and then sweep southwards and eastwards towards Paris. An enfeebled Belgian Army, holding the sector from Ypres to the sea, was all that lay in their path.

THE YSER

In mid-October 1914 the Belgian lines followed the route of the Yser river and Yperlee canal for thirty-five kilometres from Nieuport to Boesinghe, a small village just north of Ypres. From a defensive viewpoint the positions were good. The river was twenty metres wide with embankments on both sides. Between Nieuport and Dixmude it ran through the Polders: flat as a billiard table and only a metre or two above sea level, its main features apart from the river were man-made: a canalised tributary of the Yser feeding water-borne traffic to and from Ypres, and a two-metre high embankment on top of which ran the railway line serving the coast.

The river failed to stop the German assault; by 26 October, after a week of repeated thrusts, the battered remnants of the Belgian Army had been forced from its banks. They retired to the last real but feeble obstacle in Flanders: the Nieuport–Dixmude railway embankment. The position was now as critical as at any time since 4 August. To make matters worse the Belgian artillery had been reduced to 100 rounds of ammunition per field gun, and Allied reinforcements were still unavailable. With their main body of troops massing with the French for a joint counter-offensive astride the Lys in northern France, the British dared not weaken their already meagre defences around Ypres by sending men to help in the Yser sector.

With the situation approaching breaking point the Belgians now placed their trust in one of the most ancient of military tactics: inundation, a highly effective method of slowing or

blocking an advance by flooding the potential battlefield. On 22 October 1914 a small-scale inundation of about four square kilometres stemmed a determined German advance – at Nieuport, a town which had seen it all before. This small success, and the long-awaited arrival of a small French force, spurred Belgian military engineers to extend the scheme: to flood far more land than had ever been necessary in the past five hundred years.

Apart from the Yser river, the Polderlands to the south of Nieuport were criss-crossed by two other water systems: a series of navigable canals and a complex network of drainage ditches and evacuation canals which displaced excess rain and seawater during wet periods and also irrigated the land in summer. The key to the entire labyrinthine water system was a complex of locks and sluices on the tidal section of the Yser in the heart of Nieuport. It was these locks that maintained the fine balance of water levels over tens of thousands of hectares of Polder land. But inundation was not just a case of opening all the valves at once and hoping for the best; whilst desperately seeking to flood the greatest area in the shortest time to halt the German advance, it was equally imperative that the Belgians kept their own defensive positions dry.

Having made the decision to inundate, it soon became clear that there was a serious problem: the Belgian Army were entirely unacquainted with the lock, sluice and drainage systems both at Nieuport itself and in the surrounding area. What was needed was local knowledge – but most of the inhabitants of the region had already fled. With incredible good

The man who helped save the Channel ports and in so doing played a key role in the creation of the Western Front: Nieuport lock-keeper Henri Geeraerts

The inundated Polderlands photographed from Nieuport on 5 June 1915; the waters are confined to the north side of the Nieuport-Dixmude railway by the embankment

fortune an old Nieuport lock-keeper was traced; he advised the Belgian Army which gates and sluices to open and close, and when and where to build barriers to contain the resulting flood. On 29 October, when the coastal sector defences were hanging on by a thread, the sluices of the old Furnes canal were opened by Belgian engineers, allowing the rising North Sea tide to charge through, flow around the town of Nieuport to the south and burst out across the Polder plain. Over a period of three nights, under shellfire, the sluices were opened at high tide and closed during the ebb. Water seethed out across the lowlands, and was unable to return. The lock-keeper had also identified twenty-two critical drainage culverts beneath the Nieuport–Dixmude railway embankment. These were firmly sealed, restricting the rising waters to its north side – the direction of the invasion. As the waters rose, the Germans strove desperately to break through before their route was

decisively blocked. Against all odds, the Belgians prevailed – the coastal route to the Channel ports had been closed.

The inundations eventually formed a huge shallow sea reaching fifteen kilometres inland to Dixmude and covering thousands of hectares. Waist deep, it would become a permanent feature for the remainder of the war, ruling out all hope of further major hostile offensives across the Polders. The Germans, dismayed but undeterred, made the only tactical move possible by shifting farther inland; accordingly, the inundations were also further extended by flooding part of the sector between Dixmude and Ypres. The waters now lapped against the edge of the Ypresian clay plain itself, enhancing the defensive barrier of the canalised Yser river which connected the two towns. With every bridge destroyed and no physical means at hand to cross the canal, it was enough of an obstacle to force the Germans, still resolute in the quest for victory before winter, to

French troops in primitive 1914 trenches before the formation of the Ypres Salient

push yet farther inland to the south – towards Ypres – beyond the edge of the Polders and onto the plain where the first gentle ridges swelled from its uniform smoothness. Here, the Germans knew that inundation was impossible, but with every passing day it was becoming a narrower sector in which to fight; south of Ypres the French were reinforcing and securing the front between the Franco–Belgian border and La Bassée, so as winter approached the sole remaining battleground now lay between the French town of Armentières fourteen kilometres to the south of Ypres and Boesinghe, three kilometres north. Liège, Namur, Brussels, Antwerp, Ostend – all had fallen. The next target was clear: Ypres. And it was the last chance for a German victory in 1914.

THE FIRST BATTLE OF YPRES

YPRES! It is not easy to convey what this word meant to the British Army. It was a symbol – as Verdun was to the French – of the tenacity of the race, of the certainty of victory.

C J Macgrath, 1920

German troops had already closely examined Ypres before the first battles took place there. Having dropped a few shells into the market place to announce their imminent arrival, and quell any thoughts of resistance amongst the locals, they had actually been in full possession of the town as early as 7 October 1914. After this fateful day it was not until October 1918 that the beleaguered city would at last lie beyond the range of German guns. In 1914 twenty thousand troops had marched in, forced the people to pay a levy of 75,000 francs, and sent out reconnaissance parties towards neighbouring Poperinghe. It was when these scouts returned to report approaching British forces that the Germans chose not to continue their subjugation. Having

been in occupation for three days they left, marching out to take up temporary residence on the slopes of the Passchendaele Ridge overlooking the town and its road and rail routes to the north, south and east. The gently undulating spurs which spread finger-like from the ridge were soon to become intimately known to a generation of young men from a dozen nations: Pilckem, Frezenberg, Bellewaarde, Broodseinde, Messines, Westhoek. The part they were to play in the First Battle of Ypres – and indeed the whole of the war – was crucial.

There was no doubt that German forces were still rightly confident of victory despite their setbacks on the Aisne and Yser: they knew how hard hit the French and Belgians had been during the first few months of war, and how small were the British supporting forces arriving in the sector. Drawing reserve troops from other parts of the front they doubled their fighting strength in front of Ypres. In the knowledge that road and rail communications in northern France were excellent, they believed that if the enemy could be defeated here the Channel ports and the Pas de Calais – and perhaps Paris itself – might still be theirs in time for Christmas. Further encouragement was derived from the knowledge that the British had suffered severe losses to their small professional army, especially during the Mons battle and retreat, and had no immediate reserves to call upon.

My recollection is of a damnably long, wearying bewildering trek in the wrong direction, punctuated by periods of intense unpleasantness and a huge mass of indigestible rumours. Maps were non-existent; we had only been issued with maps for an advance, and we soon walked off those! For many days the Company map was a French motor touring map, which I was fortunate enough to 'borrow' from an unlucky refugee motorist. I don't think I am in any way exaggerating when I say that no junior regimental officer had any real idea as to what was happening. The general impression was that, for some reason, the enemy was always round our flanks, that he had far greater numbers of men and machine-guns and heavier artillery. This outflanking business always meant getting out of nasty situations; it ended abruptly on September 6th; to us, at the time, it seemed quite unexplainable. We lived without information, fed on rumour, so I don't think it is incorrect to state that the regimental officer who took part in the retreat really knew least about it all.

Lieutenant B K Young,
7th Field Company, RE

Reinforcements from the now calmed Somme and Aisne sectors were known to be arriving daily in the northern battlegrounds, but the German numerical superiority still looked overwhelming. A better opportunity for victory was unlikely to present itself, and to fail now would mean waiting until the following spring to launch another offensive; it could be guaranteed that by then large numbers of fresh troops drawn from British territories worldwide would have arrived at the front. And there was another fear: without a final victory in Flanders the Germans might also be faced with the possibility of heavy fighting on two widely separated fronts – against Russia to the east and France and Belgium to the west; such a complication had to be avoided at all costs, so no postponement to the Ypres offensive would be allowed. Besides, the Kaiser himself expected a decisive victory before Christmas. At home, German newspapers boldly trumpeted that the advance on Paris might have been delayed but the 'March on Calais' was about to begin - and the 'March on Warsaw' would follow.

And so, on 19 October the German army streamed down towards Ypres. Although the outnumbered British were too weak to stand their ground in the last act of open warfare on the Western Front for almost four years, every available man took part in a scrambling and often confused defence, fighting alongside the French, stopping gaps, skirmishing through woods, fighting from hedgerow to hedgerow and farm to farm, whilst all the time dropping back closer and closer to Ypres. This grinding, exhausting and desperate mêlée was the First Battle of Ypres – and within it the great German offensive withered and wasted away. The enemy force may have been numerically superior, but many were troops who had been trained in haste, for a meagre six weeks, before being thrown into battle; at Ypres they met a small but highly professional force of British regulars, well led, and even in defence inculcated with the spirit of the offensive. In Germany First Ypres was to become known as the *Kindermorde* – the Massacre of the Innocents.

When the fighting eventually subsided on 22 November, the old British Expeditionary Force had been almost destroyed, half of its establishment were dead or wounded, and their French Allies had suffered equal losses. As for Germany, she emerged from the battle a whole army lighter, and the colossal casualty lists ruled out further action for the moment. Time was no longer on anyone's side. As the grip of winter closed upon the land, the first stabilisation and

Ypres from Passchendaele. The German view from Passchendaele brewery in April 1915 illustrating the immense observational value of holding the ridge tops

definition of the trench lines began, as exhausted troops put down their rifles, took up the modest spade and began to dig. Unknown to the world the war of movement was over, and in the mud, snow and frost of a Flanders winter the foundations for the greatest siege in military history were being laid.

Perhaps out of a sense of frustration the German artillery began the process of the total ruination of Ypres from their ridge-top vantage points. The Germans were clear in their intentions: the struggle was not over yet; until they could regroup and push home the next offensive the hold on the amphitheatre of ridges would not be lost; beneath the enemy gaze the British too determined that not even a square metre of ground held by the BEF and their Allies at that time would be relinquished. By Christmas, the Ypres Salient, a fifteen-kilometre, sickle-shaped sweep from Boesinghe in the north to Ploegsteert in the south, had been born. For the next four years blood would be daily shed somewhere within its boundaries.

THE FIRST WINTER – THE SLIDE INTO STAGNATION

The British Expeditionary Force, with the help of French and Belgian Allies, could indeed be satisfied and proud that the German onslaught had been brought to a standstill in the face of massive odds, but the old Force was become a mere spectre of its former self. It now faced a Flemish winter in primitive trenches and hastily prepared field fortifications.

The weather, ground conditions and an appalling lack of equipment conspired to make life wretched for the men in the line in front of Ypres, but the situation was made infinitely worse by the denial of permission to withdraw even a few metres to drier ground; the troops were ordered to hold the positions from which the last enemy attack had been fought off, regardless of their tactical suitability.

For the next week we were on night-wiring in front of Ploegsteert Wood and St Yves. Winter had really set in and the infantry had even greater difficulties to contend with in the awful and all-pervading mud – many of them were still wearing the pre-war pattern shoe and spat; the mud just sucked these off at every step. I remember seeing two men bending down and start lifting a stretcher with a wounded man – all that happened as they tried to lift was that the stretcher stayed where it was and the two men went steadily into the mud. As stores came up the Scottish regiments were given boots and short puttees.

Trenches, wire, dugouts, etc., as known in 1914, were very primitive articles to those of twelve months later. Of tools and stores, we had practically none, and the majority of the few tools that could be collected were of the 'local' pattern and not suited to either the British infantry or the task in hand. The winter was spent by us in what really amounted in brief to 'helping the infantry make bricks without straw.' This recital of mine hardly conveys the general wetness, muddiness and inadequacy of our so-called front line with its miserable cubby-holes called 'dug-outs'. The weather was desperate – rain, frost, snow and mud were our portion. Of the infantry of those days it is impossible to speak too highly – even at the end of the year only one company

German officers enjoying a comfortable life on the ridge tops

of a battalion at a time was ever out of the line, and even then that company was used of a night as a working party. We Sappers were so few and the Divisional line so long, that our small efforts were necessarily lost to some degree when compared with all the multitudinous tasks that cried out for accomplishment.

Lieutenant B K Young,
7th Field Company, RE

Most of the British positions in front of Ypres were quite inappropriate for a lengthy stay, particularly during winter months, but the pleadings of infantry commanders in the line fell upon deaf ears at GHQ; in their opinion the trenches were temporary and a spring advance and breakthrough simply a formality. It was only matter of

Neat, clean, dry and very well built German trench

months away – 7 March 1915 was the date chosen. Until this time the Commander-in-Chief required 'as much pressure as possible' to be brought upon the enemy.

Meanwhile, across no man's land, the Germans had been far-sighted. Having advanced thus far they felt no loss of face in making small withdrawals to better positions. Safer and drier in their hillside and ridge-top residences they were able to gaze down upon the miserable British and French, who could do nothing but pray for frost to stiffen the cloying Flanders mud. In one of the many ironies of the war, these same sodden, overlooked positions would give British engineers a critical advantage when the war beneath the trenches began – but for the moment – and not for the last time – the weather was as much the enemy as the Germans.

What did the infantry do at Ypres? Nine-tenths of the time they were fighting nature, the remainder they were fighting Germans; and all the time that they were fighting nature the German from his vantage points on the high ground could look down into their very boot-tops, so the toll of life was high.

Captain Hugh Pollard, 1920

Trench warfare now started in earnest: trench pumps, loophole plates for observation and sniping, wire entanglements were gathered together, along with any kind of machinery, lightweight if possible, that could help the troops to dig, bore and scrape their way to a position of relative safety and shelter. Britain was combed for any kind of hand pump which might help keep water levels down, and contracts went out to manufacturers for urgent supplies. Suitable weaponry was also still unavailable to fight this new static war.

On the 18th [November 1914], the Company moved to Gorre, a somewhat squalid village some two miles behind the Givenchy–Festubert Sector, which was held by the Meerut Division. Here a factory for hand-grenades (as many as 450 jam-tin bombs per day were made), trench mortar ammunition, and charcoal braziers, was started. The grenades and mortar bombs were somewhat crude affairs, and the latter were extremely apt to explode at the muzzle of the mortar, which was either a wrought-iron tube or a hollow wire-bound piece of timber. Classes of infantry were instructed in the art of throwing the hand-grenades, but pupils generally were not enthusiastic!

Major H W R Hamilton,
20th (Field) Company Indian
Sappers and Miners

Improvisation and experimentation such as this was typical of the British attitude to conflict, and 'unofficial' fabrication of all kinds was to be continuous throughout the Great War. Indeed, the military engineer was about to come into his own. Since the Peninsular Campaign of the early nineteenth century, British engineer officers had been actively encouraged to suggest and devise potential improvements in equipment from their personal experiences in the field. There was never any shortage of enquiring minds in the Corps – in 1820 almost half of Britain's qualified engineers were Royal Engineer officers.

The Great War was to produce fertile pastures for the inventive, and during the four years of fighting literally thousands of ideas were despatched from the front lines to the home depot of the RE in Chatham for consideration. Each was fed through the Royal Engineer Committee, where its respective merits were debated. If an initial approval was granted, the contraption would be built and rigorously tested, both in Britain and in the field, and if satisfactory, an official order was likely to follow. Trench warfare guaranteed that many an extraordinary and imaginative suggestion was put forward. From the development of the most complex machinery to the holding power of the humble nail, nothing was considered to be beyond experimentation and useful modification. As a simple example of the scope of this process, in 1916 alone, when it may be thought that a thoroughly proven model would have long been officially selected, eight varieties of wire-cutters were tested and compared. The most mundane of objects, the humble sandbag, was also scrutinised. There were designs for waterproof paper bags, vegetable fibre bags, canvas bags, rotproof bags, white bags for use in chalk, and special bags with which to roof surface shelters. Someone tried to invent a 'noiseless pick', others a trench catapult; there were even rocket-propelled grapnels for dragging barbed wire entanglements from the German lines. As the trenches of Flanders became a fixed component of the landscape nothing was to escape review and experiment.

SECOND YPRES

On 22 April 1915 the Second Battle of Ypres

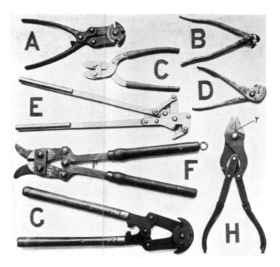

Illustration from an RE comparative test of wire cutters, spring 1916

REFERENCE.

. Cutters, wire, small, Mark V.
. Beauchamp pattern, with horns.
. Stokes pattern.
. Ironside pattern.

E. A long steel cutter.
F. A long cutter with wood handl.
G. Cutters, wire, large, Mark I.
H. Holtzappfel & Co. cutter.

erupted upon the fields of Flanders. It had precisely the same aims as the offensive of the previous November, and came even closer to a breakthrough for the Germans. The attack commenced with the first use of poison gas on the Western Front. Although entirely experimental it was a great success – but the Germans remained unaware of the fact until it was too late to take decisive advantage. The gas attack had been waiting to be launched for several weeks but the wind had stubbornly remained unfavourable. On the morning of 22 April it had again been too light to safely release the chlorine vapour from cylinders in the front lines, and the Germans were forced to wait many hours before conditions altered in their favour. Only in the late

British dead in a captured trench, 2nd Battle of Ypres 26 April 1915

afternoon was it deemed safe to open the valves. Curious and anxious eyes peered from loopholes in the Allied trenches to see streams of greenish mist rolling over the pastures east of Langemarck. The attack caused instant mayhem and an eight-kilometre wide gap opened up in the French Algerian lines. But the combination of late timing and a strenuous defence by recently arrived Canadian troops on the right of the gas attack meant that there was simply not enough time for the Germans to exploit the surprise before night fell; as the light faded Allied reserves were rushed in to fill the breach and hold off further German infantry assaults. More gas attacks followed in subsequent days, and all were endured, but at terrible cost.

It is widely believed that had the assault on the first day of battle taken place in the morning instead of the evening, leaving a full quotient of daylight for the infantry to exploit the effects, Ypres – and Belgium – would have fallen, with dire consequences for the Channel ports, and ultimately Britain itself. It was not only Belgium

Ypres and the Menin Gate in ruins, 1917

which was being defended; the muddy ditches of Flanders were to be the forward defences of the British Empire itself.

As the Second Battle continued, a series of defeats and tactical withdrawals for the British, French and Canadians resulted in the arc of the Salient contracting, and contracting again before the German force was finally spent. The positions which both sides came to occupy on 25 May 1915, the last day of battle, were to remain theirs for the next two years. The front was now fixed, the war of movement in the Salient was over, Ypres was a ruin, and a huge mutual siege had begun.

31st May 1915. As it was such a quiet morning we came back right through Ypres which was indeed a scene of desolation. I don't suppose in the whole town of well on to 20,000 inhabitants there is one single house unharmed. Most have one or two holes, even in the suburbs; round the Place practically all are levelled to the ground. The famous Cloth Hall where William II was to have been

crowned King of Belgium last November is a roofless shattered ruin. The barrel organ cylinder which used to work the famous Carillon was lying at the foot of the clock tower. Half a dozen houses were burning briskly as we passed and in fact the only live Belgian we saw belonging to Ypres was a half-starved cat. No words or even photos can express the havoc caused in what was once the show place in western Flanders.

Major S H Cowan, OC 175 TC, RE

ARTILLERY IS KING:
THE SALIENT 1915–1917

Despite the triumph of holding off the first two German onslaughts of the war, the position in which the British found themselves at the end of June 1915 was no more a happy one than before. Quite simply, they had underestimated the potential scale and duration of the conflict and its nature, and had certainly not expected to be in the invidious and rather shameful position of still being stuck beneath the gaze of the enemy after nine months of fighting; indeed, after Second Ypres even more Allied positions were now located on low and wet ground.

The war of guns, which began at this time and intensified week-by-week for the next two and a half years, was unparalleled in military history, and with the principal lines of attack and defence now firmly fixed, it soon began to seem that the artillery might be capable of winning the war on its own. Dependency upon its destructive powers was ultimately to become practically absolute on both sides. For the first few months following the formation of the new Salient the German gunners held the upper hand; an unfor- givable shortage of ammunition on the British side had restricted even retaliatory shelling to emergencies only, condemning the troops to sit and suffer in their primitive trenches and shelters.

Men are learning now, and indeed have learned, that when ordered to dig they must do it with a will in order to escape heavy loss from shell fire. Digging is as important as shooting. The country being easy to dig in, the Germans get quickly right underground, making head cover good enough to save them from any shell which does not hit directly.

49th Div CRE papers, Spring 1915

New artillery practices quickly evolved. At first the guns were used to fight troops, with shrapnel shells employed against infantry attacks across open ground, and high explosive to bludgeon the trenches. Then, as their numbers grew, guns fought guns with counter-battery fire. Increased precision in gunnery was inevitable, and area shoots followed, intense bombardments designed to obliterate a farm, a trench, a road junction, or a larger chosen patch of ground and everything which lay within its boundaries; the barrages which preceded each stage of the major offensives of 1917 were the ultimate example of this. Once an attack was underway there was a further development, a finely tuned co-operation of man and metal known as the creeping barrage, where the infantry sheltered behind a moving wall of shellfire. Finally, the decision was made to seek out and destroy not only the surface features but also the dugouts, subways and tunnels designed to protect men. The advent of the delayed action shell, which burrowed deep into the ground before exploding, made sure that even the deepest dugouts were not entirely safe havens. The appetite of the guns was *never* to be satisfied.

The key to artillery success in the Salient was observation. From their vantage points the German spotters were able to observe the whole of the British front, its reserve and support lines, communication trenches, tracks and roads, making daylight targeting and ranging straight- forward.

That's the worst of the Ypres Salient. He [the German] has perfect Artillery Observation from Wytschaete, St Eloi, Hill 60 and Bellewarde Ridge. And we are downhill everywhere – even at Hooge there is rising ground in front of us so we have to depend upon observing from our own trenches for the close work and from Aeroplanes and Balloons when we shell further back. How we all curse the SALIENT.

Major S H Cowan, OC 175 TC, RE

After dark, when the forward areas were known to be alive with activity, the German gunners could rightly feel confident that every round they fired was likely to find its mark. By contrast, the British were everywhere downhill gazing up towards a foreshortened horizon, their gunners requiring balloons or aircraft for spotting enemy movement and positions beyond the ridges. And then there was the problem of logistics, funnelling masses of supplies and huge numbers of troops into the narrow confines of the Salient. Every item of war materiel had to be fed in via routes that were known, overlooked and pinpointed by the enemy gunners. Nothing could be transported in daylight. The Germans on the other hand enjoyed excellent road and rail communication from outside the arc of the Salient to the west, north and east. Supplies could be moved close up to the front under cover of the ridges at practically any time of the day or night. They had space, and plenty of it. Sheltered in this way, large gangs of enforced civilian labour were employed to supply the forward areas, and even to work on defence lines well within range of hostile fire. Across no man's land the British were cramped, overlooked, and restricted to using military personnel for any and every job which had to be done. The result was a thin ribbon of destruction snaking around the town of Ypres, hugging the central contours of the nearest spurs of the ridge system.

The most important aspect of this early period of positional warfare was the extension and completion of the system of opposing defensive earthworks. By the end of May 1915 an unbroken trench line, effectively an unbroken pair of fortress walls with no vulnerable flanks to attack, stretched from the North Sea coast at Nieuport-Bains to the Swiss frontier. In this new form of siege warfare barbed-wire entanglements replaced ancient ditches and moats, and machine gun positions and snipers' posts, the fortified bastions of old. Eventually, any movement above ground during daylight was tantamount to suicide. Stalemate settled resignedly upon the Salient. The troops began to develop an intimate acquaintance with every traverse, sandbag, ditch, and shattered tree; farms, roads and trenches, in fact every aspect of the landscape was re-named with a familiar homely label as the British Tommies dug and delved to make their positions into 'homes', which were to be far less temporary than they were led to believe. The Ypres Salient, a tiny blood-soaked shard of Western Flanders, became an emblem of fierce British pride, with the motto 'Thus far and no farther'.

After Second Ypres small limited assaults and trench raids became commonplace all around the Salient, but it was those places with the greatest value for observation, such as Hill 60, the Bluff, St Eloi, and Hooge, which became the hotspots. These small hills and low ridges often forced opposing lines closer and created bulges in them, miniature salients from which

the Germans could best see every movement behind the Allied lines. To drive them out a new tactical approach was needed. Engineers would have to consider the possibilities of dislodgement of fixed positions using ancient siege warfare tactics, and it was in these few intensely localised positions that the embryonic underground war began to gestate. Ultimately it would encompass almost every sub-sector around Ypres. From the beginning of 1915 until the 'great push' in early summer to the late autumn of 1917 – the Third Battle of Ypres – military mining was to become a principal preoccupation for thousands of men.

When open warfare reached stalemate and the long front between the North Sea and the Swiss Jura solidified as both sides grew exhausted, the discarded and almost forgotten techniques of siege warfare received a new lease of life. As the enemy could not be attacked on the surface, he was attacked from under the ground. At key points along the front, mainly dominating ridges, men dug towards the enemy like moles – in narrow galleries, shored up with timber to prevent the tunnels from caving in, and set mines to blow up his trenches and thus breach his defences and open the way for our storm troops. While men laboured above ground with picks and shovels, wire cutters and explosives, below ground the pioneers went about their work, exactly as in the times of Frederick the Great.

Oberstleutnant Otto Füsslein,
Kommandeur des Mineure,
4th German Army

The curtain was eventually to come down on military mining over two years later on 7 June 1917 with the Battle of Messines Ridge, by any standards a brilliant success, and due in no small part to the shattering effects on morale caused by the detonation of nineteen great mines in combination with the greatest artillery bombardment the world had yet seen. The infantry clash was abrupt by comparison to earlier battles, with the ridge falling in a matter of hours rather than the usual weeks or months, and casualties on the attacking side 'astonishingly low', a fraction of those expected. It was rightly hailed as a triumph – the first true British victory of the war. But much was to happen beneath the fields of Flanders beforehand.

Chapter II

FROM SIEGE WAR TO WORLD WAR

The Art of Mining requires a perfect Knowledge both of Fortification and of Geometry; that by these previous helps, the Engineer may be qualified to inform himself in the Nature of all Heights, Depths, Breadths, and Thicknesses; to judge perfectly concerning all Slopes and Perpendiculars, whether they be such as are Parallel to the Horizon, or such as are Visual; together with the true Levels of all Kinds of Earths. To which is added, a consummate Skill in the Quality of all Rocks, Earths, and Sands in general; the whole accompanied with a thorough Knowledge in the precise Force of all sorts of Gunpowder.

Henry Manningham, 1756

From the dawn of time man has been driven by a desire to gather together and protect his family and possessions. The earliest tribal groups built primitive fortifications to defend against hostile attack, and as these groups became larger and more sophisticated the natural progression was to build ever larger and more sophisticated fortresses. To an invader, however, the more impressive the stronghold, the greater the 'prize', and the keener the desire to conquer. As defences evolved from timber pallisade to stone built forts and castles with ditches and moats, assailants found that forward planning and time was required to conquer their objective – the era of the siege, the first form of organised warfare in history, had begun.

Having first tried negotiation and threats, siege tactics included starving the enemy into surrender by blockade of supplies or, before the appearance of gunpowder, a frontal attack on the fortress using siege towers or ladders. Breaches

in defensive walls could also be created using siege engines of the throwing variety such as trebuchets, catapults and ballistas, or battering rams. A cat, sow or mantlet might also be employed. These were siege engines resembling a house on wheels with an immensely strong roof to deflect missiles such as stones, arrows, molten lead or boiling oil, beneath which engineers could work unmolested as they began dismantling the fabric of the fortress at ground level. Tunnelling beneath the walls might also be undertaken from here. The main drawback was that when such a machine was wheeled into

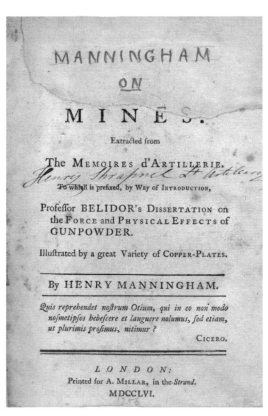

Henry Manningham's early British treatise on Military Mining. Note the signature. The book was once the property of Lieutenant Henry Shrapnel, inventor of one of the most effective anti-personnel weapons of war, the Shrapnel shell

Before gunpowder. Bringing down the walls by under- mining and the 'burned prop' process

position, it was perfectly obvious to the defenders what was about to take place, and the all important advantage of surprise was lost.

Apart from the cunning plan or stratagem – the Trojan Horse being the best known example – the most efficient way of effecting surprise was through mining. The beginnings of military mining as an integral part of siege operations are lost in antiquity, but it was to become as important a weapon as the sword, spear, pistol or musket was to infantry engagements – and also to continue practically unchanged for millennia. However, although early chroniclers were assiduous in describing the design and usage of their 'high-tech' siege engines, military mining was so common a method of attack that few felt it warranted the effort of a detailed written description. The recording of materials, construc- tion methods, and the 'mundane' practicalities of mining were therefore sadly ignored in print for many centuries – until the arrival of gunpowder.

In 2000 BC the Egyptian Army were already bringing down fortress walls by undermining, and by 850 BC the Assyrians had a special 'Corps of Engineers' organised for the same purpose. Unsurprisingly, the earliest texts are Roman and come from an engagement in Etruria, a region of Italy just north of Rome. At the siege of the hilltop fortress of Fidenea in AD 430, Roman miners burrowed into the mountainside to emerge with cohorts of infantry within the town itself. To achieve such a direct penetration to the heart of a fortress was unusual, however; it was also a risky business as the defenders might well

have become aware of the tunnel and be waiting with a 'welcoming' committee for it to break surface. The most common method of forced entry was to attempt to create larger and conse- quently safer access points for storming parties by bringing down part of the fortress structure itself – the walls.

The ancient Assyrians had been unusual in having a dedicated corps of military miners; in other armies there were no training schools or texts on siegecraft, and knowledge was gained by experience and word of mouth. Military mining, although apparently simple, was not quite as straightforward as it seemed. In a classical siege, the siegemaster first selected one or more critical points in the defences, such as a corner tower or a main wall; and from a position of safety, preferably at a point out of sight of the defenders and out of reach of their missiles, the tunnel was begun. To achieve rapid progress such tunnels were usually shallow, taking advantage of softer ground near the surface, and rarely more than two metres deep. It will at once be seen that deep moats were a considerable barrier to a tunnelled attack, as were fortresses constructed on solid bedrock. Once the target had been reached, undermining of the founda- tions began by enlarging the end of the tunnel to form a chamber. Inside, the masonry was shored up with baulks of strong, dry timber, and when complete these were packed around with brushwood which was then set alight, often with assistance of pitch or tallow (once, at Rochester in 1215, with the help of a herd of fat pigs). As

A countermine before the advent of explosives showing the moment of breakthrough into the offensive mine gallery

the props burned through and collapsed, the unsupported section of wall above would in turn fall through into the void. A breach had been made. The attacking infantry, mobilised and ready for the assault, swarmed through into the fortress. This is known as 'burnt prop' mining. As long as the geology was favourable, i.e. the ground was soft enough to tunnel through, military mining was a simple, effective and reliable method of bringing a siege to a successful conclusion – if you had the time, money and patience.

However, apart from ground conditions, the success of a mine attack also depended upon whether the defenders inside the fortress had detected the existence of the offensive mine or tunnel. If not, and the attack was unexpected, the game might be all but up for the besieged; on the other hand, if they had become aware of the enemy tunnelling, defenders were perfectly capable of stalling the siege by driving their own tunnels – counter-mining – to intercept those of the attackers, preferably at a point before it was too late, i.e. before the enemy reached their walls.

If they then could locate and break into the attackers' tunnels, it was possible to fight them off hand-to-hand underground. If successful, the tunnels could then be blocked and permanently defended, thereby rendering them inoperative and forcing the attackers to begin tunnelling elsewhere or think of an alternative scheme. Hand-to-hand battles underground were a grisly business in the dark, confined and stifling space

of a mine gallery, but other ingenious methods could be used to drive the enemy out without a face-to-face encounter. It might be possible, for instance, to divert a watercourse to flood the hostile workings and drown the attackers (this was chronicled during the Siege of York in 1644 and attempted several times during the Great War). Ingenuity encouraged by the desire for self-preservation went further: at the siege of Themiseira by Mithridates in 68 BC, the defenders introduced tigers, bears and hives of angry bees into the enemy galleries. Even forms of asphyxiating gas were used.

At the siege of Ambracia, by Fulvius, 189 years before our era, they had not the precaution to carry away the earth which was excavated from the gallery, or to spread it about; and the besieged observing this indication, carried on a defensive mine, which meeting the besieger's mine, filled it with smoke by means of burning feathers in a cask made of sheet iron, one end of which was pierced with a great number of holes, and the access to it prevented by long javelins; in the other end was introduced the mouth of a pair of bellows to drive out the smoke.

Professor I Landmann, 1815

THE ADVENT OF EXPLOSIVES

The mine produces an effect in the ranks of the besieger far greater than the fire from the ramparts. The imagination exaggerates the danger, ever appearing more formidable as it is mysterious and obscure. It is in vain that the bravest of besiegers attempt to push on the attack and overcome at all price the obstacle which impedes their advance. Yet a handful of men, by a slow, dangerous, and most difficult process, conquer, where numbers and courage succumb – a striking example of the superiority of industry and skill over force. And now a struggle is commenced and carried on amidst silence and darkness. The besieged, who cannot avail himself of such large charges as are fired by the besieger, still retains on his side all the advantages of that science which foresees, observes, calculates, and regulates every-thing. His attentive ear is directed to all the points by which the besieger can advance.

Professor I Landmann, 1815

With the advent of gunpowder, mine warfare became a somewhat more volatile affair. The opportunity to use explosive charges was clearly an advantage. However, although valuable in attack, gunpowder was equally useful in defence, adding immensely to the capability to ward off both surface and underground assaults. Most importantly, it gave the defender the chance to destroy hostile tunnels and their

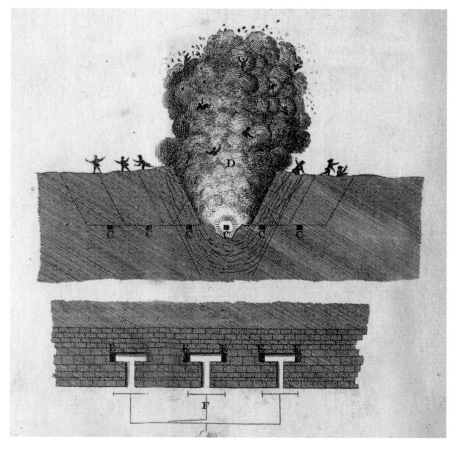

A Manningham diagram showing underground galleries and the effects of a mine being 'sprung'

occupants by an underground explosion known as a *camouflet*, and in particular to undermine and destroy enemy positions before they reached a critical position, i.e. outside the walls of a fortress. When conditions and time allowed, permanent defensive tunnels could also be put in place long in advance of an attack, to be quickly charged with powder when necessary – a tactic which was first used as early as 1497 at Salses in Rousillon in southern France. It was to become a standard universal practice in the eighteenth and nineteenth centuries.

The *camouflet* was an explosion calculated to limit damage to a restricted area underground without destroying surface works, and by luck and judgement obliterate both the enemy and his tunnel. *Camouflets* certainly helped to avoid frightening hand-to-hand fighting, but the tactic was of course also reciprocal, and could be taken a step further – it might equally be employed by attackers to destroy countermines laid by defenders – using mines against mines against mines. This was a new terror in an environment where both sides were already blindly stalking each other, reliant solely on sound to locate their foe; with *camouflets* neither side could know which moment might be their last.

The development of the gunpowder mine came surprisingly late to Europe, almost 200 years after the first appearance of the explosive in the western hemisphere. One of the earliest documented examples is credited to John Vrano, who used black powder to fire a celebrated coun-termine against the Turks in about 1433 during the Siege of Belgrade. It was news of his success which led to the deliberate development of underground defensive strategies using explosives. A celebrated and influential action took place in 1509 during the Siege of Padua by a combined force of French, Germans and Italians. The Venetian defenders, under attack by artillery, calculated that by the time the enemy guns could rupture their defences, it would be possible to arrange a surprise 'welcome'. Chambers were rapidly excavated beneath their own walls – and mines laid. When the enemy artillery eventually created a breach and the massed infantry were swarming over the tumbled masonry, the defenders sprung their mines, wiping out the storming party almost to a man.

In the early days gunpowder, being relative-ly rare, was prohibitively expensive. Its wide-spread use in military mining came only towards the end of the fifteenth century when it became available at an affordable price, and gradually the use of explosives in underground attacks became commonplace. Despite the growth of artillery in the sixteenth and seventeenth centuries, mining continued to be a key siege-breaking technique, simply because it was often far more efficient and swift than other methods. Early artillery pieces, although undoubtedly terrifying for those on the receiving end, were ineffective and inaccurate except at close range, and gun barrels soon wore out. For this reason gunpowder mines continued to be integral to siege warfare even as improvements in artillery took place. Indeed, the military mine would remain a deadly weapon for another three hundred and fifty years, until the era of permanent fortresses was over at the end of the nineteenth century.

THE RENAISSANCE

The Renaissance brought with it the dawn of a golden age in the arts and sciences, and a new spirit of experimentation in the art of war. Beginning with the Italians in 1540, fortification underwent a metamorphosis, transforming from art to science, and a new creativity was seen in military architecture. Mine warfare was to be fully incorporated into the new approaches.

Strategists now began to specialise in planning for underground offence and defence, working alongside military architects in designing surface works such as bastions, ditches and shellproof buildings in place of vulnerable towers, castles and keeps. The combination of the military mine alongside new and increasingly powerful and accurate artillery pieces meant that in devising defensive positions engineers had to do some radical rethinking. Lofty fortresses were now easy prey to improved guns and gunnery. Their replacements were to be squat structures, hugging the ground, presenting a smaller target for missiles, and much more robust. Towers were replaced by multiple bastions, spacious and low constructions accommodating defensive cannon, designed not only to fire back at attackers, but also to offer mutual cross-fire support for each other, thereby leaving no part of a fortress unprotected.

Some of these great new strongholds might have looked impregnable to artillery and infantry attack, but finding a defence against mining was still a knotty problem. Instead of the castle's high walls, deep ditches now encircled the entire fortress. Without walls to bring down it was they, not the fortress itself, which became the offensive miner's primary target. From 1670 all new fortresses incorporated permanent systems of countermines which spread like probing fingers from within the safety of the citadel far beyond its walls and ditches. Lined with brick or masonry, these tunnels were designed to last for centuries. The magnificent designs of military engineers such as Sebastien le Prestre de Vauban and Cormontaigne incorporated permanent defensive tunnels specifically to possess an immediate subterranean advantage over any potential enemy mine attack. Many were vast and complex works, with such strength in depth that an assailant was sure to be forced to fight a prolonged underground battle no matter how determined and numerous his force of tunnellers.

When attack and defence were equally resolute, the scale of mine warfare could become prodigious, making sieges a lengthy and costly business. As an example, in May 1667 the Turks besieged Candia, the ancient Venetian capital of Crete. During the first six months, 618 mines and countermines were fired, causing 12,000 casualties on the Turkish side alone. The town, defended by the Venetians, already had a highly

Complex web of defensive tunnel systems protecting the walls of an eighteenth-century fortress

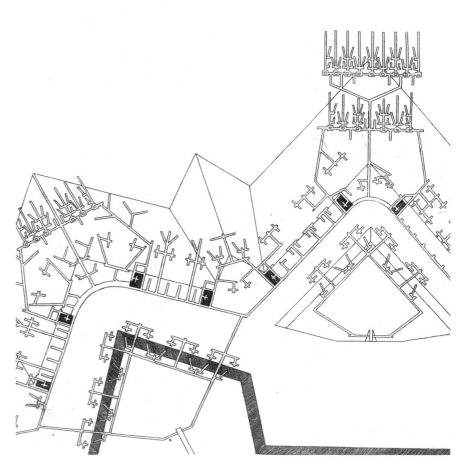

developed system of inbuilt subterranean defences outside the fortress. Almost every underground Turkish approach was detected by the defenders in their stone-built listening galleries, and tunnel after enemy tunnel was entered and destroyed by the Venetians, who on several occasions even managed to steal their enemy's powder charge. In 1668, during the same siege, a mine of eight tonnes was blown – by far the biggest in history at the time.

At the end of the year the Venetians alone had used almost 1,500 tonnes of gunpowder. Again during the same siege, another vitally important aspect of prolonged underground conflict using explosives was well demonstrated – the psychological effect of mine warfare. After two years of constant subterranean activity both sides at Candia became noticeably paranoid about being undermined. This was illustrated by the action of a division of seaborne French troops who arrived to bolster the Venetian defence. They made an auspicious start with a daring sortie from the fortress which drove the Turks from their trenches for the first time since the siege had begun, but as the Turks fled a few barrels of powder accidentally exploded in a nearby gun emplacement. The French, who for the last two years had heard gruesome stories of the terrible losses to mines at Candia, mistook this explosion for yet another mine, panicked, turned, and fled, leaving the Turks to regain their positions. With the French gone confidence could not be restored and a Venetian capitulation followed. The effects of extensive mine warfare on morale demonstrated by this story were reflected many times in later campaigns, and would become a highly significant and influential characteristic both above and below ground during the Great War. In fact, so powerful was the influence of mines on morale during the fifteenth and early sixteenth centuries that in some campaigns the besiegers, having successfully placed their offensive mines despite the attentions of countermining, were known to invite the enemy to inspect the charges in the hope of inducing a surrender!

It may be thought that given the expansion of military mining during the sixteenth century and its almost universal employment (the tactic first came into use during, and was later to dominate, the Hundred Years War of 1346–1453), all Renaissance armies would have had their own dedicated mining units, echoing their Assyrian predecessors 1,400 years before; but this was not so. Many military engineers struggled to persuade their leaders of the benefits of a permanent tunnelling corps. Even the mighty Vauban, who took part in forty-eight separate sieges (the first at the age of twenty-three), and directed forty-two of them himself, failed in his efforts to persuade Louis XIV to sanction the raising of regular engineer companies for the French military. As in many other armies, Vauban's miners were forced to remain outside the military infrastructure, being raised for siege work as and when they were needed. In 1740 Vauban's book on siege warfare, *The New Method of Fortification*, outlined his principles of military mining. It was to become a classic work, and the tactics and designs he advocated dominated the science of permanent fortification from the seventeenth to the nineteenth centuries. The fundamentals of Vauban's approach were in no way new – the basic tactics of military mining had remained the same since the time of the Pharoahs – but he improved and developed the art by paying special attention to the integration of surface and sub-surface structures and procedures, and by adapting each to suit the contours of the landscape and its geology; a feature that was to be significant in the application of military mining in the Great War.

TEXTBOOK MINE WARFARE

Mining had become a textbook operation by the close of the eighteenth century, well documented and closely studied. But little had changed: as in ancient times the besieging force needed first to reach the optimum position from which to make their underground strike at the target. For centuries this was done by 'sapping' (a term deriving from the Italian for spade, *zappa*). A sapper was the name given to the military engineers who dug 'parallels', systems of connected lateral trench lines – saps – which gradually approached closer and closer to a fortress, whilst at the same time offering cover from defensive fire. When the last parallel had been completed to the satisfaction of the siege-master, a mine was placed and blown in advance of the most forward position, not to destroy enemy emplacements, but to create a defensible and protective crater from which the next and hopefully final stage of the attack might be launched. After blowing, the crater was then 'crowned' by occupying and fortifying its elevated 'lip', an operation which gained both extra height for observation and cover from hostile fire. A 'crater trench' or 'mine trench' was dug around the lip, and this formed the most advanced surface position before the infantry assault itself took place. If a wide front of attack was required, several craters might be blown in this way and connected together. Now, sheltered from enemy fire and sight, the extra depth which the craters afforded made them the perfect place to begin driving the main offensive mine or mines towards the enemy's defences.

When the fortress to be attacked had no countermine system, there were two purposes for which mines might be employed by a besieger: as a place to begin galleries to gain access to the ditches for infantry storming parties, or to attack the scarp and counterscarp revetments – the front and rear walls of the deep ditches which protected almost every fortress. Ditch interiors were designed so that the entire sunken area could be swept by annihilating defensive fire – a formidable barrier for attacking infantry. As this defensive fire made it perilous simply to use ladders to descend one side of the ditch and scale the other, mines were used. Their purpose was not to destroy the selected area by blowing it to pieces – but to 'bridge' the ditch. The miner was concerned therefore not in blowing up the ditch walls, but blowing them downwards and inwards to create a ramp of earth and rubble, thereby allowing troops to swarm from one side of the ditch to the other without the need for ladders.

However, it was often not possible to cross a ditch if only the counterscarp (outer wall) was blown down, and it was clearly impossible to blow down the scarp (inner wall) if one's miners could not reach it. There was a way to overcome the problem: a small gallery was driven to a point behind the masonry of the counterscarp, and a chamber made; the powder was placed, the mine gallery was tamped, i.e. blocked behind the charge to stop it blowing back down the tunnel, then exploded in the usual manner. The aim was to blow a hole through which miners could emerge, cross the ditch floor and commence a second gallery in the scarp. Emerging from the newly blown hole they bolted across the ditch (whilst the enemy were still hopefully in a state of surprise) carrying thick planks or beams which were then sloped against the scarp wall to protect the attackers from missiles and shells fired or rolled down from above. For protection from flanking fire, a barrier of gabions or sandbags was built. The whole construction resembled a small slope-roofed shed. Under this elementary cover the miners could begin the final stage of their work: the piercing and blowing

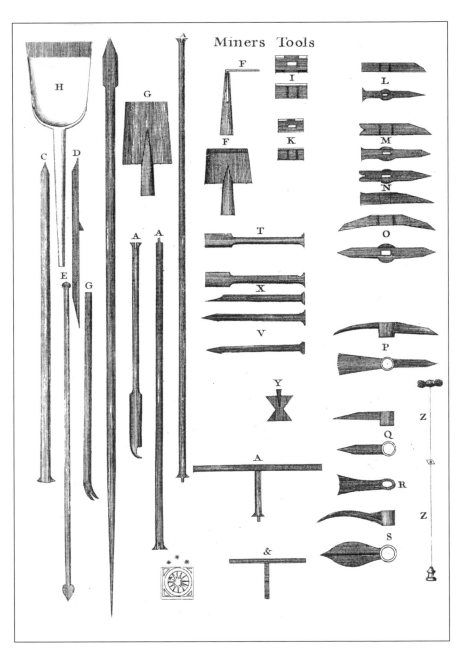

Miners Tools

down of the inner wall. It was a hazardous operation. Sometimes, to assist the men who were to run the gauntlet carrying their wood and tools across the ditch under fire, a small cannon was brought to the end of the counterscarp gallery to fire across the ditch. This was intended to puncture the masonry of the opposite wall, weakening the fabric and thus assisting the miners to burrow inside the wall more easily and swiftly. The hole could also offer a shelter of sorts inside which the next stage of tunnelling was commenced.

Even when the ditches were water filled, mining was still used. Here, the aforementioned cannon tactic was peculiarly necessary. Having

Tools of the trade for an eighteenth-century military miner

opened the initial tunnel through the counter-scarp wall, a small breach was blasted into the opposite scarp above the water's surface. The miners then crossed in little punts to install themselves, limpet like, to the inner wall. Whether wet or dry, crossing the ditch was one of the most hazardous tasks in warfare.

In every mining operation against ditches the most critical objective was to charge one's mine with the correct quantity of explosive; too little would fail to blow down the ditch walls, too much might produce a crater instead of a ramp, severely complicating things for the infantry by slowing the assault and creating easier targets for defending muskets. In the worst cases the offensive mining team could be forced into digging new tunnels in an alternative location. This careful calculation of explosive quantity and effect was to be equally critical to the success of mining in the Great War, where the engineers had to take into account not only the destruction of the surface target, but also the vagaries of the local geology.

MILITARY MINING IN THE INDUSTRIAL AGE

As the nineteenth century progressed, mine warfare became less and less called upon in conflict as protracted siege operations became less common, but several actions proved that

there was no diminution in its value, including brief forays in India, and during the Crimean War.

At the Siege of Sebastopol in 1855 over eight kilometres of galleries were driven and hundreds of thousands of kilograms of black powder used. British engineers enjoyed little underground involvement in the Crimea, but extensive French and Russian endeavours showed mining to be as important as it had always been – for specific instances. The second half of the century saw a host of technical improvements, especially in ventilation and mine rescue apparatus, and advances were made in the design of boring machines to place small countermines (bored mines were actually first used at Candia in the 1660s). The experiments were largely theoretical as mining was overshadowed by the two most important military developments of the nineteenth century – the rifled gun and the invention of more powerful explosive alternatives to gunpowder.

The advent of rifled artillery threatened the military miner with complete extinction. Coming into use for the first time during the American Civil War (1861–65), the new weapons were capable of firing an explosive projectile over far greater distances than ever before and with much greater accuracy and effect – it was the most serious threat to the fortress for centuries. In the

A rare British underground episode of the nineteenth century. Captain G W W Fulton, Garrison Engineer at the Siege of Lucknow, seated at the end of a British countermine 'like a terrier at a rat hole' lying in wait for native enemy miners to break through, June 1857

past when accuracy and range had been limited and guns needed to be positioned close to their target to be effective, defenders had sometimes been able to use mines against artillery; rifled barrels meant that hostile guns could now be located several kilometres away – clearly an impossible distance for miners to cover.

As artillery further developed and improved it was felt that even the mightiest stronghold could not withstand a prolonged long-range bombardment by heavy modern ordnance; in consequence there was a natural decline in the study and practice of mining in favour of building ever stronger fortresses using the latest technology – steel reinforced concrete. The long history of military mining seemed to be coming to an end at last, and in many influential circles a general belief grew that the miner, although employed from time to time as a specialist, would be unlikely to play a major role on the battlefield ever again. No one suspected that the underground war was patiently awaiting its apogee, that the greatest siege in history was waiting in the wings, and that all the ancient and fundamental principles would still hold good during a period when technological advances allowed mankind to begin to contemplate and envisage something which had previously been unthinkable – total self-destruction.

WORLD WAR IN REHEARSAL: THE RUSSO–JAPANESE WAR

Of all the conflicts immediately prior to the Great War it was one in which the British Empire played no part other than an onlooker that offered by far the best indicator of the coming deadlock on the Western Front. Seldom thought of today, the Russo–Japanese War of 1904–5, fought mostly in Manchuria and Korea, was one of the greatest armed confrontations the world had ever seen. Although some of its aspects were reminiscent of ancient siege warfare, many of the battlefield conditions, strategies, and much of the weaponry were almost identical to those which would be seen in France and Belgium less than a decade later. As on the Western Front, observers witnessed static trench warfare, massed infantry attacks against fortified positions defended by machine-guns, barbed-wire and artillery, and an array of underground attack, defence and shelter devices. In many ways the Russo–Japanese War was a precursor to the Great War, and spectators from a dozen nations carefully noted the successes and failures of the belligerents.

Fort Ehr-Lung. One of Port Arthur's protective outworks captured by the Japanese by mining

Significantly, the military miner played a key role in one of the most critical actions of the war. At the rocky citadel of Port Arthur (now Lushun, the premier naval base of the People's Republic of China) on the Liaoting Peninsula in southern Manchuria, the town and its outlying protective forts had been seized by the invading Russians, only to be besieged by the Japanese who considered themselves the rightful owners. Six months of bombardment, infantry assault, and Russian counter-attack had led to tens of thousands of casualties. The forts of Chi-Kuan, Ehr-Lung and Sung-Shu had ample concrete head cover to cope with most of the available Japanese artillery, eighteen eleven-inch howitzers which were not state-of-the-art, and it was clear that the Russians were perfectly capable of holding off further infantry assaults, perhaps for months. In mid-November 1904 the Japanese turned to military mining as the final option. An underground attack was pressed forward in conjunc-

Port Arthur: general view of Fort Chi-Kuan and its destroyed counterscarp

tion with continued frontal assaults, and as a result the horrific lists of dead and wounded barely diminished. In one fort alone the Russians hurled an average of 2,000 grenades each day to beat off enemy infantry. Over a period of six weeks more than thirty kilometres of saps and over 600 metres of tunnels were dug, and dozens of offensive mines blown. The combination of men and mines proved too much for the Russians; despite furious defensive countermining each of the three forts crumbled and fell. The mine which finally ended the siege was fortunate – it also detonated the contents of a magazine, totally demolishing the emplacement. Port Arthur capitulated on 2 January 1905. In this one action alone Russian casualties were 31,000 and Japanese losses exceeded 60,000.

The conflict was scrutinised by military onlookers from Britain, Austria, Germany, France and America, and each nation produced its own official history. All agreed that it had been the use of military mining that had turned the tide for the Japanese at Port Arthur. Equally, all recognised the continuing important role that mining might well play in future wars – should they resemble this one. Yet by 1914, and despite the recommen-

dations of countless advisers and observers, the lessons learned at Port Arthur had been largely discounted by European tacticians, in the belief that any future continental war would be brief and decisive, firstly because of technical advances in modern weaponry, particularly artillery, and secondly because European armies had simply become too powerful to allow prolonged siege conditions such as those witnessed in Manchuria to develop. In an official War Office publication, produced less than five years after the Russo–Japanese conflict, the Royal Engineers restated their opinions on military mining.

The latest example of a siege – that of Port Arthur – only serves to confirm the fact that subterranean warfare may have to be employed in similar cases in the future, and to further emphasise the necessity for training in peacetime of special troops for this service. Mining was used by the Japanese but only to a small extent, and only when it was discovered that without its assistance the capture of the forts was impossible. It seems probable that if the Japanese had made greater use of mining on an organised plan, the final capture of the fortress would have been in no way delayed, and the enormous losses caused by the disastrous attempts at assault would have been avoided. The Russians also made very little use of countermining, of which they gave such a splendid example during the siege of Sebastopol fifty years earlier. Owing to the small amount of mining and countermining done, to its improvised nature and to the apparent lack of coherent system in its application, the siege of Port Arthur throws little light on the subject as compared with that of Sebastopol. Neither the Japanese nor the Russians had an adequate armament of modern siege artillery, and it is impossible to say what new methods of attack may follow the improvements in artillery that have marked the opening of the 20th century. It is quite safe, however, to assume that mining will still have its role and, from time to time, its opportunities, whether the occasion for military mining arises suddenly, finding both sides unprovided with suitable material, or whether it occurs in a regular siege, where the attack may have all the mechanical resources of the period at command, and the defence a complete system of countermine galleries, the general principles governing the action of both sides will be the same as they have been hitherto. As regards the actual process of mining, the only changes to be anticipated are the development of rapid boring tools, and of high explosives for special purposes. At all times subterranean warfare is a tedious operation to the attacker. In no species of warfare is a clear cool head, combined with decisive and energetic action, more required than in the conduct of operations of this nature.

Military Engineering:
Mining and Demolitions, Part IV, 1910

These were to be prophetic words written shortly before the greatest siege in world history. Importantly, the lessons of Port Arthur led the British Royal Engineers, more in theory than expectation perhaps, to begin planning a recommended future organisation of headquarters staff, mining units and working parties, plus an outline for the necessary construction methods, tools and equipment for underground conflict. Studies included ventilation and detonation techniques, calculations of charges, and their explosive results. In fact, they were devising a template of the system which was to be employed when German mine attacks near Christmas 1914 would force the British into rapid retaliation and the subsequent vast escalation of underground warfare.

However, it was not only the siege-like mine-assisted victory at Port Arthur that would inform future tactics on the Western Front. The Russo–Japanese War threw up another curiosity for military engineers. During the Manchurian winter of 1904/5 in the Sha-Ho Valley and around the village of Li-Chia-Pu, the lines of the Japanese and Russian forces were fixed a hundred metres apart, a prophetic vision of the future Western Front. Here, in the Sha-Ho Valley, portentous but largely unreported events took place: tunnelling techniques were being used against field defences – mines against trenches. In the eyes of all but the military engineers of the observing nations, this was treated as an anomaly. It was also reported as being the first time that mines had been used against trenches, but this was not true.

During the closing stages of the American Civil War, trenches, redoubts and 'bomb-proofs' forming the siege lines in front of Petersburg, Virginia, became a target for ex-coal miners in the Union ranks of the 48th Pennsylvania Regiment. A 156-metre long gallery was dug with the aid of modified ration boxes for spoil removal, and shored with locally cut timber. At the end of the gallery a chamber was constructed beneath the trenches of the Confederate forces which was filled with 3,636 kilograms of gunpowder. At 3.00 am on 30 July 1864 the fuse was lit, and at 4.45 the mine eventually went up – the delay caused by the fuse fizzling out, and having to be relit in the gallery itself. The defending South Carolinians suffered three hundred casualties, and the resulting ten-metre-deep crater allowed the Union troops to surge through the Confederate lines.

Mining was even used in much more limited conflicts of the modern age. During the Boxer Rebellion of 1900 – an anti-foreign uprising in China – the capital Peking (now Beijing) lay for fifty-five days under siege by the rebel forces known as 'The Righteous and Harmonious Fists'. They too sprung a number of mines, two of which exploded beneath the offices of the French legation. The action raised eyebrows and created a gentle ripple of interest in military circles, a ripple that was not to last. None of these subterranean events were considered worthy of note in Europe. Just a few years later far-sighted officers such as Captain A Genez of the French *Génie* were less sanguine.

Without drawing general conclusions from these episodes of war, it may not be rash to predict that in certain circumstances mines may be used in the attack and defence of fieldworks. Everyone knows that the Siege of Port Arthur restated the value of mine warfare. Mine warfare relies upon a long duration; can we imagine that a European war will be long enough to create an environment for a significant underground struggle? Let's say that in the next continental war the probable duration will be long enough to allow us to imagine a mine war; let's hope we will be on the attack. But if a battle causes a retirement where we need to defend the 'Boulevards de la Patrie' then let's use every method we have. Mine warfare is one of them. Attack and defence by mining should undoubtedly be practised constantly during peace, the lessons to be drawn from it are invaluable.

Captain A Genez,
Histoire de la Guerre Souterraine, 1914

MINE PRACTICE IN PEACETIME

Until the Russo–Japanese War the Japanese, along with the rest of the major world powers,

Japanese mining exercises at Kokura in 1906. A crater in dry geology

had largely neglected the practice of military mining. The last time it had been employed was during the Satsuma Rebellion of 1877. In Japan, the great moats and ditches surrounding Shogun castles had all been deliberately constructed to give protection against mining, yet in common with the European powers, the modern Japanese Army in the newly-dawning twentieth century favoured new technology and the rapidly delivered blow, rather than a slow subterranean approach.

Port Arthur alerted the Japanese to the continuing value of mines, and during the year following the end of the war, 1906, large-scale mining trials took place at Kokura – the first of their kind in Japanese military history. Only one foreigner was allowed to observe, an Englishman, Colonel C V Hume, RA, the British Military Attache in Tokyo. Hume noted that:

...during the last twenty years mining has been much neglected in most European armies, and it has been the custom to train only from eight to twelve men per company of engineers in this branch of their duties. Russia alone has consistently kept it up.

Colonel C V Hume RA, War Office,
February 1907

Colonel Hume's report on the 1906 Japanese trials was full of useful information for the British, including how to cope with wet trenches, protection against gas in underground mines, the application of various boring techniques, and a comprehensive section on the nature of mine explosions. Considerations of geology – soils and subsoils – had been a particularly important aspect of the exercises, and of course were of great relevance to any considerations of military

Kokura mining trials 1906. A crater in wet clay soil

Japanese tunneller in a typical mine entrance in a trench

mining. To demonstrate the effects of different ground conditions, the testing ground at Kokura had been deliberately chosen to include geological variations. On the right flank the ground was 'light clay, dry and friable', whilst on the left the clay was water-saturated – the latter resembling typical Flemish conditions for shallow mining, and of direct relevance to future mining in Flanders. It contained much information which could have been profitable in the early days of mining in 1915 – if it had been possible to apply it. Unfortunately, none of the lessons appear to have been directly learned and applied by the RE in the opening days of the world war.

A most curious example of the attitude of most military engineers to underground warfare on the eve of war comes from a most unlikely source: the 'father' of British Great War mining himself, Major-General R N Harvey RE, who effectively co-founded, organised and ran the tunnelling companies throughout their most active period. In the years leading up to 1914 Harvey regularly addressed officer students at the School of Military Engineering at Chatham, the home of the Royal Engineers. In 1913, only a year before war broke out, the then Major Harvey RE delivered a series of important and comprehensive lectures on Fieldworks, Permanent Fortification and the Organisation of Field Companies. His talk on fortification incorporated the era from the pre-gunpowder period to the present day and spoke of all the major develop-

ments in defensive design through the ages, the technical advances in artillery, and the evolution of fortress construction methods, citing examples from the Crimean, Indian, Russo–Japanese, Franco–German, South African and Peninsular wars. In his lecture military mining is mentioned just once as a weapon of war, and even then only in passing. For the next four years, he was to be involved in little else.

A Japanese mine blow against trenches and field fortifications at Kokura

Chapter III
SAPPERS AND MINERS

Well may it be asked, what is a sapper? This versatile genius is, as Shakespeare has already answered, 'Not one, but all mankind's epitome', condensing the whole system of military engineering, and all that is practical and useful under one red jacket. He is the man of all work of the army and the public – astronomer, geologist, surveyor, draughtsman, artist, architect, traveller, explorer, antiquary, mechanic, diver, soldier, or sailor, ready to do anything, go anywhere; in short, he is a sapper.

Captain T W J Connolly,
Quartermaster of the Royal Engineers, 1869

The British, being an island race and never subject to foreign invasion after 1066, were to have far less subterranean experience than many other European armies. The English Channel had always been a formidable barrier and the minds of British military architects needed to concentrate on little other than coastal defences for homeland security. However, since the sixteenth century the Crown had begun to develop fierce ambitions that were not to be satisfied by focussing solely on domestic matters. By 1900 the imposition of a European order on the world was considerable, and foremost amongst the world's Imperial powers were the British. Their cultural influence based upon military might spanned the globe, and British military engineers, the sappers, would have a major role to play in prosecuting and preserving Imperial aspirations.

Rigorous study of military mining techniques and strategies in the British Army began not long after the publication of Vauban's influential treatise on fortification. In the mid-eighteenth century John Muller, Professor of Fortifications and Artillery at The Royal Military Academy at Woolwich, was fully aware of the military transformations taking place in Europe. He recognised the need for a comprehensive revision of all aspects of fortification design in order to keep up to date with progress – not least because every country beyond the English Channel was a potential enemy. Upon his recommendation, a warrant was granted by King George II for the construction of a permanent training ground at Woolwich. Muller called for bastions, ditches, ravelins and glacis; all the complications of a modern fortress. If proof were needed, here it was – the days of castles, towers, keeps and high walls were gone for ever. He set down the necessities of his training ground in great detail.

[It should be] of the largest dimensions the ground will admit. Each front shall be made of earth and turfed, and to consist of two demi-bastions, two flanks, and a curtain between them, with a ditch, a ravelin, a covert way, a place of arms and a glacis, and this front shall be attacked every other summer under the direction of the engineers belonging to the military branch of the ordnance with all the form and regularity that is used in a real siege. Parallels shall be drawn and trenches opened, and batteries shall be raised by the besiegers at proper distances and in proper places. Mines shall be made by the besieged to blow up the batteries, and the besiegers shall also carry on mines to make breaches. The whole attack to be traced by the engineers assisted by the chief master of the school.

Professor John Muller, 1741

In 1757 Professor Muller published his own treatise on military mining. *The Attack and Defence of Fortified Places* was to become the British engineer's 'handbook' for almost seventy years. At the time of its publication, the Corps of Royal Engineers had not yet been formed. An Office of Ordnance, which comprised both engineers and artillerists, had existed since 1415, but this was made up of officers only; the artisans and labourers who actually carried out military mining and fortification works were civilians, and hired locally. They were untrained, poorly equipped, badly paid, and naturally loath to work under fire. Unsurprisingly, discipline on active service was appalling.

It was only in 1772 that the first regular military engineers were established following a 'mutiny' of hired part-timers who had been taken out to drive tunnels at Gibraltar. The new body, the Company of Soldier Artificers, comprised craftsmen of every trade from carpenter to blacksmith – the antecedents of today's sappers. Now accepted as soldier artisans they were at last paid from Government defence funds, thereby making them subject to military law. In 1787, by warrant of King George III, the old Engineer Department became the Royal Engineers, and almost at the same time the Company of Soldier Artificers had grown sufficiently to warrant a new title; the Corps of Royal Military Artificers. Confusingly, the British Army now had two engineer corps, one of officers, the other of NCOs and private soldiers, which only ever met on military assignments.

Despite these various reorganisations, standards of work remained appalling. This was to change in 1812 after a characteristically forthright expression of dissatisfaction by the Duke of Wellington. During the Peninsular War the Duke had seen for himself the valiant work of the French engineers, the Génie, and by comparison was gravely disenchanted with that of his own sappers. He let his feelings be known in plain words to the War Office, noting that 'their bravery far exceeds their knowledge; so much so that they are very often killed in battle before they can learn by experience'. Wellington suggested that there should be a new organisation within which training in military engineering of not only officers, but also NCOs and private soldiers could take place. In a letter to Lord Liverpool he voiced a further opinion.

I would beg to suggest to your Lordship the expediency of adding to the Engineer's establishment a corps of sappers and miners. It is inconceivable with what disadvantage we undertake anything like a siege for want of assistance of that description. There is no French Corps d'Armée which has not a battalion of sappers and a company of miners. But we are obliged to depend for assistance of this description upon the regiments of the line; and although the men are brave and willing, they want the knowledge and training which are necessary. Many casualties among them consequently occur, and much valuable time is lost at the most critical period of the siege.

Wellington to Lord Liverpool, c. 1812

It worked. The Corps of Royal Military Artificers were officially re-titled The Corps of Royal Sappers and Miners, and specifically charged with their own clearly defined responsibilities: a miner was to dig tunnels and undermine walls, just as he had done for centuries, whereas a sapper was to practise the ancient art of 'sapping', the digging of trenches to allow the artillery or infantry to approach close to a fortress in preparation for an assault. In the same year, 1812, the Royal Engineer Establishment was set up at Chatham. The Artificers continued to exist separately until a final reorganisation took place in 1856 when the Board of Ordnance was abolished and all engineers were absorbed into a single organisation which combined officers and sappers for the first time – the Corps of Royal Engineers. By this time, however, the new Corps had already earned their original and highly apposite battle honour: *Ubique* – everywhere.

THE NINETEENTH-CENTURY ENGINEER

Following the financially crippling Napoleonic Wars it was decided that the British Empire should be secured by 'ruling the waves', and it was soon the British Navy which loomed largest in the hearts and minds of the public. After Waterloo in 1815, a series of distant expeditions and 'small wars' of Empire punctuated the century. There was one exception. The Crimean War of 1854–5, by far the longest and most bitter of the Victorian wars, was a conflict that combined eighteenth-century infantry techniques – squares and volleys – with nineteenth-century technologies. It was to become a study aid for the British Army well into the future. Every aspect, the deployment of troops, the use

ONE OF THE OLD BRIGADE

Sergeant-Major Hanson RE, a veteran of the Crimean Campaign

of the heaviest and most up-to-date artillery, and the application of military mining, was minutely examined, and the lessons learned firmly built in to British military education and engineering culture.

For the Royal Engineers, the late nineteenth century was to be a time of development and experiment based upon practical experience in the field. This was the age of worldwide British engineering triumphs, the era of Isambard Kingdom Brunel, of the industrial revolution, and it was an equally golden period for the RE. Many of the most senior engineer officers were elected Fellows of the Royal Society, the premier scientific 'academy' in the United Kingdom, and their technical achievements both during and between conflicts, were – and still remain – arguably without parallel. Amongst a longer list than it is necessary to mention, are the Survey of India, several Boundary Commissions (including the surveying and plotting of the 49th Parallel in North America), the irrigation of millions of hectares of southern India, the first Nile Barrage, the Ordnance Survey of Britain and Ireland, and countless building projects ranging from docks and sewage works to cathedrals, prisons and museums.

With such wide-ranging talents the Royal Engineers had rightly become responsible for

every scientific development and technical role in the modern British Army, to the point where war could not be waged without them. Through the efforts and vision of men such as Sir Charles Pasley RE, the creator of modern military engineering, the foundations for learning and experiment were laid. Amongst an array of other accomplishments, Pasley was effectively the first person to conceive the idea of adult education by insisting that Royal Engineers of all ranks should be able to read and write. Education bred curiosity, adaptability and creativity, and it remained high on the RE agenda throughout the nineteenth century.

The Abyssinian War of 1867–8 is an excellent example of Royal Engineer aptitude in action. Compared to the scale of the operation, the object of the campaign had been rather prosaic – to free several foreign missionaries and envoys imprisoned by the local potentate, 'Mad' King Theodore. The expedition was commanded by Sir Robert Napier RE, and despite having such an apparently undemanding goal, the remoteness of the battleground and ruggedness of the landscape made extreme demands upon practically every aspect of the RE repertoire; no more so than in actually reaching the place where the action was due to take place – there were no roads. Apart from road making, the engineers' tasks were to include transportation (elephants were brought from India for the bulk of this work), photography, sinking wells, supplying water, building piers, bridges, huts, tramways and railways, and all telegraphy and signalling arrangements – as well as fighting. A vast amount of experience and knowledge was amassed, all of which was used and further developed in subsequent military campaigns: the Ashanti War of 1867–8, in Afghanistan in 1878, and Egypt in 1885. Amongst these foreign excursions and their inter-war 'civil' works, the RE were also building home defence works on a grand scale.

In the early 1900s new technology, especially in automatic weapons and artillery, had finally pushed most nineteenth-century conflicts into the shadows. Of the most recent campaigns the South African War of 1899–1902, although initially inflicting severe defeats on the British, was a useful pointer towards the future with new ideas such as photo-reconnaissance, wireless telegraphy and balloon observation being tried out in the field for the first time. Much was also learned in this mobile campaign from the innovative tactics of the enemy, the Boers. But it was the Russo–Japanese War, a war in which the British role was that of passive observer, which was most to influence military engineers across Europe. Despite the detailed reports and official histories, it had little effect on the British approach to military mining, which continued to be intermittently taught on manoeuvres.

SIEGE PRACTICE AND THE ROYAL ENGINEERS

Although there had been but few opportunities to use the skills of the military miner on active service, regular siege practices took place throughout the nineteenth century in Britain. Indeed, after Waterloo they became almost an annual event and every few years a substantial exercise was carried out in which military mining played a major role. The Royal Engineers' headquarters at Brompton Barracks, Chatham – the traditional home of the Royal Engineers in Kent – was the scene of much of this activity, in and among its old Napoleonic fortifications. These fortifications had been designed in the 'Vauban style' as a protective barrier against a potential French assault upon the Royal Dockyards on the River Medway. Their low bastions were protected by systems of deep ditches with steep almost vertical scarps – perfect models for siege practice.

In 1844 and 1848 practical mining exercises were held beneath The Duke of Cumberland's Bastion, which formed part of the Chatham Royal Dockyard's defensive positions – the Chatham Lines. The next substantial practice mine attack was held in 1868 against neighbouring St Mary's Casemates, another part of the old Napoleonic defences. These exercises were based upon the

Cover page of the report on the RE Siege Operations at Chatham in 1877

lessons learned in the Crimea a dozen years earlier, and nine mines were sprung – a limited application by later standards.

In 1877 the manoeuvres were on a much grander scale. Close to the 1868 site, the sappers again attacked and defended old permanent fortifications on ground which had become known as the 'New Ravelin'. Practice mines were sprung, craters 'crowned', and defensive ditches and moats blown in. Another set of manoeuvres followed in the summer of 1878. The exercises were of course designed not only to test attacking capabilities, but equally to practise defensive mining techniques – especially countermining and listening. Finely detailed records were kept by both 'attack' and 'defence', and nineteenth-century RE reports show a close resemblance to the Mine Registers and Weekly Mine Reports found in 1914–18 tunnelling company war diaries. The largest and most comprehensive manoeuvres before the outbreak of war took

'Springing' an 11,000lb charge on 'The Lines' in front of Mill Road, Gillingham, 1877

'Crowning' an 1878 practice crater at Chatham. Note the new mine galleries being driven. Practice mines were dug in exactly the same location in 1914-1918

place during the summer of 1907, once more near Chatham, in the Kentish countryside around the villages of Borstal, Snodland, Luton and Horsted. The premise for these operations was the traditional one: that England was under attack by foreign forces from the continent.

[The country was to be] considered as connected to France by an isthmus of land bounded by straight lines from the North Foreland to Calais and from Beachy Head to the Mouth of the River Somme, the frontier being represented by the present English coastline.

Report of Siege Operations at Chatham, 1907

There were two forces, Redland defending and Blueland attacking, and each was to practise the very latest in siege techniques putting into action all the lessons learned from the world's most

Four big blows during the major manoeuvres at Chatham on 23 July 1907

recent major conflicts in South Africa, Manchuria and Korea. The manoeuvres had been preceded by a 'Preliminary Siege Staff Ride' to decide upon locations, the units to be involved, and the sequence of events. Among the twelve officers of the Directing Staff who took part in the ride was Lieutenant-Colonel G H Fowke RE. Fowke, who had served in South Africa and also been an official observer during the Russo–Japanese War, came from a long and continuing line of Royal Engineers, and would later become Engineer-in-Chief of the British Forces in France, in supreme control of British military mining on the Western Front.

The Chatham area had once more been chosen not only for its proximity to the Royal Engineers' HQ, but because the dry chalk ground was favourable for a time-limited exercise, and because of the fine selection of disused permanent fortifications available for destruction. Once more, mining played a key part in the exercises. Unlike artillery fire, the precise location and effect of a mine explosion could be carefully controlled, and between 1 July and 20 August 1907 twenty-six mines and *camouflets* were blown in the Kentish countryside, making it the most comprehensive practice mining operation in British history.

In addition, an extraordinary number and variety of field fortifications were built, including the latest designs of gun-pits and shelters for the Royal Artillery. Balloons and searchlights were also tested, observation positions set up, trench railway routes planned, and telegraphic communication systems devised and built. The subsequent report makes it clear that ideas and designs from recent conflicts had been closely studied and adapted, including Japanese trench designs from Manchuria, Russian field works from Port Arthur, South African blockhouse systems, and Boer trench shelters. As for mining, although the techniques practised mirrored all those for the previous fifty years, these exercises, only seven years before the outbreak of the Great War, would probably stand some of the young officers involved in good stead to face more severe tests on the Western Front.

From the mining viewpoint the exercise notes are exhaustive and cover every aspect of the ancient art. A most telling comment is made by Lieutenant Colonel B R Ward, the Commanding Royal Engineer of the Blue (Attacking) Force, who yet again reiterated what had been said and largely ignored time and again by military engineers for over a century.

If, as seems not improbable, mining operations are likely to be frequently undertaken in future wars, I would suggest that the trade of miner be re-introduced into the Corps of Royal Engineers.

Lieutenant Colonel B R Ward RE,
October 1907

It had been several years since the last such exercises had taken place. On 15 October, in his summary of conclusions on the siege exercises, General the Hon. Sir N G Lyttelton, Chief of the General Staff and arbiter of the findings of the final report, was clearly sceptical about precisely how much importance should be attached to military mining as an integral part of modern future warfare.

...practical experience with modern appliances was entirely wanting. The gift of imagination is, therefore, essential to anyone who attempts to obtain from such manoeuvres precepts for siege warfare in the present day, and we must guard against attaching to our experiences in manoeuvres more weight than they deserve.

General the Hon. Sir N G Lyttelton RE, 1907

The Russo-Japanese War had encouraged the consideration of many aspects of modern siegework by military engineers, promoting a brief resurgence in interest in sapping and mining. In 1908 an RE Committee had recommended that two Fortress Companies and one Siege Company should be specially trained in siege works, including mining, but although the appeal persisted faintly, the Corps' mining regulations, including gallery sizes and patterns of equipment standardised since 1870, were to remain unaltered and undeveloped until 1914. Proof of this limited continuity of training can be found in the last mining exercises of the pre-war era. As late as June 1913, two RE companies, the 20th and 42nd, carried out a set of siege operations near Lulworth in Dorset. This time the target was a small purpose-built section of fort. Mining was again practised. It followed the same old fashioned patterns: digging parallels and saps to within striking distance of the target before placing the mines. In his report of the exercises Major G R Pridham RE noted that the major benefit were the lessons learned about subterranean sound location – listening underground. However, it was clear that a great deal of thought had been put into the planning and reporting of the exercise and consequently, although small-scale, it offered far more information than any of its predecessors.

Unlike Chatham, with its well-drained chalk, the geology of the Lulworth site was not so favourable. It was a 'treacherous' mixture of waterlogged sand and clay to a depth of three and a half metres; not unlike conditions which would be encountered in Flanders in only eighteen months time. Water and water-bearing strata were amongst the miners' worst natural enemies, and both were present. The conditions made removal of spoil difficult and required some sort of pumping apparatus to evacuate water – an operation which was noisy, labour intensive and where the equipment itself occupied precious space in the cramped galleries. Pridham carefully noted all this, and that the wet mines were unhealthy and far more uncomfortable to work in than the dry chalk galleries at Chatham.

A number of other significant observations emerged from Lulworth that would be of great relevance to the future war in Flanders. Note was taken of the size of timbers best able to withstand the shock of an underground explosion, and

experiments using self-contained breathing apparatus for protection against poisonous gases underground were devised – both were aspects which had not been thoroughly reported upon previously but which were all to receive the most serious consideration in the Great War. One observation was very surprising: Major Pridham noted that almost all the equipment supplied for the exercise was of an obsolete pattern; strangely, whilst advocating that improvements should be made in all other aspects of mining, for some unexplained reason he considered this to be 'unavoidable' – a typically British reaction of make do and mend. This would almost certainly not have been the case had a dedicated mining corps been set up on one of the numerous past occasions when it had been advocated.

Perhaps the most relevant of all observations for the future world war concerned the use of bored mines, the design of boring equipment, and the after effects of underground explosions. On the Western Front more lives would be claimed underground through the effects of *camouflets* than any other underground action. At Lulworth, a Medical Officer and War Office

Plan of the last RE siege exercises before the Great War, Lulworth, June 1913

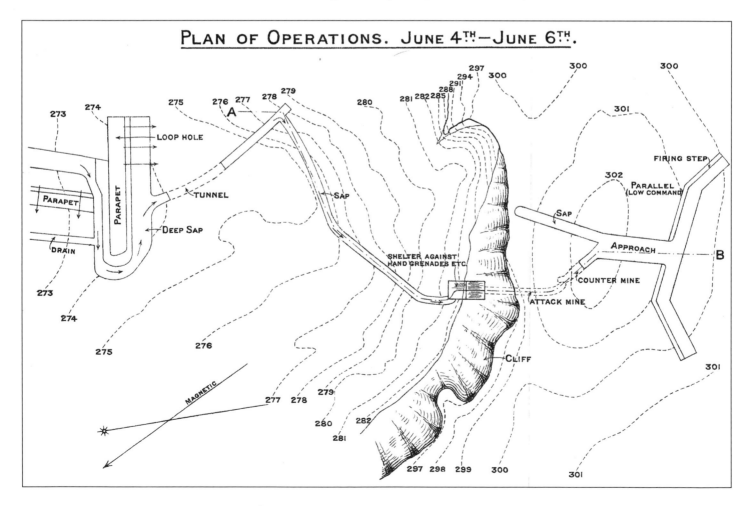

chemist were on hand to study how long poisonous gases remained absorbed in the earth following the explosion of a *camouflet*. Significantly, it was the chemist's opinion that the ground could remain dangerously suffused with lethal carbon monoxide gas, a by-product of all explosions, for days and even weeks – another piece of critical information which could inform the British miner on active service.

As for blowing mines as opposed to *camouflets*, the charging instructions issued in the standard textbook, *Military Engineering Part IV, Mining and Demolitions*, 1910, were followed to the letter at Lulworth. The results matched the figures, and therefore the expectations. Exactly the same tables of calculations were successfully used on the outbreak of mining during the Great War, but would require radical re-writing as new forms of high explosive and ever larger and deeper charges were brought into use.

What of the German training? It had been more meagre than most of her European competitors. Prior to world war, the German Army had last practised military mining on manoeuvres in 1890, working from handbooks such as the *Mineur Exercir und Dienst-Reglement* (1866), a highly detailed manual of underground warfare, again based largely upon lessons learned from the Crimean War. It was still in use when Europe erupted into war in August 1914, although a new shortened version specifically revised for trench warfare was distilled soon afterwards. Examining both British and German training regimes, there was no doubt who should have been best prepared for the war underground.

WORLD WAR: AUGUST 1914

On Thursday 30th July, the Commandant's lawn was again the scene of a gathering, this time of ladies only, all of whom were members of the RE branch of the Mothers' Union, and had accepted Mrs Capper's kind invitation to a few minutes of peace and quietness in the beautiful garden. Tea was provided, and the usual lawn games played, but it is said that the temporary absence of many husbands from their homes and the unpleasant rumours of probable further and longer absence prevented many from being present.

The Sapper, August 1914

Mobilise! It seems as though it were all a dream now that the rush is over. The RE Depot at Chatham had its share of it, but the

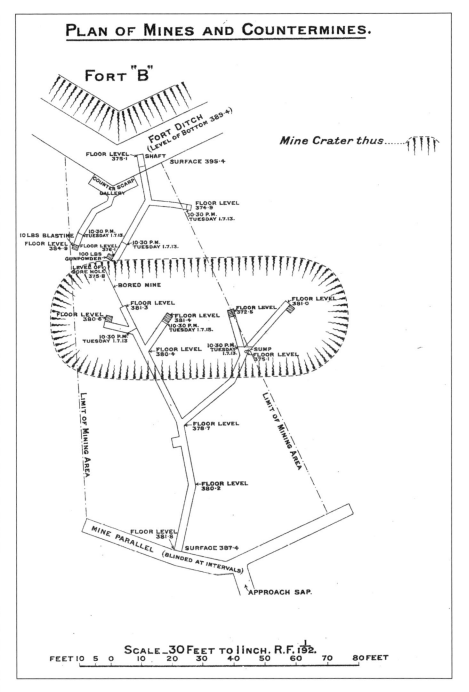

clock-like method in which it was all got through was marvellous. The RE Band for once had to put aside their instruments and become issuers of clothing and equipment to the hundreds of unallotted reservists who joined at Chatham. Warrant officers and senior NCO's strengthened the staff of the recruiting office to cope with the rush of recruits, while others swamped down on the horse owners in the district and gathered together all the best of the gee-gees.

The Sapper, September 1914

Lulworth plan showing mines and countermines

The day arrived when there was no time left for exercises. War with Germany was declared on 4 August 1914. It had been signposted for some time and the general standard of readiness, contrary to the popular belief of the British nation, was perhaps not as good as they might have been led to expect, but this was more of a political fault than a military one. None of the belligerents were expecting the kind of conflict which ensued. Germany, apparently so well prepared for war, had been given prior warning by many advisers of the potential nature of a large European conflict, not least by Colonel Csicserics, an experienced and respected Austro–Hungarian observer of the Russo–Japanese War. He suggested that in the future, modern battles would be extended both in space and time, and that the swift comprehensive victory which was forecast – and

expected – was unlikely to materialise. The Schlieffen Plan, the great sweeping thrust driving all before it, certainly showed no acknowledgement of the many warnings received during the previous ten years. But it was too late now. War had been declared and there was no turning back.

Not for many years had the cannon of contending armies been heard in Western Europe, and the people's rulers, with the arrogant ambition which comes of full bellies, accumulated power, and much wealth were eagerly anxious to draw the long white swords which they were wont to rattle so threateningly when dealing with the humble and meek, and which were rusting in their scabbards. And so they went to war. They, the people, proceeded to kill each other

Sapper volunteers in training at Chatham in 1914

New Expeditionary Force

wholesale with the terrible engines and machines which they had been busily perfecting during the long years of peace. The best brains of civilisation had been engaged on the invention and manufacture of these machines, for great wealth and honour accrued to him who could devise and construct improvements in the man killing equipment of armies, and each nation jealously competed with the other in the provision of these things. The success of these marvellous engines of war has been astounding and the numbers of lives lost, and the amount of blood shed, far transcending anything in history, has provided ample testimony of the cleverness of the human race in devising means for the extermination of humanity.

Captain Matthew Roach MC, 180 and 173 TC, RE; Killed in action, 2 July 1916

At the outbreak of war, the establishment of the Royal Engineers amounted to 11,109 men and 1,128 officers, comprising both regular and territorial soldiers. At least two of the old Militia companies had survived the radical reform of the army that created the Territorial Army in 1908; these were the Royal Anglesey and Royal Monmouth engineers, both of which were to serve with distinction in the coming years. By 1918 the establishment of the RE, including regulars and territorials, was to stand at almost a quarter of a million men: 225,540 other ranks and 11,830 officers.

The Royal Engineers, jacks of all trades, masters of many, adept at most, were variously organised. At the sharp end were the Field Companies, two to each infantry division, composed of able, skilled men who would advise on all matters technical, and engage in front-line work such as demolitions, bridging, field fortifications, and so on. They served everywhere, alongside the infantry.

ENGINEERS – the wise men of the army. They teach the ignorant infantry how to carry sandbags, barbed wire, bath mats, etc, and how to work intricate machinery such as picks and shovels.

Anon, *Made in the Trenches*, 1916

Immediately prior to the war there were fifteen Field Companies: thirteen serving at home, and two on foreign service; by the Armistice, the total number serving in all theatres had risen by an

A group of sapper volunteers

order of magnitude to 199. Field Squadrons, similarly trained, were attached to cavalry divisions. Reflecting the limited role the cavalry were called upon to play during the war, Field Squadron numbers rose from a single company to just five. All but two of the thirty-one pre-war Fortress Companies were serving in Britain or in the colonies. Effectively civil engineers, their main function was to ensure that coastal fortifications at home and border defences abroad were constructed and maintained. The odd two were sent to France to serve on lines of communication, although several sections were soon to be drafted into mining. Other functions were handled by various sub-units of the RE: the Signal Service, the Postal Section, Depot, Survey, Railway and Balloon companies are just some examples.

All ranks of Royal Engineers were highly trained. The officers continued the technical and scientific traditions of the Corps, with NCOs as 'foremen', and the men – the sappers – as tradesmen specialists. Those skilled at a trade and 'fond of horses' could enlist as mounted sappers in a Field Squadron, living partly the life of a cavalry soldier and partly that of an artisan.

A typical sapper 'advert' from the 'Wipers Times', a newspaper printed and published from 'offices' tunnelled within the ramparts of Ypres

SAPPER Bros Ltd.
CONSULTING ENGINEERS.
LAND DECORATORS.
EXCAVATING CONTRACTORS.

Contracts Accepted In
France, Flanders and Gallipoli.

Buy One of our Up-to-date 17in Proof Funk-holes.
NOBODY SHOULD BE WITHOUT ONE.
—o—o—o—o—

TELEGRAMS : " UBIQUE."   TELEPHONE : " 102, VISITUS."

A pictorial evocation of sapper skills – but curiously lacking the tunnellers

Sappers are taken almost entirely from the Artisan classes, each candidate being required before joining to pass a qualifying test in his trade. The following list give the established trades for sappers: blacksmiths, boilermakers, bricklayers, cabinet makers, carpenters, clerks, coopers, coppersmiths, draughtsmen, electricians, engine drivers, engine erectors, fitters, platelayers, plumbers, printers, rivetters, sawyers, shoemakers, surveyors, gas-fitters, harness makers, instrument repairers, joiners, lithographers, masons, metal turners, moulders, painters, paperhangers, pattern makers, photographers, plasterers, tailors, telegraphists, telephonists, tinsmiths, wheelwrights, whitesmiths, woodturners.

The Royal Engineers at Work and Play, 1915

In 1914 the RE categorised their range of work under the following headings: ballooning, bridging, electric lighting, explosives, field and siege equipment, railways, sound locators and acoustics, electrical and mechanical equipment, miscellaneous, postal service, signalling, submarine mining, survey and instruments, telegraphs, water supply. During the war camouflage, forestry, meteorology, war and messenger dogs, cinema and gas were just a few of the extra columns that would be added to the list.

When the British Expeditionary Force landed in France in August 1914 it consisted of five divisions: four infantry and one cavalry. Each was to have its complement of engineers.

The Royal Engineers were represented in the Force by a 'Brigadier-General, Royal Engineers' (Brigadier-General G H Fowke) attached to General Headquarters with a roving commission and no staff except a single clerk; by a 'Colonel, Royal Engineers' on the staff of the two headquarters (Colonels S R Rice and A E Sandbach); by a CRE (Lt. Colonel) with an adjutant and a clerk in each infantry division; by two field companies to each division and a field squadron with the Cavalry Division; and by two fortress companies on the Lines of Communication.

The History of the Corps of Royal Engineers, 1952

Fowke was given two 'attached' officers, Major R N Harvey and Lieutenant Colonel J E Edmonds. The latter was to become none other than the British official historian of the Great War, but both were to play a role in the underground struggle, but it was especially Harvey's contribution that would be fundamental to British subterranean dominance and success in the years to come.

GERMAN ENGINEERS: THE *PIONIERE*

Although the pre-war German Army was over twice the size of its British counterpart, the proportion of engineers was almost identical, being 3.2 percent and 3.7 percent respectively. The organisation of the military machine however, was a perplexing maze: few officers, let alone the ordinary soldiers, understood its structure, which was complicated by the subdivision of Germany and its wider kingdom into twenty-four *Länder* or territories, each with its own independent Army Corps. German military engineers were designated as *Pioniere*, and the forces of each *Land* incorporated one or more *Pionier-Bataillone*. In total there were thirty-four such battalions, representing states such as Bavaria, Prussia, Lorraine, Silesia and so on. Eight were designated as home-based *Festungsbataillone* with duties which included the upkeep and extension of border fortresses. Alongside them were the 'technical troops' of the *Ingenieur-Korps*, a group composed entirely of officers whose responsibilities included maintenance of fortresses and signals, electric lighting and demolitions. The *Ingenieur-Korps* also incorporated the *Festungsbauoffiziere*, the Corps of Fortress Constructors, a home based unit whose

personnel could be ordered to other engineering units in the event of war. Finally, there were the *Versuchkompagnien*, specialist units which were brought in to solve specific technical problems.

The German *Pionier* was not quite the same as his British namesake, the pioneer. British Pioneer Battalions were a new idea, with some historical antecedents, which had been developed in November 1914 as the war of movement began to falter towards stasis. Each new division, either territorial or 'new army', which was subsequently added to the BEF, benefited from the services of a Pioneer Battalion. Equipped and trained as infantry, but provided with specialist training and technical tools, the British pioneers were to have a dual function in supporting the frontline infantry as fighting troops and in carrying out tasks such as entrenchment, wiring, revetting, draining, and building roads and tracks. At least half the men in these battalions were recruited on the basis of their acquaintance with the pick or spade; the other half were skilled men drawn from the building trades. Some RE personnel were also known as pioneers, but these were effectively apprentice sappers.

[Pioneers are] Intelligent men, with a certain amount of education, though not proficient in a trade, as well as men of certain minor trades. They are put to work as assistants to skilled sappers and are given opportunities to become skilled tradesmen. When they have

A group of German Pioniere *behind the lines in the Ypres Salient*

thus learnt a trade they can be examined in it; if they pass, they are allowed to become sappers, and are then eligible for engineer pay according to their trade efficiency.

The Royal Engineers at Work and Play, 1915

German *Pioniere*, however, were required to fulfil two roles: the functions of the technically trained and skilled engineer, and the ability to serve as infantry. Both British RE and Pioneer Battalion men were also trained to fight, but their roles were separate, one providing specialist services, the other mainly labour. The longer the war went on however, the more the work of the two units coincided. The amalgamation of all these functions in the role of the German *Pionier*, the man who would be called upon to fulfil the role of tunneller for the German Army, was to have disastrous implications for their prosecution of mine warfare.

The basic unit of the Royal Engineers was the Field Company. With an average establishment of six officers and 211 other ranks it was subdivided in the same way as an infantry company, with four sections. All shared a central pool of tools and equipment. A *Pionier-Kompagnie* consisted of six officers and 262 other ranks subdivided into three sections each of which was equipped to work independently of the other two. The duties were almost identical to their British counterparts, but the *Pioniere* were also to be given the extra and heavy responsibilities for operations with asphyxiating gas, 'liquid fire' flamethrowers (*Flamenwerfer*), and trench mortars (*Minenwerfer*). By the end of 1917 there were over 700 Pionier companies in the German Army.

Neither the *Pioniere* nor, despite all their pre-war training and outside advice, the Royal Engineers went to war suspecting they would need miners; after all, was not modern war a war of movement? By the time hostilities on the Western Front ceased in November 1918 an estimated 110,000 men had spent a large proportion of their war service in conflict underground.

The skills of the sapper: a view to the future

REMARKABLE EXAMPLE OF THE GOOD THE ENGINEER'S TRAINING WILL BE AFTER THE WAR.

Chapter IV
MINE WARFARE, TUNNELLERS AND *PIONIERE*, 1915

Mine warfare is without doubt, an excellent way of training officers and men, it develops initiative and a sense of personality. The problems to be resolved are various and call for instant decision, the caprices of powder and the trickiness of soils demand constant study, the anxiety to guard against surprise stimulates listeners and observers, the deductions to be made in regard to the distances of sounds strengthen the judgment, and the old stager will form a correct opinion from one single fact where a beginner would fall into error. Attack and defence by mining should undoubtedly be practised constantly during peace, the lessons to be drawn from it are invaluable.

A Genez, *Capitaine du Génie*, French Army, June 1914

The onset of trench warfare took everyone by surprise. The lack of provision for it necessitated a degree of radical and rapid rethinking by GHQ. Organisation, equipment and training were all to be reassessed, and so too were tactics. By the close of 1914, underground warfare was being considered seriously as an option to help break the growing stalemate, albeit on a localised level, on the Western Front. The first British mine was intended to help launch an attack by the Indian Dehra Dun Brigade near Festubert in December 1914. A shallow twelve-metre long tunnel was driven close to the opposing German parapet, and charged with nearly one hundred kilograms of guncotton. However, the mine was destined never to be sprung, thanks to enemy mortar fire destroying the trench from which it was to be blown. Another early venture took place near Armentières just south of the Salient.

I think I took part in the earliest mining which was at Rue du Bois on the Armentières-Lille road where the lines crossed. This was in January 1915. The trenches there were only about 30 yards apart. I was a subaltern in the 20th Fortress Company and was sent with my section to put in a mine to protect their trench against alleged mining. The infantry were up to their necks in water. It was a pretty gloomy business. We started sinking this shaft and it filled with water, so we pumped it out with hand pumps – lift and force. We got down about 10 feet or so. It was heartbreaking – I hated it. But I had to keep my men going. The Boche saved us. We were making a lot of noise with spiling [a specialised method of timbering in tunnels and shafts]. The Boche opposite us were Saxons, rather friendly, and they put up a notice on a blackboard 'No good your mining. We've tried. It can't be done.' The notice was in English. I reported this to my OC and it went up to HQ and they stopped the mine.

Major General F Gordon Hyland, 20th Fortress Company, 171 TC, and later Controller of Mines, 3rd Army

Just a few kilometres to the north in the Ypres Salient, the mine war had also started. Although the trench lines had not yet settled upon the trace which they would occupy after the Second Battle of Ypres in May 1915, and there was still mobile skirmishing in the area, some sectors during the winter 'closed season' were static enough for small mining schemes to be attempted. In January and February it was the French *Génie*, not the British sappers, who were first to join battle underground at the soon to be

The crater resulting from one of the earliest mines in the Salient, blown under French trenches on Broodseinde Ridge in early 1915

Sprengtrichter Bro

infamous Hill 60, and also at Broodseinde Ridge, scene of several bloody infantry confrontations at this time. Here, the Germans blew a crater seven metres deep and twenty-five metres in diameter beneath the French lines. On 3 February near St Eloi the 3rd East Yorkshire Regiment were the first Tommies to be 'lifted' by a German blow. Although tiny by comparison to later standards, the sense of shock and fear which had accompanied mine blows for centuries remained undiminished, and the call for vengeance and protection was immediate. 'Retaliation' came just two weeks later on 17 February when at Hill 60 Lieutenant White's

'amateur miners' from 28th Divisional Engineers blew the first British mine in the Salient; a very small affair, and in fact the culmination of a scheme started by the French. However, with these two minor actions mine warfare – and its accompanying psychology of fear – was firmly established in the Salient.

The first serious German mine attack against British troops occurred a few days afterwards on 21 February 1915 when a hundred-kilogram blast at Shrewsbury Forest left the 16th Lancers with five officers and seven men killed, twenty-nine wounded and eleven missing; a heavy and abrupt loss. As the news spread a palpable shiver of

The earliest known British mine plans, showing the work of Monmouthshire miners before the formation of the tunnelling companies

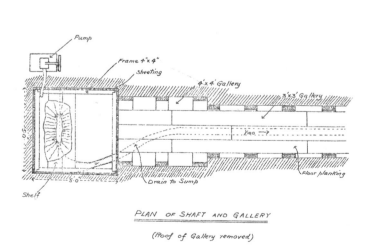

PLAN OF SHAFT AND GALLERY

(Roof of Gallery removed)

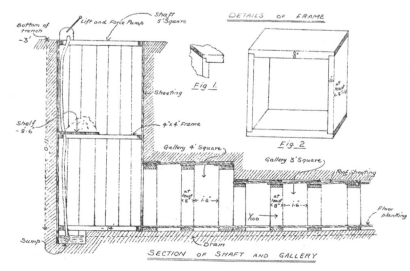

SECTION OF SHAFT AND GALLERY

nervousness passed up and down the line. GHQ were fully aware of the need for protection against hostile tunnelling and had already consented to Divisional and Brigade engineer commanders instigating their own defensive response; but they were also looking to offensive British mining as a useful method of injuring enemy morale and as an adjunct to future surface attacks.

Throughout the winter period it was not mining which preoccupied the army, but security. Most of the engineers on both sides began the process of developing defensive systems in depth with a minimum of three trench lines, front, reserve and support, plus strong points, barbed wire entanglements and communication trenches: the embryonic linear fortress of trench warfare. As this web of parallel systems appeared, the concept of no man's land, a phrase so commonly used today, was born: that strip of ground between the opposing belts of barbed wire, where men could explore and labour only at night, and even then with dubious safety. The German blow at Shrewsbury Forest changed outlooks considerably. Messages demanding more men for defensive mining flew from Battalion, to Brigade, to Division, to Corps and on to HQ. There was nothing they could do except give permission for infantry commanders in the line to make the best of the talents and skills available amongst their own ranks.

EARLY MINING IN THE SALIENT

Official proposals for raising specialist mining units had been made as early as November 1914 as the Salient first began to take shape, but came to nothing through not only a lack of trained men but troops in general. Early British mining was done on a local basis – trench by trench – by groups of men selected from infantry units with an abundance of civilian miners in their ranks. These small teams of about fifty-five men came to be called Brigade Mining Sections and were often led by a RE Field Company officer. With such meagre resources the brigade miners' work could only be small-scale, but was extremely valuable in being for some time the only available counter to the German threat. From January 1915 they contrived both to defend British trenches from underground attack and to harass the Germans wherever possible with a few offensive mines of their own. After the arrival of dedicated and organised tunnelling companies in the Salient in the early spring of 1915, brigade miners were regularly attached to

A rare photograph of a Brigade Mining Section at work on an entirely uncamouflaged British shafthead. Wez Macquart, January 1915

the new 'specialists' for instructional purposes, mainly in listening and defensive mining techniques, but also in the strange practice of 'clay-kicking'. They continued to work alongside but independently of the tunnellers until early 1916, when the Brigade Mining Sections were finally disbanded. Fortunately, their experienced miners did not all return to their infantry battalions; a large percentage transferred to the RE and continued their underground careers, actually fleshing out the ranks of eight tunnelling companies.

Ventures in the early days of 1915 have been described as 'individual', with the quantity and quality of mining schemes being woefully inadequate to have any effect on German superiority. It was crystal clear that at this stage there was no overall 'grand plan' for this style of warfare. Both sides had only the most rudimentary equipment although it was initially quite satisfactory for pushing out short and shallow tunnels to the opposing trenches – if they were close enough to warrant the effort. From twenty, to a rather surprising two hundred yards was the rough distance where mining might be considered feasible. To select potential targets 'local

Early 177 TC mine plan; the Sanctuary Wood workings

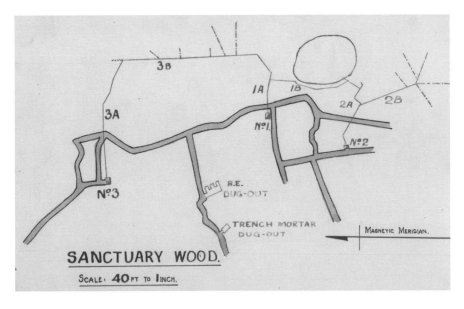

knowledge' was needed. HQ demanded information from the only men who could possibly know, the front line troops themselves.

Fifth Corps. 23.2.15
Reference to your G.757 – the German trenches are closest to ours at the following points:
On right of 23.a. opposite 27th Division, about 40 yards, opposite 24 the German trench is about 30 yards from ours.
Opposite 28, the enemy have run a sap to within about 50 yards from us.
Opposite 32 the enemy are within a few yards of us.
Opposite right of 33, and right of 35, the distance is about 50 yards.
Opposite 44, the Germans are only 20 yards from our trench.
Report to Major-General Bulfin, Commanding 28th Division, February 1915

Even from the earliest days of mining the German *Pioniere* believed that the Royal Engineers, thanks to their regular pre-war siege exercises, were more experienced, more skilled, better equipped and better resourced than their own miners. This view was certainly not shared by many RE officers in 1915. In fact, the uniquely clandestine nature of military mining conspired to persuade both sides of the superiority of the other for a long time, and, although this was a baseless supposition for the British, as no one could actually know the true state of enemy work without seeing their plans or entering their tunnels, it acted as a spur, encouraging engineers to work harder so as not to be 'left behind' and wide open to being blown up – or as the engineers called it, 'lifted' – at will by the Germans.

By the end of February 1915 mine warfare was already gathering a momentum of its own, developing and spreading at a rate at which Brigade miners were unable to respond, and it was the enemy who were instigating almost every new attack. If there was to be any possibility of competing, let alone integrating underground and surface warfare as GHQ desired, a radical British move was required

From The Sapper *magazine: A mine blown by 2nd Field Company RE early in 1915*

MINING BY 2ND FIELD CO., E.L. R.E.
THE START OF THE MINE.

THE END OF THE MINE.

First Corps Memorandum outlining the imminent organisation of special tunnelling companies, 18 February 1915

I consider that 1915 was a year of preparation. There wasn't much to show except the fact that the infantry were holding the same line which they had taken over in 1914, in spite of the fact that the enemy had been trying to blow them out of it almost continuously. Most of the offensive mining of 1915 was devoted to what I call ornamental destruction, which is the demolition of individual snipers' nests, OP's [observation posts] and MG [machine gun] outfits. These were frequently fired to celebrate some day of public rejoicing, Brigadiers' birthdays, and so on, but in no connection with any infantry operation. This sort of mining is perfectly useless for ending a war; it is very unsettling for the occupants of the posts blown up, certainly, but the straf [bombardment] which always followed made our trenches most unhealthy.

Brigadier General R N Harvey, RE,
Inspector of Mines, 1929

THE TUNNELLING COMPANIES AND 'EMPIRE JACK'

The inspiration behind the creation and mobilisation of specialised mining units in the British Army can be largely accredited to the ambition and drive of one man: John Norton-Griffiths. Before the war this self-made entrepreneur, MP, millionaire and businessman was already prominent, rejoicing in the nickname of 'Empire Jack'. In his Wednesbury constituency his campaign slogan carried a simple, direct and typical message.

> For beer or for wages
> You never will lack
> If you plant all your votes
> On to Empire Jack

On the outbreak of war, Norton-Griffiths had been a civil engineer with his own large and successful firm, Griffiths and Co. The company was internationally renowned and had worked in Britain, Canada, Africa and Argentina on railways, bridges, buildings and docks. A glance at his *curriculum vitae* would also reveal a degree of military experience. At the turn of the century in the South African Field Force, Norton-Griffiths had served with Brabant's 2nd Division, and later as Captain and Adjutant of Lord Roberts' bodyguard. John Norton-Griffiths was one of the Great War's most colourful, unsung characters; his achievements in both civilian and military life were so remarkable as to be almost fictional. An unidentified writer who worked closely with him for three years after the Boer War encapsulated his personality and summarised the sentiments of most people who came to know 'Empire Jack'.

Mr J Norton-Griffiths was not a man of action, he was action itself. His energy was dynamic, almost elemental. I have heard him called sometimes a slave driver by people who knew little of him. Such an epithet means only qualities of brute force, without intellect, and of this he had plenty, but for him, the thoughts, the schemes had no value unless they were transformed into acts, and transformed immediately. His imagination, sharpened by an acute quickness of perception, made him see at once in the embryo of a project its ultimate realisation, and seemed to communicate a spark which called for immediate deeds. He had no time to work out details; difficulties

Major John Norton-Griffiths in his role as inspector/ procurer/recruitment officer and controller for the 'Moles'

did not exist. This effervescing energy was often the despair of his collaborators who could hardly keep pace with him, and their work was not rendered any easier. But he was of such a genial disposition, his ways were so attractive, that he used to obtain from everyone, the utmost everyone could give. His capacity for work was tremendous. Quick tempered, impulsive, ready to give his sympathy, he was always willing to help or oblige, but men who lacked enthusiasm, slow at work, difficult to rouse, were of no use to him.

Anonymous author, c. 1930

Officers (above) and men of the 2nd King Edward's Horse. Norton-Griffiths is seated front right

THE 2nd KING EDWARD'S HORSE

Now Quartered at the White City.

A GROUP OF THE OFFICERS

Left to right (seated): Hon. Gideon Murray, Colonel Craddock, who is in command, and Major Norton Griffiths. Among others in the back row are Major Murray, Major Hodder, Captain Hogg, Captain Deller, and Lieutenant Frazer

MEN OF THE RANK AND FILE: A SCENE ON THE DRILL GROUND

Apart from his civil accomplishments, Norton-Griffiths was also celebrated for being instrumental in forming a Yeomanry cavalry battalion before war broke out. Advertising worldwide for old friends and employees, mainly from his South African days, he created in July 1914 the 2nd King Edward's Horse, paying for much of the billeting and equipment from his own pocket. The 1st King Edward's Horse was also a Yeomanry battalion made from 'colonial' volunteers; it never accepted the existence of its rival, yet Norton-Griffiths' band of 'chums' would become one of the few privately raised units to be officially incorporated into the British Army.

One achievement for which Norton-Griffiths has never been properly celebrated was the foundation and formation of the Comrades of the Great War, a non-political veterans' association. Its primary aims were to care for dependants of the fallen, for war veterans suffering hardship, and for the promotion of a continuing bond of friendship after the war was over. The idea was formulated during a conversation with a sergeant in a trench near Ypres in 1915; by 1918 the Comrades was fully formed, raising money and caring for soldiers and their families all over Britain. Norton-Griffiths was to resign when the committee began to use his brainchild as a political football. The Comrades were not to disappear, however; they amalgamated with other smaller organisations and changed their name. Today the Comrades of the Great War are better known as the British Legion. However, it is as the driving force in the formation and organisation of specialist mining companies – to be styled Tunnelling Companies – that Norton-Griffiths made his most direct contribution to the world war.

Norton-Griffiths' military mining career originated in a sewer. In 1910 his company had worked on part of the London Southern Low Level Sewer Contract, and in October 1913 they secured another tunnelling project, a section of the Manchester Main Drainage Scheme, and this work continued throughout 1914. Both projects entailed driving tunnels through the thick layers of clay subsoil that lie beneath the streets of each city; although Norton-Griffiths was not to know it at the time, these conditions were a reasonable simulation, and in the case of London, an almost exact match, of the clay soils later to be encountered in Flanders.

By November 1914 it had become clear to many that the war was not going to be over by Christmas; with his military experience and a civil

engineer's mind, Norton-Griffiths appreciated that if a prolonged and relatively static struggle lay ahead the ancient siege technique of under-mining the enemy might once more be profitable. No details of the ground conditions in Flanders were known to him, but if the clay subsoils were favourable he imagined that experts like his sewermen might be able drive mine galleries using a unique north country method known as clay-kicking. The system involved the manipula-tion of a modified spade known as a 'grafting tool' which was worked with the legs, or 'kicked'. It had proved its worth in Manchester, Liverpool, Preston and hundreds of other sewer, road and rail projects that required cutting through clay subsoils. The special method was an adjunct to traditional pick and spade work, but was espe-cially useful in tunnels which were too small to swing a pick. In all cases, kicking was less exhausting, and far more swift and efficient.

Observing the war becoming more siege-like with each passing week, Norton-Griffiths wrote to the War Office with an offer to assemble a company of 'moles' – a term he used to the annoyance of the Army throughout his military career. There was no reply – the letter had been ignored, filed under 'M' and forgotten. When, however, the Germans planted and blew ten small charges under the Indian Sirhind Brigade at Le Plantin near La Bassée in northern France on 21 December 1914, it was found that no units for retaliatory or protective mining could be mustered by the already overstretched RE Field and Fortress Companies. As news of the mines spread along the line, concern amongst the infantry deepened – were their positions suscep-

Norton-Griffiths' sewermen beneath Barlow Road, Manchester, February 1915. Note 'spits' of clay in the truck and the clay-kicker seated rear centre

tible or perhaps already undermined also? It was critical to make a response. Back in the War Office someone recalled the note on 'moles' and passed it to GHQ. It was received with scepticism. The suggestion that untrained and therefore undisciplined civilians might be taken to the front and set to work on one of the most hazardous tasks in warfare was too much; such men could surely neither be relied upon nor controlled.

The crisis deepened in early January 1915 when intelligence reports suggested that the Germans might be embarking upon a systematic mining offensive. On the 26th fears were confirmed as twenty more enemy mines caused heavy losses, panic and confusion at Cuinchy, also near La Bassée. Although the charges were small by later standards, a considerable length of front-line trench was lost, and despite counter-attacks by the Guards Brigade, was not regained. The new threat was now more than serious, but little could be done to help as the scale and growth of trench warfare was already testing the RE beyond their limits. The only two engineer units trained in siege techniques, the Fortress Companies, already had a section or two on mining work near the Belgian border, and the rest of the Royal Engineer establishment could offer only minimal assistance. The Brigade Mining Sections, newly formed and locally deployed, could have only limited effectiveness. Specialist units were sorely needed.

Back in Whitehall Kitchener, the Minister for War, having heard of the resurrection of the 'moles' letter, interviewed Norton-Griffiths personally in his office. The meeting resulted in an immediate demand for 10,000 clay-kickers. It was an impossible request to fulfil – there were perhaps a thousand or two in the whole country. But Kitchener's commendation of Norton-Griffiths' scheme was enough to set wheels in motion. The War Office wired GHQ that it was now willing to send a draft of Norton-Griffiths' uniquely skilled men to the front – were they in a position to agree? Despite grave reservations about putting untrained civilians into uniform – especially if any were independent-minded Scotsmen – the answer was a desperate yes – send 500 immediately.

On 13 February 1915 Norton-Griffiths was furnished with the rank of Major RE, given authority to cross the Channel, confer with GHQ in France as how best to organise and equip the potential new units, and personally inspect the ground at the front for suitability. The same evening he reported to General Fowke, the Engineer-in-Chief at St Omer, and next day accompanied Fowke's assistant, Colonel Robert Napier Harvey RE (later Brigadier-General and Inspector of Mines), to Bethune before going on to further meetings at Givenchy, where the British mining 'troubles' had first begun.

At every stop Norton-Griffiths had to explain his obscure 'moles' proposal. The furrowed brows of his audience illustrated the hopelessness of attempting an explanation in words, so a mime performance was given, with the new Major lying on the floor and mimicking the actions of his sewermen at work. Thus the upper echelons of the British Army were initiated wide-eyed into the mysteries of clay-kicking. The displays were greeted with amusement and scepticism but a degree of general enthusiasm. It was no more than 'Empire Jack' expected – and no more than he needed.

Discussions about how the moles might be organised within the British Army were equally lively. An early proposal had been to form mining sections within existing Field Companies, but it had been noted from the 1905 report on the Russo–Japanese War, and in all subsequent siege exercises, how important autonomy was to all units engaged in underground warfare. Responses to enemy action had to be immediate, and decisions taken on the spot, so authority and decision making must also be localised. There was also the problem of employing men without so much as a single day's military training. The existing Brigade Mining Sections were hard at work harassing the enemy already. Although small in number they were working well and as a close-knit team; it was considered best to leave them alone. If Field Companies with their myriad duties were also to play host to tunnelling, an activity which was likely to demand round the clock labour with highly specialised skills and specific material needs, there might be conflict. An alternative had to be devised. It was therefore decided to create a body of new and fully distinct specialist units under the direct control of the Royal Engineers. On 19 February 1915 the tunnelling companies were born.

Norton-Griffiths was given carte blanche to develop his new units of moles. It was a unique post; no other officer in the BEF other than the Commander-in-Chief himself had such a free hand to go wherever they wished and do whatever they wanted. For a little over a year Norton-Griffiths would put all his energies into the task, bearing a workload which after his departure in 1916 would be shared by half a dozen men. However, it was no chore; imbued with the spirit and enthusiasm of the adventurer and given the 'freedom' of the Western Front, it was precisely the kind of pioneering challenge he relished. The first step was to get some of his moles to the front.

As with everything Norton-Griffiths did, this first action – like all those which followed – was executed at breakneck speed. Having set up a 'Tunnelling Depot' at 3, Central Buildings, Westminster, his London office, he set off for Manchester. The principal contingent of clay-kickers would be a party of his own employees from the sewer contract. On Thursday 17 February 1915 twenty men were selected and removed from their work beneath the streets. The following day they arrived at Royal Engineers HQ at Chatham. Eighteen were passed and attested. In his diary Norton-Griffiths listed the names of the first moles to go to war.

> Left for France taking first 18 Moles. They were divided as follows:
> 1st Party – 66875 Stamper H, 66865 Banford R, 66876 Barker W C, 66874 Large G, 66870 Welsby F
> 2nd Party – 66863 Carrington F J, 66864 Brown A, 66874 Berry H, 66862 Jones G, 66872 Smith H W, 66861 Williams C
> 3rd Party – 66871 Keen R W, 66867 Gibson R, 66868 Jameson J, 66869 Murphy D, 66860 Ransom S
> 18 in all with one officer, Sec. Lt. L A Barclay RE, transferred.
> Major J Norton-Griffiths, RE, 1915

By lunchtime the following Monday the men were in uniform, equipped with thigh-length gum boots, a knitted khaki balaclava helmet plus a sleeveless leather jerkin, and as part of the embryonic 170 Tunnelling Company were grafting not Mancunian but Flemish clay near the spot where it had all started eight weeks before: the French town of Givenchy. None of the men had received any military training whatso-ever, they were incapable of marching, drilling or saluting, and were more likely to call an officer 'mate' than sir; the mechanism of a rifle was a total mystery. Harry Mosley was in one of the early contingents.

> I was a National Reservist, a clay-kicker. I was a lad of 16 and worked on building the railway from Leeds to Huddersfield. They

170th Company.

Officers.

Lieutenant Lacey.
2/Lieut.L.A.Barclay.

Specially enlisted Tunnellers.

Regtl. No.	Rank	Name	
	Sergeant	R.Miles	
*66875	Sapper	H.Stamper	*Foreman
66865	"	R.Banford	
66876	"	W.C.Barker	
66874	"	G.Large	
66860	"	W.Stafford	
66870	"	F.Welsby	
* 66863	"	F.J.Carrington	*Foreman
66864	"	A.Brown	
66874	"	H.Berry	
66862	"	G.Jones	
66872	"	W.H.Smith	
66861	"	C.Williams	
* 66871	"	P.W Keen	*Foreman
66867	"	R.Gibson	
66868	"	F.Jameson	
66869	"	D.Murphy	
66860	"	S.Ransom	

The first men to arrive in France – the nucleus of 170 Tunnelling Company

showed me how to clay kick for laying drains and so on underground. I volunteered and went into the Yorkshire Light Infantry. We were training at Hythe. Norton-Griffiths came. All the men were paraded 'Take two paces to the front' – he called out some names. I wondered where he'd got mine from. We stood out and were mustered – we were all miners. Norton-Griffiths went round each company calling out names, and the men stood out. They put us on parade then, and marched the others away. He told us to get ready as we were going away and that we were going to be specially enlisted tunnellers for a job that he knew we could do. We were the people he wanted. We weren't volunteers. We all jumped at it though, when he told us the figure we were going to get – from a shilling a week to six shillings a day! I got six shillings a day right from the start. They mobilised us. I was in the first tunnelling companies to go to France.
Lance-Corporal Harry Mosley, 170 TC, RE

Being only a teenager, Mosley was not precisely Norton-Griffiths' preferred material. He was looking for a different class of man, older, wiser, and steadier, but trained professional clay-kickers like him were a rare species and none could be overlooked. Norton-Griffiths' own hands-on mining experience around the world had taught him that stability and dependability underground usually came only with experience; having seen the early reports of underground warfare at the front, and the psychological effect of mines on surface troops, it was clear that the stresses of tunnelling were likely to test the nerves of even the stoutest civilian miner. It was absolutely true. In the future his moles would face more intense, more constant, more insidious, more prolonged and potentially more barbaric dangers than any other branch of the services.

Recruiting qualified workers was one thing, but it was equally necessary to employ experienced mining men in command. The task of finding them was not an onerous one. The British Empire was at its peak and spanned the globe. Mines owned and operated by British companies existed in almost every colony. The younger generation of engineers employed in lower management level were keen to enlist and 'do their bit' for King and Country, and if they could bring their professional experience to bear, all the better. The most appropriate unit for such men was clearly the Royal Engineers; for a miner, the

1915 tunnelling officer hopefuls on the steps of what is today the Royal Engineers' Library

choice could only be one of the new tunnelling companies.

I belonged to the Institution of Mining and Metallurgy in the student grade. They sent out a circular stating that they had been asked by the War Office to recruit their members for the new tunnelling companies of the Royal Engineers. I replied I would like to transfer to a tunnelling company. I don't think I mentioned this to anyone. In about a week I was told there was a telephone call for me. The signaller said it was from GHQ. I took the phone. A voice said, 'This is Colonel Norton-Griffiths, the IMM have suggested your name for the tunnellers'. I said I did not think signals would let me go. He replied, 'Do you want to be a tunneller?' I said, 'Yes, sir'. He said he would arrange at once for me to go to 171st Tunnelling Company who were not far off. The Brigade Major said it was nonsense to suppose I could transfer when I told them. In a few days the transfer came through, my surprised CO was told it was not open to argument.

Lieutenant Brian Frayling, 171 TC, RE

NO. 39 (TUNNELLING OFFICERS) CLASS.

A. I. Beveridge.   C. Y. Bruce.   F. G. Herdman.   W. Stewart.   E. H. A. Joseph.   N. S. K. McCallum.

B. J. Gillard.   B. J. Lambie.   S. Butler.   E. Barker.   H. M. Eddowes.

Like his moles, the first officer recruits were assessed personally by Norton-Griffiths, and many went equally untrained in military matters straight to the front. Military tuition was to be an osmotic process, with clues garnered from the regular soldiers who surrounded them, and by trial and many errors. Few knew what kind of life they were heading towards or what their duties would be. And none imagined it would be such a thoroughly clandestine affair. Although the 'glorious deeds' of the infantry were regularly reported in the press, tunnelling was to be a furtive and secret occupation almost from the start. There were few press reports from which to glean information, and neither the staff at Engineer HQ at Chatham nor GHQ in France knew anything of the work except to tell prospective officers and their men where to report for duty.

There had been no time for military training or unit establishment in Britain; indeed, having crossed the Channel one tunnelling company was actually formed on a railway platform in Boulogne. Introduction to the trenches, however, of which so much had already been heard at home, was universally anticipated with excitement. Many found the contrasts to be stark.

The mess-room of the 180th seemed like a haven of rest. I arrived just in time for dinner which I thought surprisingly good. After the meal I was shown to my billet and here was another pleasant surprise for I found that I had been allotted a cosy little room in the house of an old French couple. There was an old-fashioned bedstead with a tempting display of white linen. A few easy chairs, a table, and a bureau completed the furniture. On the walls were hung old prints and pictures and numerous crosses, crucifixes and rosaries. I crept into bed with a sigh of luxurious contentment and was soon fast asleep.

27th November 1915. One's first visit to the trenches must naturally be a supremely wonderful experience. The firing line, the battle front had a compelling attraction to which few healthy males are insensible. It appeals to the old fierce combatant instincts which are always slumbering close up to that very thin veneer of artificiality with which centuries of what we somewhat vaguely termed civilisation has clothed us; a veneer of acquired habits, a veneer compounded of conventionality, false pride, blatant conceit, effeminate fastidiousness and a plethora of hastily manufactured social laws. With this thin crust we have encased ourselves and have learned to talk with smug complacency of 'culture' and 'progress' and with the pitying arrogance of conscious superiority of 'savagery' and 'barbarism'. And all the while underneath this polished exterior the primitive instincts, the primordial passions have been smouldering and spreading and gathering strength by suppression. Then war comes and smashes the flimsy armour that we thought so strong. We stood stripped and shorn of artificiality and cant and the passions that shook the contending armies were the passions of our cave-dwelling ancestors in the dim, red dawn of human history. These were the thoughts that flickered through my mind as I awoke to my first day of war.

I started out in the dull, grey chillness of a November dawn on my first trip to trench-land. The thoughts and longings of a year were to be crystallised in fact. Accompanied by another officer, a chap named Thorburn, who had spent some years on the Rand, I left the grimy war torn little town and headed up the long straight paved road. The road was torn and rutted by shellfire and transport traffic until it almost resembled a cart track on the Karoo. On either hand was a countryside of indescribable desolation. Where once had been green, smiling pastures and well-tilled fields was now a dreary waste of weeds, an unkempt wilderness of yellow grass and cankerous undergrowth. Here and there piles of debris, brick and plaster and protruding beams, marked where the homely cottages of the peasantry once stood. Now not a peasant was to be seen. They had fled before the terrible, all destroying tidal wave of war and the little homes which had sheltered them for years had been pounded to shapeless heaps by the roaring guns. Everywhere was solitude, dreariness and ruin.
Captain Matthew Roach 180 and 255 TC, RE,
27 November 1915

Having benefited from a period of military training at home with a battalion of the Duke of Cornwall's Light Infantry, officers like Matthew Roach had been transferred straight to the front. But his was an unusual case; most prospective tunnelling officers recruited in Britain arrived without military experience, receiving only a week's basic instruction in Chatham before being assessed for suitability. As time passed and the appalling nature of the tunnel war was understood by Engineers HQ, selection became ever more careful. Those who failed to pass the rigorous tests for attachment to the tunnellers were assigned work in other RE units such as Field or Signal Companies. For the other ranks, the clay-kickers themselves, joining up was a relatively straightforward process. Each prospective tunneller passed through Chatham to be sworn in, kitted out and prepared for embarkation to France and Belgium.

I had to proceed to St Mary's Barracks, Chatham. I travelled down on the train to London with an old school chum called Knowles. I had dinner with him and he paid for it – it was the first time I had had a bottle of beer on a train. As a youth I had been Lads Brigade, so I had had some experience in training and drill. The recruiting bloke was trying to straighten all these miners up, and trying to teach them how to form fours and slope a rifle. Half the time he'd tell them to go back with the left leg and they'd go back with the right – they couldn't drill them into it because some of the miners were 50 years of age. I used to be dismissed because I could do it. Anyway, we knew we wouldn't be there long because we hadn't gone to fight, we'd gone to work.

Sapper Hubert Leather 175 TC, RE

You had to laugh at some of the antics. Drilling was a shambles. It was not their fault of course, quite a lot of them seemed to me to be old men, and they had come straight from the pits, I believe. But our regular sergeant-majors were horrified. I can see their faces now. I think the problem was that their pride was hurt in failing to make anything like soldiers of the miners. With normal RE recruits we had time to get them into shape – weeks and months – but with the miners it was so urgent to get them out to France that a few days was all that could be spared. It was all right for me, I was a volunteer and I don't think I had the same sense of history and pride in the Corps as the old stagers. The frustration of it! The language they [the RSMs] came out with had to heard to be believed; I'm sure even miners had never heard half of what was yelled at them day in and day out. It made no difference though, they knew they were going to the front in a few days, and were going to dig not drill. I saw a lot of tunneller drafts pass

through and every time I wondered if they ever drilled again during the war.

Drill Corporal Frank Parsons, RE

Later there was more breathing space for training, more time to shape recruits, and for inculcation into army ways. A tunnelling officer would spend five weeks on a basic tunnelling course, including a period learning mine rescue, with other ranks receiving an introduction to military life, mainly on the barrack square. The skills which the army required most urgently, however, were already built into the tunnelling recruits, with their backgrounds in practical mining and engineering. They might have known little of military etiquette but arrived with a strong sense of underground discipline, a familiarity with confined spaces, an intuitive camaraderie, and the miners' innate ability to work hard in cramped and uncomfortable environments. Many were also trained in timbering, explosives, the dangers of mine gases, and rescue.

We had a Regular CO, the other officers were from mines all over the world. Although the first draft to the company had been clay-kickers, the rest were coal miners. These came from all the coalfields of Britain. I soon formed the opinion that in a difficult situation underground one Geordie from Durham was worth two of any other kind. The Durham miner had had a hard upbringing in narrow, wet seams. It was a Geordie who, on enlistment, was naked in front of the medical officer who asked 'Have you been circumcised?' 'Oh no, Sir,' replied Geordie, 'That's just fair wear and tear.'

Lieutenant Brian Frayling, 171 TC, RE

Actually, many commanding officers held that those men who had received no military training at all were easier to handle underground. Norton-Griffiths had always felt this way, his opinion and recommendation being that careful selection of men was all that was required.

The men are mostly from the mining districts and have been transferred from line regiments. Thus I have a good many Royal Scots in my party. There are also some specially enlisted men who have worked for municipal corporations on sewers, etc., and they act as foremen. They are very useful men, but, as they have had no military training, they are quite unfamiliar with Army methods. That, however, is a minor (not miner) detail on this job.

Lieutenant Walter Gardner, 172 TC, RE,
1 April 1915

One of the most curious ironies was how the hastily recruited and uninitiated military mole could become omnipotent once below ground. Whilst in the trenches the tunneller was, of course, subject to the same regulations as all his infantry colleagues. But should a Brigadier, General – even Sir Douglas Haig himself – visit a tunnel system without a tunnelling officer being present, such luminaries would fall under the immediate authority of the most lowly soldier. In this most hazardous and particular environment, the tunneller was king, and must be obeyed.

Following another of Norton-Griffiths' early suggestions each Army was to have its own Mine School behind the lines. For the Salient the 2nd Army School was at Proven, near Poperinghe. Here, officers and NCOs were put through several courses on a rotational basis to avoid over depletion of the unit, and although instruction was fairly basic as most learning was done in the field, technical courses in listening and mine rescue introduced the student to the more esoteric aspects of the work.

Once the decision to form the tunnelling companies had been made, it was imperative that ranks should be quickly bolstered, bringing them up to a full working strength as soon as possible. The aim was have enough trained tunnellers in each of four sections to work three or four headings constantly, day and night. Eventually there were two establishments: higher, with a total of 550 men, and lower, with 325. At first, the numbers of civilian mining volunteers fell short of requirements, so Infantry Brigade Commanders in the field were asked to submit the names of men under their command with mining experience who could be offered a transfer to the tunnellers. Even the Brigade of Guards did not escape the request.

JOINING UP – THE TUNNELLING MEN

On joining up tunnellers who were not applying as officers were assessed at Chatham. They were required to state the number of years they had worked, the positions held, where and when they had last been employed underground and whether they possessed any mining certificates, before being segregated into two groups according to experience and skill.

The key workers were to be the 'face-men', those who did the actual clay-kicking and timbering, with a secondary group known as 'mates'. Mates could be 'timbermen', 'baggers', or 'runners-out' and were responsible for assisting in timbering the gallery, bagging the spoil and getting it out of the tunnels. In practice, however, all took turns at kicking. A third group, those who had held posts as foremen in civilian life, were usually recruited as NCOs, and became known as 'gangers'. Stiffening would come from warrant officers drawn from regular army Royal Engineers, CSMs and CQMSs with years of pre-war experience. The company worked under a regular Royal Engineer Major or Captain as Officer Commanding (OC), with four section officers, professional engineers, holding the temporary rank of subaltern. Each officer was furnished with a servant, or 'batman'.

Face-men received six shillings a day, an excellent wage for a working man at the time; a mate received two shillings and tuppence. Both rates were considerably higher than that of the average infantryman, whose daily pay was a meagre one shilling and threepence. Harry Mosley was posted to 173 Tunnelling Company, one of the first to make a start in Flanders. On his first night at the front the young man was given responsibility for No. I subsection of No. 4 section, and assigned the apparently simple task of having his men carry the necessary kit to the trenches ready for work to begin the following day.

FIELD SERVICE POST CARD.

(For use of Tunnelling Companies only.)

I am { pretty well / absolutely } fed up.

I have { paid / not paid } my mess bill.

I have had no rum for { ....days. / ....weeks. }

No....................Section is the best.

I hope to get leave in 19 { 17. / 18. }

Signature only...

Date......................................

22608/Bx451—126m 10/16   B.S. & Co. Ltd.

Tunneller's non-standard version of the ubiquitous Field Service Postcard

The first night we went in we were given a guide. I had to take the men up and when I got to a certain landmark I had to start to take them in extended order [single file]. About twelve men, every man had an implement, a piece of timber, hammers, picks, to be taken to where we were going to put the mine down. I didn't know where we were going or anything. I sent them off in order of ten paces. When I got the last man going I went up front but it took me a long time to catch up. You could hear the bullets going ping ping over your heads. When we were going up Taffy Davies lost the connecting file. It was dark, and the ones following behind lost the others. When I got there, there were only three men. I went down looking for them and I came across an officer. He said 'What are you doing here? What do you belong to?' I said 'Tunnelling Company'. And he said

'Tunnelling Company?' I said, 'Yes, we're going to put some saps in around here.' So then he said, 'Get back, we're expecting an attack at dawn'.

But I'd no need to tell my men to go back – they'd all gone back! I was able to follow their tracks by all the tackle – they'd thrown it all away on the way back.

Lance-Corporal Harry Mosley, 173 TC, RE

It was not the last time that the tunnellers would make unilateral decisions on active service.

TUNNELLERS AND *PIONIERE*

You are probably thinking what a splendid, heroic body of men they must have been, who did these things. And you are right, my friends! But it was all created painstakingly out of nothing. Mining warfare had not been taught in the German Army since 1890, and only a few older pionier officers knew anything of this art which had been practised on the training grounds virtually unchanged since the days of Frederick the Great. When the War came, everything had to be learned again from the beginning.

Oberstleutnant Otto Füsslein,
Kommandeur des Mineure,
4th German Army

German *Festungsbataillone* were the first to begin mining on the Western Front. It was a natural step to send troops trained in siege tactics underground, but as with the British it was soon found that there were far too few trained personnel to cope with the expansion of mining in 1915. The shortage led to Divisions and Regiments organising their own 'Berg' or 'Stollenbau' companies composed, like the British Brigade Mining Sections, of infantrymen with civilian mining experience commanded by an officer with an engineering background.

The foresight and efficiency with which the Germans planned their surface war was strangely absent when it came to military mining. Command structures and working practices were totally different from those of the British, lacking unity, coordination and continuity. Mining had hardly been exercised by the German Army for decades before the war, and although the British were certainly only a little better prepared for underground conflict they began, largely through the efforts of John Norton-Griffiths, to bring together trained civilian miners, to take geologi-

The major British mining sectors in the Salient and their German counterparts

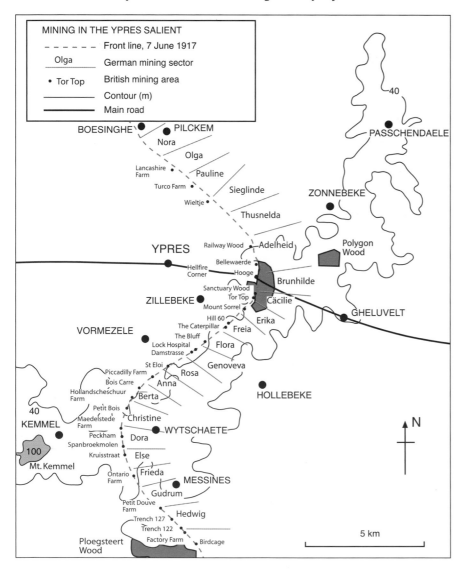

cal advice, and to think on a grand scale far sooner than their enemy.

The primary consideration in military mining is the promotion of a close familiarity with one's ground. In pre-twentieth-century mine warfare this was never a problem; the attentions of a besieging force were fixed on one immobile objective, the fortress, until it was either captured or the siege was broken. Under the mutual siege conditions of trench warfare on the Western Front the battleground was indeed fixed as in earlier times, but the fighting troops were not. The Royal Engineers believed that in order for mining to be effective a tunnelling company must know their sector intimately, and only time and experience on and under the same piece of front could achieve this. The obvious course of action was not to attach tunnelling companies to mobile divisions, as were most field companies, but to designate tunnellers as Army troops thus making them relatively 'immobile'.

The British eventually had five Armies on the Western Front, each of which was made up of Corps, Divisions, Brigades and Battalions, units that were permanently attached to their host Army. When on active service Corps and Divisions remained relatively stationary but their smaller offspring, Brigades and especially Battalions, moved in and out of the line in different sub-sectors regularly, constantly on the move yet remaining within their respective wider Army boundaries.

A battalion might therefore find itself serving in a particular area for a period and then be transferred to another sector, possibly several kilometres away. This relief system was deliberately planned to prevent infantry becoming 'stale', to avoid units remaining for long periods in sectors more dangerous and stressful than others, and to allow new arrivals to acclimatise in a quiet 'nursery' area before moving to less temperate quarters. As Army troops British tunnellers were deliberately divorced from this relief system; they were allotted a sector and stayed there, defending their own underground 'patch', whilst the infantry units in the trenches above came and went. Action and reaction underground was often executed in alliance with the wishes of the local Brigadier or divisional Commander, but the tunnellers' field of activity remained firmly fixed for long periods. The nascent Salient was shared with the French until the first week of April 1915, when the whole of the area from Armentières to Boesinghe came under British 2nd Army authority. It was to remain their responsibility for the duration of the war.

The German *Pioniere* were unable to benefit from any of the advantages enjoyed by their sapper counterparts. The German Army Staff, working from a revision of the eminently practical, functional and, until March 1916, entirely appropriate 'Old Mining Regulations' from the 1870s, were content with the flying start made by their tunnellers, but they had not considered it necessary to draw up a separate structure for the formation, command and organisation of specialist military mining units. This condemned their tunnellers to labour within the rigid military framework of the Division to which they remained permanently attached. It was to prove a crucial error.

Tunnellers camp, Dickebusch. One of the homes for many men working underground at St Eloi, Hill 60 and The Bluff

Although engaged in tunnelling, the Pionier was still classed as a surface combatant. When reliefs took place he was required to move on with his infantry colleagues, leaving the workings to new men who, perhaps not knowing the underground system in that sector,

172 TC Officer at rest in his hut at Dickebusch

British officers of 172 TC letting off steam after a hard shift in the St Eloi and Bluff tunnels

had to 'learn the ropes' afresh. Even if relieved by men familiar with the ground, incomers suffered from disorientation as the workings naturally expanded over time, and a period of re-familiarisation became obligatory. The system was disastrous, interrupting important works and bringing confusion and exasperation to mining commanders. There were further complications. In addition to mining, *Pioniere* were also required to perform some of the other duties of a front-line infantryman, fighting if necessary, repairing and extending surface earthworks, and doing the essential 'housework' demanded by trench warfare. The result was that some underground workings

could be left unprogressed and empty for days, even weeks, making continuity of work at best patchy and at worst non-existent. There were in fact too many diverse units doing too little work without a firm central independent control. To cap it all, the infantry used a spell in the mines as field punishment for miscreants.

In the early days of the underground war in Flanders, there were no mining units. Mining companies were formed of volunteers drawn from army units, mainly miners, tunnellers and specialist tradesmen, commanded by mining engineers, engineers from other disciplines and other officers with relevant skills. There was no time for elaborate training away from the front. We learnt our trade by battling with the earth, the water and the enemy, mastering the art of sinking shafts, driving tunnels, blowing charges, listening, and everything else that mining entails, in particular working with machinery. Lectures given by our officers and training carried out in the companies ensured that the knowledge and experience of individuals was shared. Soon, however, the miners were recalled to the homeland. In the end – and there were ultimately fifteen, mostly self-formed, mining companies operating in Flanders – we had virtually no miners or craftsmen, and the officers, apart from a small number of mining engineers and deputies, were lawyers, teachers, post office administrators and students.

> Oberstleutnant Otto Füsslein,
> Kommandeur des Mineure,
> 4th German Army

Tunnelling officers of German Pionier *Company 324*

Difficulties were later compounded by the recall of many experienced military miners from the front lines to the Fatherland to cope with shortages of coal, metal ores and other commodities desperately needed by the German war machine. Everything was to change in May 1916, when a unified and systematic approach to German mining was put in place. Not unexpectedly, it emulated the British model.

APPROACHES TO MINE WARFARE, 1915

Field fortification presupposes a defensive attitude, and, though recourse to it may under certain circumstances be desirable, IT MUST ALWAYS BE REGARDED AS A MEANS TO AN END, AND NOT AN END IN ITSELF.

Manual of Field Engineering, 1911

Offiziere der Pionier- (Mineur-) Komp. 324.

n links nach rechts: Aff.-Arzt Zehl, Lt. Müller (Max), Lt. Wichmann, Lt. Kirsch, Lt. Müller (Moritz), Lt. Hülsenberg.

This statement illustrates precisely the attitude of those responsible for military mining in the British Army. The fear and panic triggered by two months of poorly opposed German mine attacks in French Flanders in early 1915 provoked GHQ, on the formation of the tunnelling companies, to insist on a purely defensive tactical response. It worried many, not least the gung-ho Norton-Griffiths, that offence was being relegated to secondary importance. For the first year of war the British were apparently 'on the back foot' underground, and certainly receiving far more punishment than they gave.

What the Germans did not know was that since the day of their formation in February 1915 the tunnelling companies had been *ordered* to pursue a predominantly defensive policy. It was known and accepted by the British that for a while this strategy might entail serious enemy molestation, but they believed it would pay off and ultimately permit the launch of much more damaging major offensive schemes. Mines HQ had decided that offensive mine warfare could only be successful if derived from a position of defensive strength. The Germans had no inkling of their enemy's perceived inferiority; in their eyes the British had made a creditable first response – to them the simple fact was that their

Pioniere were superior miners, and their duty now was to keep the pressure on by increasing the numbers of men and of offensive actions. Indeed they continued to score far more successes throughout 1915 and into the spring of 1916, erroneously thinking that they had nullified any possibility of substantial British offensive mining schemes.

The *Pionier* officer signalled to his Feldwebel. 'They are quiet!'
Now, hundreds of thoughts reel through their minds. 'What are they up to? Are they ready? Will they fire the charge now? And take us and all our explosives with it?' Their faces are tense as they spur on the *Pioniere*.
'This is it!'
The *Pioniere* know exactly what they mean: this is a race against time, against death. Faster and faster they move the bags of explosive forward. Has the enemy barrage started yet? That would be the sign for firing the charge. The reply is passed down from the surface 'No!' The detonators are placed and firing wires rolled out through the tunnels to a dugout. Tamping! Sandbags are passed down, hundreds stacked in front of the charge. The *Pioniere* are still thumping the

Pioniere-Mineure of 352 Company at their billet Villa Glück Auf near Messines

wall in a confusing rhythm. The *Pionier* officer raises his hand and everything stops. The grumble of the pumps cease. The Feldwebel squats down next to the officer who lies motionless on the floor:

'What's going on?'

'They are working! They are working again!'

The message is passed back through the gallery; pumps restart, the thumping on the wall begins once more. Work continues and the tamping grows yard by yard.

'Everybody out!'

Men creep out of the tunnel and disappear into the darkness one by one. The officer checks the leads.

'They're OK.'

The closest dugouts are warned, the infantry moves back. Dawn is breaking. The first skylarks rise sleepily from the grass. Suddenly...the earth lifts; a dull thump reverberates through the waking countryside ...deep in the guts of the earth the *Pioniere* have won the race, and the tunnels of the enemy have been destroyed.

Leutnant Otto Rubicke, 2 *Kompagnie, Pionier-Battaillon* 28

As the British continued to concentrate on the installation of defensive mine systems, the Germans became convinced that their *Pioniere* were overwhelmingly superior at underground warfare, reading report after report about successful mine blows, but without wondering why the British, whom they had long thought of as being better equipped, better led and better trained, were not responding more effectively. As far as the Germans were concerned the facts stood for themselves, and there was clearly no need to change an organisation which was apparently working perfectly well. Complacency reigned. The British, with a clear goal, trained men, and a well-organised autonomous command structure, grasped the opportunity with both hands. It was indeed the very success of the German *Pioniere* which led to their downfall. The problem was not a lack of skill, determination, or gallantry, but of organisational foresight. German commanders, quite content in the belief that their men held the upper hand below ground, were happy to maintain the structural status quo – a status quo which ruled that *Pioniere* remain infantrymen. The decision was to prove disastrous.

The situation was to be forcibly changed in May 1916 with the formation of a dedicated and thoroughly reorganised German mining corps which resembled the British model. The new units were called the *Pionier Mineur Kompagnien* or simply *Mineur Kompagnien*, and more than fifty had been formed by the beginning of 1918. In the Ypres sector they would be led by a talented and far-sighted officer, Oberstleutnant Otto Füsslein. But by the time Füsslein took over it was already too late. The great plan to blow the Messines Ridge had been hatched, and the ultimate fate of the German mining corps was already sealed. The tables were turning, and in 1916 the British were to blow 750 mines to the Germans' 696.

What the Germans really lacked was a John Norton-Griffiths.

Oberstleutnant Otto Füsslein, Kommandeur des Mineure

Chapter V
KRIEGSGEOLOGIE: GOING UNDERGROUND

Although mining had been going on for nine months before I took over the appointment of Inspector of Mines, I did not realise that geology had anything to do with military mining. We were not mining very deeply in those days, and naturally if we came to a wet place, if the Germans were mining we continued, and if it was wet we pumped; but there was no geological science so far as that was concerned. It was when we came to deep mining that its importance was obvious.

Brigadier-General R N Harvey, 1919

When the European nations went to war, none of them expected that they would need advice from geologists, scientists trained in the wider understanding of the earth's surface and subsurface conditions. Yet one man, Captain Walter Kranz, a German engineer attached to a *Festungsbataillon* stationed at Strasbourg, had insight. By 1913 Kranz had already written of the necessity of understanding geological conditions for any foray into France. As a geologist, he knew that if the battlefront was to be along a 650-kilometre frontier from the English Channel to the Swiss border, then it would need to take into account the stark lithological contrasts between the wet Flanders plain and the hard crystalline rocks of the Vosges mountains; but as the enactment of the Schlieffen Plan in 1914 already pronounced that the German armies would avoid the most complex terrain, Kranz's advice was left on the back burner. However, with the first expression of trench warfare in late 1914, and the growing need to find adequate supplies of drinkable water by methods other than dousing, by early 1915 the German High Command had fully awoken to the need for

frontline geologists. These first military geologists – *Militärgeologen* – were to apply scientific principles to the war effort – but on the Eastern Front – providing advice to the general staff on aspects as diverse as road metal, drinking water and landslides. Kranz's concept of the value of geology in warfare – *Kriegsgeologie* – had been born.

GEOLOGISTS AND MINING

Until the Great War the objectives of military miners had traditionally been large and clearly defined – forts and castles – with the besieger often better equipped and outnumbering the besieged. On the Western Front armies found themselves facing an enemy with roughly equal resources spread over a vast area, possessing not one but thousands of potential objectives, each of varying tactical value.

It became immediately clear to both British sapper and German *Pionier* that successful military mining even on a flankless battlefield demanded precisely the same preconditions as it had for millennia: that the position of the objective was fixed, that it was within reach, that it would remain immobile, that there was enough time to carry out the work, and that the ground between the attacker and the objective was mineable. This meant that the surface soils and the strata beneath – the local geology – could be easily worked and excavated with normal tools. Trench warfare in the British sectors of Flanders, Artois and Picardy at least, abundantly satisfied all these requirements. In Flanders particularly, the key was geology, and is the starting point for any discussion on mining.

In 1915 the war underground in the Salient was not necessarily guided by geologists. The

German establishment of *Kriegsgeologen* grew throughout the year but much of their work was theoretical, and those men engaged in actual geological work at the front were in junior positions; they were expected simply to advise, but not supervise. For example, although the German 4th Army was responsible for the Ypres Salient, their geological staff were remote, based in Lille, and working from the laboratories of the eminent French geologist, Professor Charles Barrois. Other German geologists sent to the front occupied lowly positions; their opinion was not sought by High Command.

At the outbreak of war the British Army had no geological staff whatsoever. In early 1915 tunnelling company commanders requiring information about soil conditions were recommended to visit the nearest *préfectures* for maps produced before the war by the Belgian Geological Survey.

British military geologist Lieutenant W B R King

Yet in the nineteenth century different conditions applied. Then the Royal Engineers had a reputation for both practical and theoretical engagement in all aspects of military engineering, with officers routinely instructed in geological techniques by notable geologists such as Alexander Henry Green, Professor of Geology at Oxford. Following Green's death in 1896, the study of geology was lost to the RE, such that by the outbreak of the Great War it had faded from view.

It was the chronic need for water in both the Dardanelles and on the Western Front that led to the appointment of Britain's first geologist in uniform. Lieutenant W B R 'Bill' King, who had worked for the British Geological Survey, was an infantry officer serving with the Royal Welsh Fusiliers. At the request of Major General W A Liddle, Director of Works at GHQ, and following a recommendation by his former employers, Bill King was to become the first British geologist to receive a military assignment in his own profession. Seconded to Major-General G H Fowke, the Engineer-in-Chief of the BEF, he was put to work in Flanders and Artois exploring for water. In Flanders, King tackled the problem of polluted water supplies – surface waters contaminated by poison gases and the human detritus of war – and also determined a way of tapping the clean water-filled fine sands that lay beneath the clay plain; on the Somme he examined the effect of fluctuating water levels in the porous, freely draining chalk rocks, and was able to predict how far the RE needed to sink boreholes to permanently tap the sweet waters at depth. For a year King worked in isolation.

In May 1916 the Australian Mining Corps detrained on the Western Front at Bailleul. The three companies of 'Diggers' joined the Canadian 'Beavers' who, arriving a little earlier, also formed three tunnelling companies. A single New Zealand company was also formed, but were to work mainly in the Vimy and Arras sectors of Artois. This reinforcement was a great shot in the arm for the British moles who had been hard at work underground for over a year. Most of the newcomers were already experienced in civilian mining and were immediately attached to RE Companies for instruction in the art of military mining – a very different proposition, as they were quickly to discover. All of the new units were under overall command of the British Engineer-in-Chief, General Fowke

With the Australians came Major T W Edgeworth David FRS. Professor of Geology at Sydney University, David was an influential scientist who had helped raise and recruit the Australian Mining Corps. The Corps had originally been bound for Gallipoli, but before they arrived on the Peninsula the Anzac positions had been abandoned, and the miners were diverted to France. Welsh-born David, at 58 already advanced in years, was attached to Mines HQ and became the most senior British military geologist in the Great War. He was to work under Brigadier-General R N Harvey, the recently appointed Inspector of Mines. Harvey's role was to bring order to the apparently endlessly expanding and complicated underground war; under him, the complete mining operation would be re-organised and coordinated, charges would no longer be blown without good reason, and no scheme would be considered without consultation with other relevant and complimentary branches of the Army. He was eventually to administer his duties through three Assistant Inspectors, and locally through a Controller of Mines for each Army in the field.

Whilst with Harvey, David had a roving commission. His role was principally that of geological work in relation to mining and dugouts, and providing practical advice and trouble-shooting where necessary for all the British armies in the field; together Harvey and David made a potent force that offered a focused direction for British mining efforts. In practice, although King was attached to the Engineer-in-Chief at GHQ, with a remit to concentrate upon water supply, both he and David were also to work closely together within all the British sectors of the Western Front. For two and a half years both men, assisted from September 1916 by another Australian geologist, Lieutenant Loftus Hills, used test bores to ascertain water levels and soil types, ultimately incorporating them into a series of highly informative geological maps intended for the use of the British armies in Flanders.

Professor David was already a well-known public figure when he arrived in Flanders. He had achieved celebrity by accompanying Sir Ernest Shackleton on the Antarctic Expedition of 1907–9, and had himself led the party that had been the first to reach the South Magnetic Pole in 1908. The arrival of such a high-profile figure on the Western Front caused quite a stir within British tunnelling companies.

23rd May 1916. An Australian Tunnelling Company is to take over this sector. They have already been here several days and are being initiated into the mysteries of mining on

Major T W Edgeworth David FRS

The man who ran the British mining 'game', Brigadier-General R N Harvey

the Western Front. Men and officers are doing their shifts in the trenches and the officers have practically taken over their sections from us. They have with them a Major 'Dr' David who accompanied Sir Ernest Shackleton to the South Pole. He was the geologist of the expedition. I believe he is a Professor of Geology at Sydney University, at any rate he is undoubtedly a geologist of considerable note. He is one of the most likeable and interesting men I have ever met. He recounts his South Polar experiences with a vividness and quiet modesty that is charming and at the same time absorbingly interesting. From what I can gather he will have charge of some Artesian well sinkings which the 1st Army are commencing. Another interesting fellow is Kennedy who was surveyor to the Mawson expedition. The men are a far superior lot to ours but I think will need careful and tactful handling as they have been subjected to very little military discipline and are very much imbued with the Trades Union spirit.

Captain Matthew Roach 255 TC, RE

Another 255 TC officer, Captain H R Dixon, was to work very closely with David as an Assistant Inspector of Mines. In his memoirs Dixon recalled the humour and charm of the 'professor', especially in dealing with lower ranks.

It was said that he was the politest man who ever came out of Australia. I can still remember his method of addressing his Batman: 'Johnson, I have left my Sam Browne in my billet. I wonder if you would mind stepping over for it, that is if you have time'. The gentle tone of his voice it is impossible to explain; but it will readily be believed that David was loved by all who knew him, and he speedily became one of the best known characters in the Army.

He would come back to the office having been sent for by the General to discuss one of his technical reports, and remarked quietly 'Well, well, it didn't hurt so much that time.' It was a standing joke between us that his attitude to the General was that of a small boy going in to see the headmaster. His reports were always first written out, and once he came back very sadly, because the report had all to be re-written. 'The General says nobody on the General Staff knows anything about

geology, and that I am not to use any technical terms. He asked me if I could expect anyone over there to know what an anticline [a broad arching fold in rock strata] is!'

Captain H R Dixon, 255 TC, RE

Even the Inspector of Mines himself, Brigadier-General Harvey, was awed by David being placed under his command.

Harvey said to me 'Do you know Professor David?' I said 'Oh, rather, the explorer chap.' 'Well, he's Major David now. He was up at GHQ and I called him in to see me. There was this tall man – he stood strictly to attention. I said 'You have done a lot of exploring?' 'Yes, sir.' 'Do you like it here?' 'Yes, sir.' Then I said to him 'Look here David, for Christ's sake sit down and stop embarrassing me by standing to attention. You have done 20 times more in your life than I shall ever do.'

Lieutenant Alan Reid, 172 TC, RE

The British military geological establishment remained at an apparently meagre total of three throughout the most of the war, in contrast to the German organisation of an estimated 250 men on all fronts. For the British, it was not until the underground war was effectively over that two more geologists, transferred from tunnelling companies, joined them in the autumn of 1918 – Lieutenant G A Cook of the 2nd Australian TC and Lieutenant C S Homan of the 3rd Australian TC. This establishment of five were to advise on geological conditions during the Allied advance in 1918.

The greatest success for the British tunnellers and their geological advisors was to come in June 1917 when the Messines–Wytschaete Ridge was captured in the most effective and successful battle of the Great War. Understanding geology played more than a major role in prosecuting the huge coordinated mine offensive which launched the first attacks.

If German geologists with military training had, immediately after the beginning of mining operations, at the latest in 1915, made a thorough survey of the whole Wytschaete salient, and if our *Mineure* from the beginning would have checked their advice tactically and technically, and if found correct would have followed this with all available means, the British would never have been so successful with their Wytschaete explosions – in spite of their excellent technical equipment and enormous willpower.

Walter Kranz, 1935

MINING THE FRONT: TACKLING GEOLOGY

As Kranz well knew, the Western Front is not geologically uniform. As the war progressed, the British armies expanded to fill a sector from the Salient to the Somme, an area which straddled two distinct geological regions of Europe. The dividing line is the Marqueffles Fault – a set of fractures formed when parts of southern Europe were tortured into the Alps by the collision of the Indian subcontinent some 60 million years ago. By this accident of earth history another dividing line was also created; a line that defined the chalk uplands of Artois and Picardy from the wet Flanders plain. This line was to be as significant as any in the history of the Great War. It is one of the most obvious features of the Western Front, a much contested piece of high ground overlooking the Douai plain, and one of the bloodiest of all battlefields – Vimy Ridge.

To the south-west of Vimy, past Arras and Cambrai and down to the Somme river where the British-held sectors ended, the underlying geology is all chalk; a soft, pure-white limestone

Left: German miners picking and bagging in chalk. A few timbers have been installed to prevent roof falls known as 'slabbing'

overlain by a complex of soils created during the last ice age. These surface soils – collectively known as *limon* – were easy to dig and provided many a 'funk-hole' for troops in the trenches. Beneath them the chalk was strong and dry, so tunnelled galleries hewn with picks in the traditional way were self-supporting, with added timber being only necessary to prevent 'slabbing' – the collapse of sections of roof. But with this strength came relative hardness; each strike of the pick invited a ring, particularly where the

Below left: British subway in chalk country. Note the height of the gallery and lack of timber support

Below: British chalk tunneller working on the chamber for the Hawthorn Ridge mine on the Somme

Fallen slabs of roof in the Vimy Ridge chalk workings in 1995. Note channels cut into walls to take supporting timbers without encroaching on gallery space. The wood has long since decayed

metal tools found the intermittent lines of tough flints so characteristic in chalk strata. To dig silently in chalk was impossible, and totally clandestine work was only achievable by driving galleries at great depths where it was hoped the enemy might not have a listening presence, a tactic which could never be guaranteed; or by being painstakingly careful in the excavation and digging at rates which might be so slow that the whole project was rendered ineffectual. In a war which depended much upon silence and secrecy for success, the enhanced transfer of sound in chalk was a critical aspect. In several sectors no attempt at all was made to work quietly and a deadlock developed below ground similar to that on the surface, with the tunnellers of both sides knowing precisely where their opposite numbers were located. In this case the goal was to ensure that the enemy always knew that wherever he was digging a rival and hostile presence was never far away, and any offensive action would be swiftly responded to in kind.

A second problem was the porosity of chalk, as its fine pores allowed easy percolation of water. Bill King's work showed that during the winter the level of water saturation rose dramatically as rain drained down from above. It flooded mine galleries and also created mudbaths of the once dry soils above. A third hazard was the very whiteness of the material; if left unhidden, spoil

from underground workings gleamed brilliant white in the sunshine – and was the simplest of clues that mining was taking place nearby for even the most inept aerial observer.

There was also another somewhat bizarre difficulty to be faced when tunnelling in chalk: its very whiteness underground. Even the light of a single candle was so brilliant within an entirely white and reflective tunnel that miners could occasionally suffer from a form of snowblindness. Darkened goggles could be requisitioned to combat the problem.

North of the geological dividing line of Vimy Ridge lies the clay plain of Flanders. This is defined by a layer of heavy clay of variable depth, but up to 130 metres thick. The Ypres Clay, the *Argile de Flandres*, is, like its London equivalent the London Clay, eminently suitable for tunnelling. Alike in every way, both Ypres and London clays are blue-grey when freshly cut, oxidising a dull-brown, and both are a plastic material. Plasticity produces movement, as the fine minerals that make up the clay have a structure that expands to absorb moisture, and contracts upon drying. Mine galleries in clay could therefore be driven with relative ease – and silence – but had to be regularly supported with timber to prevent collapse. The moisture absorption aspect was a severe problem for tunnellers; it led to expansion of the tunnel walls that could exert huge pressure on timber supports.

The Ypres Clay was formed in a tropical sea that flooded northern Europe tens of millions of years ago. Later environmental changes led to the laying down of a set of different sediment types – sands and silts – above the clay; the nature of these beds of sediments was to materially affect the course of the Great War in Belgian Flanders. The Passchendaele Ridge system represents such strata laid down on the Ypres Clay, and is composed of a complex mixture of ephemeral sands, clays and silts. The British geologists knew that these strata – together known as the Paniselian – could be unpredictable, with for example a bed of dry clay adjoining on the same contour a seam of saturated sandy clay. Local variations like this needed careful mapping as their various geotechnical characteristics exerted powerful influences over the success or failure of military mining activities, and indeed surface actions.

Directly overlying the pure Ypres clay at the base of the ridge is a layer of more sandy clay, the Paniselian Clay, which was curiously named 'bastard blue clay' by the miners. This damp, but

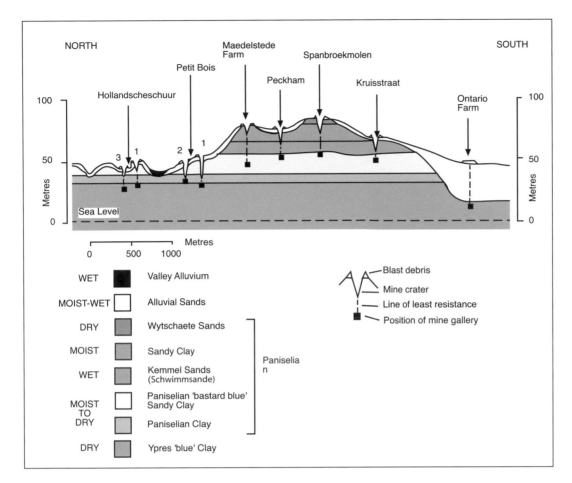

NORTH

Geological section through the Passchendaele Ridge showing the complexity of soil types faced by the tunnellers

not sodden, unit lay beneath the upper saturated sand layer of the Passchendaele Ridge system; where it existed, this layer became the most favoured medium for mining by the British, as the admixture of sand lessened the plasticity, and therefore lowered the pressures exerted by easily-expanded purer clay on timbered galleries. Proving the presence, depth and thickness of the various strata was a task requiring borehole testing, and this became one of the primary duties of British geologists. The bores not only determined the depth to militarily significant strata, they also ascertained the fluctuation in the seasonal water table, which was of great worth, both for King in searching for drinking water supplies on the Somme, and for Edgeworth David in gauging the suitability of geology at depth for offensive tunnels, infantry subways and dugouts in Flanders. Boring commenced in a systematic way in May 1916, but it was not until after the Third Battle of Ypres in 1917 that the operations became a principal preoccupation of the Australian Electrical, Mechanical, Mining and Boring Company – the AEMMBC, or 'alphabetical' company.

At this time up to 100 bores a week were being sunk, each one carefully logged for vertical alterations in strata by Loftus Hills; by the end of the war over 1,000 linear metres had been recorded. The carefully coloured records still exist in the National Archives at Kew. Ultimately, Edgeworth David was to compile his research into a set of immensely valuable maps, drawn at the same scale as trench maps, which indicated to tunnellers, pioneers, field company personnel,

A Royal Engineer boring team at work

RE Test Bore map of the Wytschaete–Messines sector. Red dots signify dry conditions, with purple dots indicating waterlogged geology

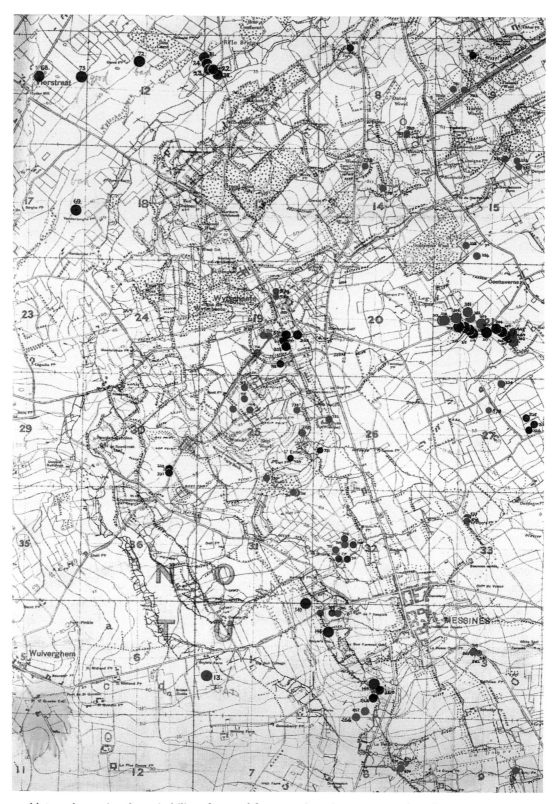

and later other units, the suitability of ground for dugout construction, with the relative wetness of the strata being simply illustrated in a colour code ranging from red (dry) to purple (very wet). These were amongst the first applied geological maps of their kind aimed specifically at military engineering – a principle still employed today by geological surveys across the world. Armed with their maps the British tunnelling companies were able to carry out the last major underground assignment of the war; the systematic construction of deep dugouts.

THE KEMMEL SANDS:
THE ENEMY WITHIN

From the end of 1914 the British occupied positions on the clay plain and the lower slopes of the Passchendaele Ridge system, with the Germans on the upper slopes and ridge tops. Sculpted by rivers and streams, over the millennia the valleys gradually filled with wet sands and gravels, whilst elsewhere heavy soils obscured the vagaries of the geology beneath. But there was one crucially influential geological unit that separated the British from the Germans both physically and tactically, and which entirely controlled military activities in both defensive fieldworks and offensive mining: the Kemmel Sands.

Found at around fifty metres above sea level, this layer of fine sands was bursting with water, trapped *in situ* by a layer of moist or dry clays beneath, and a seam of moist sandy clays above. Once the surface water reached this level, the impervious clay beneath made further percolation impossible, and although spring lines fed the streams at the base of the Passchendaele Ridge, the permanent saturation level effectively meant that the Kemmel Sands were nothing less than a layer of quicksand. To the German miners they were *Schwimmsande* – literally, swimming sands.

For those holding the upper contours of the ridges of the Ypres Salient, almost universally the German forces, the *Schwimmsande* presented a huge problem. Every attempt at constructing deep tunnels or dugouts was bound to intercept this saturated layer. As soon as a shaft broke into them, the Kemmel Sands 'boiled' from beneath, distorting timbers, and filling the workings faster than it could be excavated; in some places the pressure was so great that sands 'fountained' in

the shaft. Coping with a metre or so of this kind of ground was manageable, but at several points on the ridges the Kemmel Sands showed thicknesses of up to ten metres – a colossal engineering trial in peacetime even with the finest workforce and technical apparatus.

In an ironic reversal of fortune, the very moment military mining began in the Salient the tactical advantage of holding the high ground, which the Germans used to such great effect through observation and artillery fire, instantly became a frightening liability. Sinking through even five metres of *Schwimmsande* was practically impossible without access to purpose built, watertight, steel or concrete shaft sections – the only method which might help workings remain stable and safe. No such equipment was available to the German forces for some time. But this was not their main problem; the *Pioniere* believed that the sands were of a uniform depth throughout the Salient and that the British tunnellers faced precisely the same geological and engineering dilemma as their own troops. They did not.

For the British, still wallowing in the surface mud on the lower slopes and in the valleys, the Kemmel Sands were mainly either thin and manageable on the contour of the British trench lines, or topographically above where their tunnellers were working, and therefore effectively nonexistent. Even in places where they were problematic the British were often able to drop their shaft site back on to a slightly lower contour to find better geological conditions. Such a move was totally impossible for the Germans – unless they wished to mine from no man's land. For the *Pioniere*, there was no escape from the Kemmel Sands.

As I told you, when we went deeper in Flanders, we soon hit water. Was there not, you might ask, anywhere that the ground was firm and dry? Yes indeed, but only below the water. But at that time we were not in the clay, but in the water. For all the water that percolates down through the ground is trapped on top of the clay and the bands of impermeable material within the Ypres [Kemmel] sand. The ground is almost always waterlogged to just below the topsoil, and in winter to the surface itself. Even the high, broad ridges on which stood the once-proud villages of Passchendaele, Bezalaere, Wytschaete and Messines are sodden with water, as we found when we dug there. Only

Post-war German shaft section showing geological strata. A concrete shaft has been used to sink through the Schwimmsand *layer to the dry clay below*

German Mineure *preparing to descend into a wet mine system*

gradient, usually forty-five degrees. Where possible, entrances were concealed from enemy view either by camouflage or careful siting in a wood or ruined building. With geology being the prime influence in all forms of subterranean work, the shaft type was also subject to its control. Wooden shafts were swift and easy to sink in good, dry conditions but could very seldom be used in wet ground, without immense effort and a lot of good luck. The geology must therefore be tested before digging could commence.

When the shaft house was completed a test hole was bored with an earth auger and showed that we would have considerable trouble sinking. From the results of the borehole it was decided to use steel casings until the hard blue clay was reached. This casing was built in sections, three of which bolted together formed a circular casing eighteen inches deep. On the first ring was bolted a cutting edge, merely a nine inch section with no angle iron on the lower edge. This section was placed in position and forced into the earth with screw jacks working against the roof of the shaft house, the earth being removed by men inside the casing. When the first ring had been bolted far enough, the jacks were removed and another ring was bolted on the first one. The earth was never removed below the flange of the cutting edge at any time, and no excavation of any kind attempted during the time the casing was being forced through the soft wet sand. If

in deep valleys, such as the terrain in front of Ypres, held by the British, and to the south in the valley of the Douve, is this layer of wet quicksand absent.

Oberstleutnant Otto Füsslein,
Kommandeur des Mineure,
4th German Army

GOING UNDERGROUND

To penetrate the surface some form of adit or shaft was required. Adits – tunnels driven horizontally – were few and far between in the Salient. Some of the early British mines at Hill 60 were driven directly into the slope of the hill for shallow mining, but no significant depth could be gained unless the target was well above the adit entrance, i.e. unless the hill was of substantial height. Shafts and inclines were a better proposition. Shafts were vertical, using ladders or hoists for access, with inclines gently sloping with a flat floor, forming a sort of thirty degree chute, or built as a stairway on a steeper

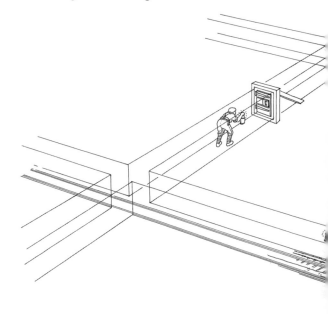

this was done, the wet sand would flow into the shaft and the soil around the shaft would fall, and in a very short time the shaft would be several inches out of line. In this manner the shaft was sunk thirty-five feet and at this depth had entered the solid blue clay. We excavated around the cutting edge and removed it and bolted a wooden collar set to the bottom of the steel casing and continued sinking in the ordinary way to the depth of 96 feet, using shaft setts of nine by three inch timber, four feet three inches square. We then built a platform at the ninety foot level, arranged frames and broke away from the side of the shaft towards the enemy lines.

Lieutenant R R Murray, 1st Canadian TC

The circular steel shaft approach was known as 'tubbing', and the prefabrication of both metal, and later concrete, rings became a necessity in dealing with sands that were liable to run or flow. Tubbing was first used on 6 May 1915 in French Flanders, at Cuinchy, near La Bassée. Here, a section of 170 Tunnelling Company commanded by Lieutenant J A Leeming successfully sank a 1.8-metre diameter timber shaft, a famous achievement in itself, through two metres of running sand to reach the dry clay bed beneath. On hearing of Leeming's success, Norton-Griffiths immediately instructed the young officer to find some sort of 'round iron

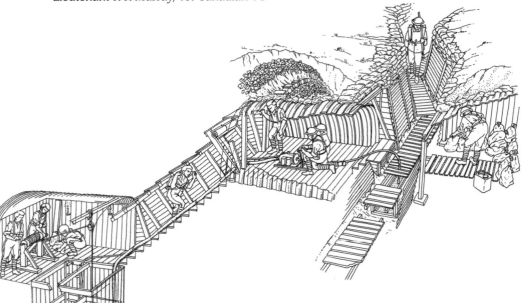

A shaft built in 'good' ground. No steel is required, timber alone can be used in the construction. The gallery from the shaft chamber at the bottom leads to the 'lateral', from which offensive and defensive galleries are driven. Note the gas door

cylinders' with which to 'tub' the interior of his shaft in order to permanently seal it from sand and water. On the strength of Leeming's achievement Norton-Griffiths then made sure that specially designed steel tubbing was bought and manufactured in France for immediate application, and also put into production in Britain for the use of his tunnellers the full length of the line.

Sectional steel shafts were to become one of the keys to success in wet ground conditions everywhere. The first French patterns, made at a factory in Lillers, were later superceded by much stronger and better purpose-made examples from Britain. They made the sinking process very simple, very fast, very dry and very safe. In places twin shafts were used, with a 5' 3" (1.6 m) diameter shaft fitted inside a 6' (1.8 m) diameter one. When the joints were sealed with strips of rubber cut from car tyre inner tubes, and the gap

Combination mine shaft using steel tubbing to negotiate wet ground to reach clay layer. Beneath, a standard timber shaft connects to the 'lateral' gallery, and defensive and offensive mine systems

A well-preserved British steel 'tubbed' shaft in the reserve line at Lancashire Farm near the Pilckem Ridge. A small doorway at the bottom (14 m depth) accessed an 'offensive' subway which led to a dressing station beneath support trenches, before emerging in the front line beyond

between the two sleeves filled with concrete, the structure could be relied upon to be strong enough to withstand all but a direct hit from a shell or mortar – but most importantly for the tunnellers in the galleries below, it was totally watertight.

Metal shafts were of course only necessary where the ground conditions were poor; as soon as the steel tubbing reached dry and stable strata at depth, the shaft was continued in timber, and built to traditional designs. If great depths of wet ground had to be negotiated two and even three sizes of shaft were used, bolted together telescopically, gradually decreasing in diameter as they probed deeper towards the clay.

If steel was available the running Kemmel Sands were no obstacle to the British, and the clay could be reached through any depth of bad ground. The time gained by using this method meant that new schemes could be started at safer points farther behind the British front line than hitherto, yet still in the confidence of reaching the target. A shaft location in the support and even reserve lines, out of sight and earshot of enemy observers, also allowed machinery which was

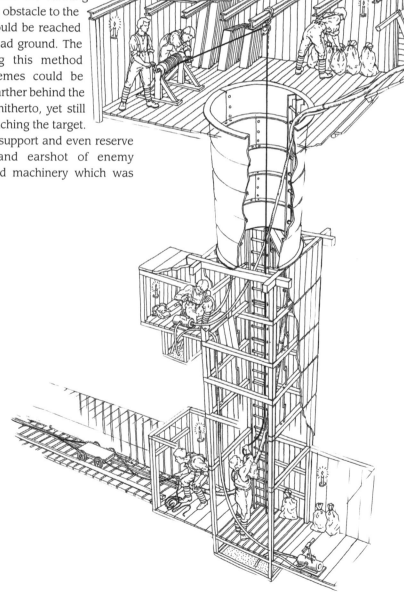

great thicknesses of wet sand and silt known as alluvials, which now lay buried deep beneath the surface. In preparing for the Messines offensive, 171 Tunnelling Company had to tackle this medium at shaft sites at Boyle's Farm, where they were sinking two shafts for the mine scheme known as Ontario Farm. The ground here was waterlogged to a depth of twenty metres, with the alluvials lying directly upon the Ypres Clay. By tubbing entirely in steel to thirty metres the clay was pierced and the driving of offensive galleries begun. After a hundred metres of gallery had been installed a further shaft was sunk another ten metres, to avoid the ancient valley floor. Now a full forty metres below ground level, progress towards the target continued without a problem. Yet around 180 metres from the shaft the face of the tunnel cracked and burst, and a rush of yellowish quicksand reclaimed over thirty metres of gallery before it was finally stopped with a timber dam. The tunnellers had broken through the ancient valley floor into the sopping alluvials above; following the advice of Edgeworth David to go deeper still they continued, pushing forward with an incline from the dam, and even-

too noisy for front-line work to be safely used for pumping, lighting and ventilation.

But the Kemmel Sands were not the only geological problem faced by tunnellers in Flanders. Over the millennia the small rivers and *beeks* which had shaped the Passchendaele Ridge system had laid down in their ancient valleys

Technical details of British tubbing and how it was sunk with screw jacks

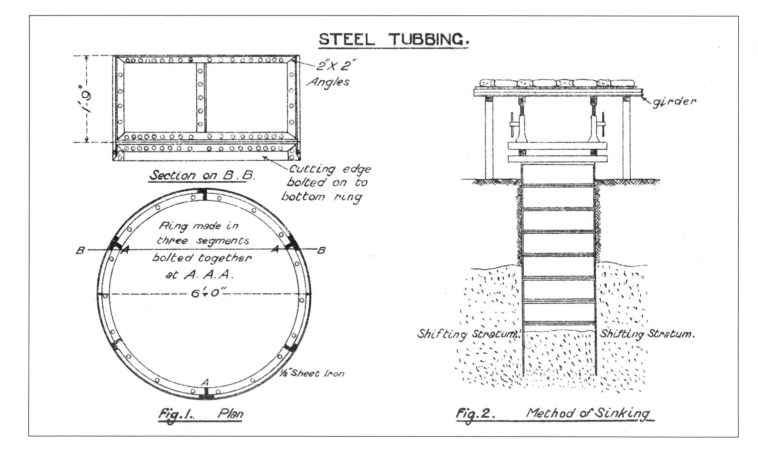

STEEL TUBBING.

Section on B.B.

2"x 2" Angles

1'.9"

Cutting edge bolted on to bottom ring

Ring made in three segments bolted together at A.A.A.

6'.0"

⅛"Sheet Iron

Fig.1. Plan

girder

Shifting Stratum.

Shifting Stratum.

Fig.2. Method of Sinking

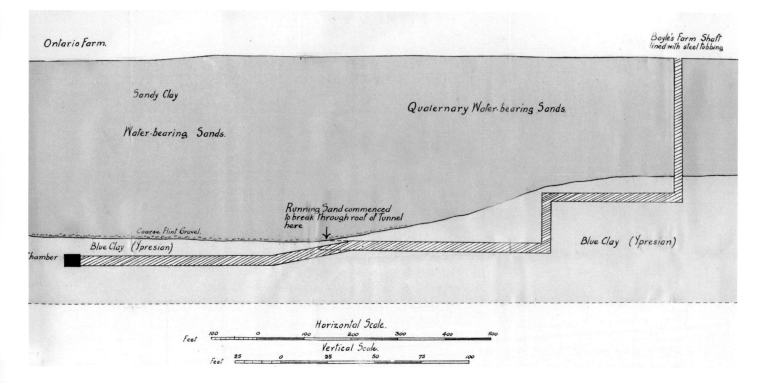

Problems with irregular strata at Ontario Farm showing how the gallery pierced the running sand layer and had to be taken deeper with an incline

tually reaching the target and charging the mine.

It was in large part the combination of the early innovation of tubbing, and the quality of British geological advice which sealed the fate of the German *Pioniere* in the mine war. Trapped upon the ridges they struggled to unlock the secret of sinking through the *Schwimmsande*. In the meantime the British were driving forward new schemes all around the Salient.

DRIVING THE TUNNELS

Having successfully reached the optimum depth, tunnelling proper could begin, with galleries being driven towards the enemy lines by the clay-kickers. The inviting blue clay that so attracted the British also had drawbacks: as we have mentioned, some sort of physical support was essential to avoid collapse. For strength and safety almost all galleries in clay in Flanders – both British and German – used 'close-timbering', the construction of a continuous 'box' of wooden 'setts' forming the floor, roof and walls and fitting tightly together, inside which the miners worked. As a general rule, only the minimum amount of timber necessary to support the earth was used in 'attacking' tunnels. Both sapper and *Pionier* advanced their tunnels in a similar way, carefully cutting the face ahead to the precise shape and size to admit the insertion of the next 'sett'. Progress was made in this stop-start manner, moving forward sett by sett towards the target.

Timber and gallery sizes were also practically identical; they were universally uncomfortably small, requiring all tunnellers to move around in a painful crouching position for hours. Those unused to this kind of work, such as attached infantry working parties, were astonished at the conditions.

I faced many a shell and sniper, but I never liked mining. It was stuffy, filthy, oppressive, dangerous – just...frightful. You were down there on your hands and knees for hours on end, part of a long line of men passing bags back between our legs. You couldn't stand up as the saps were only about four feet high, if that. And you couldn't stand up when you got out, having been in that crouched position for hours. It was the most tiring and painful work I ever did on the Western Front, and although they were safe from shot and shell, we didn't envy the miners who were doing it day in, day out for months. I faced many a shell and sniper, but I never liked mining!

Private Donald Hodge,
Royal West Kent Regiment

By July 1916 the British had standardised the interior dimensions of all their workings to just three sizes:

1. Ordinary galleries (offensive or defensive tunnels): 4' 3" (130 cm) by 2' 3" (69 cm)

GALLERY SETTS

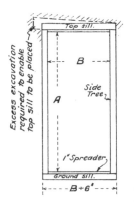

Purpose	A	B
Main subways	6'·6"	3'·6" or 4'·0"
Dug-out passages	6'·4"	2'·9"
Inclines — 1/1 Vertical Timbering	6'·4"	2'·9" to
Normal Timbering	4'·10"	4'·6"
Mine galleries Normal size	4'·10"	2'·9"
Minimum	4'·3"	2'·3"
For Demolitions	4'·3"	2'·3"

Suitable Dimensions.

Cases, 7 to 11ins. wide

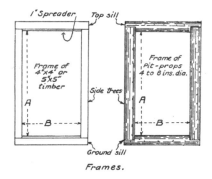

Frames.

2. Galleries near the shaft bottom or for the first 75-100 metres: 5' 0" (152 cm) by 2' 6" (76 cm)
3. Galleries for communication of men: 6' 0" (183 cm) by 3' 0" (91 cm)

The dimensions were devised to achieve the maximum driving rate; the smaller the tunnel (up to a point) the quicker the progress. These gallery sizes represented the most efficient balance.

British mining setts were made from timbers with simple 'stepped' joints; the Germans, however, persevered with the nine-teenth-century mortice and tenon system throughout the war. According to the Royal Engineers, this gave the sappers a further advantage as the German sett both took longer to assemble and produced more noise in the process. In testing the designs the RE also found that so much wood was cut away in fab-ricating the joints that the completed German sett was also rendered considerably less resilient to fracture than the British pattern, making damage by *camouflet* or pressure from swelling clay walls more likely.

Methods of excavation also differed. Whilst the Germans habitually used traditional miners' tools, small picks and mattocks, from February 1915, the British employed Norton-Griffiths' clay-kickers wielding small, super-sharp 'grafting tools'.

Underneath the surface in the Flanders Plain is a strata of blue clay. It was through this tough substance that most of our tunnels were driven. The miner lays on his back at the tunnel face and digs more by pressure and leverage on the surface with a small sharp spade. He will tie sandbags round his boots or a wad of rubber cut from an old gum boot or motor tyre to muffle the sound he makes in digging. The men call this operation 'kicking' and that describes it suitably. There the man works for hours on end steadily kicking his spade into the tough clay, loosening lumps of the stuff and throwing it behind to his mates. Two of them fill the stuff into sandbags. One of these pushes a small rubber tyred trolley

Typical British gallery sizes and timber dimensions. Note cut out at top left to allow 'cap' or 'top sill' to be inserted

Johan Vandewalle illustrates the cramped nature of listening post galleries at Mount Sorrel, where even a minor constriction could mean entombment. Note how the tunnel has been driven immediately above the distinct change in geology from dry sand to wet sandy clay

German method of timbering using mortice and tenon joints, plus fixing wedge

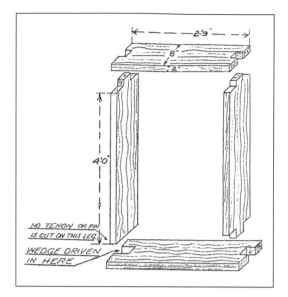

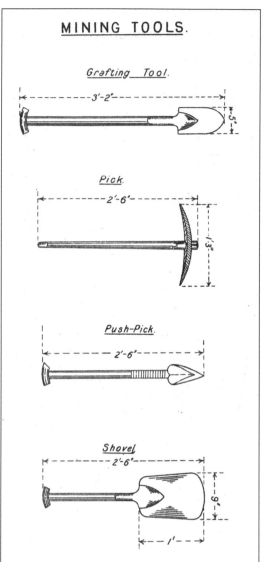

Right: Basic British mining tools at the time of the outbreak of war

loaded with clay filled sandbags back along the plank floor to the shaft bottom. Here the bags are slung on a pulley-hook and hauled by windlass to the top. The miner at the face cuts into the wall of clay ahead a few feet at a time then he stops to insert four pieces of stout timber already sawn to the required lengths to form a box inside which he works. The timber is usually two inch plank and about nine inches wide. The two side pieces have a step sawn out of each end; the floor and roof timber sit on these steps. In this way the timbers cannot slip around from pressure of clay from above, or on the side or from below; the pressure just jams the box tight.

Company Sergeant Major J Lyhane,
172 TC, RE

Morticed mining timber used in a German dugout near Merckem

Progress was usually made in nine-inch (23-cm) stages – the preferred width of mine timbers – using hardwoods wherever possible for strength and greater longevity in the damp conditions. The advantages of clay-kicking were not only that the power generated through the legs made progress far swifter and used less energy, but the grafting tool was pushed into the ground, making excavation a practically silent process. With a pick or mattock the clay had to be struck; the firmer the ground the more forceful a blow was required and the more noise was produced. The choice of tool, however, seemed to be left up to the individual. In some German tunnels a device resembling an oversized 'apple corer' was used to drill holes, in the same way that a carpenter uses a brace and bit, before the final tunnel shape was trimmed to size with a push pick ready to receive the timbering. This was

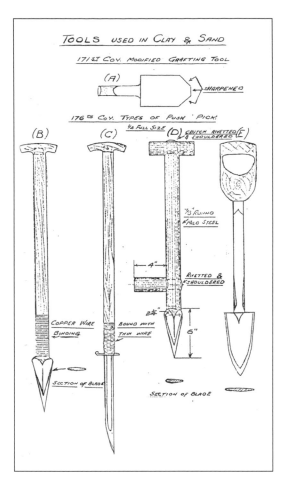

just as silent a method as clay-kicking, but much, much slower, and uncommon. For obvious reasons the predominant German use of picks throughout the war was an invaluable piece of good fortune for British listeners.

There were further curious differences in working practices: Company Sergeant Major Lyhane noted the British use of rubber-tyred trolleys. By the end of 1915 all mines used trolleys, with self-oiling roller bearings, running on tracks. In fixing the wooden rails to the gallery floor the sappers employed screws specifically to avoid unnecessary noise; inexplicably, it was found that the Germans often nailed their tracks to the floor creating yet more unnecessary

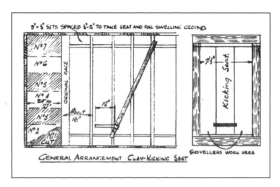

commotion. Practices such as these were clearly avoidable, but the *Pionier* was also hampered by matters over which he had no control. As the war dragged on and the Allied naval blockade of Germany bit harder month by month, the supply of many essential mining commodities inexorably dwindled. Rubber for hosing, waterproof boots and tyres for trolley work in both trench and mine took second place in the supply chain to the only weapons capable of breaking the blockade – submarines – the U-Boats. Pleadings from *Pionier* commanders fell on deaf ears – their men were forced to do their best with what was available.

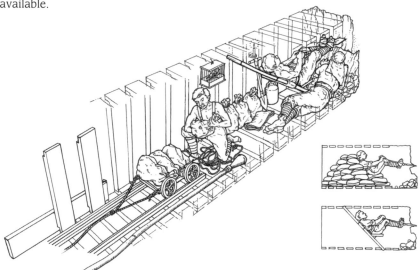

Left: 'Home-made' tools manufactured for specific geological conditions by the RE

Below: A clay-kicking team at work, with kicker, bagger and trammer

A German Pionier *working in clay with a small mattock whilst a 'mate' fills sandbags with spoil*

Far left: Clay-kicking arrangement with timber seat showing sequence of digging each spit of clay from bottom to top of gallery

CONSTRUCTION AND TIMBERING

When the first British military mining in the Salient had begun in early 1915, construction design was left for each section to decide how best their skills could be employed in that particular spot. Timber, the most essential element after the miner himself, was not issued from store but cut locally as required to the specifications of individual commanders. Like the RE Field Companies and their personal bomb factories, some mining companies fabricated their timber mining frames or setts on site, whilst others organised their own workshops behind the lines using locally 'sourced' machinery. The speedy growth of mining during 1915, however, meant that standardisation of equipment and materiel was essential, and by the middle of 1916 all timber was supplied cut to the sizes mentioned earlier and delivered to forward dumps from RE depots, ready for infantry fatigue parties to carry forward to the mines.

As shafts sank ever deeper, so working practices had to alter. Each geological layer had its own geotechnical characteristics that governed the type of construction best suited to cope. Some shallow tunnels constantly dripped and dribbled water, filtering down from shell holes on the surface, whilst others were dry. However, all were uncomfortable, stuffy, cramped and dim. Hill 60, one of the Salient's most mine-riddled sectors, was typical of the damp conditions in the sandy ridge tops.

> The wet gave a lot of men chest trouble. There was plenty of rheumatism. The galleries were then disinfected – about the end of 1916 – and better sanitary arrangements were put in. And men didn't like drinking the chlorinated water, so every dugout had a can catching drips from the roof. The surface was littered with corpses and excreta, but seeping through 30 feet of sand filtered out the germs. The MO's were horrified when they heard. I got an MC just for being there.
> Captain William J McBride, 1st Australian TC

Early workings were shallow, up to about ten metres below the surface; later, when coordinated offensive mining schemes were initiated, tunnels could be up to forty-five metres deep. At this depth, working far beneath the Kemmel Sands, the galleries were seldom wet, but driving through the stiff Ypres Clay created a host of different problems.

> It was a dirty, dangerous and exhausting job. There were sectors in the tunnels where the clay wall pressure was so terrific on the timbers that they snapped like matchsticks, almost as fast as we put them in. The ventilation was terrible – even the bits of candle we used to stick on the timbers for light would burn very feebly because of the lack of oxygen. It was a ghastly business and you never saw a staff officer down in that inferno where we poor devils laboured.
> Sapper Frank O'Callaghan, 1st Canadian TC

Such timber trouble was a common problem in 'the deeps'. The introduction of moisture to the dry Ypres blue clay, via the damp air of a newly driven tunnel caused a rapid swelling of walls, floor and roof – it was an almost irresistible force. In an effort to counteract the effect, heavier section timber setts were fixed, and if successful used throughout that system; if not, the tunnellers might remove certain timbers to leave gaps through which the clay was allowed to swell, being carved away like cheese daily from behind the remaining setts. Eventually the clay would cease swelling, and 'settle'. In the most severe cases the tunnel was reinforced with steel girders spaced at standard eighteen-inch (46-cm) centres. During the long run up to the Messines Ridge battle several mines had been completed and charged for over a year

Unstained blue-grey clay indicates a very recent roof failure in the Petit Bois workings near Wytschaete, probably caused by the removal of hydrostatic support when the gallery was drained. The ruddy colour is created by rusting steel beams

Far left: Petit Bois. A single 'leg' or 'side-tree' in a close-timbered by-pass gallery snapped by clay pressure. Note the convex bowing of other timbers

Left: Spaced setts in a gallery to allow for expansion of the blue clay

Timber dimensions, arrangement and spacing showing relative strengths. No. 1 was used as the 'control'

before they were finally exploded. In these cases the problem of timber degradation became commonplace, necessitating frequent maintenance in replacement of timber elements – an extraordinary degree of labour and care was expended on workings that were simply awaiting instant destruction when the mines were blown. In good mining ground like the more sandy 'bastard blue clay' at the base areas of the ridges where there was more stability and inertia, progress was quiet, rapid and straightforward; bastard blue clay was a tunneller's dream.

At Mount Sorrel, Tor Top, Sanctuary Wood and in the shallower tunnels of Hill 60 the geology was different again, and both sides worked mainly in the firm, compressed sand of the upper contours of the ridge system.

I used to console myself by thinking, 'you've nobody to thank but yourself for being here', because miners were a reserved occupation. At Hill 60 we cut the sand out with a bayonet, never used a pick – never saw one. I didn't do any clay-kicking at Hill 60, it was all sand. Using the bayonet was simple as easy as cutting cheese. You'd cut a hole and make room for your sill, get it in level – the floor went in first – then the two uprights or legs slotted into the sill, and then the top one slotted in the same way. Shove a sandbag or something in behind to keep it tight.

Sapper Hubert Leather, 175 and 252 TC, RE

Type No.	DESCRIPTION.	Approx. Relative Strength.	Approx. Relative Timber Consumption.
1.	9"x 3" FLAT 3' SPACING	1	1
2.	9"x 3" FLAT CLOSE CASED	1 1/3	1 1/3
3.	4½"x 3" ON EDGE 3" SPACING	1½	1
4.	4½"x 3" DOUBLE ON EDGE 3" SPACING	2	1 1/3
5.	6"x 3" ON EDGE 3" SPACING	2 2/3	1 1/3
6.	6"x 3" DOUBLE ON EDGE 3" SPACING.	3½	1¾
7.	9"x 3" DOUBLE ON EDGE 6" SPACING.	6	2
8.	9"x 3" DOUBLE ON EDGE 3" SPACING.	8	2½

View through crown hole into Mount Sorrel tunnels. The workings are dry and timber decay advanced. These are typical conditions for the upper layer of the Passchendaele Ridge

Work in sandy ground was easy, quick and practically noiseless, with large kitchen knives, bayonets and entrenching tools being commonly employed. As a result tunnels could extend much farther than in sectors with different sediments, reaching as far as the enemy reserve lines in some places. As the sand was damp, firm and stable, it was also often practically self-supporting, and therefore needing less timbering than clay. With no swelling action to combat galleries were often timbered just enough to offer a calculated degree of protection against remote *camouflets*.

Temporary shortage of standardised timber probably led to this use of pit-prop 'legs' and sawn 'caps' in Bridge 6 dugout near South Zwaanhof Farm

Most systems in sand installed a protective timber sett every eighteen inches (46 cm), but as the mine war expanded and timber supply became increasingly unreliable, with deep offensive work taking preference to other schemes, setts were gradually spaced farther and farther apart in an effort to eke out resources. The already borderline eighteen-inch (46-cm) spacing first expanded to forty-two inches (107 cm), and later to forty-eight inches (122 cm), offering almost no protection against enemy blows. One of the most widespread comments found in war diaries is 'work stopped due to lack of timber'. This could be due to a variety of causes.

> I wired the Brigade and asked for a carrying party of 120 men to bring up from our dump to the trenches, a matter of two miles, some material. Brigade wired back to say 120 men would report to me at 8pm that night at the dump. I sent down a guide to lay out their loads and guide them back up. Well, they turned up all right in charge of an officer and the guide asked him to file the men past and take up their loads straight on. Unfortunately, the sporty old Hun commenced to sling a few bangs there just at that moment, so instead of 120 loads being taken only 75 filed up past. The remainder, including the officer, had vanished; not hit, but merely 'missed'. Well, that wasn't too bad, but when that party arrived at our sap head, there was only ten men and only five of them had a load.
>
> Lieutenant Oscar Earnshaw, 177 TC, RE,
> 17 April 1916

SUPPLYING THE TUNNELS

Mining, although often receiving special consideration, had to take its turn in the queue for timber which was in huge demand on the surface for trench revetments, duckboards, roads, tracks, dugouts, railways, tramways and hutting. Vast amounts were consumed in everyday trench life on the Western Front. In 1917 in French forests alone the British Government was maintaining two RE Forestry Battalions comprising around 2,200 men, plus fifty-six companies of the Canadian Forestry Corps, and 13,000 unskilled labourers (mainly Chinese Labour Corps, Indian troops and German prisoners of war). Ready sawn timber was also being imported from Britain, the Baltic, America and Canada. Between April 1917 and November 1918, over one million tonnes of sized

German Pionier *dump with massive piles of sawn timber for mine and dugout use*

timber was despatched to the various armies at the front.

Having reached France the wood had to be delivered, and when it came to supply, conditions in the Salient were unfavourable in every way for the British miners. Whilst German stores arrived relatively unmolested from behind the ridges on the outside arc of the Salient, timber, and every-thing else for many British mines had to be funnelled nightly into the narrow pocket around Ypres, and then on by road or track to the workings at Railway Wood, Sanctuary Wood, Mount Sorrel and Hill 60. The main exit routes out of Ypres were pinpointed every day by German artillery with a few ranging shots in readiness to open up on the steady streams of transport beginning their delivery rounds after nightfall. As tunnellers worked a round the clock shift system they faced their own chaos.

> Most of our casualties were getting to and from the job – Hellfire Corner and Idiot's Corner. The Germans would get the range during the day and then bombard when we were due to come through. We changed shifts on the Hill between 9 at night and 2 in the morning – about a mile to walk. We never marched up, each man chose his own pet route and went up independently. We had 300 casualties at Hill 60, including those going to and from the line.
> Captain William J McBride, 1st Australian TC

Unlike the almost permanently encumbered infantryman, tunnellers were not required to take part in the fatigue parties that delivered supplies, or to carry any salvaged materials back at the end of the shift. But this was not the only 'perk': tunnellers and their attached infantry received a generous rum ration – much more than the single tablespoon a day allocated for the rest of the army. Given the damp, dim, poorly-ventilated, arduous and permanently

perilous conditions under which the men worked, rum was considered an essential adjunct to the health, efficiency and mental welfare of the tunnelling companies. Hardly rationed at all, rum became a lifesaver.

> Conditions that first winter [of mine warfare] of 1915/16 were very uncomfortable. I don't suppose any troops anywhere else had the discomfort we had in the Ypres Salient. In the infantry no individual would stay [in the line] more than two days. We had no reliefs. We were there all the time in the wet and mud. The thing that held us together was rum. No one knew what we were up against, so we could get anything we liked from stores. Our miners had big mugfuls of rum every day. When the rum ration was being dished out I'd hold out my mug and then look away so that he went on pouring.
> Captain Basil Sawers, 177 TC, RE

An earth 'slide' in an entrance to the unfinished Martha House dugout system near Zonnebeke. The neck of the ubiquitous rum jar is visible at the foot, and ready-notched timber in the fore-ground

However, some found equally useful external uses for the enhanced rum ration.

When I was with the tunnelling company I couldn't believe the amount of rum we got. You weren't allowed to store it because the army were afraid of bartering, and some men getting too much of it. Well, we could have too much anytime we wanted. I used to keep mine in my water bottle – always full it was, and swop it for other comforts: bread, cheese, a bit of cake – nobody ever said no! But I used it on my feet too. Never got trench foot, never no trouble when I rubbed my feet with rum every day. I had the best little pair of feet in the army.

Trooper Albert 'Smiler' Marshall, Essex Yeomanry, attached 170 TC, RE

SURVEYING; WHICH WAY TO THE FRONT?

Knowing precisely which way to dig was no easy matter once the tunnellers were below ground. In normal civilian applications, mine survey was a complex task; the introduction of the obstacles of war did not help the issue.

From the earliest days of trench warfare the military surveyors of both sides produced accurate trench maps, based at first on the existing Belgian surveys and later using military surveyors to create more detailed maps showing trench lines, natural features with military implications, and communication routes. This information was vital to the success of the trench war on the surface, but below ground things were a little different. At first, for the British at least, there were no accurate plans of the underground workings, and this was a serious omission.

When he took the field, John Norton-Griffiths immediately insisted that commanding officers of tunnelling companies should keep detailed, up-to-date plans of all workings, and cajoled GHQ into supplying the necessary equipment to help them achieve it, such as box sextants, miners' dials and levels. Soon, the keeping of meticulous mine plans became the norm, showing rates of progress, distances between entrances, depths and dimensions, and the location of the workings in relation to mine craters and one's own surface features. Galleries were carefully marked relative to the projected positions of enemy tunnels detected by listening. But these mine plans, if they were to be of any real use, had also to show the position of the enemy trenches above, because it was within those lines that the tunnellers' targets lay. In trench warfare it was no simple thing to know precisely how far away

A British miner's dial used to maintain correct direction underground

German Mineure *using their version of a miner's dial at a Messines shafthead*

The importance of survey and careful plotting of tunnels. German Mineure *consulting plans below ground*

one's enemy was. An officer could not get out of his trench and walk across no man's land with a tape measure, so the normally straightforward task of calculating distance by simple triangulation was problematical.

Aerial photos were used but they were not sufficiently accurate in all cases. The method employed to verify the distance between the lines was as shown in the sketch, but it was not easy to find points A and B from which C could be seen without the observer being seen. We employed a more direct, but dangerous method (not looked upon with favour by the authorities) i.e. crawling over no man's land on a dark night with a graduated string as far as the enemy lines, the string then being withdrawn and measured. On one

occasion an officer was shot in the head whilst going over, and had the presence of mind and the courage to mark the spot where he had finished before returning. The measurement was then completed by another officer.

Lieutenant Arthur Eaton, 171 and 184 TC, RE

Eventually, a dedicated survey officer for each company relieved the need for other tunnelling officers to concern themselves with anything but efficiency and progress. Maintaining a gradient for drainage in underground galleries was also a part of his job, as was following the correct bearing so that the tunnel did not deviate from its course towards the target. Such a mistake could have serious consequences and lead to weeks or months of wasted effort.

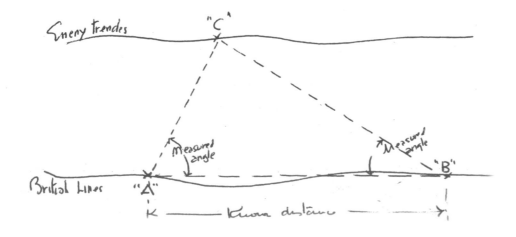

Lieutenant Arthur Eaton's hazardous triangulation method of measuring distance to the enemy front line by crawling across no man's land with a graduated string

The head of a German mine system. Like their British counterparts, the Pioniere *also used trolleys for spoil removal both above and below ground*

The mining engineer officer is constantly visiting the men at work, checking the direction of the tunnel or gallery with a mine surveyor's instrument, which is something like a surveyor's theodolite with a compass attached. It is set up at the bottom of the shaft on a low tripod and levelled. The required bearing, as previously determined and plotted on a plan of the mine, is found on the graduated circular plate of the instrument. The sights are clamped to it and a mark is made on that bearing on the roof timber at the tunnel head. This forms the centre line for direction. The face worker just inserts each extension of his timbering centrally on his direction mark.

Company Sergeant Major J Lyhane, 172 TC, RE

One of the most important requirements for the timberman was to have standardised and unvarying timber sizes. As long as all the timbers were identical in width all was OK, but a mixture of widths created great difficulties not only in cutting the tunnel to the correct size but also maintaining a straight course. The straightness aspect was important as most tunnels would be driven directly towards the target whenever possible, although in sectors known to have a strong defensive enemy presence dog legged workings were sometimes employed to effect a 'flank attack'. These were used more commonly in chalk areas where noise was more of a problem than in clay, and demanded highly precise surveying to maintain correct line, depth and distance.

DEALING WITH SPOIL

In both sinking shafts or driving galleries there was one logistical nightmare that could severely compromise the secrecy of the overall mining scheme: the removal and disposal of spoil, the 'waste' earth produced by tunnelling. With increasing aerial reconnaissance being utilised specifically to identify mine sites through spotting spoil heaps, this problem became acute, and large numbers of unskilled men were employed to make sure that disposal was carried out with the utmost speed and care.

The infantry played a major role in the success of tunnelling schemes and no company could carry out their duties without the assistance of large numbers of men who were attached to the tunnellers from infantry battalions. Such men might be 'borrowed' for several

months, with extra injections of labour being drawn whenever necessary from other units who were serving outside front line duty. Underground work was labour intensive; even a 325-man company might require 300 attached infantry to carry out the multitude of unskilled jobs, including delivery of equipment and materials, winching bags up shafts, pumping water out of the mine, or blowing air in. The most unpopular work of all was spoil removal.

We dreaded being told off for duty with the tunnellers. They came from all over the place – the accents were so broad that I don't know how they got on together: You had men from Cornwall, Wearside, Lancashire, Scotland, Wales. The Welsh were hard to understand but the Wearsiders were a damned sight harder! The officers were more civvy than military – construction or mining engineers I suppose, but they all seemed an unmilitary lot. They were all very sure of themselves and very unsure of you. They had a very superior attitude – they were the upper class and we were the labourers – and we were treated as such – just useful nuisances!

There was just enough room in the tunnels for two men to pass, one with a bag coming out and another one empty handed, or sometimes with a lump of timber, going in, so you had two rows of men constantly moving. The timber was usually stacked near the entrance.

Some mines had a day store for bags in a

shelter off the trench, where there was a damned great heap waiting for us every evening, but usually we had to cart them out of the tunnel and sometimes hundreds of yards away to dump them in shellholes or old trenches. Before it grew light the whole lot had to be covered up with soil or whatever was handy. If a hole was not full and could be used again for more stuff, the RE rigged up a wooden frame affair with a cloth fixed to it which was put over ready for the next night – camouflage. And we had to cover over our footsteps because there was this obvious trail of mud leading from the tunnel to the dump; we broke it up a bit with brooms and then spread stuff like garden sweepings over it. There was always an officer who would check – he was very particular. Jerry would see the trail from the air, you see, and if he suspected you were mining he would blow the place to hell.

Our lot only worked at night. The bags were stacked in sort of lay-bys in the tunnels or outside in shelters waiting for us to move them after dark, and they were often sopping wet. They were a bugger to get hold of – and keep hold of. We got plastered from head to foot in this slimy clay – you couldn't avoid it. Then afterwards you had to try to get dry and stay warm. You couldn't clean yourself –

trying to wipe the stuff off your tunic just spread it about more – it was like wet soap. It started blue but when it dried, it dried virtually white. We fetched up looking like ghosts. New blokes in the line would look at you, and you could tell they were thinking 'what the hell have these blokes been up to?' Being young, I was curious to know where all the muck was coming from, but I never did get to see the end of a tunnel.

> Private Bert Fearns, 2/6 Battalion,
> Lancashire Fusiliers

More often than not spoil was lifted from the tunnels either via vertical shafts or up inclines, gradually sloping tunnels without steps. Making sure spoil was removed at least at the same rate as it was produced at the face was essential; there was little enough space in mine galleries without having backlogs of spoil-filled sandbags. Invariably the hoist for this job was a simple and reliable windlass worked by two men. Hand powered geared winches might also be found in particularly deep or difficult mines, but one of the golden rules of British military mining was 'keep it simple'. There was no point in employing equipment, particularly expensive electrical or mechanical kit, which could do far more work than was practically necessary. There

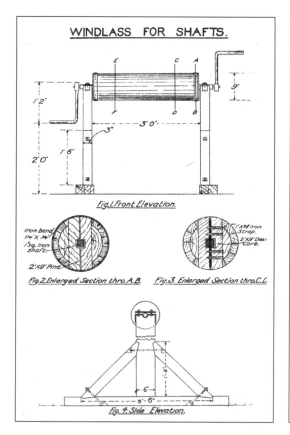

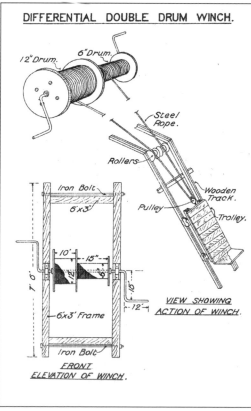

The windlass: a simple and reliable mechanism for hoisting sandbags up shafts and inclines

Double drum winch for lifting or lowering heavier loads

In exposed positions trench tramways ran underground for concealment of spoil removal activity

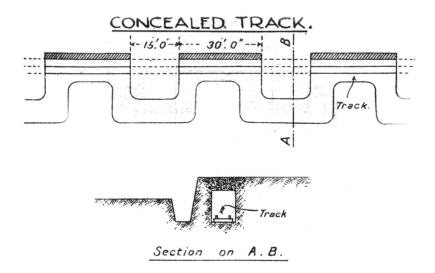

was no need to complicate matters; in the Army musclepower was abundant, dependable and reliable – complex equipment was not.

Removal and concealment of spoil was made much easier in rearward positions by the close proximity of a trench tramway network. Even in forward sites, covered tramways could be built by the tunnellers for bags to be transported back secretly and safely each night for concealment behind farms and in natural hollows, often several hundred metres behind the line. In rare cases, spoil was removed to the rear areas using a monorail system of suspended buckets. In places where disposal was particularly awkward, grouped craters were blown at night behind the parados, by 'drilling ten-inch holes for charges six to eight feet deep and nine feet apart'. The craters were camouflaged with a specially designed screen and then connected to the trench by a

covered sap by which route the spoil could be taken and dumped in safety and secrecy.

Military mining was a pursuit which demanded meticulous time and motion studies to achieve maximum efficiency and careful analyses were regularly made of how many 'faces' were being worked, how fast the clay-kickers were progressing, and how many bags needed to be lifted to keep the work moving at the maximum rate of progress. The results helped determine the number of auxiliary shafts and inclines required for a project, the kind of windlass or winch needed, and how many men constituted the most economical use of human energy. With geology as the universal key, mining operations had to be finely tuned in every department. Once underground, however, the silent war would rely on the nerves and skill of the tunnellers themselves.

German covered tramway for spoil removal at shafthead

Both sides used monorail systems. This one, in use near Messines, is a German example

Chapter VI

THE SILENT WAR

Hill 60. We'd scores of fellows every shift listening below ground with geophones. You could hear the Germans walking sixteen paces towards you and sixteen away from you; could hear them spit, drop soil when working, and so on. We used to take compass bearings from all the different people who could hear them along the gallery, and from where the readings converged we knew pretty well where they were.

Lieutenant B C Hall, 3rd Canadian TC

The underground war was principally one of stealth; a deadly game in which both attacker and attacked sought to outwit their opponent, predicting their movements without giving away their own positions – and killing without compunction, emotion or hesitation. There was no room for chivalry or mercy in mine warfare; it was kill or be killed. The work could never be hurried. Every aspect demanded calmness, efficiency and silence, for even an inadvertent cough could lead to death, if not of themselves, then of others. Giving way to alarm and panic encouraged loss of confidence in comrades, and then a man's usefulness would be over. The tunneller had to remain ever conscious of danger, ever alert, ever quiet, ever in control, and ultimately, ever fatalistic.

There were ways of achieving immunity from underground attack without going underground oneself; one could instigate an infantry advance to permanently capture the lines which enclosed enemy mine workings; a sequence of heavy and persistent bombardments could be delivered in the hope of destroying personnel, shafts and equipment as a deterrent to further work; or a raid could be carried out to find and destroy suspect sites with mobile explosive charges. All were tried many times with varying success. In fact there was an obvious, effective, indeed infallible, solution to the problem: shifting one's positions rearward out of range of enemy tunnellers and their mines. Even a fifty-metre retirement might guarantee the safety of front-line troops, at least for a period, and would often have been enough to scupper most major hostile schemes, either in progress or even completed. The practice, although often advocated by both sides, was hardly ever used.

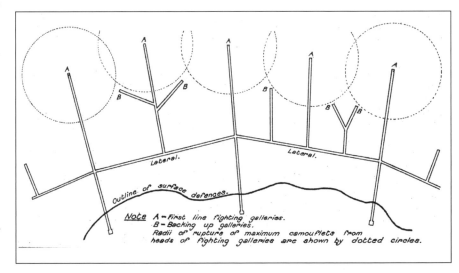

British defensive fighting system showing the utility of a 'lateral' gallery

Whilst offensive mining operations were carried out against enemy surface features – trenches, machine gun positions, pillboxes, and redoubts; defensive mining (also known as protective mining) was used in response to a hostile underground threat. In offensive work silence, and the speed of progress to a point beneath the target, were the primary considerations and if a combination of both could be achieved the chances of

97

success were greatly enhanced. Tunnellers engaged on defence had different priorities: they had no concern with surface features but concentrated entirely upon calculating where their enemy was, where he was going, how quickly he was tunnelling, and how to stop, or at least arrest, his progress. The sole targets in defensive mining were the enemy miner and his workings.

To achieve underground superiority the first task was to put in place a carefully planned and developed system of defence. Where a position was considered to be of vital importance a protective listening system, devised along exactly the same lines as those of the ancient fortresses, could be installed before any enemy activity had been detected, thereby placing the defenders a step ahead. But such premeditated work was rare; it demanded manpower and materiel which could scarcely be spared from sectors where mine warfare was actually in progress or expanding. The vast majority of defensive tunnel systems tended to evolve organically according to known or perceived threats. In the first instance it would plainly be signs or sounds of hostile mining which prompted a response. That response was absolutely obligatory – neither side could take the risk of allowing any position to be undermined without opposition. The tunnelling war had begun precisely in this apparently benign fashion, but the long-term consequences were inevitable: once mine warfare had successfully been started on a geologically favourable and static battlefield – such as the British sector of the Western Front – a rapid escalation in underground activity was bound to result. The first successful German mine attack at Christmas

1914 had been all that was needed to set a subterranean leviathan in motion.

Once underground the miner effectively engaged in a game of blindfold cat and mouse. Every action in offence or defence was controlled by the knowledge of what one's unseen enemy had already done, what he was doing at present, and an educated guess as to his future plans. This knowledge could only be gained by listening.

I sense that you wonder how we were able to hear so well. As you know, sound travels further through solid ground and water than through air. Thirty or forty metres down, you can hear a stake being hammered into the floor of a trench as clearly as if you were beside the man driving it. Dry sand, on the other hand, tends to deaden sound. Your ears gradually learn to interpret the sounds that reach them through the earth, recognising their origin, direction and distance away. That noise is coming from our trenches; but what about those dull thuds? Someone above us is tapping a shoring frame into place. To the right, someone is working cautiously with a pick, and to the left another is stabbing into the face with a bayonet – there, he has just dislodged some clods of earth. Further away there is a humming sound – their electric ventilators are working. Then a buzzing sound: aha, they are using a drilling tool! Thus the sounds come to life for those who know how to read them.

Oberstleutnant Otto Füsslein,
Kommandeur des Mineure,
4th German Army

RE officer with a listening stick as used by civilian water companies for locating leaks

LISTENING WITH INTENT

With luck, surface and aerial observation might offer an indication of the starting points of enemy tunnels, but they could of course give no clue as to the scale or plan of the system. Listening for the underground activities of the enemy was the only key. Yet in early 1915 tunnellers had no listening aids, except for the old and uncomfortable favourite of immersing an ear in a water-filled biscuit tin or Dixie on the floor of a trench or gallery, in the hope of picking up enhanced vibrations. It was no surprise that things were so primitive; on mining exercises as late as 1913 the RE still employed the bizarre method of driving wooden pegs into the ground and biting on them to pick up sensations through the teeth, and the first formal listening aids to be used on the Western Front – London Water Board 'Listening Sticks' – worked on the same principle. It was therefore not uncommon to find a tunnelling officer arriving back from leave with his own kit. Often it was a doctor's stethoscope. Listening was one of the most critical parts of the tunnellers' work and any newly devised device was worthy of consideration.

> The strain on the morale of the infantry occupying sectors which are known to be mined is a terrible one, especially if they have no engineers to combat the stealthy attack. For the hundreds who are killed, buried, or injured from enemy mines there are thousands who suffer mental strain from the mere suspicion of their existence.
>
> Captain H D Trounce, 181 TC, RE

The army could not expect 'Tommy to be shot at from the surface, boofed at from above, and blown to Hell from below' as John Norton-Griffiths so aptly put it. Being those most likely to be 'lifted', the infantry, aware only of dangers which were magnified tenfold by a fear-fuelled imagination, were naturally desperate to know what might be happening beneath their feet, and equally desperate for a defensive response from their own engineers.

> The mine was exploded at 'stand-to', 6.15 in the morning when every man in the line was at his post. This accounts for the very heavy casualties we suffered. I received the news in the early morning. I made a hurried meal and hurried up on the motorcycle to find out the extent of the damage and see if anything could be done. A tremendous artillery bom-

bardment was in progress as I proceeded up the communication trench. Arriving in the firing line I found the infantry, a Bantam Battalion of the HLI in a very perturbed and nervous state. They were new to the firing line, it was I believe their first term of duty in the trenches and some of them were cowering in their dugouts and shelters seemingly petrified with fright. It was not a pleasant sight. Personally I felt rather disgusted but I suppose their terror was natural for there is nothing in warfare more nerve-racking and demoralising than the explosion of a big mine at dawn.

> Captain Matthew Roach MC,
> 180 and 255 TC, RE

Without technical listening aids for early warning it was a question of improvisation. Many infantrymen, particularly those who had been miners in civilian life, preferred to trust home-made devices rather than the word of a young and perhaps inexperienced sapper officer, even though a protective mine system in their sector might be instigated on his recommendation. Nocturnal infantry listening patrols in no man's land revealed a surprising amount of information about shallow workings. From saps and shell holes it was possible to detect the sound of winches, bellows, pumps, digging, and to know with certainty whether they were hostile

The Protected Mine-finder for Use in Sounding for Enemy Mines

Records have not yet revealed whether Mr Heath Robinson's listening system was ever employed

More black mining humour from the 'Wipers Times'

CLOTH HALL.
YPRES.

Great Attraction This Week

Messrs. INFANTRY, ARTILLERY & Co.
Present their Screamingly Funny Farce,
ENTITLED:
BLUFF
THIS FARCE PROMISES TO BE A GREAT SUCCESS AND A LONG RUN IS
EXPECTED.
—o—o—o—o—

QUARTERMASTER & COMPANY

The World's Famous Back Chat Comedians
(A GREAT SHOW.)
—o—o—o—o—

A STIRRING DRAMA,
ENTITLED:
MINED
A MOST UPLIFTING PERFORMANCE.
—o—o—o—o—

ALL THE LATEST PICTURES.

ENTIRE CHANGE OF PROGRAMME WEEKLY·
—o—o—o—o—

Best Ventilated Hall in the Town.
PRICES AS USUAL.

---

or friendly. For the troops manning the front line it was a different matter. Such shallow tunnels could often be attacked from the surface too by planting and blowing charges in holes. Deeper workings on the limit of audibility for the human ear were more problematic.

My men were mainly Nottinghamshire miners, some of whom reported to me that they were sure the Boche was working below our trenches. Some sappers came along to investigate and said it was highly unlikely as the ground was too wet. However, my mining boys rigged up a contraption consisting of an 18-pounder shell case into which was inserted a bayonet running through the base. The lid was the lid of a tin of a cigarette case and was connected up by a wire to the top of the shell case, and the contraption was put on the floor of the trench. My fellows spent hours holding the tin to one ear and the lid to their teeth and were absolutely certain that mining was going on. During my next spell they told me that all was quiet, which was suspicious, and I got authority to move my platoon at night to a trench 50 yards behind. And sure enough our forward trench went up with a bang accompanied by trench mortar fire. A full story was put up to Brigade, but I gather the RE were not impressed with our home-made mine detector.

Lieutenant Colonel A Hacking,
8th Battalion, Sherwood Foresters

On 'emergency' duty day and night during a spell in the line, the first warning the duty engineer officer was likely to receive about enemy activity underground would invariably come from the men in the trenches. Scares and rumours were rife, particularly during the hours of darkness when all was quiet and the mind was free to dwell on 'uplifting' thoughts. Most were found to be false alarms, but it was the tunnelling officer's duty to investigate all reports of suspicious sounds. This was a job carrying great responsibility, and if experienced listeners were on hand to assist they would not be ignored as a valuable second opinion.

A Canadian officer and myself were in a dugout on the other side of the cut [railway cutting] when a corporal and two men came down to say they could hear noises like creaky truck wheels underneath their little shelter. We reported back to HQ at Larchwood and they sent two Durham men up – miners trained in listening and Proto work. The Canadian officer, the corporal, the two Durhams and myself slithered over in the dark and got into this place. The two Durhams knelt down, plugged their ears to the ground, listened for about ten minutes, then got up on their knees again and looked at each other. We were breathless with suspense. The first man got up, looked at his mate and slowly, ponderously, said 'Rats.'...'Aye', said his mate, 'fucking'. So we blew a small charge just to be on the safe side and to satisfy the infantry.

Lieutenant William McBride, 1st Australian
Tunnelling Company, Hill 60

There were many such stories; men chopping wood, wiring, even digging graves, were sometimes found to be the culprits, but it was undeniable that simply the threat of enemy mining caused profound anxiety, and unwarranted panic could be quick to spread through no more than a few injudicious words. Finely tuned technical equipment would soon arrive at the front, but before the advent of reliable kit, tunnelling officers often had to be devious in calming the troubled breasts of the infantry.

As most of these alarms were abortive and in any case sounds were difficult to interpret, I made a box similar to the ones I had tested at Cambridge and Chatham containing a battery and headphones attached to an iron spike for

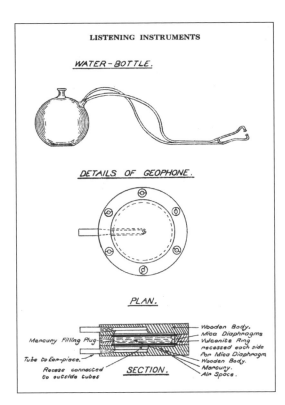

LISTENING INSTRUMENTS

WATER-BOTTLE.

DETAILS OF GEOPHONE.

PLAN.

Mercury Filling Plug.
Tube to Ear-piece.
Recess connected
to outside tubes

Wooden Body.
Mica Diaphragms
Vulcanite Ring
recessed each side
for Mica Diaphragm.
Wooden Body.
Mercury.
Air Space.

SECTION.

driving into the ground. It produced various noises at will which I duly interpreted like a fortune teller, because the trench occupants would seldom if ever rely upon my superior listening ability without an instrument. We christened it 'The Wind Box' and it proved a blessing in dealing with false alarms.

Captain G R Cassels, 175 TC, RE

By the spring of 1916 all tunnelling companies had a selection of efficient technical aids to choose from. The French geophone, the American Western Electric, and the German Siemens Halske machines each worked on the principle of magnifying sounds through sensors and earphones. They were a great improvement on the naked ear and great care was taken to ensure that the infantry gained confidence by demonstrating just what the new fangled machines could do.

The geophone was small and could be put into a coat pocket. With it one could hear the earthworms crawl and ants walk. Listening to a pin drop shocked the eardrum. It was a great aid in reassuring infantry who heard noises. We would invite them to use the geophone to confirm there was no sound of mining. Hearing the background noise they would say it seemed to them that a dozen Germans were tunnelling just underneath. I

would then tip an earthworm out of a tin and invite them to listen to it crawling around. To clinch the matter I would release the ant and left them to listen to it putting its feet down. On the geophone it sounded like an elephant walking around in lead-soled boots.

Lieutenant Brian Frayling, 171 TC, RE

The geophone, the most efficient and consequently the most favoured machine used by the British, worked on the amplification of vibration. Two wooden sensors containing a quantity of mercury trapped between two mica discs were connected to a doctor's stethoscope. An earpiece served each disc, making the machine stereophonic. The operator moved the discs around on floor, wall or roof of the gallery until a 'balance' of sound was achieved in each ear, and from this a reliable bearing could be taken of suspect noises with a simple compass. The geophone was a highly effective modern reincarnation of the more primitive listening techniques employed many centuries before: pressing an ear against a shield on the ground, hanging metal water filled vases in galleries, which hummed when enemy miners were active, or using a drum with a few pebbles on the taut skin – each was based upon amplification of vibration.

An early water bottle listening aid and its advanced and highly efficient successor, the geophone

A geophone in use. Two sensors were employed to establish the direction of hostile sounds, one alone was used (still with both earpieces) to determine distance

THE SILENT WAR

With so many people listening in, the fundamental ambience of a tunnel system was obviously silence. Sign language was commonplace, and verbal communication in anything above the faintest whisper was outlawed – if the enemy were close by even subdued speech could be clearly heard through listening devices, so a hushed calm was expected at all times.

One day whilst listening with a Geophone I was startled to hear quite distinctly the sound of voices coming seemingly through the clay. There was no one in the mine but myself and one listener, and he was sitting close by. I watched his lips but they did not move and I felt a most uncomfortable tickling sensation running up my spine to the roots of my hair, for I knew that the sound of voices could only mean that the Germans had a gallery close up within a few feet of ours. I was very much perturbed at the discovery until I reflected that they must have been there some time and that their very presence proved that there was no immediate danger from a blow. Thus reassured I sat for some time with the instrument to my ears rather enjoying the novel experience.

Captain Matthew Roach MC, 255 TC, RE

Getting close enough to the enemy to hear conversation might have been initially nerve-wracking and highly dangerous, but it allowed a lot of information to be gathered, and not only about tunnels.

At Mount Sorrel often we ran up within a few feet under the surface so as to obtain better information of enemy troop movements, and with an area so full of shell holes, care had to be taken not to break the earth surface, for this would have been fatal. It used to make us feel sometimes like a mouse nibbling at cheese bait in a trap. We had some listening posts right underneath their front line, only a few feet below, and we had men who could speak German for that. We had to be very quiet and talk in whispers, and some of the listeners who could understand German used to have some fun taking down their talk.

The RE Headquarters sent us down some Russians, supposed to be Russian miners who could speak German. There were four of them. We had come up to six or eight feet from the surface right underneath the German front line – we had run up a bit too quick, contours of the land, and we knew we were very thin. We had the Russians in there. It had to be very quiet – there was only supposed to be one man listening in a listening post at any one time, using a geophone. We had them in there and they had been a few hours on duty and I went along to one of these listening posts. Long before I got to the post I could hear these fellows chattering away, and I found the other two chattering away. I couldn't do anything with those Russians, I really couldn't. I sent them away as useless.

Lieutenant John Westacott,
2nd Canadian TC

Below: Two British listeners with geophones detecting sounds from the same German hostile gallery

Below far right: Top – training. A listener learns to detect and note the direction of noises from the centre of a listening circle. Bottom – the system in action: taking bearings of sounds of enemy activity from several listening posts

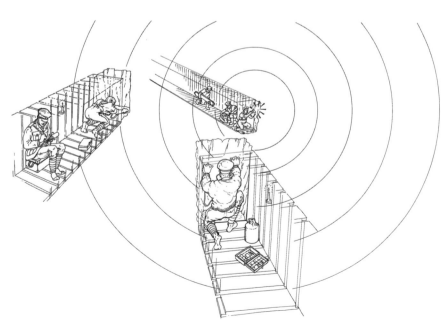

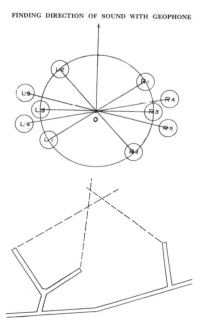

FINDING DIRECTION OF SOUND WITH GEOPHONE

German Mineure *listening with a Siemens Halske device in a small clay gallery. Note the British tunnellers' friends: the tell-tale cleated German boots*

German speakers were on hand to be drafted in when speech became audible, just as English speakers were on the other side of no man's land. To maintain maximum silence, men suffering from colds or coughs were put on other duties until the problem had cleared, and in most British mines the standard army pattern of noisy cleated boots were outlawed beyond a certain 'safe' point, with tunnellers wearing plimsolls or just thick socks elsewhere.

At the tunnel face a clay-kicker bound his feet in sandbags to muffle the 'kick', whilst in particularly wet galleries rubber boots were a standard issue for all. Careful footwear selection was apparently not always common practice in German tunnels, and British officers often cited the commotion created by heavy enemy footwear as one of the significant factors in the eventual British dominance underground. For added sound insulation, floors were covered with sandbags or spread with sand to muffle footfalls, and blankets were hung at regular intervals along galleries to further deaden noise. In one unusually efficient mine, the German system at Mount Sorrel captured in June 1917, some tunnels were found to have been carpeted with rugs and mats from nearby cottages; in another, pairs of bedroom slippers were found. So, silence was the key, and those who failed to observe the basic and very simple rules were likely not only to have a short tunnelling career, but also to place in jeopardy the lives of many of their comrades.

It was a strange state of affairs for anyone outside the tunnelling companies to comprehend. Whilst one side was striving to keep quiet, the other was desperately willing them to make a noise, and straining every sinew to hear it. Indeed, without noise there was no enemy to fight. Yet silence could never be assumed to indicate that the enemy was not present. It was therefore the listener, not the man who placed or blew the charge, who held the key to life and death underground.

The lives of dozens of tunnellers rested upon total attentiveness and correct interpretation of sounds. Extreme care was taken in the selection of men for this most vital of duties. Alone in a cramped listening post and under immense psychological pressure due to the nearness of the enemy, the imagination could become overactive to the point where the sounds of normal bodily functions such as the beating of the heart could easily be mistaken for the regular thud of a miner's pick. Even the slightest inadvertent movement of a toe inside a boot might be picked up by the geophone and mistaken for enemy mining. Sounds of surface shelling, disturbingly regular in some areas, had to be filtered out by the natural talent of the listener, as did those emanating from the galleries themselves such as timber creaking under pressure, or water dripping. In very wet galleries even the ultra sensitive geophones became useless, as each tumbling droplet sounded like a lead weight falling to earth. Yet in less damp systems even these sounds could be filtered by the best of listeners. Some men were found to possess an almost instinctive talent for extraordinarily accurate eavesdropping, being able to ignore all the other myriad noises of trench warfare save those of the enemy *Pioniere*, and those found to possess the talent were pigeon-holed as specialists. Some men were able read a book whilst listening at their post without affecting concentration. Listeners need not have begun life as tunnellers, but could come equally from infantry or artillery; suitable men were attached to tunnelling companies for the duration.

In the most active sectors large numbers of men would be listening at the same time, taking compass bearings of suspected hostile sounds, and producing listening reports which were later collated and compared at HQ. Whilst calculating where the several separate bearings coincided could give a remarkably accurate position of the enemy, only the listeners' experience allowed him to gauge distance. With the aid of the geophone's 'artificial ears' the trace of a hostile tunnel could be followed as it progressed, and the digging speed of the enemy measured. At Mine Schools behind the lines new listening devices and captured enemy equipment were tested for their properties in every type of geology. The results, *Tables of Listening Distances*, were published and circulated so that each company knew which device was most appropriate for the soils in their particular sector.

In an effort to mimic front line conditions when training new officers, a 'Mining War Game' was also devised whereby two teams were pitted against each other underground. Here, they listened, plotted and located sounds, calculated charges and pretended to blow their enemy to kingdom come – before it was done to them. In allowing men to learn without risk by first-hand experience in a competitive, authentic and compelling environment the game was to become a great success.

ORGANISING THE LISTENERS

On 23 October 1915 John Norton-Griffiths had advocated the setting up of specialist listening centres for each company. At this time many listeners were still being attached from local infantry Brigades; when their unit was relieved, these trained, valuable and trusted men were replaced by inexperienced newcomers who had to learn the art afresh. Norton-Griffiths planned to solve this problem by attaching them permanently to tunnelling companies. He also devised a design for a 'listening circle' for training new recruits, but the idea was soon to be developed much further into specialist Mine Listening Schools, one for each Army. Companies in the Ypres Salient would eventually be served by a branch at the Second Army Mine School near Proven.

The distances for effective listening depended on geological conditions; harder rocks such as chalk carried sounds much farther than dense clay. In March 1916 the Listening Schools gave a table of average listening distances for underground activities in differing geological conditions as a provisional guide for officers.

(With geophone)	Chalk	Blue Clay	Sand & loam
Picking	250-300'	50–70'	30–40'
Dirt falling (careless)	60'	25–35'	8–12'
Walking (enemy)	55'	10–15'	8–10
Dragging sandbags	55'	10–15'	6–10'
Talking	30'	4– 6'	3–5'

(With unaided ear)	Chalk	Blue Clay	Sand &Loam
Picking	100–150'	35–45'	20–30'
Grafting	—	10–15'	8–12'
Dirt falling (careless)	35'	10–15'	4–6'
Walking (enemy)	30'	5–8'	5–8'
Dragging sandbags	25'	6–10'	4–6'
Talking	12'	3–4'	2–3'

Mining Notes Number 12, 24 March 1916

The Listening Schools were to reduce these figures in just a matter of months, and British listeners became adept at picking out the activities of their underground enemies at even closer distances. The geophone was the most significant factor in reducing these figures and buying the tunnellers time.

RESULTS OF LISTENING at Listening School
Broadly speaking, the results of several weeks' experience in the Blue Clay [Ypres Clay] proves that the geophone picks up working sounds to a greater distance than previously supposed. This is very significant and a revised table should be obtained for circulation as soon as possible. Recent results show the following for Blue Clay:
Walking in nailed boots – heard with
    geophone at 63 feet
Walking in muffled boots – 20'
    (Sometimes heard)
Dragging sandbags – 30'
Talking – 20' (Variable according to voice)
Dirt falling – 40'–60'
Shovelling – 60' (heard but not distinguished)
Filling bags – (falling dirt) – 40'–50'
Picking – nearly 200'
            War Diary, Major R S G Stokes, RE,
Assistant Inspector of Mines, 20 August 1916

Missing from these tables is the installation of timber; an essential process in clay, and a noisy business – especially where the ungainly German mortice and tenon joints were used.
    Norton-Griffiths was to take the development of listening one step further, proposing that posts should contain remote electrical listening devices, and not men. These instruments were

to be connected to equipment resembling a telephone exchange housed in a centrally located dugout, where one man could monitor as many as twenty-five individual posts. The concept was eventually adopted, and seismomicrophones and tele-geophones took the place of the human ear in a great many mine schemes along the front; the German *Pioniere* were to use an almost identical method. Again, geology was the key to efficient use; each device had to be calibrated to suit the nature of the ground at the point where it was located, and the distance at which sound was required to be detected.
    Being Army troops with a fixed territory, each tunnelling company soon became intimately acquainted with their 'patch', organising duties to suit local conditions, geological, tactical and

Mount Sorrel. Plan showing T-shaped listening posts and the radii of rupture of British and German camouflets. Hatching indicates destroyed galleries

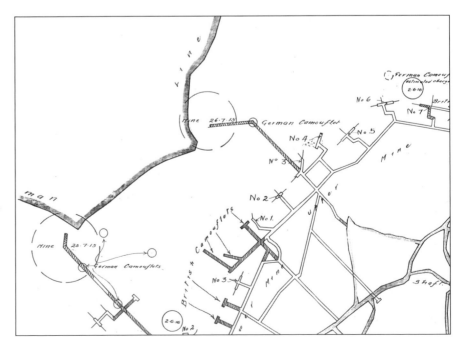

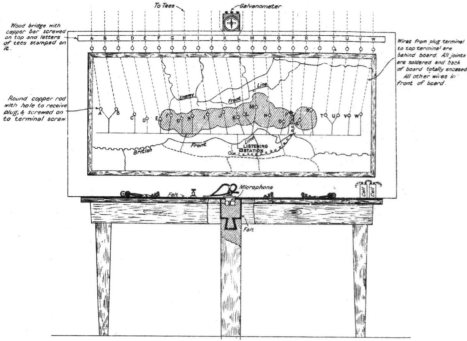

Above: A typical central listening station table with cables connected to tele-geophone and seismomicrophone sensors in twenty-two listening posts. Each post has its own terminal. Potential enemy activity is scrutinised by plugging in the headphones on the table top. The Galvanometer ensures electrical continuity in the cabling is visibly maintained

Right: An apprehensive-looking British officer in the Hawthorn Ridge mine chamber in the chalk country of the Somme

The new men of course, they were not used to it, they hadn't seen any warfare at all, just sent out from Canada and some from the States, practically green. It was hard for them, they weren't up to the other men who had all seen service.

It's very hard to stand there with the geophones round your ears and listening, listening all the time. Men used to crack up, they didn't like that job at all. An officer would be jumpy and he'd come back and do a lot of grousing, and we didn't like that, we had to put up with what we'd got! But you could tell a man's nerve had gone. I used to put in a confidential report to the CO and they would be got out at night and back to headquarters and the doctor. That's all we could do.

Lieutenant John Westacott,
2nd Canadian TC, at Mount Sorrel

logistical. Listening was included in the plan, and the duration of spells underground varied according to how perilous the individual post was considered to be. In sectors where the lines were very close, enemy tunnels might originate from points well behind the front lines for safety and secrecy reasons. It was of course critical to obtain as early a warning as possible of hostile schemes, and the nearer one was to the source, the sooner one was informed. Listening galleries therefore sometimes extended beneath no man's land, under the enemy front line to the support trenches, and occasionally even to his reserve lines.

In these positions the most dangerous aspect of the work was not the listening itself but reaching and leaving the post noiselessly, passing beneath hostile trenches and through the invisible maze of enemy tunnels beneath no man's land. To maintain the critical continuity of work, men were relieved *in situ*. In leaving a post in these tiny forward listening tunnels it was necessary for one man to lie flat on the gallery floor and allow the incoming listener to crawl over his body to take up his duties. Whereas in normal work a three-hour listening spell might be expected, in such perilous forward posts it was reduced to one hour on and four off. Not everyone was up to the task.

Noise was the thing. We had one or two cases of men who would break down and say they couldn't stand it – go all to pieces – and ask if they could go out before their shift was over.

One of the most desirable but dangerous points for a listening post was close to an enemy shaft. Here a good listener could pick up all the information needed to decide precisely what stage the hostile mining had reached, simply by the sound of the enemy windlass. Long winds with short periods between them meant that the shaft itself was still being sunk, as heavy loads were being lifted; larger pauses between each lift signified that the shaft was complete and a gallery was being driven; and a greater period of descent compared to lift showed that materiel – possibly explosives – were being carefully lowered. The one thing the listener did not wish to hear from this or any other point was silence. Silence often signified one thing and one thing only; an enemy mine was charged and ready to blow at any time.

In the labyrinthine workings which gradually developed beneath no man's land, calmness, concentration and experience were required to determine precisely what information a listening

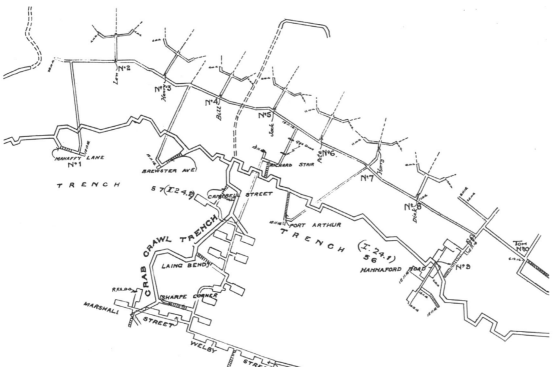

The dugout, lateral and listening system at Tor Top. Dotted lines from listening posts indicate pre-drilled holes for electronic listening devices and/or camouflet charges – 'torpedoes'.

instrument was picking up; were the sounds friendly, or were they hostile? Major R S G Stokes, Assistant Inspector of Mines from early 1916, and later Controller of Mines for the Third Army, was already an experienced tunneller when he took up his post, having been a mining engineer in civil life. He had begun his war service as a subaltern in 174 Tunnelling Company, winning a Military Cross in the late summer of 1915 for an exploit which had required great *sang froid*. Detecting a nearby and incoming hostile gallery, Stokes calculated that the German tunnel would not collide with his own workings but just, and only just, pass by. In the event the enemy were so close that talking could clearly be heard – the gallery was literally within centimetres of the British workings. When the Germans had passed over and beyond his post, Stokes blew.

After the war, Harvey referred to his assistant as 'the most capable man I have ever met'. Stokes was also the most meticulous observer and recorder in the Inspector of Mines' department. One of his first moves as Assistant was to make sure that any clay-kickers who were wasting their time working with standard mining techniques in the harder chalk of Artois and Picardy were transferred to areas more suitable for their skills – the clay-rich sectors of Flanders. Throughout the Salient he also instigated the 'silent period', long used on individual schemes, to coordinate listening sector by sector in all mines.

Brigadier-General R N Harvey's highly respected Assistant Inspector of Mines, Major R S G Stokes, photographed in Russia in 1919

Hill 60. There are listening posts and geophones at all desirable points, and the listeners are apparently intelligent men who have mostly been at listening school. But in these complicated workings there seems to be peculiar need for properly regulated listening periods, say two per day, of about half an hour, when all work and movements are stopped, and when four or five officers are listening simultaneously from chosen points, recording all sounds heard with synchronised watches. The policy of wholesale simultaneous listening was found most profitable in chalk systems and would be equally applicable to Hill 60 where the range of hearing is good. The 'cost' of this listening would be possibly one foot per day, and the chances would be good of gaining some knowledge of the position and policy of the enemy.

War Diary, Major R S G Stokes, RE, Assistant Inspector of Mines, 5 March 1917

Stokes' 'cost' refers to the extra distance which could have been driven in offensive galleries if work had not been halted for his listening period. It was essential to vary the timing of these periods so the enemy did not 'cotton on' and stop work himself at the same time. There was the usual hitch of course: both sides used the same strategy in the same places, so listeners were not only required to note detectable sounds but also the times when they ceased, and for how long, thus indicating the enemy's quiet period. At such times it was clearly crucial to make sure to stop all one's own tunnellers working within a certain radius. Three times a day at pre-arranged, coordinated but varying times, all activity ceased for a mile or so around. Everybody listening underground was ready with geophone and compass to note the bearings of any and every noise and to record its nature. The enemy could be above, below, ahead or behind the listeners, or trying to outflank their opposition on either side. The listening reports were then rushed to the Senior Trench Officer's mapping dugout and plotted on an overall plan – a plan that would indicate the enemy's activities and perhaps save the lives of infantry occupying the lines above. From these sounds alone a projected plan of enemy workings could be drawn up.

In both defence and offence secrecy was obviously paramount. Mine plans were not permitted to be taken beyond company headquarters, no one except tunnellers were allowed underground without special dispensation from GHQ, and the need for caution with careless talk was incessantly drummed into infantry working parties, despite the fact that they were never allowed into inner reaches of mine systems. Mining was such a slow, dangerous and laborious process that months – even years – of work could be wasted by scraps of information finding their way across no man's land. If the Germans had discovered that the British were going deep in the summer of 1915 for instance, the complexion of the subsequent two years of underground conflict would have been very different.

But with tens of thousands of men involved in mining in one way or another it was practically impossible to keep things totally covert. Curiously, Norton-Griffiths believed that men talked too much when on leave – especially when having their hair cut. But not all opinions were based upon such simple supposition. On 22 March 1916 just before the detonation of the first 'deep' British mines at St Eloi – mines which altered the course of underground warfare firmly and permanently in British favour – suspicions were running high.

Had to hurry down to Vlammy [Vlamertinge] in the afternoon to organise a relief party to go out and recover a GS wagon which had been ditched last night...I strolled over to a farm and was a little astonished to be told by our Belgian hostesses that there was going to be an attack at St Eloi *avec des mines* in three or four days. Naturally, I knew this to be perfectly true and equally naturally I had to reply *'Vraiment, mais je n'en sais rien: peut etre qui sait?'* Still it is a bit sickening to find such secret doings common property for, what is known to a Belgian is almost certainly known to Fritz. Or at least that is what most of us believe.

Major H S Cowan, 175 TC, RE

ON THE OFFENSIVE

Offensive mines could not capture and hold positions on their own, but were used as a shock tactic to help secure strategic points, usually salients or high ground, and fired in association with an infantry, mortar and artillery attack. Although often used in minor operations, offensive mines were equally appropriate as an adjunct in launching large-scale attacks, for example on the Somme on 1 July 1916, and at the Battles of Arras and Messines Ridge in 1917.

The essence of successful offensive mining was surprise, and its achievement depended as much upon the nature of the ground as the silent working practices of the tunnellers, and of course the overall secrecy of the project. Before entertaining any hostile ambitions however, a degree of confidence, if not superiority, had to be attained in defence, which is precisely what the British strove to do throughout 1915 and 1916. There was no point in attempting to mine a target where it was known that the enemy had a strong underground presence; success was only possible if their attention had either not been attracted at all, or that one's defensive system was so well organised that the enemy was unable to countermine without being discovered and destroyed beforehand: he might suspect offensive mining, but he must not be allowed to discover it. The British could never have achieved total underground dominance without first nullifying the hostile threat through thorough defensive procedures (as well as solving the riddle of the running Kemmel Sands). An unyielding and comprehensive defensive strategy allowed them to work with confidence and ultimately to tunnel at depths far greater than the Germans thought probable. It took time and patience, and left the officers commanding several of the tunnelling companies wondering if they would ever be able to strike an offensive blow.

It cannot be said that the British superiority was entirely of their own making, however. Working practices on both sides of no man's land were diverse, and each side applied two totally different strategies in mine design and construction. The British almost universally employed 'laterals' – tunnels which ran parallel to the trace of the trenches above, and to which entrance inclines and shafts from the surface were connected. All listening posts reaching forward beneath no man's land were also driven from laterals, as were fighting tunnels and often galleries to some of the great offensive mines. Even if two or even three levels of tunnels were employed, each was served by its own lateral gallery wherever possible. The benefits were obvious: firstly, a lateral system helped to ventilate the tunnel complex by delivering a draught of precious fresh air via the numerous shafts and stairways. This flow is produced naturally in workings with multiple entrances by air descending one entry point, the downcast shaft, and exiting from another, the upcast. Secondly, in having so many entry/exit points

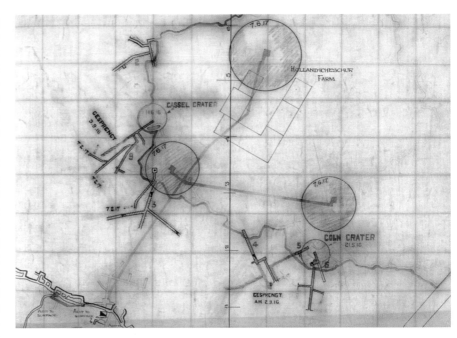

laterals offered a choice of escape and rescue routes in case of emergency. By contrast, a surprising number of German mine systems in the Salient remained similar to the earliest British workings, consisting of a single shaft serving a single gallery at the end of which lay a branched cluster of listening posts. It was a method that offered no natural ventilation – and only one exit route. After the St Eloi blows in March 1916 the decision to install laterals was made by the Germans, but pressures to find and neutralise the British deep offensive mines meant that those few which were put in were insufficient and too late to form a credible counter-measure platform.

VENTILATING THE TUNNELS

As a tunnel extended beyond the range of natural ventilation, a sufficient and reliable air supply to the face was required. Although shift duration could vary between companies, the average practice was to employ four shifts of six hours each, with four men on face work, kicking, timbering and bagging, another four tramming – hauling the spoil back to the shaft on trolleys – two men on hoisting, and a further two pumping. Every litre of air which the working section consumed in the cramped tunnel had to be supplied from the surface. Should this supply be interrupted, oxygen levels quickly dropped and efficiency suffered along with the health of the tunnellers who, grafting hard, soon became light headed and listless before developing severe migraine like symptoms. The somewhat shocking rule of thumb was that as long as the

The Hollandscheschuur mine scheme showing forked German listening systems without lateral galleries, in red. The blue British offensive tunnel can be seen to pass safely deep beneath. The British defensive system is not marked

The reliable and effective Holman Air Pump delivered air on both the forward and backward stroke of the handles

Right: Alongside blacksmith's bellows, the rotary fan was the standard early-war mine ventilator for British workings

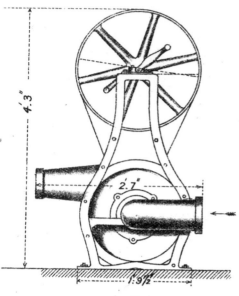

VENTILATION OF MINES.

Rotary Fan

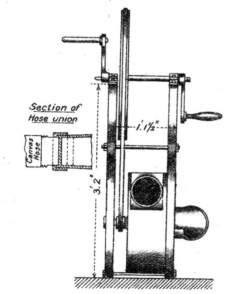

Section of Hose union

candles did not go out through lack of oxygen, it was safe enough to work.

A junior officer was detailed to monitor the air pumps at all times. The earliest pumps – which some considered to be the best on account of their quietness – were 'won' from local smithies.

One of the big difficulties in driving the long tunnels was in ventilation. At 60 [Hill 60] we had two men working a big blacksmiths bellows with a long line of stove pipe leading to the face. In the early days we had candles for light, and often there was so little oxygen that they would only burn with a tiny blue flame. Later we got rechargeable storage batteries, which was a great improvement as one candle would use up as much oxygen as six men.

The infantry, two men usually, would pump away on the bellows. You knew straight away if they had stopped because the air got even worse very quickly – your senses are attuned to everything down there – but you couldn't shout out for them to get back to it; they couldn't hear you for one thing, and we weren't allowed to talk in anything but whispers, so one man would have to go back, tell the officer that the air had stopped, and he would go and give them hell. You can't work without air.

Sapper H Mawson, 3rd Canadian TC

Oxygen consumption of candles was a problem which troubled GHQ. Yet although electric lighting began to be installed in some tunnel systems towards the end of 1916, candles were to remain by far the most common light source. They had certain benefits over electricity. Apart from needing no technical servicing, which meant they were reliable, they took up less valuable space in the gallery. And having four, six or eight hours' duration, tunnellers could tell roughly how long they had worked by the rate of burning – and consequently when it was time to knock off. Tunnellers naturally had access to an endless supply of candles and other similarly valuable, rare or desirable commodities which

were often unavailable to their infantry colleagues. Apart from being a useful currency for bartering with the Tommies for cigarettes, food and other comforts, officers found some items of tunneller's stores particularly handy *pour encourager les autres*.

> ...a packet of candles to a sergeant would materially accelerate the bag shifting, while the offer of a few lengths of 9 x 3 to the OC to prop up his dugout would probably increase the size of our required carrying party, to which party the promise of an unauthorised tot of rum, of which we always had a generous supply, would infuse added energy.
>
> Anon, 250 TC officer, 1927

By the spring of 1916 many deep galleries in the Salient were well over 300 metres long, and sufficient and reliable air delivery was crucial. At the Conference of Second Army Tunnelling Company Commanders on 27 July 1916, Major Stokes was particularly concerned about this issue.

> The whole ventilating question is in a very indefinite state and I think this is largely due to lack of fundamental facts, which should be obtained at once as to the capabilities of standard machines. The question is more urgent in Second Army since the long extension of galleries is a certainty and now in progress. Present knowledge of the air requirements are also very hazy. Text books say 20 cubic feet per minute for a working man and 1 cubic foot per man quiescent.
>
> Major R S G Stokes, RE

In shallower workings it was possible to create extra natural ventilation in certain 'safe' tunnel sections by drilling numbers of vent holes to the surface through the roof using a 'Wombat borer', a screw-like, small-diameter boring machine. In deep mines this was of course impossible, and lengths of three-inch (8-cm) diameter armoured hose connected to electrical or manual air pumps or bellows fed air both to the face and to intermediate stations along the tunnels. The use of armoured hose was deliberate; it offered the best chance of a continued air delivery should

Electrically lit French mine workings

German mining equipment captured by British tunnellers near Fricourt on the Somme, 1 July 1916. Some of the kit is of British manufacture

miners be trapped behind a collapse. However, the problem of achieving a totally efficient and unfailing supply was ultimately found to be insoluble and in the end each company or section did the best they could with the equipment available. The tunnellers, as always, accepted what was offered and carried on.

MINE AND COUNTERMINE

In all offensive mining it was obligatory to have a considered and comprehensive plan of attack before starting a scheme. It was far better to go into action expecting hostile intervention rather than with blind optimism, and the greatest attention was paid to studying and anticipating the likelihood of enemy activity, be it offensive or defensive, by listening, noting and reporting: how strong was his presence, how close was he known to be, when was the last time he had been heard, at what depth were his galleries? The countermine war was similar to a pre-battle artillery bombardment on the surface – it was designed to destroy emplacements and limit retaliation, and ultimately to entirely neutralise all enemy action to allow an offensive to be launched; the difference was that this battlefield was entirely subterranean, the emplacements were tiny tunnels, and one could seldom observe the results of one's labours. A path literally had to be cleared for the advance of the offensive tunnel, and kept free by blowing in every enemy gallery before it drew close enough to become a threat. This demanded finely tuned listening,

careful collation of information, speed of action, and a chilling determination to strike without mercy. It took enormous coolness and detachment to blow at the most opportune moment – before your enemy blew you. To destroy anything underground, one needed explosives.

In military mining there were several roles for explosives to play. The two primary purposes were to destroy surface features with 'overcharged' or 'common' mines which broke the surface and formed a crater, and to crush enemy galleries with 'undercharged' mines – *camouflets*. The *camouflet* was a controlled explosion designed to be powerful enough to wreck a hostile gallery and kill its occupants. The rule was that it should not shatter more ground than was absolutely necessary nor be powerful enough to crater the surface. Confusingly, mines which cratered the surface were also called *camouflets* when used defensively. Such mines were usually planted in shallow tunnels where surface cratering was unavoidable.

The preferred position of underground attack was from beneath. This was as much for psychological benefit as practical; the fact that one side had managed to undermine the other's subterranean defences sowed seeds of anxiety and potential panic, both above and below ground. In the early days of the underground war, before concerted defensive systems had been installed, the tunnellers were naturally influenced by the great anxiety of their infantry colleagues. This osmotic transfer of nerves often led to defensive

The hazards of exploration. Part of a 8,000lb mine charge of Ammonal in rubberised bags found in the chalk tunnels beneath Vimy Ridge. This mine has since been made safe by the Durand Group

camouflet action being taken sooner than was necessary – blowing before there was a real need to do so, and thereby both giving away one's position early and destroying stable geology. But with time and experience came knowledge and confidence, and with them came the opportunity for the cold-blooded, calculated killing that epitomises the underground war. It was a murderous ritual which both sides came to recognise and accept as a part of everyday activity.

> The 'jumpiness' which all new troops are subject to at first had its influence on us, as on the troops above ground; and in the month or two previous to my joining the company sometimes a mine had been fired when probably by delaying it a little longer we might have secured more satisfactory results in damage and casualties to the enemy. That condition, however, wore off and we very seldom blew any mine unless we had the most certain evidence that we could get a good toll of Germans. We would frequently hold our mines for several days or a week or two, and when the listeners reported that the enemy could be heard in sufficient numbers in their tunnels just near our charges, we would connect our double set of electric leads to dynamo exploders or blasting machines, push handles home hard, and lift them to a higher sphere of operations.
>
> Captain H D Trounce, 181 TC, RE

Then there was the practical advantage of blowing a *camouflet* from beneath the enemy. Every blow, large or small, created a variable 'sphere of destruction' according to the size and nature of the explosive charge used. This sphere represented the area of subterranean territory shattered or shaken by the explosion; the downward 'kick' of an explosion is naturally far less damaging than the vertical or lateral effect. This meant that one's own galleries were far more likely to survive the blow if they were beneath the enemy because a smaller charge could be used. Occasionally, if the danger was especially acute, it was necessary to fire a heavier charge than one might have wished in order to shatter larger areas of suspected enemy workings. These defensive mines (recorded as heavy *camouflets*) were not only likely to pierce water bearing levels should they be present, and to crater on the surface, but would also destroy considerable portions of one's own system by their much larger sphere of destruction. They were avoided where possible.

> I decided to lay a charge. The Germans were quite close to our listening post, only about six or seven feet away I thought, and before commencing I strictly admonished the men to maintain absolute silence and to work as quietly as possible. I made the necessary arrangements for the passing down of the tamping and explosive, posting the men, about 40 of them, at regular distances in the drive, and went down myself to lay the charge. I had decided to put in 600 pounds of ammonal. The packing of the explosive, the fixing of the electric leads and detonators, and the tamping of the charge with about 50 feet of sandbags occupied the whole night and the grey dawn was breaking when I got back to the surface tired, dirty and wet to the skin but very well satisfied with the way the work had been done. All was now in readiness for the blow but I decided to wait till night so as to allow the Bosch to get a little nearer. Being quite 'played out', I went back to my dugout and had breakfast and a short nap.
>
> Bell, the officer who was to relieve me arrived at 6.30pm and after warning the infantry I took him underground to convince him that the enemy were actually there. We could distinctly hear them burrowing away and decided to blow at once. The trenches were cleared by the time we got up and I at once connected the exploder, turned on the current and pressed the button.
>
> A mighty column of red flame 80 feet high leaped up out of the earth with a dull heavy roar. It was a splendid, but terrifying sight. The ground rocked and swayed beneath my feet and the air was thick with flying lumps of earth. Then from both the opposing lines, starshells and flares commenced to soar skyward lighting up with a weird grandeur the tremendous cloud of white smoke which hovered over the crater. I could not help feeling a twinge of compunction for the poor German devils I had blotted out with such horrible suddenness and certainty, but I soothed my rebel conscience with the reflection that war was war, and that if we had not blown them they would most certainly have got us in a very short time.
>
> Diary of Captain Matthew Roach MC
> 180 and 255 TC, RE, 11 February 1916

Such mines were used only *in extremis* in the Salient. Here, where the geological conditions were so varied and critical, it was more common to use the most limited charge possible. In some areas, however, the preferred method of defence was to make certain that much of the geological territory beneath no man's land was so pulverised by heavy blows that it was only with the greatest difficulty that either side was able to construct galleries.

In workings beneath the saturated Kemmel Sands, the difficulties were magnified by the need to finely calculate the charge so that the enemy was destroyed without puncturing the waterladen stratum above. If a camouflet was accidentally overcharged whole systems could be lost, either temporarily or permanently, to inundations of water and quicksand.

There were two basic techniques used in *camouflet* fighting with limited size charges. The first was to plant a charge in the tunnel itself, in a listening post or in a small spur which was specially dug towards suspect enemy sounds, just as Captain Roach's men had done. This was the preferred method in tough ground such as hard clay, or the resilient chalks of Picardy.

loose detonators were inserted in every third or so remaining tin, to be exploded by the general shock. The electric leads were run back to the shaft and surface. The fuse was only meant as a standby, and was only long enough to reach the tamping so as to be accessible. To the end of the instantaneous fuse was attached a length of time fuse to allow it to be spitted and then to reach the surface in safety.

Having run the leads and fuse back as requisite, the tamping would be done. It is obvious that the explosion will seek the easiest path, and therefore one has to give the charge a solid backing or tamping to prevent it blowing down the gallery like a shot out of a gun. This tamping should be one and a half times the distance of solid ground to be broken through, i.e. for twenty feet, say thirty-five feet of tamping. Laying the tamping was a lengthy and arduous job; filled sandbags, lowered from the surface had to be dragged in to the face and stacked as tightly as possible. A tamped distance of thirty feet would require the best part of a day's work.

Lieutenant Walter Gardner, 172 TC, RE

A mine chamber in the process of being loaded, packed tight with explosive in waterproof tins. Any small gaps were filled with guncotton slabs

The charge would be stacked against the face, all tins packed closely together and touching. An electric detonator, connected to leads (all connections carefully made and taped with rubber for insulation), would be inserted into the powder of one of the tins. Another common detonator, crimped on instantaneous fuse [orange coloured, and crisscrossed with thread so that it could be recognised by feel in the dark], would be inserted in another tin, and in case of a large charge

The second somewhat specialised method was more applicable in softer ground, especially in the sandy ridge and spurs of the Salient, and required the services of a 'torpedo'. Torpedoes were a special self-contained explosive charge housed in a tube, and designed specifically for *camouflet* fighting. Kept in a store holding about ten at the rear of tunnel systems, at least one was always prepared for action, fully charged, primed with a detonator, and ready for instant use.

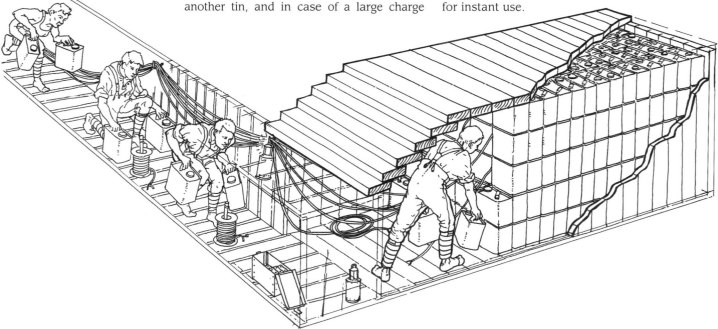

If one or other heard his opponent working, the direction and level was obtained and a torpedo which carried over 100 lbs of explosive in its tube which measured about 8 feet long and about 8 to 10 inches in diameter, was set in a hole bored by a special auger. The angle of the hole was drilled to the correct position to strike the enemy workings. Then this torpedo was wired back to an exploder, galleries were blocked off to resist the explosion in our own galleries – this was done by sandbagging [tamping]. The infantry on top were warned, then the exploder tested and the torpedo fired. Often the enemy heard

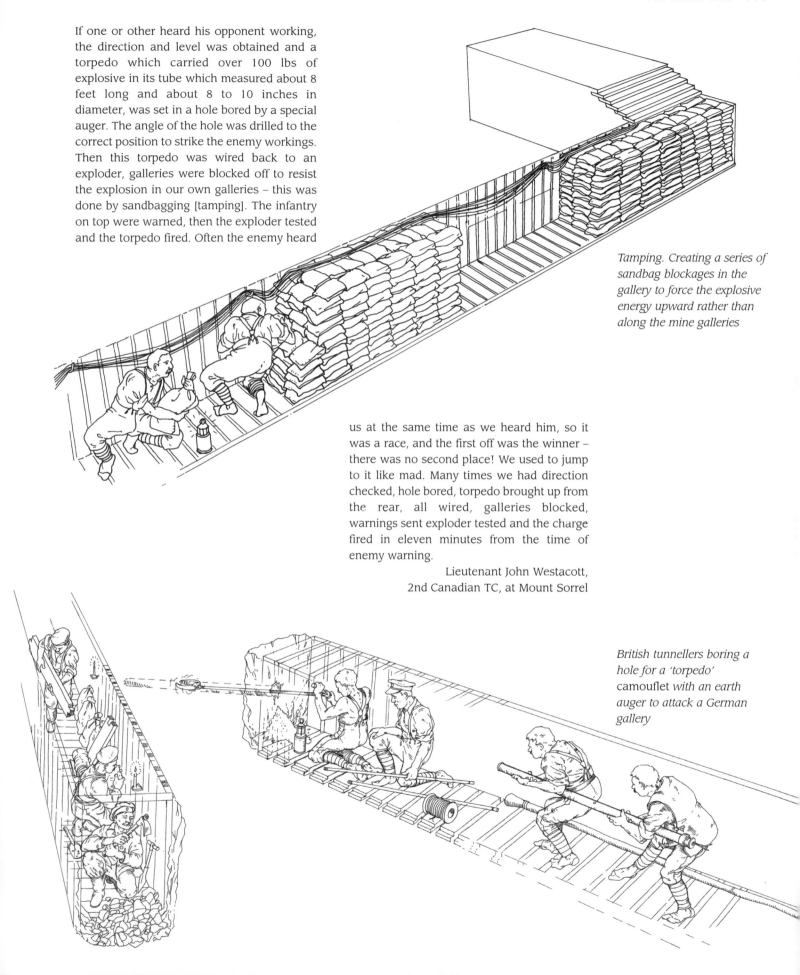

Tamping. Creating a series of sandbag blockages in the gallery to force the explosive energy upward rather than along the mine galleries

us at the same time as we heard him, so it was a race, and the first off was the winner – there was no second place! We used to jump to it like mad. Many times we had direction checked, hole bored, torpedo brought up from the rear, all wired, galleries blocked, warnings sent exploder tested and the charge fired in eleven minutes from the time of enemy warning.

Lieutenant John Westacott,
2nd Canadian TC, at Mount Sorrel

British tunnellers boring a hole for a 'torpedo' camouflet with an earth auger to attack a German gallery

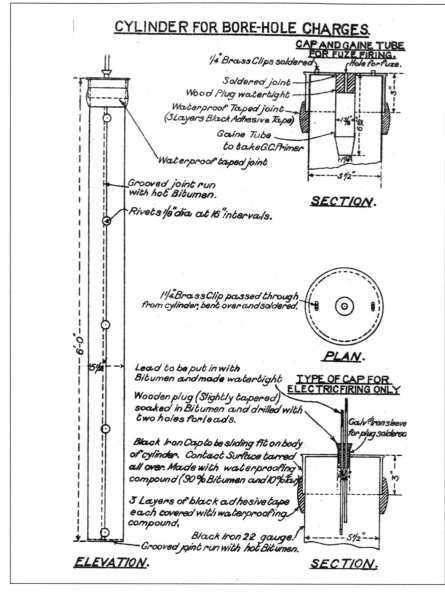

CYLINDER FOR BORE-HOLE CHARGES.

The British 'torpedo' used for camouflets *in soft 'drillable' ground*

EARTH AUGER.

The standard earth auger used to drill holes for torpedoes

Naturally, damage could not be restricted solely to enemy workings when a blow was made, but no *camouflet*, except in the direst emergency, should do more damage to one's own gallery than that of the enemy. After a blow, going back into the mine was an obligatory but dangerous business. It especially took a peculiar kind of courage to re-enter a gallery after an enemy *camouflet* had been blown. Apart from the danger of carbon monoxide gas, which will be covered in the next chapter, the tactical permutations of *camouflet* fighting were as elastic as the miners wished them to be, and neither side could ever be sure that only a single charge had been placed.

It was early summer 1917 at Railway Wood. We had a listening book, and we used to hear noises at the same time every day. We never could understand what it was. They [German prisoners] told us that these were the times when their officer came on his rounds, so then everybody worked like mad, and made the noises we could hear! We worked like hell to plot our next blow to catch that officer. We had a system when we had a blow. We kept track of them, let them come on for about a week. We had two galleries which joined in a fork. We loaded up both and tamped them. One went off about 10 pm and the other at 4 am. We learnt later from our German prisoners that the first blow got a couple of German miners in the face, and the second got their rescue party of thirteen – killed them all.

Captain Basil Sawers, 177 TC, RE

Having re-entered the mine after a blow, any damage was immediately repaired and preparations made to tackle future enemy approaches. For the vast majority of tunnellers during the war, this rebuilding period might be the only time that they witnessed the grisly results of their handiwork.

Where miners had been killed underground and pulverised by the explosion as happened so often, the water oozing into the tunnels was often discoloured with blood, and after a time the whole area became repulsive with the sickening stench of decomposing bodies. But mining was just like a game of chess: one had to anticipate the opponent's moves. If one made a false move one was usually 'for it'.

Captain R S Mackilligan, 178 TC, RE

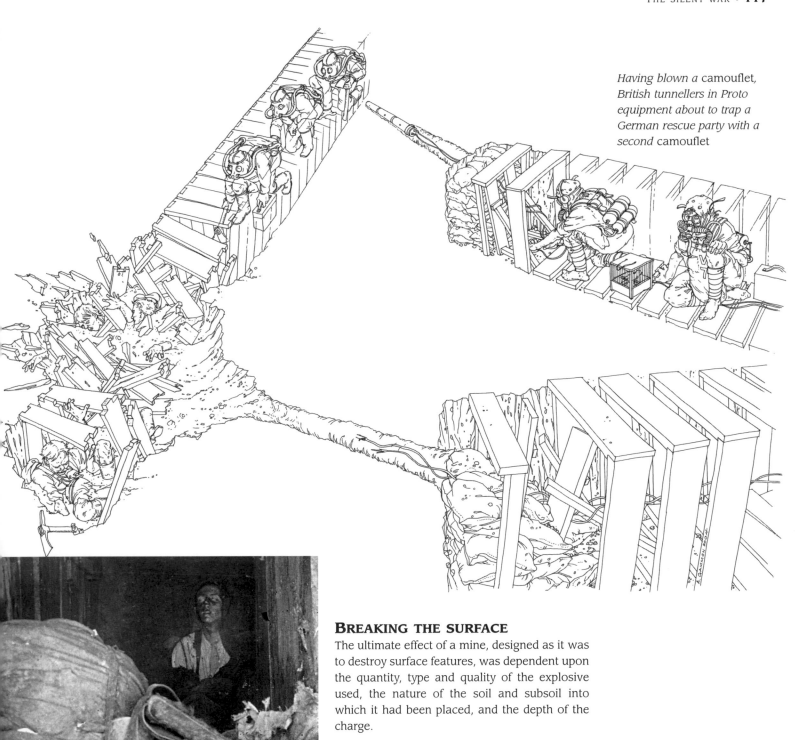

Having blown a camouflet, *British tunnellers in Proto equipment about to trap a German rescue party with a second* camouflet

BREAKING THE SURFACE

The ultimate effect of a mine, designed as it was to destroy surface features, was dependent upon the quantity, type and quality of the explosive used, the nature of the soil and subsoil into which it had been placed, and the depth of the charge.

For a period of nearly two years our lives centred in possible enemy action, aeroplane photographs, changing shifts, Company strength, listening reports, geophones, water levels, clay, chalk, timber, exploders, detonators, explosives. And of these, explosives were one of the most important. From the day I joined the Tunnelling Companies in April 1915 to the day we fired our last mine, we thought and dreamed explosives and their

The horrific dream of every tunneller. The result of a camouflet *in a German gallery*

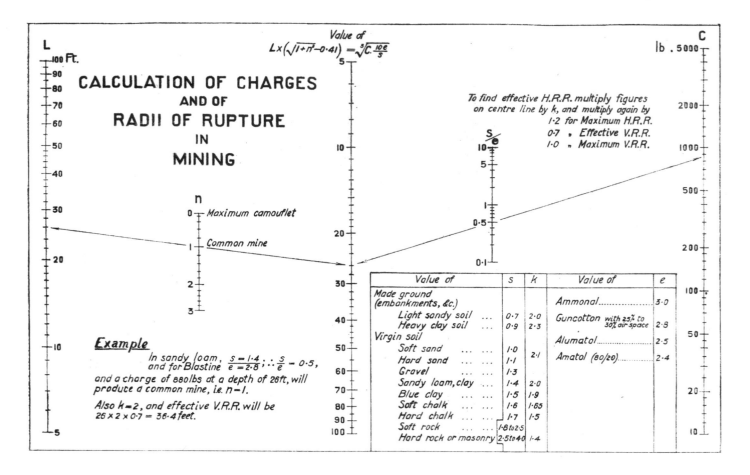

CALCULATION OF CHARGES AND OF RADII OF RUPTURE IN MINING

Value of

$$L \times \left(\sqrt{1+n^2} - 0.41\right) = \sqrt[3]{C \cdot \frac{10e}{s}}$$

To find effective H.R.R. multiply figures on centre line by k, and multiply again by
1·2 for Maximum H.R.R.
0·7 " Effective V.R.R.
1·0 " Maximum V.R.R.

n
0 — Maximum camouflet
1 — Common mine

Example

In sandy loam, $\frac{s=1\cdot4}{\text{and for Blastine}} \frac{s}{e=2\cdot8} \therefore \frac{s}{e} = 0.5$, and a charge of 880lbs at a depth of 26ft, will produce a common mine, i.e. $n=1$.

Also $k=2$, and effective V.R.R. will be $26 \times 2 \times 0.7 = 36.4$ feet.

Value of	s	k	Value of	e
Made ground (embankments, &c.)			Ammonal	3·0
Light sandy soil ...	0·7	2·0	Guncotton with 25% to 30% air space	2·8
Heavy clay soil ...	0·9	2·3		
Virgin soil			Alumatol	2·5
Soft sand	1·0	2·1	Amatol (80/20)	2·4
Hard sand	1·1			
Gravel	1·3			
Sandy loam, clay ...	1·4	2·0		
Blue clay	1·5	1·9		
Soft chalk	1·6	1·65		
Hard chalk	1·7	1·5		
Soft rock	1·8 to 2·5			
Hard rock or masonry	2·5 to 4·0	1·4		

Calculating mine charges of various explosives and their effects in different geologies. VRR= vertical radius of rupture; HRR= horizontal radius of rupture

effect. Black powder was the first, followed by wet guncotton and then Blastine, and finally Ammonal. Of these Ammonal was by far the most satisfactory. The first explosive used by Hickling in the shallow mine at St Eloi was gunpowder. It was always necessary to carry substantial amounts of explosive in the forward area and it was difficult to find storage protection for it. Guncotton had inferior cratering properties and furthermore it gave off large quantities of carbon monoxide gas. It was replaced by Blastine, which was quick acting and more effective. Ammonal became the standard. It was easy to handle, was quick acting and generally met our requirements. It was common hearsay that you could fire a bullet into it and it would not detonate.

Lieutenant F J Mulqueen, 172 TC, RE

Overcharged and common mines, exclusively laid by officers, were put to use in a variety ways to suit local circumstances. For example, they were blown beneath the enemy front line as a 'shock tactic' to launch to a trench raid, or employed for the destruction of trench redoubts or pillboxes. However, when it was decided that hostile mining progress was overwhelming and could not be controlled adequately by *camouflets*, heavy charges were also blown to cause havoc underground. These would naturally blow through to the surface due to the size of charge, and tunnellers were particularly pleased if the crater appeared as an irregular shape, i.e. elongated rather than round; this was conclusive proof that a portion of the blast had also blown down enemy tunnels before erupting, thereby doing greater damage and necessitating more repair work.

During the Great War around thirty-six different types of explosive were employed by the British alone for mining purposes. All produced slightly different effects in action. Explosives generally fell into two classes, low and high. Low explosive has a form of combustion which gradually burns through the charge, producing large amounts of hot gases under pressure and giving a slow 'pushing' explosion; with high explosive the action is much more rapid with the complete charge combusting at the same moment. In this case the gases are produced suddenly at enormous pressure and heat,

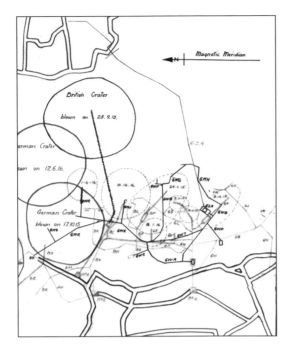

177 TC plan of mine galleries in a small portion of their Railway Wood sector. Green markings show a shallow fighting system with camouflets; brown a deeper defensive system, and the single yellow line traces a deep British offensive gallery from an underground shaft at 62A

firing, or a slab of guncotton which was incorporated into the charge. Being stable and safe Ammonal had no rivals in military mining – and with its speed of detonation being neither low nor high, it also produced the perfect 'lifting' effect. The only drawback was that Ammonal was hygroscopic, i.e. it readily absorbed moisture, a condition which might seriously impede or even prevent detonation. The problem was solved by supplying Ammonal in water-proofed rubberised bags or sealed petrol tins.

The blow itself was a tense affair. Tunnellers

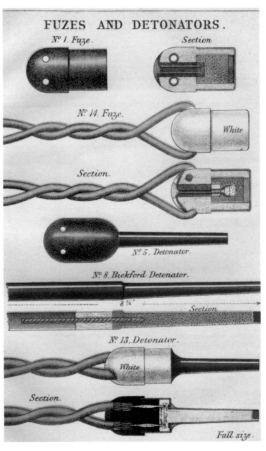

Standard fuses and detonators used by the RE in military mining

creating a rapid shock wave – a sharp blow rather than a push. The two different products might therefore ultimately create exactly the same amount of energy, whilst each produced a very different explosive effect and result. But in mining it was the 'lifting' effect that mattered: mines were being placed ever deeper, and therefore had an ever greater amount of earth to lift in order to break the surface and crater. This necessitated the use of an explosive which was neither too low nor too high in nature.

After a great many tests the tunnellers' preference was a fairly new product called Ammonal, an ammonium nitrate-based grey powder which was three times as powerful as gunpowder. Ammonal was especially popular because unlike gunpowder based explosives, it could not be set off with a naked flame, or even a bullet. A standard detonator and primer was required for

Crater comparisons following explosive tests at Chattenden, near Chatham, 1915

Section of a British practice mine blown at Wisques on 20 June 1916

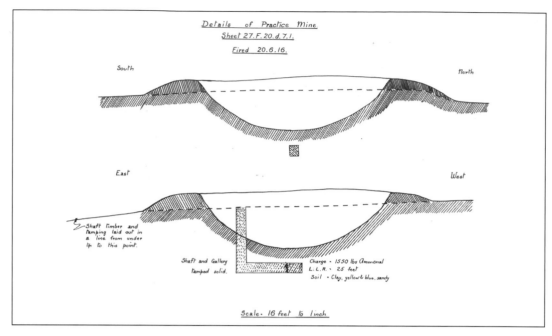

A practice mine being 'sprung'

were responsible for making sure that all the necessary parties had been informed of the reason for the blow, the timing of it, what the artillery might do afterwards, and that trenches and dugouts were cleared of infantry to the sappers' estimated safe distance.

The tamping process satisfactorily completed, the leads were extended to a point in the reserve trenches about a hundred yards in rear from which the mine could be fired in safety. The infantry were then warned to evacuate the front line trenches for some distance on either side and the bombing squads were held in readiness to resist the enemy should they attempt to occupy the crater. The battery was connected and everything was ready. When the button was pressed a huge mass of earth seemed to rise between the two firing lines as though some gigantic mole were at work underground. Then it burst with a dull heavy boom and a pink-white mass of flame leaped skyward.

For a few tense seconds the air was full of earth and stones. When we could safely look we saw where once had been level ground a yawning crater 30 feet across wreathed in yellowish eddying smoke. Then every short range weapon on the German lines seemed to open fire on the spot and trench mortar shells, rifle and hand-grenades and bombs were hurled into and around the cavity making an ear-splitting and indescribable din and rendering the occupation of the crater by either side utterly impossible. Our infantry

The 'mushrooming' of twin practice mines blown in preparation for the Messines attack of June 1917

Royal Engineers examining the results of the deep practice charge at Wisques

quickly regained their positions in the trenches and soon the mad bombardment ceased. When we left shortly afterwards our infantry had already commenced driving a sap to the crater edge from which they could bomb out any of the enemy who might try to occupy it. Returned to billets tired but happy, had a good sleep and went to bed.

Diary, Captain Matthew Roach, 180 and 255 TC, RE, 30 November 1915

As in many earlier centuries, craters were highly prized by attackers and defenders alike, and it was critical to try to capture the elevated rim following a blow, particularly that nearest the enemy if possible. As the mine was sprung, the earth driven up into the sky fell back to create a raised piece of artificial topography, the crater lip, which in a flat country like the Salient offered greatly enhanced observational advantages. It was essential to capture the lips without delay, but storming and holding a crater was fraught with difficulty. The moment one side gained the upper hand, enemy grenades, artillery, mortar, rifle and machine gun fire was rained upon the position turning it into a miniature cauldron of

Left: Rubberised, waterproof bags for explosives. Petrol tins were also widely used

Below: Calculation of risk to surface troops from the fallout of debris from a heavy mine blow

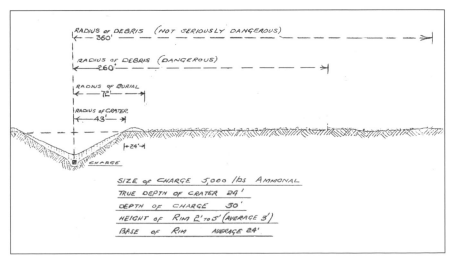

Crater in no man's land, equidistant between the opposing front lines. This blow would have destroyed both hostile and friendly galleries in the area, and made future tunnelling difficult in the shattered ground. Cuinchy, 1915

hell. Once inside the rim, there was little chance of escape until night fell.

The St Eloi Craters were big mine craters, held in turn by the Germans and then by our troops, each side holding a crater for only a day or two at a time. Nobody could hold such a position for long, as they were all wiped out. The pits of hell, we called them, and thousands of lives that were lost in those pits,

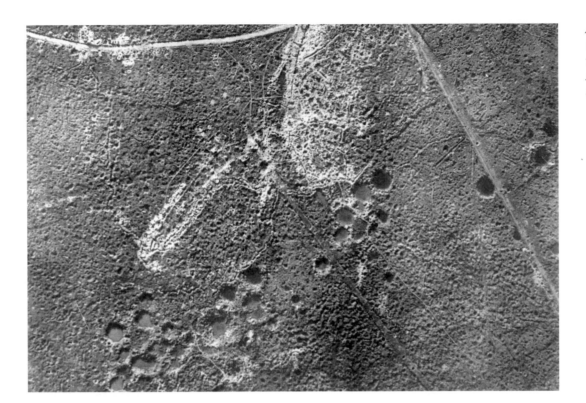

Aerial photograph showing the proliferation of mine warfare in the Railway Wood sector. The craters lie almost exclusively in no man's land

for nothing; months and months of fighting there for positions that were absolutely no good to any side. In the crater that I went into twice, both times with about 30 men, 10 came out the first time after 48 hours holding the crater, and 3 came out the second time after 24 hours. They were packed with dead bodies of both sides, and the smell was awful. We often had to place bodies over ourselves to save us from the shrapnel, and when we fired

The yawning gape of the huge Bluff craters. The British front lines can be seen skirting the forward crater lips with no man's land and the German trenches beyond the wire

our machine guns at those waves of Germans coming over, it was like mowing down hay. I got recommended for a commission for holding these craters, a commission in the field. Then I went back to Abbeville and went through instruction for sapper officer for about a week. I thought I was having quite a rest from the front line trenches and I got sent up to 4 Field Company – the next night I was outside wiring exactly where I had been in the trenches! Didn't think much of that! Then the next day the CO said I had to join the tunnelling company.

Lieutenant John Westacott,19th Canadian Infantry and 2nd Canadian TC

For both the RE consolidation parties and the infantry, crater fighting was possibly the most hated and bitter form of battle of the war – and in it the Germans had no peers.

On one occasion I had the pleasure of over-running a crater of our own under the German wire, the most appalling strain that any man might have to undergo in any form of war. It had to be done immediately after the mine went up, while the stuff was still falling – we all rushed the crater lip and worked around towards the German's side. Fighting in craters was worse than going over the top. The ground had been fought over and was littered with bodies. They had been disturbed to such an extent by the mines that they often disintegrated, Craters were themselves covered in bodies, themselves covered in maggots from head to foot.

Lieutenant Kenneth Anns, 7th Battalion, East Surrey Regiment

But there were equal dangers below ground.

One of the craters from 172 TC's 27 March 1916 blows at St Eloi, immediately recaptured and fortified by the master crater fighters, the Germans

Chapter VII

ENEMIES BELOW

N-G [Norton-Griffiths] came out to breakfast at 8.30 and he took us in his Rolls-Royce. We looked in first of all at the CE's [Chief Engineer's] office where I heard two more officers and some of the special Tunnellers were on the way. Several of our men have been badly 'gassed' lately through entering a mine too soon after an explosion, so special rescue apparatus like divers' is on the way out. Carbon Monoxide is a product of all explosions. You can't hear it, see it or smell it. First of all I'm told you have 15 seconds of supreme elation, then your knees give way and unless you are got out in say 15 minutes more it's a bad job. However, if one carries a mouse or a canary in a cage with one when expecting gas the wee beast feels it first and one has a chance to run. We are buying mice!

Major S Hunter Cowan OC 175 TC, RE,
28 April 1915

Whether on the surface or underground, all explosions, even rifle fire, produce a variety of gases, principally hydrogen, carbon monoxide and methane. In a surface shell burst gases dissipate quickly into the atmosphere, but in the confines of a mine system all are trapped, saturating clean air in the galleries and impregnating newly shattered ground. The most dangerous of these gases for the Great War tunneller was carbon monoxide (CO). Whilst hydrogen and methane disperse rapidly CO, being approximately the same density as air, is prone to remain trapped in fissures or pockets of broken ground for weeks and even months after a blow. It was one of the most serious problems the tunnellers faced, and a glance at a tunnelling company war diary will instantly show that the number of casualties from gassing far exceeded those caused by the destructive action of enemy mines or *camouflets*. Positive action was needed to counter this threat.

THE SILENT KILLER

Invisible, tasteless and odourless, CO was unknowingly inhaled. It displaced oxygen in the blood, and the process was cumulative, resulting in body tissues being gradually starved of oxygen and energy. Death, when it came, was painless, gentle and insidious, but it was a terrifying process. In low level concentrations men could be entirely unaware of the presence of CO, allowing them to penetrate deep into a tunnel system before being affected. As little as 0.1 percent CO in air was dangerous, and it was found that a man at rest in an atmosphere of 0.15 percent CO would be affected after two hours, reducing to about forty minutes if working strenuously. A concentration of 0.2 percent caused loss of consciousness in around twenty-five minutes, and 0.3 percent in ten to fifteen minutes. If the gas was present in large quantities, a tunneller could be unconscious in a matter of moments – with little warning. The early symptoms were giddiness, shortness of breath and palpitations; the effects were exaggerated by the slightest exertion, and confusion followed. There was then a loss of power in the limbs. When this stage was reached very little further exertion would induce loss of consciousness.

The after effects of CO poisoning could also be serious. Oxygen starvation caused deterioration in the nervous system and long-term or permanent mental damage was possible.

Headache of a peculiar throbbing character is complained of by nearly all who have been gassed. Pain in the pit of the stomach, and vomiting and fluttering and palpitation of the heart, with breathlessness on the least exertion, are also complained of. Trembling is frequently seen. The patient generally complains bitterly of cold. Convulsions may be met with. On recovering consciousness men are frequently dazed, confused and stupid-looking. Other men become delirious, struggle and fight, talking in an incoherent manner, shouting, laughing or crying. Care should be taken that these men do themselves no harm when they are being removed on the stretcher. Others again become very drowsy, great difficulty being experienced in rousing them.

Memorandum on Gas Poisoning in Mines, 1923

Although CO was produced in every explosion, the amount given off varied greatly according to the type of explosive used. For instance, guncotton gave off far more than gunpowder, which in turn gave off more than Ammonal. A critical feature was the condition of the charge. If old or damp, an incomplete or slow detonation was likely, and this created much greater quantities of gas than a dry charge which produced a complete detonation. *Camouflets* were particularly dangerous. When a mine was blown and a crater formed, a substantial proportion of the poisonous gases produced escaped into the atmosphere as the explosion broke the surface. However, this too was dependent upon atmospheric conditions. Should the air be still, in attempting to capture the newly blown crater infantry were warned to avoid the depths of the hole, specifically to evade the effects of CO before it dissipated, indeed, in such circumstances the gas could also be dangerous in newly blown artillery-derived shell holes. In underground blows designed not to crater, there was no escape route for the gas; it was trapped either in the newly shattered ground itself, or in the mine galleries. This was an entirely deliberate tactic. If men were not killed by obliteration, entombment, or concussion of the blow, CO was likely to be waiting quietly and invisibly to claim their lives.

I mentioned that the wind had been up round our way, and a couple of days ago, I discovered that Fritz was working so close to us that he could not have been more than 6 or 8 feet away from where we were working. We had been working quietly and listening for him underground for some time, as we thought he was about somewhere underground. When I could hear the pick going against the side and the muck being shovelled up, he was pretty near – so near that when I put my ear to the side of the gallery I could feel it vibrate. He evidently did not think we were so close and of course in that case by keeping quiet we stood to give him a bad knock. So we decided to put in a charge and boost off. We put in 150 pounds of guncotton and blew them up. What a nice game war is! However, they would have done the same to us and we would have been caught like rats in a trap.

The worst part of it was getting down into our galleries again with the danger of gas from the explosion. We negotiated one gallery safely and explored it, but the other was more difficult to enter again. We had one try with Proto safety apparatus and a canary, but the canary died as soon as we got a little way into the gallery. Later on my sergeant and I said we would like to go in and see how bad things were. The sergeant came with me and I told another man to stay at the bottom of the shaft and keep in touch with us. We went in slowly and cautiously and got 200 feet in when I decided we had gone far enough as it was gassy. I had no sooner started back when my head started to throb and I felt myself being overcome by gas. I said to the sergeant 'Come on man. We'll have to go for it. I'm nearly done.' He said 'So am I sir.' I crawled along that 200 feet feeling my sense giving way every second and expecting to lose all power in my limbs any moment. I yelled for help but received no reply and by this time the sergeant had collapsed altogether, and as I crawled on to the light I could see in the shaft only 50 or 60 feet away, I knew that unless I could reach the bottom of the shaft I would not make anybody hear my cries.

Gasping for breath and fighting for my life I reached the shaft and yelled for the fool who should have been at his post but had left us in the lurch. I told him to come down and help me to get the sergeant out. He came down and about 50 feet in I found the sergeant. We dragged him out and got him to the surface and with artificial respiration, brought him round, while I revived myself. All I can say is it would have been a most peaceful death from the feelings I had. I am feeling a bit dizzy today but otherwise have pretty well recovered from the shock and the effects of gas. The sergeant is still pretty shaky and will not be fit for duty for another couple of days. However, it is all in the game, and I am none the worse for the experience.

Captain Cecil Cropper, OC 250 TC, RE

Strangely, gas poisoning produced a bright pink healthy-looking hue on the face of the unfortunate victim.

The ever-fecund imagination of John Norton-Griffiths was to draw him into experimentation with CO and other deadly gases such as hydrogen sulphide which he proposed could be used as a weapon of the underground war, pumped from cylinders into German galleries. The idea was tested – successfully, with cats – but ultimately not taken up at the front.

PROTO SETS AND PROTO-MEN

In conflicts prior to 1914 mine warfare had been fought on a comparatively limited scale; galleries were relatively short and emergency breathing apparatus for rescue purposes simple and direct, with air being supplied via a hose connecting a sealed helmet to various forms of bellows. In the labyrinths of long and deep workings which appeared throughout the Salient in 1916, this method was clearly unviable. With multiple shafts, laterals, listening posts, and offensive and defensive galleries on three, four or five levels beneath the surface, some military mines were beginning to resemble civilian works in scale and it was often the case that men were trapped underground hundreds of yards from daylight. Box respirators and gas helmets as used by the infantry to counter the effects of

Smoke Helmet Apparatus.

'designed' asphyxiating gases such as chlorine, phosgene or bromine were useless against carbon monoxide, so specialised self-contained hoseless equipment as used in coal mines was acquired. The standard British civilian equipment were the Proto and Salvus breathing

British hose-fed short-range breathing apparatus. The miner carries an electric torch to avoid the danger of combustible mine gases

Far left: German nineteenth-century self-contained breathing equipment for military mining

Left: A British Engineer wearing Proto equipment

Civilian mine rescue teams recruited (and photographed) by John Norton-Griffiths. Note canary, hose and bellows kit, and electric lamps

sets and the Novita oxygen revival kit; the German equivalents being the Draeger, Tubben and Flottenatmer. Proto, Salvus and Draeger were the most common and popular. They all worked on the same system of delivering a regulated supply of oxygen from cylinders, like scuba gear, whilst exhaled carbon dioxide was absorbed by being passed through a pouch of replaceable caustic soda granules.

Staff of the earliest Mine Rescue School. The first rescue instructor, selected and brought out personally by Norton-Griffiths, was Corporal Arthur Clifford, seen here standing rear left. The equipment in the right foreground is a Novita Oxygen revival kit

Expert miners were to remain a scarce commodity throughout the war and the arrival of these reliable rescue devices saved many lives. An alarming increase in CO poisoning during the spring and summer of 1915 (one company alone had 150 cases in a six-week period, including sixteen fatalities) encouraged the British to train dedicated specialist rescue teams and create Mine Rescue Schools for each Army. The first expert instructor, hand picked by Norton-Griffiths of course, was a Welsh miner, Corporal Arthur

Clifford. All ranks within a tunnelling company were required to undergo an intensive programme of instruction in mine rescue and the dangers of CO on a rotational basis, beginning with those officers who had not completed a course during training in the UK.

The first mine rescue experts arrived on 13 May 1915 and a rescue school – a small affair by later standards – was started soon afterwards near Strazeele not far from Ypres. In September 1915 Colonel David Dale Logan of the Royal Army Medical Corps was given the task of organising rescue work and tuition in all British sectors. Eventually every Army Mine School would incorporate instruction in rescue, and in every sector where mine warfare was in progress the British eventually developed a network of rescue stations in close proximity to the mine systems they served. Every shaft or incline throughout a mining sector would ultimately be within 200 metres of one.

The station itself was located in a shellproof dugout isolated from the main mine system to avoid the possibility of gas affecting the Proto team before they could get to work, a lesson which had been learned by hard experience. The amount of equipment kept in each station varied according to the size of the system it was required to serve, but eight sets of Proto gear and four sets of Novita were the average. The main stores consisted of spare oxygen cylinders, tins of caustic soda for refilling Proto sets, extra goggles and nose clips and other spare parts and tools. The 'Proto Dugout', as it was often called, was kept clean and dry, inspected twice a week, and totally out of bounds to all but authorised individuals. Mine rescue personnel were accountable for the overhaul and maintenance of their equipment.

Standard stores kept in the dugout were somewhat eclectic, comprising: ten electric miners' lamps with spare accumulators, six canaries (or mice) with four mobile cages and two living cages, one saw, one hand axe, three life lines, two mine stretchers, one trench stretcher, a Primus stove, two tins of café au lait, six hot water bottles and six blankets. Two trained rescue men were on duty at all times, ready to respond when an enemy blow was reported, and immediately descending the mines to help those who were found to be overcome with gas or injured by explosions.

In extensive mine workings lateral galleries were fitted with special regulator doors to stop gas spreading throughout a system. The problem was more severe in British mines than German due to their routine use of the lateral, which in creating a flow of fresh air from gallery to gallery via downcast and upcast shafts, was equally liable to carry lethal gases. With regulator doors in place at regular intervals the affected section of the mine could be safely isolated whilst only slightly impairing the work of the rescue teams.

Mine rescue teams were hand picked men, with as much care being exercised in their selection as that of listeners. They did no clay-kicking, bagging or tramming – their job was rescue and nothing else. However, if necessary, Proto-men were also responsible for immediate countermining, and would have to charge and tamp *camouflets* whilst still in their very restricting rescue gear. The Proto allowed a man to work for up to two hours in a poisonous atmosphere, with the smaller and lighter Salvus kit providing around thirty minutes' protection; Salvus, being much lighter to wear, was used for 'rush' jobs, such as emergency rescue. Ultimately, almost all tunnellers would become well acquainted with all the gear. However, before receiving his special training, the average tunneller, whether officer, NCO or other rank, would have absolutely no idea how to use the strange and complicated apparatus.

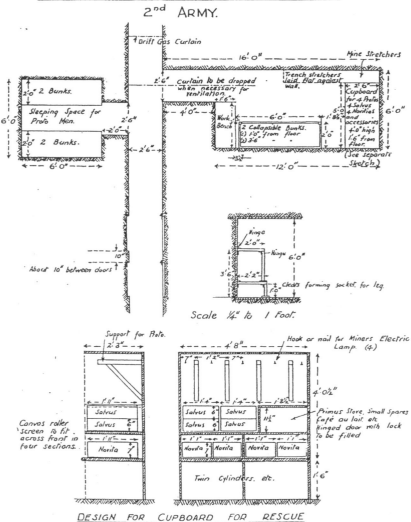

Above: Plan of a 2nd Army Mine Rescue station. A typical design found in the Ypres Salient

A Proto dugout on the Loos/Lens front. Note the two caged canaries

TYPE OF REGULATOR GAS DOOR IN MINE

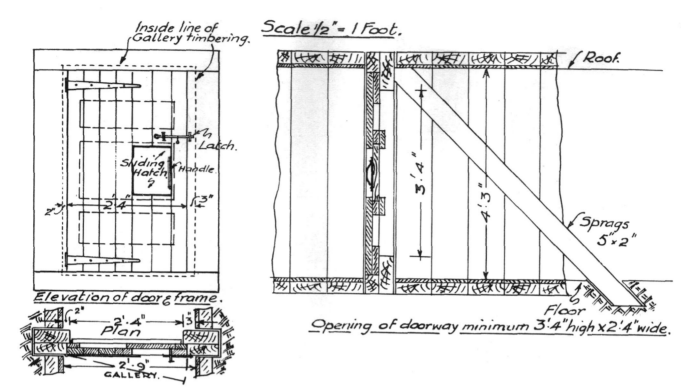

Inside line of Gallery timbering.

Scale ½" = 1 Foot.

Latch.

Sliding Hatch   Handle

Elevation of door & frame.

Plan

GALLERY.

Roof.

3'.4"

4'.3"

Sprags 5"x2"

Floor

Opening of doorway minimum 3'.4"high x 2'.4"wide.

Gas door design for isolating sections of mine systems against CO gas dispersal after a blow

An RE rescue team in training at a mine school

A fully equipped Proto-man descending a mine shaft

The Company had recently received a mine rescue apparatus known as a 'Proto' set. A telegram was despatched to headquarters for it. It arrived, but the operating instructions with it were not completely understood. Did any of the men know how to work it? They were vaguely familiar with it, but that was all.

It was an awesome thing. Heavy goggles fitted over one's eyes. A clamp closed one's nostrils. A mouthpiece connected to a bellows, which sat on one's chest. A tube led from the bellows to a steel cylinder containing oxygen. A sketch on the case showed the cylinder mounted on one's back. A gauge to record the oxygen pressure. But how did the whole apparatus work? Put it on and find out!!

Furthermore, if the Germans were breaking into the gallery there was no time to lose. A test was made, but how much pressure should be kept in the bellows? Better get going. Some person should be stationed at the foot of the shaft. Corporal Clapson was a cool person. Ideal for the job. How much gas was there at the foot of the shaft? Tie a rope around Clapson and station men to pull him out should he be overcome. A revolver and a flashlight must be carried. The bottom of the shaft seemed OK. Clapson took up his position.

Feeling very much like an overdressed Christmas tree wearing hip rubber boots, I passed the idle pump and splashed down the gallery which had at least a foot of water in it. Corporal Clapson had no idea why I collapsed. It might have been gas. Actually I had not opened the oxygen valve sufficiently and had smothered myself. He thoroughly drenched me when he pulled me through the water along the gallery. When we reached the foot of the shaft my teeth were found to be so firmly clenched on the rubber mouthpiece that the Corporal couldn't open my mouth to revive me. The nearest instrument was a crowbar. Not an ideal tool for the purpose, but better than none, and most effective. Not only did it effectively remove the mouthpiece, but it also effectively removed two lower front teeth.

Lieutenant F J Mulqueen, 172 TC, RE

Clapson was to receive the Distinguished Conduct Medal for this action – an award second only to the Victoria Cross.

LIFE SAVING UNDERGROUND

Lance-Cpl. Clapson of the 172 Tunnelling Company was tunnelling at St Eloi when an old working was struck and two officers and two sappers were slightly gassed. One of the officers went exploring with an oxygen apparatus. The officer reached the face, and finding something wrong with the apparatus turned to come out, but collapsed. Lance-Corporal Clapson took off his rope, ran in and tied it around the Officer, and dragged him out, thus undoubtedly saving his life.

The Times, 15 October 1915

Gas poisoning was not the only risk after a blow. When trapped under pressure mine gases could also become combustible. Secondary explosions of gas mixtures, although infrequent and less of a threat than poisoning, were an added problem for tunnellers to be aware of. When the detonation of an enemy blow was felt underground, all candles were immediately extinguished within a calculated area, and electric torches switched on; galleries were then evacuated until the special teams with breathing apparatus pronounced it safe to restart work. Gas explosions were at least obvious, usually occurring soon after an explosion, but poisoning could be a subtle killer often long after the event.

THE 'TUNNELLERS' FRIENDS'

As CO could not been seen or smelled, an 'early warning system' to detect gas in good time to take action was clearly essential. Lacking a reliable chemical testing kit until later in the war, tunnellers fell back upon the traditional civilian method of employing small birds and mice. In an atmosphere which would produce deleterious effects in humans in half an hour, a mouse or a canary, having a much more rapid metabolic rate, was affected in under three minutes, thereby hopefully giving sufficient warning for men to evacuate the workings. There was considerable debate as to which of the two creatures was best suited to the job, and it was left to personal preference in most companies. Canaries, the preferred choice for the majority of

Lest we forget the canaries and mice: memorial to the 'Tunnellers' Friends' at the Scottish War Memorial in Edinburgh.

tunnellers, were brought into mines in small wire cages. Colonel Logan's study into mine rescue described three distinct stages in the effects of carbon monoxide on the birds.

The first indication of poisoning: the bird rubs its beak on the wires of its cage or against its perch, shakes its head vigorously and very often brings up seed as if it were slightly sick.

The second stage is very clearly defined. The bird pants with its beak kept invariably open. Its legs are more widely separated to maintain the balance of its body, and the body being near the perch gives it a characteristic crouching position.

Just before collapsing the bird sways backwards and forwards on its perch trying to maintain its balance, till it suddenly makes a wild flight from the perch and falls into the bottom of its cage.

Memorandum on Gas Poisoning in Mines,
1923

What was not mentioned by Logan was the need to regularly trim the birds' claws – if they were left too long the canary, although dead, might not fly or fall from its perch and the tunnellers would receive no danger signal; a tunneller's life might therefore depend upon the length of a claw. Whereas it was usually obvious when a bird was affected – it fell off its perch – mice reacted differently, tending to curl up in a corner as if asleep: a sign that could easily be missed by busy miners. Thus, a general preference for canaries increased. Equipped with specialist equipment and a bird each, teams could enter 'gassy' mines with confidence. Before the advent of the self-contained breathing gear, however, rescues were a far more perilous proposition.

We floated the canaries on a board before us. One died and the other survived. We ourselves still shared the air tube. On reaching the first man we found it impossible to move him with one hand; the other was needed to hold the air tube. Rigor mortis had set in and his left foot was stuck fast in the duckboard. Only one of us could work as there was no room to pass each other. For the same reason we could not reach the face man until the first was out of the way. We reluctantly decided that it was no use risking further lives so we tied the end of the air tube to some casing and left it there to clear the air until the next day when it would be safe and two hands could be used.

On my way out without an air supply I took a breath of foul atmosphere and nearly succumbed. The second canary died. I was assisted out of the shaft but bemused by gas. I had a splitting headache and was nearly deaf but got to the road and mounted my motorbike to drive home. On the way I heard a faint cry of 'Halt' bang in front of me, and then louder and louder, so pulled up sharply, but not before I had run onto a sentry's bayonet levelled at me. Luckily it only cut the skin over my Adam's apple, but had I gone another few inches I would have had it. I must have presented a sorry sight – dripping wet, covered in mud, no cap, no tunic, unrecognisable as an officer. The sentry would hear none of my tale of woe and I was detained in a guardroom while contact was made with the tunnelling company's CO, Major Danford.

Lieutenant G R Cassels, 175 TC, RE

The gas problem was truly serious. In typical RE fashion, no stone was left unturned in the search for best practice, and tests were made over a period of months to ascertain whether canaries which were used regularly might perhaps develop a tolerance to CO. During these tests, one hardy bird was gassed thirty-three times without showing any changes in behaviour, before being honourably retired. Then there was the supply problem. Mice were much easier to procure than canaries of course, and in the first few months of mining were more commonly used. In a world where variety of work was non-existent, and entertainment when off duty minimal, they were a source of other simple diversions.

Early in mine warfare it became important to find a means to quickly identify its [CO] presence and white mice were used for this purpose. Colonies of them were kept at tunnelling headquarters in the front line and many amusing tales were told of them. The British miner is an inveterate gambler and it was a common practice to run pools on the different colonies, i.e. which could produce the greatest progeny within a given time. You have no idea of the amount of interest and discussion this created among the different shifts.

On occasions some of the mice would escape and while their life expectancy under such circumstances was low due to the large rat population, nevertheless they did find their way into extraordinary places such as the dugout occupied by the Colonel commanding the Battalion in the line. Whether that officer thought he had had too much war or that the Scotch was more potent than advertised, the record does not say. In any event it was a relatively short time before the mining officer was seized upon as culprit.

Lieutenant F J Mulqueen, 172 TC, RE

Unsurprisingly, some tunnellers became very fond of their tiny guardians, with canaries especially becoming cherished pets. Those which survived multiple actions were 'pensioned-off' and kept in tunnellers' camps well behind the line. Replacements for birds 'killed in action' or retired was obligatory. Originally canaries were either obtained locally, or an officer was sent on buying missions to various towns and cities, Paris naturally being the favourite. But they were also brought overseas from England. One enterprising individual, possibly a friend or relation of a tunneller, spotted a commercial opportunity.

Norwich Canaries – Cocks, from 6s. 6d.: Hens, from 3s. Approval. – Dick Chaney, 103, Adelaide Street, Norwich.

The Sapper, 1915

As mine warfare grew, so stocks of birds became more difficult to replenish. The army eventually took over full responsibility for supply, building a large aviary at the RE Store in Calais where birds were bred and reared, to be issued complete with cage as an item of trench equipment. Canaries and mice were not the only animals used in mine warfare, however; a section of 172 Tunnelling Company employed their mascot – a

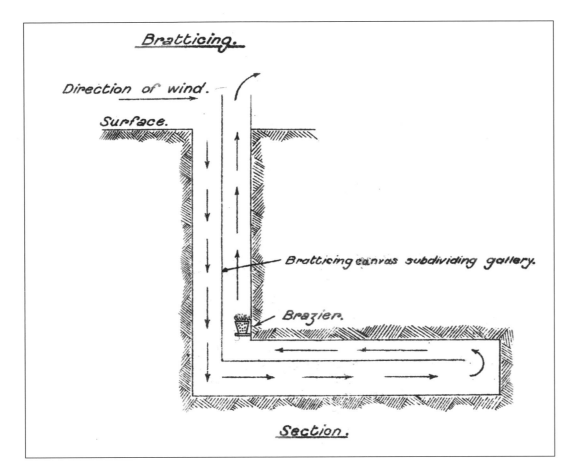

Bratticing. Clearing foul air from mine systems by assisting natural convection with bratticing cloth and a brazier

white rabbit. After a blow it was lowered on a rope down the nearest shaft to test the air. The rabbit survived many a descent until a new officer, ignorant of its symbolism and lofty position, arrived in the Company. The rabbit was not to die in action – the poor beast ended up in a stew.

Once a rescue was completed, or if possible whilst it was underway, every attempt was made to ventilate the system ready for tunnellers to re-enter and restart their vital work. Air pumps, both manual and mechanical, would be worked at full speed to push clean air to working faces, driving foul air out towards exit shafts and inclines where evacuation was often assisted by another civilian mining method, bratticing. Bratticing encouraged the flow of air within a gallery or shaft by dividing it into two unequal compart-ments using 'bratticing cloth', a heavy impervi-ous blanket material on a roll. The process was accelerated by using the truly ancient mine technique of burning a brazier near the bottom of a bratticed shaft, thereby creating 'draw' down one side of the shaft (downcast) by encouraging the convection of hot air up the other (upcast). As usual, it was Norton-Griffiths who suggested, found and procured bratticing cloth for the army.

THE OTHER SIDE

Rescues were always terrifying ordeals, but the natural bond between the tunnellers as a result of civilian mining affiliations led to extraordinary efforts being made to reach and extract gassed colleagues, whether dead or alive. The Proto-man must put all his faith in his breathing equipment; if it failed, he was almost sure to perish. But the story did not end there; military miners, whilst respecting their enemy, gave no quarter; a mine rescuer also had to contend with the fear that the enemy might have another *camouflet* ready and waiting for his team – or they might be waiting in person.

The worst part of the job was still to do. We must get down before the Germans had recovered or our work would be useless. We waited a little for the fumes to disperse then with a rope round my waist and a revolver in each hand I went down again into the thick gassy darkness. Treading slowly and warily I stole up the main drive. The fear and dread of the unseen was upon me. I was momentarily expecting to see a stab of light in the darkness and to feel a German bullet in some part of my anatomy. My trusty Corporal was following about forty feet behind. I could feel the stinging acrid reek of the fumes from the explosion in my eyes and nostrils, my head began to throb and I felt a choking sensation in my throat as the deadly carbon monoxide began to take effect. I struggled on, hoping to get soon into the purer air coming from the Boche gallery. I had proceeded about 100 feet from the shaft when I felt my brain begin to swim and reel, my muscles began to lose their power and my knees sagged under me. I turned and, weak and giddy, started for the shaft shouting a husky warning to the Corporal to do likewise.

The horrible journey I shall never forget. Every moment I could feel my strength failing and a band of steel seemed to be grinding into my forehead. When about half way back my legs gave way beneath me and I struggled on, on my hands and knees. I remember fixing my failing consciousness on the ladder, the topmost rung. When at the bottom of the shaft I became entangled in a loose rope that was used for hauling out sandbags. Then terror seized me, blind unreasoning terror, the fear of death down there in the darkness and black water, and madly I fought myself clear. I crawled into the shaft and gripped the ladder, but my strength had gone, my feet felt like huge lumps of lead that I was powerless to raise. However, my friends on top had been winding in the rope as I came back and now began to haul me up. I remember gripping that topmost rung, hands reaching out to drag me in, a confused murmur of voices and then I was slipping back, slipping back into the horror and darkness of the mine, then – blackness.

Captain Matthew Roach, 180 and 255 TC, RE

Until a particular mining sector was captured the only comprehensive factual information about enemy tunnel systems, working practice and rescue services came from prisoners. For instance, the British finally discovered the extent of German workings in the Ploegsteert to Sanctuary Wood sectors when the Messines Ridge was taken in early June 1917. They were astonished to find that only the simplest and most basic organisation existed for mine rescue. There were no central stations, only one or two Draeger suits were found in recesses at the head of shafts, and in the mines themselves there was no evidence of gas regulator doors, nor even gas blankets for protection against cloud or shell gas at entrances. In some mines special belts were discovered with which unconscious men might be winched up a shaft, but there was no sign of any form of Novita-type oxygen kit with which to revive a man once extracted. Subsequent captured documents revealed that *Pioniere* were not supplied with such equipment; German rescue teams were expected to use the oxygen in their own Draeger sets to treat affected colleagues. Much of the equipment was also noted to be of poor quality manufacture, and made with unsatisfactory materials; a state of affairs which was largely due to the lack of brass, bronze and rubber as a result of the Allied blockade.

So British tunnellers not only benefited from better equipment and organisation but soon after the Mine Rescue Schools opened a special medical service for tunnellers was also set up. Companies already had a medical officer on the strength trained in gas poisoning as well as general practice, but the serious 'wastage' of skilled, and practically irreplaceable specially enlisted miners had been a problem since the very formation of the tunnelling companies. Many men were much older than the regulation age for military service, and some had arrived at the front already suffering from a variety of miner's ailments and disabilities, all of which were to be exacerbated by the physical and psychological stresses of military mining. These men were essential to the war effort; new recruits with whom they might be replaced became ever more difficult to find, so rather than working them into exhaustion and retirement – the problem Norton-Griffiths had observed in 1915 – those found to be below par were treated by officers with specialist medical knowledge of a mining workforce, and the peculiarities of their industry with regard to health and welfare. When they were 'worn out' by underground labour and stress, the years of priceless skills and experience were often put to good use in training others at a Mine or Listening School.

FACE TO FACE

The longer the war went on, the more likely it was that British and German tunnels would meet underground. Tunnellers were finely attuned to their environment and the moment one tunnel broke into another air pressures and air flows throughout the whole system would instantly alter. The change might be imperceptible to all but the experienced miner, but it would have been immediately clear that something out of the ordinary had occurred. More often than not the meeting was sudden and unexpected.

I removed the remaining boards to find out where the water was coming from. Imagine the shock I experienced when as the clay fell away, there, not two feet from the end of our gallery was the white new timber of a German gallery. No sounds came from behind the timber but for all we knew several Germans might have been waiting on the other side with their fingers itching on the triggers of their automatic pistols. Neither of us were armed so I posted the Corporal at the entrance to the branch and went back to the surface for arms. The collection of three revolvers and a rifle with a plentiful supply of ammunition did not take long and I went below again. I found Corporal Mackenzie trembling with excitement 'They're breaking through, Sir, they're breaking through', he said in a tense whisper. I silently handed him the loaded rifle, cocked two of my revolvers, stuck the other in my belt, and listened. There was no doubt about it, from up the gallery came the sound of stealthy knocking. Signing to the Corporal to follow I crept noiselessly up the drive. When near the end I caught the flash of an electric torch through the timber. I settled myself down to await developments, both revolvers cocked, nerves tense and taut as banjo strings. I could feel the Corporal trembling beside me, not with fear for I had proved him before, but with excitement. My own feelings I can hardly describe. I felt that in a short time I should be grey-headed. Only two inches of timber separated us from the Bosch. They were doubtless armed to the teeth and at any moment we might be fighting for our lives. Tense whispers came to us though the timber. What devilry were they hatching? Perhaps they were preparing a charge. For all we knew there may be one already lit and any moment might be our last.

All sorts of wild possibilities flashed through my mind and I felt an insane desire to flee to the surface for safety. I was convinced from the stealthy way he worked, with intervals of tense silence in between, that he suspected our presence there. Flashes came through at times, but he worked for the most part in the dark, like a badger in a rabbit warren. The Corporal was beginning to break up, I thought. He plucked my arm at every fresh sound and I could feel his flesh

quivering. My own nerves were beginning to suffer and I decided it was time to act. I signed the Corporal to retire. We crept noiselessly back for some distance and I told him in a low whisper what I intended to do. We would blow one bag of Ammonal 30 pounds against the German drive. This I thought would kill all the enemy near and, not being sufficient to break the surface, would simply enlarge our drive. I instructed the Corporal to go back and fetch up the explosive with fuse and detonator attached. He rustled away into the blackness and I returned alone to my vigil.

The next quarter of an hour was the longest I had ever spent. The Germans, it seemed to me, were getting more reckless. I could hear the timber moving, then a lump of clay would drop from the roof on my side and work would suddenly stop. Whispering would come from the other side and then a tense silence as they listened. I felt that if I stayed much longer I should shout and hurl myself in upon them. The strain was becoming too great, and I knew I could not stand it much longer. With a start and a thrill I felt the Corporal's hand on my foot. He had brought the explosive as instructed. I motioned him to retire. When back some distance I told him to clear all the men out of the main drive and go himself back to the shaft. Then I fumbled in the darkness for my jack-knife. With this I cut the fuse to what I judged to be sufficient length to allow me time to get to the surface. I waited a few minutes to allow the men time to get out then lit the fuse by scraping a match-head over the core, an old bombers trick. With the fuse spitting and smoking I crept back to the German gallery. Placing the bag gently against the timber I listened for a moment. There was a rustle on the other side, sounds of whispering, and I crept away quietly.

I made no noise until I reached the main drive when caution being no longer necessary I made all haste back to the shaft. I had not proceeded more than half-way however, when there was a crash that seemed to burst my eardrums. Something like a battering ram seemed to hit me in the back and I was hurled forward on my face along the floor of the gallery. The fuse had of course been cut too short, probably in the darkness I had misjudged the length. When at last I reached the shaft I saw a sight that struck me as being supremely ludicrous. In the sump was a

Tommy (*confused by the sudden encounter*) : " Er—er—third return to 'Ammersmith ! "

Heath Robinson's humorous view of meeting underground; the truth was somewhat different

had been well armed; if things had not gone according to plan, he would have followed the strict directions learned in training.

Underground fights always followed the same pattern. The tunnels were boarded and bullets didn't ricochet off the wood. So you got two men facing each other and firing. When one man emptied his gun, he dropped down and the man behind him stepped over him and took over. You carried little automatics which were meant to shoot where your finger pointed. If the Germans broke into us we had to fight them back with guns and then blow. Eventually one side or the other had to blow – there was no question of capturing [enemy mine workings].

If we broke into them, the whole thing was organised. We had our charges ready. We did it once, but never again. When you are all on the same level, you can't get a proper seal to keep the air from going through. Result is that gas might blow back on you.

Captain Basil Sawers, 177 TC, RE,
at Railway Wood

Although the tunnellers themselves were fascinated by the prospect of a personal encounter with the enemy and recounted with glee the escapades of colleagues who had fought hand-to-hand underground, the collision of two opposing tunnels was clearly a menacing and potentially gruesome event ending in death or mutilation in one way or another. However, things were not always what they seemed, especially in the early days before meticulous mine survey and plotting had become statutory.

squirming, fighting, cursing mass of humanity, hurled there by the force of the explosion. They were fighting like wild-cats to get to the surface, panic stricken and terrified by the shock. Two men were stuck in the ladder like Siamese twins, both on one rung, neither able to move. I burst out laughing, rather hysterically I think, and then proceeded by shouting and cursing to restore some sort of sanity among that struggling mass.

Diary, Captain Matthew Roach MC, 255 TC,
RE, 8 April 1916

By cool thinking Roach had managed to avoid the blind terror of hand-to-hand combat. But he

And then our turn came. A telegram arrived at section headquarters from the officer on duty in the line saying, 'Have encountered enemy timber in E right – men withdrawn – please send instructions'. We had not expected the enemy at this point, which was relatively close to our line. Immediate investigation must be made. The infantry must be notified. On the way forward I called at Brigade Headquarters, saw the Brigade Major and showed him the telegram. I told him we would try to break into the gallery. Under the circumstances he decided to have the Battalion in the line and the gunners 'stand to'. In the line we went below. Sure enough a small portion of timber upright was showing. The silence was absolute. A blanket was strung across the gallery behind us. A rush of air from one heading to the other must be prevented. Lights must not be shown. Tools must not be used. They might accidentally hit the timbers. We must rely on our hands alone. An hour went by. The upright was free of earth. Still absolute silence. Careful with the roof. A small opening. Stale moist air. A cautious investigation with the flashlight. The heading was an abandoned one. It was our own. What a letdown! But the worst was yet to come – I must inform the infantry. And the Brigade Major. The Battalion commander was greatly relieved, but not so the Brigade Major. When I arrived at Brigade Headquarters I was given an unmerciful ribbing. The Brigadier stood by with a sly smile and when the leg pulling had run its course, he suggested a drink. It was a badly needed one and morale was restored.

Lieutenant F J Mulqueen, 172 TC, RE

False alarms were far from rare, but no one could be fully prepared for the horror of the real thing. Tunnel fighting bore no comparison with any kind of combat on the surface, and although men had been trained for such encounters, the instructions were far from easy to put into action simply because of the nature of the environment.

Sometimes a fight would take place in a tunnel – 4' x 3' – and in the dark you didn't know who you were fighting. The only thing was to put your hand over quick to feel if the man had any epaulettes; the Germans used to have epaulettes on the shoulder and we could tell that way. That knuckle knife was very good. One of our officers invented that. It was a specially made knife with a blade about five inches long which was fitted to a brass frame over our hand and strapped to our wrist, so when our fist was closed the knife was at right angle to our arm. It was silent in action - very handy, especially for raiding galleries.

Lieutenant John Westacott, 2nd Canadian TC, at Mount Sorrel

Which weapon to use was left to personal preference. Officers carried a Webley service revolver, or another model of their own choice, such as Captain Sawers' small automatic, but others favoured specially devised alternatives. At the Bluff Canadian listeners armed themselves with sawn off .303 Lee Enfield rifles, whilst at Railway Wood, one officer produced a wooden

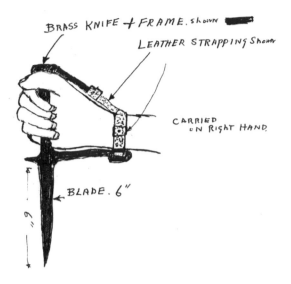

John Westacott's 'knuckle' knife – the weapon of choice for Canadian tunnellers in underground fighting

Major R S G Stokes' sketch of a cut down .303 Lee Enfield rifle, the weapon of choice for some of the tunnellers in the Bluff workings

club, finding it more handy than a knife or bayonet as it avoided the danger of a blade embedding itself in the timbers of the narrow tunnels. He also fashioned a wooden forearm shield to ward off enemy knife thrusts.

Despite the most careful listening, it was common in tunnelling the soft ground of the Salient for the existence of enemy galleries to be entirely unsuspected. As we have seen, in the case of an accidental breakthrough the first indication that all was not as it should be was the sudden appearance of enemy timber. It could equally be discovered by the blade of grafting tool, bayonet or pick touching not the expected earth or clay, but the timber sett of a German gallery itself. The revelation that only a few centimetres now separated friend from foe would have been instantaneous. If the contact had been heard on the other side, the response could be swift and deadly.

I was putting a borehole in a sap [tunnel] when the Germans must have heard me – we were working in sand and always had a 20 foot borehole for safety. I came in contact with an old gallery of ours where two of our men had been blown in some months earlier. My auger came in contact with some oak timber and made a noise. I had only taken a few paces back from the face on my way to tell the officer about this when the Germans blew. They must have been charged and ready. I was blown about 10 yards straight back along the gallery and round the corner. I picked myself up and was up that shaft like a March hare. I didn't stop to pick up tunic, shirt, watch, or anything. I wasn't hurt, only winded. I went down to the officer's dugout and he gave me half a mugful of rum. Then we'd to wait for two hours for the gas to clear before I could go down again. We were sapping there again the same night.

Sapper Hubert Leather, 175 and 252 TC, RE, at Railway Wood

By far the most terrifying ordeal was not knowing whether the enemy *had* detected one's work earlier, and primed a mine or *camouflet* ready to blow at the most opportune and deadly moment. If sounds of enemy working were audible, tunnellers could feel confident that nothing unpleasant had been arranged, but the moment the sounds ceased for more than a minute or two, hearts began to beat faster and breathing quickened. If it was decided that a hostile blow was being prepared every available man was pressed into service – including attached infantry if necessary, to beat the enemy to it.

There were always one or two miners going about the tunnels in rubber-soled shoes listening for the Germans at work. Once they were found the most careful and constant watch was kept with the object of discovering when they would be likely to blow, and then by blowing before them, nullify their work and double the effect of our explosion. When our listeners decided the Germans were packing their mine the activity in our tunnels was amazing – we must pack and blow before them. The miners, and particularly the man in charge, worked like demons. Our job as privates was to carry in the explosive in bags of about 30 lbs. The bags were loaded onto a small trolley which ran on rails; the trolley had to go down an incline to the place where the bags were to be packed. The man in charge placed himself in front of the trolley, took the weight on his back, and putting his hands on the sides of the tunnel carefully eased the trolley down the incline. Everyone worked with feverish speed and our mine was blown before the Germans had time to explode theirs.

Although the work was hard I did not mind it, as it was warm and dry in the tunnels compared often to the trenches above. My task was to pump by hand air down below to the face. It was monotonous work but if I stopped for a breather there was quickly a shout from below telling me in no uncertain terms to get the so-and-so pump working!

When down below there was always the risk of the Germans blowing one of their mines, and I was on the air pump one night when there came a dull thud, the earth rocked and for a moment I thought the tunnel would collapse. It was some distance away but our miners immediately left the face and were all withdrawn in case gas came through to our workings. The miners, who worked stripped to the waist because it was so hot, did not wait to put on their shirts and tunics before getting to the top.

Private James Taylor, Manchester Regiment

Accidental encounters with enemy timber were not uncommon, and if they remained undetected the close yet secure and secret position offered an excellent post from which much could be heard and learned, and also where a *camouflet* attack might be made at leisure. It was indeed the blowing of *camouflets* which offered the most likely opportunity to meet the enemy face to face by opening up an access route into his galleries.

Tunnellers were duty bound to explore enemy workings if the chance arose, and this would be done in the certain knowledge that the opposition might already have a rescue team underground, or on the way. However, the primary purpose of entering a hostile system was not to engage in hand-to-hand combat but to capture any survivors from the *camouflet* blow, swiftly survey the workings, and then destroy as much as possible with mobile charges, rendering existing tunnels inoperative and creating as long a period of awkward and dangerous rebuilding work as possible. Shafts were the primary target here, for if they could be reached and destroyed the enemy were condemned into sinking new ones, a task which required far more effort and time than repairing a blown gallery. It must also be remembered that unless captured plans were available, the design of enemy workings was drawn up purely by listeners' reports alone – educated guesswork; it was probable that nobody had ever seen the enemy or his workings, and quite possible that once viewed they would never be seen again.

Lieutenant John Westacott of the 2nd Canadian Tunnelling Company was to experience at first hand the terror of meeting the enemy underground at Mount Sorrel.

We decided to try to enter the enemy tunnels. Cutting away the soft wet clay and removing debris in frantic working an entrance was made in about 20 minutes. We put on our Proto sets – oxygen apparatus for breathing in mine rescue and gassy areas. Taking four sappers and my sergeant, all armed with revolvers, knuckle-knives and grenades we crawled into the German tunnel and started up the gallery. Now, Proto sets are alright for working in an ordinary civilian mine gallery,

Evidence of the horror of subterranean conflict: bullet scars in gallery timbers of the Mount Sorrel tunnels where Lt John Westacott and his men fought for twenty-four hours

but crawling along or bent over in a war time tunnel of 4 x 3 feet is not so good – and fighting in a Proto set is an art to be learned. Although the German tunnels were a bit larger then our own, the size was still very small. So, in the dark with our torches we crept down the German tunnel towards the blown in face. We found no bodies there. We returned the way we had come and went farther up to find out more of their system. Going towards the German front line for 40 or 50 yards we came to a fork, with another tunnel leading at an angle towards our lines, so we knew then that this must lead to the workings we had blown in at point A. We went down the tunnel and found the face blown in and the bodies, or parts of, two Germans. We also heard our party clearing an entrance and this was done in a few minutes.

As we had gained so much enemy tunnel I decided to try to have a go and destroy as much as we could without too much loss to our own men. I instructed the party to prepare two heavy charges, and for an NCO and a sapper to carry them and follow us some distance behind. My party of six then set off back up the German tunnel knowing that we should most likely run into trouble as the enemy would certainly send in a rescue or fighting party after two explosions. With myself leading and my sergeant behind me followed by four sappers, all in single file, we had just started down their main tunnel when we heard and then saw torches coming in the distance towards us. Their heavy boots made such a noise and they were shouting or talking very loud. The atmosphere in the tunnel was still thick with dust and gas from the explosions. Not knowing how many of them there were I decided it would be best if we came back and wait just past the fork junction to see what would happen. We waited for a few minutes with our torches out and all quiet. The suddenly there appeared through the semi-darkness with their torches blazing in front of them, seven Germans, first a sort of NCO armed with a revolver, then five armed with revolvers and grenades, and the last was a junior officer also armed with a revolver. For a moment I thought they were coming down the tunnel straight at us, but no, they decided to go down the other tunnel.

They still were making a lot of noise con-

sidering the job they were on. My thoughts went to my own two men who were coming up the tunnel with the two charges – they would run right into the German party. We waited until the Germans had gone a few yards past the fork so as to get enough room to get up behind them, then we crept in our stockinged feet silently up behind the enemy in single file. Ever so quietly we gained on them and in a few seconds I was only about four yards behind the last man, the officer, and then all of a sudden they saw the torches of my other two men coming towards them. Thinking they were their own men from the face they shouted in German, and they all stopped. Then, as no reply came they jabbered a bit amongst themselves for a second or two, then the NCO in front fired a shot down the tunnel, Back came a shot from my boys right on the second. So now, being only a few yards behind the enemy I put on my torch and so did my men behind me. The Germans were taken completely by surprise, absolutely trapped, with their enemy in front and behind them. The man in front of me, who was the officer, turned round half facing me and with my torch shining in his face, he had his revolver pointed at me in a second; but he sort of hesitated, no doubt struck dumb by the grotesque sight of a hooded body coming at him. It must have been an awful sight for them to see us in a Proto set in that dim semi-darkness. I shot him before he recovered from his shock. At the same time keeping my body in a down to the floor level to allow my sergeant in a crouching position to shoot over me, and the others behind to fire over us. This was something we had practised in training.

The German party never had a chance, their NCO was shot in the leg and my sergeant kicked his revolver out of his hand, but he rolled over, grabbed his gun again and was starting shooting, so the sergeant shot him again. The fighting did not last more than perhaps two or three minutes, then one of the Germans shouted 'Kamerad' and we soon disarmed the three enemy left standing. But the Germans fought well and hard, and if they had not been subject to such bad luck in getting trapped, they might have won the fight and killed the lot of us. The casualties were Germans: one officer, one NCO, two men dead; three captured alive, one very badly wounded; Canadians: three men wounded, one badly. The last two sappers of my own party in the rear never fired a shot but both got hit themselves.

We knew the enemy would be sending another larger rescue and fighting party so we laid our first explosive charge on a time fuse 50 yards up the main tunnel from the fork, dropped one near the fork itself, and ran as fast as we were able with our Proto sets still on to our own tunnel entrance. We had just reached the entrance when both charges went off and knocked us all flat on our faces with the enemy tunnel caving in at the back of us, catching the last sapper of our party and trapping him in falling debris and timbers; we pulled him out but one of his legs was broken. Getting back into our own tunnels we laid an explosive charge. This completed the blowing of the enemy tunnels and we knew we had stopped all the German works in that direction for a few weeks to come.

Lieutenant John Westacott,
2nd Canadian TC

Westacott later had another more deadly encounter at Mount Sorrel, when he and a complete section of his men were trapped underground during a surprise German surface attack which captured the British front line trenches. Unknowing, the Canadian tunnellers emerged unconcernedly from a shaft at the end of their shift, to be spotted by the Germans. Diving back down the shaft and sounding alarm bells as they went, they blew in several other entrances to the tunnel system, and waited. The Germans piled down after them, and one of the most grisly battles of the war took place.

Fighting with grenades, pistols, rifles, and hand-to-hand with knives, bayonets and even razor sharp spades in the tiny galleries, the encounter was horrific. Westacott himself was almost to lose an arm, whilst sixty out of eighty of his shift were killed or wounded. The struggle lasted almost twenty-four hours – and then stopped just as suddenly as it had begun. When the tunnellers plucked up the energy and courage to tentatively peep out of a shaft again, they discovered that the Canadian infantry had recaptured the trench.

Both British and German miners had many encounters where enemy galleries were entered but no personal contact was made. In an unusual meeting of mines, as opposed to miners, Lieutenants Syme and Cooper of 172 TC, and their OC Captain Clay Hepburn, won notoriety by coolly stealing the charge from a German mine chamber which had been accidentally discovered at the Bluff. The procedure of pilfering the 1,350 pounds of explosive had to be done in total silence over a period of two days, and in the full knowledge that the mine might have been blown at any time. During the process it was equally essential that the delicate and dangerous detonators were not damaged, and that electrical current was preserved in the many cables spread throughout the charge; a break in continuity would have brought an investigating team to repair the problem. The extracted charge was reused by the British in one of their own mines a few months later at St Eloi. The possibility of 'mine theft' increased as systems became more and more complex. It was countered by installing remote microphones inside charged mine chambers specifically to pick up the sounds of potential enemy breakthroughs. If unidentified noises were detected, down would go the plunger.

As if working underground was not enough of a problem, the furtive nature of tunnelling created problems on the surface. Infantry units in the trenches would often change during the night, the new troops being uninformed and therefore unaware that engineers were at work beneath their feet. On appearing from their secret entrances in the morning it was not uncommon for tunnellers to be challenged as to their identity. On several occasions officers were marched off to a dugout at bayonet point and questioned. Their explanations were sometimes greeted with incredulity by inexperienced young infantry officers, until a visit to the tunnels themselves proved the truth of the matter. Some tunnellers were arrested several times in this way. They found it more amusing than annoying – except that the infantry never seemed to apologise for their errors.

Chapter VIII

THE MINE WAR DEEPENS, 1915–1917

It was a frightening sight for a novice as we left the shelter of a semi-demolished house and moved into the open to see the bursting shells to the northeast in front of Ypres and the hundreds of Verey lights extending to the north and south. The situation was not relieved by the frequent whine of bullets passing close by. Eventually we arrived and reported to Lieutenant Hickling, whom I found to be a first rate fellow. The place was alive with men. Hickling showed me the shaft and heading and the mine which he had laid, but it was not completely tamped. The electric leads ran behind a rather stout wall to a cellar to the north. The exploder was ready and waiting, but it was not connected. Hickling gave me complete instructions, introduced me to the Battalion Commander and departed. It was then I realised how deficient I was. I had graduated in civil engineering and knew nothing about mining.

Lieutenant F J Mulqueen,
172 TC, RE

A tunnelling company shift leaving billets and climbing into their own transport to be taken to the front

Cowan's and Cassels' men: a section of 175 Tunnelling Company RE

In mid-February 1915 Norton-Griffiths' moles had arrived at Boulogne at a time of deep crisis for the British. It had been over two months since the first German mine attacks, and the infantry were crying out for protection the full length of the line. The new men were immediately transported to the battlefront where their skills were most needed – to Givenchy, where it had all started in December 1914. It was a rude awakening; having spent less than an hour in the front line and already been shelled, mortared and sniped the tunnellers were keen to get underground.

The first eight tunnelling companies formed on the Western Front were designated with the numbers 170 to 177, continuing the numerical sequence of existing regular RE units. Each was allocated a sector between La Bassée in northern France to Ypres in Belgium – the only sectors for which the British Expeditionary Force was responsible at that early stage in the war. They first started work in French Flanders – at Givenchy, Cuinchy, Rue du Bois, Fauquissart and Houplines, but farther north in the still primitive British trenches of the Ypres Salient, the infantry were also suffering from the German superiority in mining and artillery. It was imperative to get tunnellers underground to give the troops both protection and confidence.

There were few dissenting voices at GHQ to the formation of the new companies, but complications were expected in the line, and they duly emerged: one of the problems was that regular RE officers given the responsibility of leading the

new companies had little or no experience of military or civilian mining, or indeed working with civilians at all. All were anxious, or perhaps curious, to learn, but a number simply regarded the prospect with horror. In April 1915 Major S H Cowan, an experienced regular RE officer who had been in France since 14 August 1914, was ordered to command the newly formed 175 Tunnelling Company.

MINING SAPPER (on seeing worm): "All right, don't swank; we're follering yer."

16th April 1915. Without any previous warning at 8.45 a.m. I was ordered to hold myself in readiness to form and command No. 175 Tunnelling Coy RE. Orders is Orders but to be quite honest I was absolutely disgusted. If I had been given half a chance of saying so, I'd certainly have taken it but, there, it came as an Order, straight out of the General's head as I have since learnt. Trench warfare with shells and overhead bombs has always seemed to me sufficiently arduous even for a trained RE Company, but these new Coys have only one RE officer and 12 NCO's to 8 other officers and 300 men, some of whom are specially enlisted civilian navvies or sewer men and the rest miners or such sort, transferred from the infantry out here.

17th April. Called in at Blandy's Chateau and made him drive me back to St O [Omer], where I spent the day trying to pick up information from Wace about the tunnelling job. The more I heard about the actual details of the work, the less I seemed to like it.

Major S H Cowan, RE

The companies were practically autonomous from the start, but to become fully effective time was required: time to familiarise themselves with the peculiarities of their 'patch', and time to determine the capabilities of their men in an environment where no one had had a single day's prior experience. The immediate and primary task was to make sure that personnel

Coalminers: their skills were particularly useful in the harder chalk areas

and materiel were delivered where and when they were needed. In the early months the process was not helped by having to satisfy the requirements of three separate authorities. At this time Army, Corps and Divisional commanders all had a say in their employment, but whilst one would want purely defensive mining, another might require support for a minor attack, and a third could have ideas for a massive offensive blow. With too many masters confusion reigned, and mining schemes became piecemeal and uncoordinated. Some influential schools of thought believed that a scattering of large numbers of small projects would confuse the enemy; it did not, but at least with the combined knowledge and imagination of the many experienced civilian engineers being drafted in to help command the new companies, foundations were being quickly laid for a healthy and sturdy system. Fortunately, the Germans were completely unaware of the British confusion, were content with the start they had made underground, and saw no need to develop a longer-term mining strategy.

AN EFFECTIVE FORCE EMERGES

Throughout the spring and summer of 1915, the enrolment of experienced men continued. Having detailed selected staff from his private business to recruit miners and sewer-drivers throughout Britain, and to liaise with the War Office directly, Norton-Griffiths attended to the most crucial task of personally organising and scrutinising the underground work at the Front. He was effectively a one-man Commander, Inspector and Controller of Mines. Activity was frantic from the start, but it soon became clear that far too few men were arriving at the Royal Engineers' Depot at Chatham to fill the ever-expanding needs in France and Belgium. Furious and disappointed with the Army and his operatives in Britain for their lack of effort, Norton-Griffiths decided to do the job of augmenting the ranks of his moles himself.

In 1914 mining was a significant business in Britain. In the north of England alone over 250,000 men worked in the coal and mineral mines of Lancashire, Yorkshire, Cumberland and Westmorland. Norton-Griffiths ordered his agents to draw mine owners and managers together at regional meetings, where he personally explained the crisis in his own inimitable fashion. Signs were posted at collieries throughout the country asking for volunteers. Where others had failed, Norton-Griffiths could always persuade employers to make men available. When pits reported a shortage of miners due to many of their workforce having already joined up as infantrymen, he obtained their names from Colliers and Miners Associations and tracked them down through the regiments. After the great flood of enlistment at the beginning of the war, by mid-1915 substantial numbers of civilian miners were still undergoing infantry training in the UK; Norton-Griffiths' people gradually sifted and selected the best; many were taken on in this way – but it was still insufficient. But Norton-Griffiths was also well aware that thousands of potential tunnellers were already on active service overseas. Who was to say that they too were not 'fair game'?

Experienced miners with the added benefit of a little military instruction were a very valuable commodity. Norton-Griffiths knew that the temptation of six shillings a day – a rate he himself 'negotiated' for his moles, three times the pay of the infantry – would guarantee that little persuasion would be necessary to attract suitably qualified men into the ranks of his moles. All he had to do was locate his candidates and enrol them. There was a slight problem, however; all infantry transfers required sanctioning by the commanding officers of their respective battalions and brigades. When transfers were demanded by higher authority, as they had been when the tunnellers were first formed, there was no case for argument, but Norton-Griffiths was a merc Major – not even a regular soldier at that – and Generals, Brigadiers and Colonels were not to take kindly to his blatant, disrespectful and unmilitary 'poaching'.

Norton-Griffiths knew exactly where to start: if battalions had been raised in mining areas, a large percentage of their establishment were likely to be miners. For example, in February 1915 the 1st Battalion, South Wales Borderers put forward no fewer than 161 names of former colliers for potential transfer to the tunnellers – almost twenty percent of its total establishment of NCOs and other ranks. It was likely that many more units could supply similar percentages of experienced men, but no infantry battalion in the line could stand such a deficit unless the losses were replaced – and quickly. Norton-Griffiths looked upon this as the Army's problem, not his. He was a man in a hurry, with the sole desire to bring the tunnelling companies to a strength where the growing German threat could be adequately countered, and especially to a point where his moles could strike back. He refused to

be mired by anything resembling red tape, pig-headedness, pride or ignorance; the prospect of making enemies of 'buffoons' at GHQ left him entirely unmoved – he wanted his men, and he would get them.

In stormed a Brigadier and two Colonels. The Brigadier fumed. 'What the hell do you mean by stealing officers from our battalions?'

Norton-Griffiths: 'Well, Sir, tunnelling is very important.'

Brigadier: 'Important be damned. The infantry are more bloody important. If we weren't here, the bloody Germans would come and mop the lot of you up. What are you? Just a lot of bloody clay-kickers.'

Norton-Griffiths: 'Well, Sir, I've got my job to do. Perhaps you'd better report to General French. Will you have a drink? I won't steal any more of your men.'

They had a drink and N-G [Norton-Griffiths] asked him to stay to lunch, which he did, and they had a helluva do. As the Brigadier was leaving he said 'Alright Colonel, we don't mind if you take a hundred or so. But don't take any more.'

Captain Alan Reid, 176 TC, RE

It is said that Norton-Griffiths' Rolls-Royce, which the War Office had been 'persuaded' to buy from his wife Gwladys for his personal transport at the front, always carried several cases of whisky, port and claret all of which were used to 'soften up' awkward commanders. Basil Sawers, a Corporal of the Royal Canadian Engineers, and a future 177 Tunnelling Company officer, was stationed with his division in front of Messines Ridge. He was tracked down by Norton-Griffiths.

Gwladys Norton-Griffiths' Rolls-Royce with two unidentified officers and driver. The car served as a mobile office for her husband in France and Belgium until he left the tunnelling companies in March 1916, at which time it was donated to General Harvey

Somebody must have told him I was a mining engineer. Suddenly one evening a fellow came rushing into my tent saying 'There's a bloody General out there looking for you'. I went out and saw a great limousine, may have been a Rolls-Royce, and a Colonel with red tabs and a red hat. He seemed rather surprised I had never been underground before, but he seemed satisfied. I had actually worked in about 12 different mines and was studying at McGill [University]. He said, 'You'll hear in a day or two.' About three days later I heard from one of the clerks that a chit came into the office: 2Lt. Sawers to report to RTO [Railway Transport Officer] Steenwerk for transportation to 177 Company.

Second Lieutenant Basil Sawers, 177 TC, RE

Despite his exasperating eccentricities and disregard for protocol, most of the staff at GHQ realised the value of the work 'Naughty' was

doing, and that he had unique capabilities. They recognised knowledge derived from experience, and knew that no one else had either the drive or contacts to make things happen as swiftly as he could. On endless visits to tunnelling companies along the front Norton-Griffiths remained resolutely approachable, well-informed, and full of ideas and suggestions. He was always interested in new schemes, and in the welfare of his moles, particularly that of the many older men who had joined up. In several instances, knowing that his official diary was read by his superiors, he used entries to beg them to remove 'worn-out' moles from the mines, and either send them home or give them easy jobs in the rear areas. Above all, he won respect from the tunnellers and their officers because he was a regular visitor to the sharp end – the mines themselves.

Norton-Griffiths' official diary detailing mining activities and his own movements was handed in regularly to Colonel Robert Napier Harvey, the Engineer-in-Chief's assistant running the emerging mining enterprise at GHQ, and future Inspector of Mines for the whole of the British effort on the Western Front. The diary, which was entitled 'Moles', was started on 13 February 1915. It was unmilitary, sometimes irreverent, often downright rude, and was to become known as 'Punch' at mining headquarters. In it can be found detailed reports upon mining as it developed along the Western Front

An example of the 'Weekly Mine Report', a form devised by Captain Henry Hudspeth which replaced the old 'Mine Register' in the spring of 1916

			Shaft or Gallery.			Footage for week.	No. of days worked.	Nature of ground.	REPORT.
Designation of working.	Trench No. or name.	Map reference.	Depth.	Size inside timbers.	Total footage.				Circumstances affecting progress. Results of listening. Mines and camouflets. General information.
1.	2.	3.	4.	5.	6.	7.	8.	9.	10.
6	H 20	In 6 8.3			Date of feet			Bastard Blue Clay	
62A			8 2'	4'6"×3'3	28 80	14	—		
11	H 18	I 12 A 10						ditto	Charge of 2500 lbs Ammonal fired at the end of 11E at 8.30 on 3/5/16 making Crater about 100 ft diam and 20'deep radius of rupture about 100 ft All 11E, 11 E beyond 11E, and Tank lost 35 ft of 11D destroyed Enemy distinctly heard 10 left of charge on 3/5/16
11E			20'		7 1021	27	3		
11P	Branch fought at end of 11E		20'		14 20' / 21 100' / 28 114'	114	9	ditto	At 89' picked up, old NO.10 workings and 3' lower than present workings
11N	To East from 65' on 11D				14 55 / 11	66	5½	ditto	11' Tee across end
11L	To South at 50' on 11D				7 19 55	55	4	ditto	
11K	Branch to left at 102 ft on 11G				7 25 / 14 100 / 21 131 / 28 148	148	13⅔	ditto	At 87' struck enemy gallery, smashed in at 3' lower than ours bearing N50E. 25 ft of our gallery lost on the 25th by flow of mud and gallery barricaded at 120 feet
11M	Branch to left at 55 ft on 11L				14 19 / 21 74 / 28 137	137	13	ditto	
11Q	Branch to left at 36 ft on 11K				21 21	21	2⅔	ditto	Joins junction of 11E and 11M
11R	Branch to left at 17 ft on 11K				28 26 / 31 40	40	3⅔	ditto	
11V					7 38 / 31 40	8	3	ditto Blue	An attempt was made to break out at 38 ft but ground was too bad Sinking was therefore continued

throughout 1915 and into the spring of 1916 – the formative period of British underground endeavour. The diary can also be seen as the precursor to the detailed 'Weekly Mine Report' sheets – devised by Major Henry Hudspeth of 171 and 184 TC – that were to chronicle underground progress and action

But Norton-Griffiths' forthright daily jottings raised eyebrows at GHQ. The impatiently scribbled entries are interspersed with comments by Harvey and others, and even spelling mistakes are noted as if the document was the work of a schoolboy. If Norton-Griffiths ever allowed himself to be concerned by the remarks of his detractors, it does not show. The diary, whilst being absolutely blatant in opinions of others' shortcomings, is neither bitter nor nasty; it exudes enthusiasm for the job and a determination to get it done, but remains suffused from beginning to end with impatience and frustration, mainly directed at military methodology and inefficiency.

Although Norton-Griffiths rightly felt that he was doing most of the donkey work, recruiting, seeking out new equipment, devising schemes and visiting units, Harvey and his small staff at GHQ were also working hard to keep up with the burgeoning mine war and put into place a command framework for the ever-expanding tunnelling company numbers and establishments. The results of their combined labours would relieve much of the administrative pressure, and ultimately create a supremely efficient specialist corps with an immensely strong group identity and fierce pride in their work. The irony was that when the new arrangements were eventually put in place, making Norton-Griffiths' dream of a great mining offensive a reality, he himself would not be a part of the team, or enjoy the truly great triumphs in person. He was to be required elsewhere, first to shake up the Ministry of Munitions, and then on a secret mission to Romania to destroy vital oil and grain resources before they fell into enemy hands. Unsurprisingly, he earned himself another nickname whilst in the Balkans – the Angel of Destruction.

THE CHRONOLOGY OF THE MINING WAR, 1915–17

The mining war in the Ypres Salient is circumscribed by the critical events of just five key dates between 1914 and 1917. The first is the day the underground war really began, 21 December 1914, when the ten initial mines blown by the Germans at Givenchy shocked the British military into concerted action. The next, 13

February 1915, marks the date that John Norton-Griffiths received authorisation to form his Moles – the effective birthdate of the tunnelling companies. The third, 6 May 1915, although marking an apparently minor and unremarkable achievement, was the true red-letter day for tunnelling in the Ypres Salient. On this date Lieutenant J A Leeming and his section of 170 Tunnelling Company miners successfully defeated the unpromising geology of French Flanders – a continuation of that of Belgium – by sinking a spiled (sheet piled) timber shaft through two metres of running sand to reach the dry clay beneath. Records show that this single action at Cuinchy guaranteed that comprehensive deep British tunnel systems could be secretly established, as long as the Germans continued to fail to master the *Schwimmsand*

Craters and tunnels in Cuinchy Brickstacks sector in French Flanders showing proliferation of mining. Many mining sectors of the Salient were equally elaborate

layer, and that this fact was clearly recognised immediately – by none other than Norton-Griffiths. Instantly seeing the potential of Leeming's achievement, on that very day he suggested that every tunnelling company commander in the Salient should 'get into the clay'. Earth augers capable of testing the ground to a depth of ten metres, wooden-wheeled mine trucks, water pumps, and air blowers were also requisitioned. These were orders which would pave the way for almost complete British underground dominance at Ypres within a year. The next two dates – 27 March 1916 at St Eloi, and 7 June 1917 at the Battle of Messines Ridge – mark the British development and exploitation of Leeming's victory over geology.

For the British 1915 was a critical year. By June the underground war had become a private and highly secret conflict. In just three months the tunnelling companies were to move from initial formation to a dominance of the ground conditions. By the end of April the Germans, although surging ahead after their first energetic and triumphant forays into military mining, were already showing signs of complacency. The spring of 1915 was clearly a crucial formative period, and the learning curve was a steep one for all eight of the newly forming British companies. A good illustration of tunnelling practices at this time is that of Major J Hunter Cowan's 175 Tunnelling Company who were working in the Hooge Sector close to the Menin Road, at the same time as Leeming at Cuinchy and Lieutenant Horace Hickling at nearby St Eloi. Cowan's diary and those of his colleagues allow us to plot the birth, growth and conclusion of a single scheme in the early days of mine warfare in the Salient.

ANATOMY OF A BLOW: 175 TUNNELLING COMPANY, HOOGE, 1915

The lack of experienced men had led to some units starting work later than others. 170 to 177 Tunnelling Companies had received the green light for action in mid-February 1915 but Cowan's 175 Company was still waiting to be allocated a sector several weeks later. Many of his tunnellers were already mining, however – attached to other active companies, but Cowan was frustrated at still having no sector of his own, and also at having no knowledge of mining. His new junior officers, all professional civilian mining engineers, had been 'loaned' to other units to gain experience. Cowan was

unable to get to know them, and learn from them. He began to worry about the workload he was about to take on.

18.4.15 Nominally each of the four sections is given nice little job of its own and should be able to drive three galleries day and night for ever, being attached to the nearest Field Company for quarters, rations, cooking etc. Practically, however, a section can never find as complacent a Field Company as the ideal one above so its output falls at once to two headings. Further, every General from the Brigadier in whose area a Section may be working, the Divisional General and so on up to GHQ itself requires the very latest information as to progress etc., so the poor OC appears to spend 12 hours a night visiting the mines and 12 hours a day buying timber, getting it and rations and stores sent out, and answering questions. Somehow or other I don't fancy my own brain will stand the strain.
Major S H Cowan, OC 175 TC, RE

For a while Cowan had been suspecting that 175 TC would be posted to Ypres. His guess was to be correct; but the Second Battle of Ypres was still in progress, delaying his tunnellers from making a start. The German gas attacks near Langemarck, in the northern part of the Salient, had led to the loss of a great deal of ground. GHQ were unwilling to begin new schemes whilst the lines in front of Ypres were still fluid and undefined; in any case, they were aware that 175 TC men could be profitably employed in training and assisting other companies in other more pressing sectors. It was not an ideal way for a new OC to be introduced to a job he knew nothing about, but Cowan was not idle. He sought out documented information on enemy mining, and ordered the construction of practice shafts and galleries near 175 TC HQ at Terdeghem – as much for his own enlightenment as that of the new tunnellers who were now arriving daily.

On 5 and 6 May 1915 the British were forced to draw back from the Zonnebeke, Veldhoek and St Julien arc to a carefully chosen and well-dug line of trenches closer to Ypres; a line which was to define the Ypres Salient for over two years. The German offensive was brought to a halt on Tuesday 25 May 1915. By the beginning of June, Cowan had long ceased kicking his heels and had resigned himself to the situation, but a surprise visit by John Norton-Griffiths left him excited.

5 June 1915. Norton-Griffiths arrived full of

enthusiasm over the results of a recruiting trip he had carried through in the Midlands and North of England. He is certainly full of energy and I wonder how many Army rules and regulations he has broken or worse still promised the recruits that the OC's would break for him! It seems likely however that we shall get about 200 men in the next week or two and then we can hope to make a start on our own.

Major S H Cowan, OC 175 TC, RE

Norton-Griffiths had not been exaggerating. Three days later Cowan received the news he had been awaiting for so long.

At 12.30 General Glubb himself arrived in a great hurry. There is some very urgent work to be done at once in a village [Hooge] on a main road east of Ypres. We hold one half and the job is to get the G[ermans] out of the other, failing that they may get us out and so obtain another hill top from whence to overlook the land. It is a significant fact that all their recent attacks round Ypres have been directed on hill tops and have rested content on the same, without trying really hard to advance down the slopes towards us.

Major S H Cowan, OC 175 TC, RE

This was the green light for Cowan to start mining, and the village of Hooge on the Menin Road was indeed to be the scene of the action. The next day Cowan took Captain G R Cassels, whom he had selected to command the work, to meet the Brigadier for lunch and be introduced to the scheme. It was a meal that Cassels would never forget.

Captain G R Cassels who was in charge of the first big mine to be blown in the Salient at Hooge in July 1915

Major S Hunter Cowan OC 175 Tunnelling Company took me through Ypres to a convent. Here we met a General who gave us a plain lunch but who regaled us with apricot brandy found in the cellars. He told us of a plan to tunnel under the German trenches at Hooge and blow up a chateau there. As Hooge was at the apex of the Ypres Salient it was considered a most dangerous job and whoever undertook the work was to be a volunteer. The apricot brandy was extremely potent and its effect such that I would have accepted an assignment in Hell, and as it turned out, in volunteering, I had indeed accepted such an assignment.

Captain G R Cassels, 175 TC, RE

YPRES.   HOOGE.   Aug. 1915.

Looking North East from Hooge stables. Bellewaarde Lake in middle distance

My most priceless photograph. Hooge Chateau, taken over the parapet of our front line, with the Bosch 50 yards away

The dreaded Hooge sector photographed by Lieutenant Robin Skeggs, 3rd Rifle Brigade

A typically humorous view of front line conditions at Hooge by Robin Skeggs

Trench in early morning before the housemaid had been round

Cowan and Cassels asked for a map of the Hooge sector. A two-inch (5-cm) square plan was produced which showed two wavy lines and a few houses. It was hopelessly inadequate. A reconnaissance trip was suggested.

> 9.6.15 We were walking across fields at about 200 yard intervals 'so as not to be worth even one shrapnel' as the Brig. put it. It is a firm rule that no single person walks about. After about a mile he stopped and pointed out the scenery – Hill 60, Hooge, Bellewarde Ridge. He said, 'If a sniper does fire get down into the corn and crawl' so on we went and got into the wood unnoticed by any missile. We were conducted up a muddy zig-zag communication trench, then along more trenches under a road by a tunnel and so into another trench which smelt at times of dead cow. They said it *was* cow. There we borrowed periscopes and at last beheld our objective 50 yards away.
>
> Major S H Cowan, OC 175 TC

In the Hooge sector the opposing front lines were almost within whispering distance of each other; it was regarded as *the* hotspot for the infantry, where snipers abounded, trench raids were frequent, and shelling was more fierce and relentless as anywhere on the Western Front. Much of the rest of the newly forming Salient had suffered relatively little damage from artillery as at this time shells were still being used sparingly. Targets were carefully selected, the policy being to restrict heavier bombardments to particularly important areas. Hooge fell squarely into this category. Cassels surveyed a ruined village and a maze of battered and confusing trench lines.

> It was a small village in ruins on top of the ridge, Hooge meaning height, astride the Menin Road. On the north side of the road was a chateau with a separate annex standing in its own grounds by a large wood. Behind the chateau was Bellewarde Lake. In front of the chateau and east of the village proper were the racing stables with the names of the horses still in place over the stalls. The stables were at the very apex of the salient. They were actually in our front line. The trenches were shallow and primitive, even the front line ones, and to reach the front line some tunnels had been driven under the road and part of the ruins. No Man's Land between us and the Germans was littered with blackened corpses. Many men, mostly Germans, had been buried in recesses off the communication trenches and the stink was abominable. The flies flew in swarms. Our objective was to sink a shaft, then tunnel under the chateau and annex and blow them up.
>
> Captain G R Cassels, 175 TC, RE

An early 177 TC plan of Hooge tunnelling showing Cassels' crater top left, the 'disused original' tunnel from the cellar of Bull Farm, new dugouts beneath the Menin Road, and a fresh offensive tunnel on its way towards the German lines.

The stables were chosen as the starting point for the tunnel. Although somewhat exposed, any work would be sheltered from fire and view by the remaining walls, and it also had the advantage of being the nearest building to the château. Within hours of beginning work Cassels' sappers struck problems: the sandy ground was waterlogged. Despite piling with metal sheeting and attempting to stem the slipping earth with Scotsmen's kilts, the shaft had to be abandoned. An alternative site was found in the cellar of Bull Farm, a nearby house on the edge of the Menin Road. Working from this point required a longer tunnel, but the depth of the cellar immediately saved one or two

HOOGE.

Scale :- 40ft to 1 inch.

metres of shaft excavation. Cassels' men made a good start but soon became concerned about the enemy overhearing their work, so one of the sappers prepared the shaft timbers with dovetailed joints, avoiding the need to hammer them into place.

> Our luck held and we got through the green sand and struck the blue clay at about 35 feet down. We sank further, well into the clay and started the gallery. It had been intended to go deeper and then make towards the chateau and annex but observation showed that the Germans were not holding any in strength, but there was still some coming and going to and from the annex. They had, however, brought up civilian labour and often we could see top-hatted contractors moving about to the west of the chateau. One of the German latrines was partially in sight and one day observing a top hat protruding above the trench and the owners posterior below, the remainder of his anatomy being concealed, I could not resist borrowing a rifle and having a pot at it. I scored a bull and we were all delighted to see the top hat bobbing about as the wounded Hun made for the rear, Another chap nearby shot his hat off as he ran.
>
> Captain G R Cassels, 175 TC, RE

The gallery was initially seven feet (2.13 metres) high by two feet six inches (0.75 metres) wide reducing to four feet (1.22 metres) by two feet (0.61 metres) as it approached beneath the target. It was fully timber lined and listening posts were constructed in branch galleries along the route. The work of the listener was critical to the success of the operation. At specified intervals Cassels' tunnellers laid down their tools whilst he tried to locate the sounds of the enemy. It soon became clear that German miners were also operating.

> On no account had you to speak above a whisper, and you had sandbags wrapped around your feet and you had to walk as quietly as you possibly could because we knew that they were on the game as well. It put the wind up us. We had to send for an officer and he came down and had his listening stick, his geophone. There would be a consultation among the officers, what was best to be done when the Germans were found working underneath.
>
> Sapper George Clayton, 175 TC, RE

Push pick. The type of tool used by Cassels' men to complete the Hooge gallery, and by all companies working in clay to 'finish' the tunnel after 'kicking'

Clay-kickers had been employed at the shaft end of the Hooge gallery, but as they delved farther progress slowed to a snail's pace as grafting tools were put aside in favour of pear-shaped 'push picks'. The small scoop of earth which the tool carved from the face was allowed to fall only a few centimetres.

> Even this sounded like a ton of bricks in the eerie silence. Everyone wore gumboots which had to be well fitting, and speech was limited to the faintest whisper. Progress was painfully slow, the maximum being only a few feet per day. It was eerie enough to be working in the quietude of a tunnel, lit only by the occasional candle, the whole place dark and damp, often soaking wet, and the acid smell of wet clay or sand. Wondering whether one might break through into a German tunnel, or worse still, whether German miners might break through into ours behind us cutting off retreat to the shaft. Whether the Germans might set off a mine and blow us all up. Whether a surface attack would develop and we would emerge from the shaft into enemy hands, or they would throw hand grenades down it. Perhaps they would use gas and it would seep down into the tunnel.
>
> Captain G R Cassels, 175 TC, RE

The original plan had been to destroy two concrete German redoubts by branching the gallery and planting one mine beneath each target. However, the tunnel, although originating from a fairly deep shaft, was already quite shallow as it had been dug on a steeper than normal gradient to help drainage. German activity in the trenches above could now be plainly heard. To go farther and consequently still shallower by branching would be risky and might jeopardise weeks of gruelling work. They had driven fifty-eight metres; Cassels decided that it was enough; he calculated that if the gallery was formed into a T-shape at this point, and planted with a heavier charge than originally intended, it should blow up the larger redoubt and bury the smaller one.

For the blow itself 3,500 pounds (1,590 kg) of the then new explosive, Ammonal, had been ordered. On 16 July 1915, three days before zero, it had still not arrived. Cassels begged other tunnelling units for anything they could spare, gathering 700 pounds (318 kg) of Ammonal from HQ, 500 pounds (227 kg) of gunpowder from nearby Maple Copse tunnels, and 200 pounds (91 kg) of guncotton from other generous sources including the artillery. Then the Ammonal arrived. Cassels decided they would use the lot. The mine was going to be far bigger than he had planned.

As the great day dawned, twenty-four detonators were prepared and distributed throughout the charge. Half were connected to wires leading to two exploders in a communication trench at a safe distance from the mine, the others to traditional match-lit 'instantaneous' fuses, in case of electrical failure. The ends of these fuses had only been brought to the head of the shaft – if there was a failure and Cassels had to light them, he would almost certainly be buried alive. The charge was tamped with tons of sandbags firmly packed into the galleries to stop the blast losing part of its energy by blowing back down the tunnel. Now, no more could be done underground.

As zero hour approached the electric leads were tested every few minutes with a weak torch battery to ensure they were in circuit. Just before zero hour the circuit failed and I had visions of the Hun having broken into the mine head and cut them. Another officer, a corporal and I hurried back along the line of leads and suddenly a shout went up from the corporal. He had found both leads broken where a German shell had burst. Hastily we repaired them, tested, and found them OK, and connected them to the two exploders with only four and a half minutes to spare.

Captain G R Cassels, RE, 175 TC

Cassels was well aware that his mine was only the second British offensive underground attack in the Salient. On 17 April five mines had been blown at Hill 60 using gunpowder and guncotton – but none of them was even half as powerful as his Hooge charge. A nervous Cowan had come up to ensure that the work was complete. It was. Double-checking the resistances on the firing leads, he crept back to Brigade HQ in the reserve trenches to watch the show. Cassels contemplated the scene as he prepared the exploders.

It was a beautiful evening. Sun about to set and everything at that moment quiet and peaceful like the still before the storm. Although there was nothing but dried mud and ruins in sight, some birds were singing and a little black cat which earlier had been sitting on my knee rubbed itself against my boots. I and another tunnelling officer were standing in the short trench outside the dugout and exactly at 7pm by our synchronised watches we simultaneously pressed our exploders.

The whole ground beneath and around us sank and then rose again two or three times and then it shuddered and swayed from side to side like a ship in a rough sea. Away in front the earth opened with a huge woofing roar like a miniature volcano. Actually there was more than one explosion and it appeared we might have blown up a German magazine or ammunition store as well. Concrete, bricks, earth, sand, timber and other debris with volumes of smoke hurtled high into the sky and amidst it all we could discern a whole tree and bodies and limbs of Germans ascending then falling to the ground; but we did not wait for all of it to come down. We ran for cover as the German guns opened up too with a heavy barrage.

One wondered how anyone could survive and we began to think we had not only buried the Germans but our own troops as well for we could see none of them. We only hoped the attackers had passed safely under this and were now overrunning the German positions. Soon afterwards an officer from the front line came in to say that all was well but that we had killed some of our own men and he himself was wounded by a falling sandbag.

Captain G R Cassels, 175 TC, RE

A German eyewitness account describes that which Cassels and Cowan could only imagine.

It was the 19 July. A day never to be forgotten as our regiment withstood the test of the heaviest fighting yet experienced. Throughout the afternoon the English had maintained their slow but effective gunfire of all calibres upon the German positions. Then suddenly at 8 o'clock in the evening there was a tremble and a swaying of the ground; then a shudder. The sentry, who was still standing in position at his loophole with whistle in mouth, was hurled against the revetment and lay there stunned. Another was thrown over the breastworks. Dugouts collapsed, burying and crushing those inside. Suddenly we were enveloped in darkness and the air was full of soil and dust. From the skies came huge clods of earth, timber, wire pickets, human limbs and whole bodies; everything swirling in confusion. Trenches are flattened by the falling mass. Those who are dazed and half-conscious and cannot dig themselves out are suffocated. The English have exploded a mine – and what a mine it must have been! The central sector was about 100 metres wide and the two platoons within it were either blown to pieces or buried alive.

Leutnant Wollinsky, 6 Kompagnie,
126 Infantrie Regiment

The Hooge mine was a great psychological boost at a time when little had been going well for the British. The German positions, and the crater, were captured, and for the moment at least Hooge could be said to be firmly in British hands. Cowan revelled in the praise heaped upon his company from all quarters. Telegrams of congratulation arrived from General Sir Herbert Plumer, Corps Commanders, neighbouring tunnelling companies and many other units, one of them informing Cassels that he had won the Military Cross. Cassels, however, felt that it was his sappers who really deserved the reward. Soon afterwards the news broke that 175 TC, still being the most 'spareable' company, was possibly to be relocated for defensive work elsewhere. The news came direct from the Corps Commander General Allenby, who suggested that after the Hooge mine the King of Belgium might have been behind the suggestion 'in order to make sure of having some of his country left!'. Norton-Griffiths was delighted to see an offensive scheme come to fruition at last, and expected the success of the blow to set a precedent and change attitudes. He would continue to spit feathers of frustration, however; defence was still to be the priority – for the moment. Meanwhile Cassels, having worked on the mine for six weeks without respite, was certainly due a well-earned rest.

I was granted ten days leave with orders from Major Cowan not to forget to bring back some grouse from the Yorkshire Moors. On the way back I had packed a couple of brace in my suitcase for safety en route. On opening my

Men of the 3rd Rifle Brigade temporarily occupying Hooge crater. The bottom was filled with lime bags to counteract the smell of rotting corpses

Right above: The response. British dead on the rim of the German Hooge mines of June 1916

Right below: German infantry exploring the freshly sprung mines of June 1916

bag I found it a seething mass of maggots and ordered the CO's batman – his name was Hart – who cooked all his meals, to throw the lot away. 'No, sir,' he said with his Scots brogue, 'I'll cook the grouse for dinner.' And we duly had an excellent repast with a delicious white sauce made with wine. Afterwards I said, 'Hart, I hope you burned the maggots.' 'Nae, sir,' he replied, 'they're nae but grouse themselves, so I made the sauce with them.'

Captain G R Cassels, 175 TC, RE

Near top of Strand shewing our attempt to rebuild trenches after (a) The Firing of the Mine (b) The Bombardment and (c) The Liquid Fire attack.

Hooge trenches after the mine and the first German liquid fire attack

The German mines at Hooge. Pioniere about to descend a shaft

Cowan's and Cassels' joy was to be short-lived. On 30 July, with the assistance of a new weapon – liquid fire – the Germans took back all and more of the ground they had lost. It was the beginning of a game of shuttlecock with each side suffering scandalous losses in the struggle for a tiny morsel of the Western Front.

Tunnelling in the Hooge sector was also far from over. In June 1916 the Germans blew three mines of their own close to Cassels' crater as part of a surprise offensive which captured the village, plus neighbouring Observatory Ridge and Sanctuary Wood – the only high ground in British hands in the whole of the Ypres Salient. The Canadians clawed it all back again – except Hooge. After eighteen months of toil and bloodshed the village had been decisively lost.

HICKLING AND ST ELOI

In April 1915 Lieutenant Horace Hickling, a trained mining engineer with many years' experience, and a section officer with 172 Tunnelling Company, was working at the ruined village of St

My company did the work at St Eloi, starting roughly March 1915. There was a gap where the road came right through St Eloi, which was no man's land, right down to a cross-roads. The first thing we did was to start to put a tunnel right under the cross-roads. We did that – and ran into a cess-pool which drove us out. Conditions were terrible for the first attempt to mine at St Eloi. The weather was bad; ground very wet and sloppy with pumps going all the while. We weren't given any plan about where to start mining. We went out and stood and looked at the Mound – couldn't get up to the place by day at all because we were under fire. We had the Mound as our objective. I had Hickling with me. He was the man who did most of the digging there.

Major Clay Hepburn, OC, 172 TC, RE

Left above: Lieutenant Horace Hickling, 172 TC section commander in the St Eloi workings. Hickling was Norton-Griffiths' 'live wire'

Left below: Mining terms as explained by 172 TC

Below: The despised Mound at St Eloi, photographed (at great risk) by Hickling

Bottom: Hickling's 172 TC men – the 'pick of the clay-kickers' – resting in a St Eloi trench

MINING TERMS ILLUSTRATED.

"Good footage."

"At work on the face."

Eloi near Ypres. Mining conditions were pitiable, with wet ground at the surface and running sand beneath. And the British positions were under frequent artillery and constant sniper fire, the latter from the dreaded 'Mound', a small ancient tumulus which overlooked the British trenches and the lines of communication beyond. Tunnelling here did not make an auspicious start.

I went out with the Monmouthshire Regiment in February 1915. Most of them were miners and many of us were drafted out. I was sent home to get some boring machinery and when I came back I joined 172 TC under Johnson VC. Johnson was a regular RE and he didn't like tunnelling one bit. He scorned taking cover – he was the sort who would stand up – even from rifle bullets. He told me two or three days after I had been with him 'Look here, I don't know anything about these tunnels. You do – you take over.' Then he would go off into the trenches and try to get people to strafe the Hun – that was what he was after.

A relaxed Hickling in the lee of a St Eloi breastwork

Far right: One of Hickling's experienced kickers in a tunnel entrance at St Eloi

shallow, and when I joined the company [21 April 1915], Hickling was probing to see how deep he could go before reaching the water level. The upshot of Hickling's probing was that he decided we were working at too shallow a level and that we should go deeper. There were several advantages, the principal one being that we expected to get underneath the Hun. He found also that at about thirty-five feet we were in drier clay.

Lieutenant F J Mulqueen, 172 TC, RE

Mining at St Eloi was shallow – so shallow that Hickling was seeking some form of new strategy to escape the annoying and valueless tit-for-tat fighting at restricted depth.

I was instructed to report to Lieutenant Hickling in charge of the section at St Eloi. Hickling's section was woefully weak in Officer strength and he had been in the line for several days. I was instructed to relieve him that night. It was explained to us that the Germans held a piece of high ground known as 'The Mound' overlooking the village of St Eloi. A heading had been started from the village towards 'The Mound' and was about half way to its objective.

The first mine which was sunk was

View from the British front line across the narrow ribbon of scrub which formed no man's land at St Eloi; the German trenches are just a stone's throw away beyond the knife-rest

As at Hill 60, Hooge and the Bluff, the British were desperate to break the German hold on certain key observational positions. St Eloi's Mound was also one such place – a strategic jewel. The infantry, British and French, had been thrown into several bloody attempts at capturing the Mound since the Germans first occupied it on 10 November of the previous year, all of which came to nothing until St Valentine's Day 1915 when the British finally retook St Eloi. Exactly one month later the Germans were back in residence – and they had mined the Tommies out.

For Hickling, a patient and careful man, mines were also his solution. He first developed a small cocoon of listening posts in shallow galleries from which the British trenches could be defended with *camouflets*, and then began a group of deeper offensive mines. The plan was to distract attention from his lower tunnels by keeping the Germans constantly and fully occupied in the 'shallows'. In mid-July 1915 Norton-Griffiths' diary illustrated how hard Hickling's 172 Tunnelling Company was working to 'entertain' the *Pioniere* and safeguard their 'deeps'.

> The G's [Germans] have made repeated efforts to get at us. Hickling has blown them off each time. Since 14 April he has blown them on 23/4, 24/4, 3/5, 17/5, 26/5, 28/5, 5/6, 10/7.
>
> Major J Norton-Griffiths, RE

At the beginning of July Hickling had finished his scheme and was ready to create a major distraction.

> One of the tunnels went out under a sort of mound – that was the place we were aiming for. By the end of June we had a line of five mines under the German trenches and under the mound. I went to HQ, General Glubb, 2nd Army and asked for artillery support. He said 'You know, I've only got ten rounds per gun at the moment, for a weeks ammunition. I can't give you any artillery support. You must blow the mines – and that's that.' We could see the Germans starting [tunnelling] all over the place. I had Hickling with me. He was the man who did most of the digging there. We blew up these five mines in a row – we didn't set them off simultaneously, but dotted them here and there waiting at intervals so they didn't know where the next one was going up. I was in the trenches and I would say to Hickling 'Let that one off now... let number 3 go.'
> We were able to sit on the parapet and not

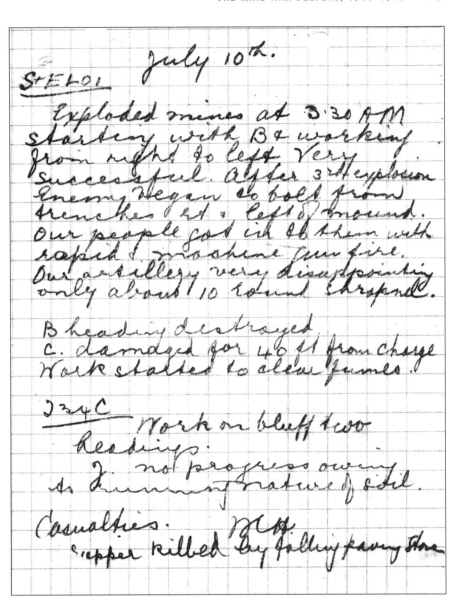

Horace Hickling's 172 TC diary entry for 10 July 1915, noting success of mines and only one casualty – a sapper killed by a falling paving stone

> a shot was fired at us. We saw the debris going up and when everything had settled down we saw the Germans haring out over the country any way they could to get away from the front line trenches. It was a very successful blow, and if we'd had artillery and attack support it would have been even more so.
>
> Major Clay Hepburn, OC 172 TC, RE

The 10 July mines were a psychological boost for tunneller and infantry alike, but unfortunately no more than that. A fierce counter-attack in and around the craters clawed back all and a little more of the British gains, and the Germans once more regained the Mound. It was no surprise to Hepburn and Hickling; without artillery support they had expected another failure. Undeterred, Hickling 'carried on'. He had more cards still to play.

One of the five mines blown by Hickling's and Hepburn's men on 10 July 1915, photographed by Hickling

The first deep mine in the Salient under construction. Hickling's significant St Eloi shaft which pierced the wet sands to reach the clay bed

Before Hickling left it was decided to sink a really deep shaft into the blue clay, known geologically as Ypresian Clay. The junction between the surface sandy clay, i.e. Paniselian Clay and the blue clay was extremely wet. The latter was heavy and close grained and it had a tendency to shed water rather than to absorb it. The setting of the timbers in a shaft under normal conditions requires considerable skill and is quite an undertaking. When one has to contend with difficult water conditions and disturbances due to enemy interference, it becomes that much more difficult. Our sappers were very efficient and we managed to seal off the water quite effectively. It is my recollection that we established a pumping station just below the junction of the two clays and then continued sinking until we reached a depth of about 64 feet.

At that depth the blue clay was quite dry and the gallery was a pleasant one in which to work. It was driven in the general direction of the 'Mound' and while at that time I was not aware of it, this heading was projected as part of a general plan to capture the Wytschaete–Messines Ridge.

Lieutenant F J Mulqueen, 172 TC, RE

On 2 September 1915 John Norton-Griffiths, by now an ardent admirer of Hickling's offensive spirit and vision, made a note in his diary.

172 Coy. Lt Hickling 'the live spark' has 2 deep shafts down 60 feet, without talking, into clay, and going for St Eloi under crater with 55 feet of head cover.

Major John Norton-Griffiths, RE

Message from Hickling to Mulqueen giving instructions for Mulqueen's first opportunity to blow a camouflet since arriving at 172 TC

The ground reclaimed. The big St Eloi crater of 27 March occupies the place where the Mound once loomed; showing German fortifications, dugouts and mine workings. Photographed on 6 April 1915

During the seven months it took to complete this first deep scheme of the war, British listeners would report absolutely no German activity at that depth. It had now been almost a year since Leeming's first successful sinking through the running sand at Cuinchy, and the Germans were still unaware of British deep ambitions anywhere in Belgian Flanders. On 27 March 1916 Hickling's five mines, four large and one small charge totalling 82,300 pounds (37,331 kg) – the first to be planted in blue Ypresian clay – were blown. At nearly seventeen metres they were the deepest fired to date – not only in the Great War, but in the history of military mining. Hickling was not there to see the culmination of his scheme having been given a command of his own (183 Tunnelling Company) on the Somme during the previous October, but he would have been proud of his tunnellers and certainly would not have failed to realise that on this day and due to his work the fate of German mining enterprise in the Ypres Salient was almost guaranteed to be irrevocably sealed. Nearly the whole of Jäger Battalion 18 was lost in the vast St Eloi craters and the Mound area was captured. But once again, not for long. The German infantry, so adept at this kind of fighting, once more retook the craters and their original line. This time they were to retain the positions for over a year, until 7 June 1917.

The historic St Eloi craters blown on 27 March 1916 photographed from the British front line on 23 September. They are all in German hands again. The dreaded Mound has ceased to exist as a topographical feature

Craters at St Eloi

The Norton-Griffiths show goes on

The St Eloi blows had given 172 TC a classic pyhrric victory if ever there was one. Although the gains were only temporary on the surface, through the explosion of the mines the tunnellers had learned two vital lessons which were to be critical for the future: the explosive effects of deep and heavy charges of Ammonal in clay as opposed to shallower geology, and the range of flying debris from big, deep charges. From these five mines new equations could be drawn up to calculate the effects of even greater charges at even greater depths. As for the infernal Mound, it was actually no longer a problem; the biggest of 172's famous five – a mine of 31,000 pounds (14,061 kg) of Ammonal – had guaranteed an end to its delinquency. It had been wiped from the face of the earth.

Both the *Pioniere* and German High Command were now suddenly fully aware that what they had thought impossible – the sinking of shafts through the *Schwimmsand* – had been achieved by the British. The most frightening realisation was that it had been accomplished long, long ago; Hickling had in fact reached the 'blue' clay at St Eloi at almost the same time as Leeming at Cuinchy, during the first week of May 1915. It was a devastating blow from which the *Pioniere* would never recover. In twelve months they had slipped from a position of robust underground authority to trailing at least nine months behind.

We wasted our effort in driving numerous shallow and wet tunnels, and had pitiful beginnings in the engagement of the enemy at greater depth, but with little immediate prospect of getting deep ourselves.

Oberstleutnant Otto Füsslein,
Kommandeur des Mineure,
4th German Army

Now, a radical German reorganisation of tunnelling policy was unavoidable. Almost before the dust had settled from the 27 March explosions, the *Pioniere* were reorganised as *Mineur Kompagnien*, with a command structure and working practices almost identical to the British pattern. The Commanders issued urgent orders to go deep wherever necessary and wherever possible – and at all costs. By the middle of May 1916 large numbers of troops had been transferred as *Mineure*, and the first German listening posts were being installed in blue clay – but it was all much too late: preparations were well underway for the fifth and final date in the fateful chronology of mine warfare in the Salient, 7 June 1917.

MINE WARFARE IN ITS FINAL PHASE

Just a week after Leeming's triumph at Cuinchy in early 1915, and a full two months before Cassels' Hooge mine, an entry in John Norton-Griffiths' war diary reveals the embryo of a plan which formed the template for the greatest mine offensive in modern history, and the most successful battle of the Great War.

12.5.15 An examination of the trench maps of 6th Div. Area and 3rd Div. area lead to the belief that if mining efforts of 174 and 172 were concentrated in front of Wytschaete on ground lying between St Eloi and Wulverghem, a good and perhaps most useful mining programme might materially help to straighten out our line. Taking Wytschaete and straightening out our line from St Eloi to Messines. The reason I suggest this for the consideration of the E in C [Engineer in Chief] is because indications point to the ground in this area being favourable for mining. Such a scheme would want some 6 weeks to complete and it should be possible for mines to break the line at say 6 given points. To do this however, a close examination of the area should be made by me first for the personal information of the E in C to discuss this with the CEs [Divisional Commanders of Engineers] otherwise the most suitable points might not be selected. From a mining point of view these would have to be combined with the tactical points as far as mining will permit. As there is so much else to do, do not propose to examine all the area unless the E in C considers there is something in the idea.

Major John Norton-Griffiths, RE

At this time, unlike the British, the German High

TRENCH WARFARE: "A GOOD BAG."

Command did not attach much importance to mining; it was a necessary annoyance, a strategically insignificant conflict which had become unavoidable but would simply trickle on – to a greater or lesser extent as at present. Even after the disaster at St Eloi in March 1916, the German Generals would continue to believe that the mine war would still reach a point of equilibrium, and it was only a matter of time before each side would be unable to make any major underground assaults. The longer it continued, the more a mutual nullification would develop. Mines could therefore play no more than a minimal part in major victories. Many on the British side were to concur. But the Engineer in Chief, General George Fowke, the Inspector of Mines, Colonel R N Harvey and John Norton-Griffiths did not. By 6 January 1916, Norton-Griffiths' grand scheme had been approved. Almost within days it began developing into an epic plan involving the planting of dozens of deep and massive mines along a thirteen-kilometre front.

A few enlightened German commanders such as 4th Army Kommandeur des Mineure, Oberstleutnant Otto Füsslein, were to be far from complacent. In December 1916 his *Mineur Kompagnien*, working furiously to counter the British deep mining threat, were to be struck another crushing blow: 50,000 German miners and many of their engineer officers would be called back to help solve the industrial crisis at home in the Fatherland. They were replaced – but by untrained infantry.

The offensive that was eventually to employ the Norton-Griffiths concept and capture the Messines Ridge on 7 June 1917, had originally been planned to take place during the summer of 1916. Norton-Griffiths had also envisaged a 1916 attack when drawing up the scheme, but the tragic and costly events on the Somme during the summer and autumn of that year forced a postponement. As several of the Messines mines were already in place by the summer of 1916, those who sanctioned the continuation and expansion of the scheme until the spring of 1917 must have been more than supreme optimists to believe that those mines already *in situ* would lie undiscovered and could be preserved for twelve months. Perhaps his unbounded enthusiasm and confidence had been contagious after all; at any event, the Norton-Griffiths show would go on.

Chapter IX
'EARTHQUAKING' THE RIDGE: MESSINES, JUNE 1917

The cauldron of the Salient. Hill 60 (left) with the Caterpillar on the opposite side of the Ypres–Comines railway cutting (right), April 1915

250 Tunnelling Company. OC Captain Cropper away to see CE. This officer is getting well into his stride and has got the big idea. Four Shaft sites have been located, 3 shafts underway. Bored to clay bed and knows his depth before starting. His object is 4 deep shafts making for Wytschaete Ridge. Excellent programme if given time. OC's 172, 250 appreciate the importance of 'earthquaking' the ridge. In addition 175 has over 600 feet already in and is now under our lines, deep in the clay. Our advantage is the enemy has to counter-mine from the higher ground being made up with running sand and loam sitting on the clay bed. Further, our previous shallow mining is a curtain, and if no company is allowed to blow the deep level game until the whole is completed, the enemy, it is very unlikely, will tumble to it.

Major John Norton-Griffiths, RE, War Diary, 20 December 1915

The Messines Ridge is, like all the other high ground north and east of Ypres, an extension of the Passchendaele Ridge system. Forming a broad plateau-like spur from the main arc, which runs from Passchendaele itself through Broodseinde, Mount Sorrel, Hill 60, The Bluff and St Eloi, it was carved by the action of the Steenbeek and Wambeek streams draining south-eastwards to the Douve river below. The village of Wytschaete – 'Whitesheet' to the British – sits atop its northern end, with Messines guarding the southernmost extension looking down upon Ploegsteert ('Plugstreet') Wood, the valley of the Douve and beyond into French Flanders. With a maximum height of around ninety-five metres, the Messines Ridge was a magnificent vantage point, and had of course been in German hands since the First Battle of Ypres in November 1914.

The Germans had heavily fortified the full length of the upper slopes with a continuation of the *Flandern Stellung*. This formidable trench and pillbox system followed the sweep of the higher

HILL 60

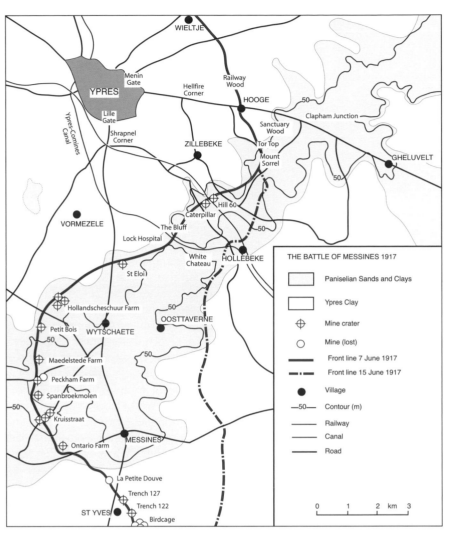

ground in front of Ypres before curving around the wooded slopes beneath Wytschaete and Messines. The front lines here – the *Wytschaete-Bogen* – drew an elegant curve westwards. Embedded within the trenches were regularly spaced strongpoints that loomed belligerently over the British lines beneath. Their purpose was to disrupt and disintegrate any frontal attack. To the British and their allies, it was another irritating illustration of German dominance of the best strategic positions in the Salient. Being downslope, British artillery fire was difficult to register on the German lines on the ridge top, and after recent lessons on the Somme it was recognised that any infantry assault was likely to be a costly proposition. But the British did not intend to attack using the traditional artillery–infantry combination. For well over a year Norton-Griffiths' moles had been working on the largest coordinated mine attack in the history of warfare; their goal – to create a man-made earthquake which would contest the forces of nature herself.

THE BATTLE PLAN UNFOLDS

From the summer of 1915 permutations for concentrated mine attacks in the Messines and Wytschaete sectors of the Ypres Salient had often been debated at British GHQ. Eventually several ambitious but localised proposals were cast aside in favour of an audacious scheme that would cover the entire front of the Messines Ridge. In November 1915 Norton-Griffiths' idea of 'earthquaking' the German front at St Eloi,

Above: Plan of the Messines Ridge battlefield for the attack of 7 June 1917 showing the ridge geology, mines blown and allied gains

Above left: Timber-braced German breastworks crossing the railway line and ascending Hill 60

THE CATERPILLAR

Hollandscheschuur, Petit Bois, Peckham, Maedelstede and Spanbroekmolen, was elevated from possible to probable. On procuring his new position of Inspector of Mines in January 1916, Brigadier-General R N Harvey, with the support of Engineer-in-Chief General George Fowke, had persuaded GHQ that parts of the mine plan were already well advanced, and that for any attack planned for the coming summer, an extension of the scheme might well have considerable strategic value. The suggestion was accepted by GHQ; the mine scheme would be expanded as far as time constraints allowed – as many mines as possible should be planted before zero day. Norton-Griffiths' plan then escalated to incorporate all the ground from Hill 60 in the north to the Birdcage sector, at the south end of Messines Ridge beyond Plugstreet Wood.

Since taking over as Commander-in-Chief from Sir John French in December 1915, Field-Marshal Sir Douglas Haig had sought to launch an offensive in Flanders. His strategic aim was to clear the Germans from the clay plain and maritime region of West Flanders, opening up a route to the Channel ports of Ostend and Zeebrugge, and unlocking the way to the rail hub of Roulers, the key arrival and distribution point of the German Army's materiel and troops. All this would be achieved by punching through the German positions on the ridges in front of Ypres before advancing along the Belgian coast at Nieuport. Originally planned for the summer of 1916, the offensive would be delayed as British

Sir Herbert Plumer, architect of the Messines attack

attention was turned towards co-operation with the French in the great Somme offensive in Picardy. In November 1916, with the Somme battles out of the way, Haig was at last free to concentrate on Ypres once more. He charged 2nd Army Commander Sir Herbert Plumer with developing plans for a series of attacks to begin in the spring of the following year.

Plumer knew the vagaries and nature of the Salient as well as anyone; he had commanded V Corps during the Second Battle of Ypres, and had spent almost all his time in the sector ever since. His minutely considered proposal was delivered to Haig on 12 December 1916. The first stage was to be based upon Norton-Griffiths' mining scheme. Plumer's concept outlined a deliberately limited offensive at Messines, employing the deep mines as a launch pad, in conjunction with an infantry attack on the Pilckem Ridge to the north of Ypres. But limited objectives did not impress Haig, who wanted a breakout from the Salient, not an adjustment of its lines. Plumer was sent back to reconsider. He was to be assisted in his deliberations by General Sir Henry Rawlinson, still engaged at this time with the 4th Army on the Somme, whom Haig had promised a command in any forthcoming battle in the Salient.

Their revised plan arrived on Haig's desk on 30 January 1917. It now proposed a sector-by-sector clearance of the Passchendaele Ridge complex beginning in the south. The northernmost sector at Pilckem Ridge – no more than a gentle swelling – would now be attacked after its more imposing neighbour at Messines had been taken. Pilckem was a low north-western spur of the main ridge complex, but it commanded the strategically important Menin Road that, running out of Ypres, bisected the Salient, rising up past Hooge and on to the broad expanse of the Gheluvelt Plateau beyond. Taking Messines, Pilckem and Gheluvelt in quick succession would facilitate the capture of the total ridge complex. Furthermore, the whole offensive was now to be linked not only with the coastal attack, but also an audacious mechanised amphibious assault against the German sea defences north of Nieuport.

But the plans for the Salient required artillery, lots of it; more, in fact, than was available. Conferring with Plumer, Rawlinson suggested that there should be a break of two or three days between the Messines and Ypres attacks to move and re-lay the guns. Haig wanted no such delay, and petulantly replaced Rawlinson with General

Sir Hubert Gough – a 'thruster' with the necessary offensive spirit. Gough was given full responsibility for the battle in front of Ypres, leaving the more cautious Plumer in charge of only the Messines plans. Inexplicably, at Doullens on 7 May 1917, exactly one month to the day before battle was to commence, Haig was to dissect his offensive again. Messines would now stand alone, and the Pilckem and Gheluvelt attacks would follow later. As the Battle of Messines Ridge opened on 7 June 1917 the other components of the original plan were left hanging on its outcome. The battle was to be a complete success and the ridge was to fall in a matter of hours. Stage one had been achieved.

Stage two of the offensive, the advance upon the Pilckem Ridge and Gheluvelt Plateau, was eventually launched on 31 July; a full six weeks later than Plumer had counselled. It could hardly have differed more from Messines. No footholds were to be gained on the main body of the Passchendaele Ridge for almost three months. Half way through the battle Gough was relieved as Commander of the 5th Army, and Plumer given overall control. The thirteen-week campaign that has become known as the Third Battle of Ypres has entered modern myth as a single word: Passchendaele – a battle that was as much a struggle with the elements as with the enemy, and fought in the most awful conditions that modern warfare could produce. The outstanding and celebrated victory at Messines was to be squandered.

BUILD UP TO BATTLE

From the spring of 1915 all activity in the Ypres Salient had been regulated by the Germans, who harassed the British both above and below ground. Constant underground fighting at the mining hotspots, Hooge, Hill 60, Railway Wood, Sanctuary Wood, St Eloi and the Bluff, soaked up new drafts of tunnellers for several months after the formation of the first eight British companies, and restricted the number of miners available for work in other parts of the sector. The formation of twelve new tunnelling companies between July and October 1915 brought more men into action, and old and new schemes, still overwhelmingly defensive in nature, began to germinate. With the approach of the second winter of war, however, conditions became so wet in the then shallow tunnel systems that both sides were forced to cease practically all work outside the hotspots, keeping just a few listening posts manned for security.

The 172 Tunnelling Company's shattering blows at St Eloi in March 1916 alerted the Germans to the fact that the British had gone deep. An investigation by eminent geologist Siegfried Passarge, a professor at Hamburg University, confirmed the fears of the *Ingeniere*, and hinted that it might not be impossible that British tunnellers were already working at depth at several other locations north of the Douve river. The question was: where? There were no reservations about the next step; the German response had to be, and was, immediate, with the dissolution in May 1916 of the old 'amateur' *Pionier* units in favour of professional *Pionier Mineur Kompagnien* organised upon the British

German 4th Army Mining Commanders near Wytschaete, August 1916. Füsslein is recognisable in the centre by his splendid moustache. On the right is Bindernagel, commanding Mineurgruppe Wijtschate

Mineur-Offiziere im B 2-Wald bei Wijtschate, August 1916.
links nach rechts: Lt. Thein, Oblt. Wassung, Lt. Santelmann, Oblt. Füßlein, Kdr. d. Mineure
Lt. Heß, Hptm. Bindernagel, Kdr. d. Mineurgruppe Wijtschate.

The German mining factory at Tourcoing showing steel formers and concrete shaft rings

Below: The head of the 'Frauenlob' shaft, built within the protection of a concrete pillbox

Below right: Remains of a German deep countermine shaft inside a shattered pillbox at Grand Bois below the village of Wytschaete

putting economic factors aside in the face of crisis, they followed the lead of their surface based colleagues and selected concrete and steel to solve the problem. A factory producing a range of technical and specialised equipment specifically for military mining was started behind the lines.

Later on we made many things ourselves in the splendid mining workshops we set up at Tourcoing: steel frames for concrete shafts, steel tubbing, concrete blocks, silent spoil conveyors and overhead conveyors, and many other things. At that time, though, in the spring of 1916, we had the same gear as the other troops, with none of the proper mining equipment and materials that were urgently needed to make rapid headway in the mud and water.

Oberstleutnant Otto Füsslein,
Kommandeur des Mineure,
4th German Army

model, working independently to the infantry. Seven units were formed before the end of the year, with another three arriving in mid-January 1917. Initially under the leadership of Hauptman Bindernagel – commanding *Mineurgruppe Wijtschate* – and from 1 September 1916 under the overall control of an experienced military miner, Oberstleutnant Otto Füsslein, Kommandeur des Mineure for the 4th Army, the German reaction was admirable - but far too late. Three huge British mines had already been laid and tamped by the time Bindernagel began work; when Füsslein arrived just a few short months later the total had reached sixteen.

The challenge for the German *Mineure* was absolutely clear. They knew that to counter the British threat – and counter it they must – the *Schwimmsande* had to be conquered. Attempts to reach the deep dry clay with timber shafts and inclines had failed many times in the past; now,

In the meantime, the British were tunnelling fast. Visitors to the Messines battlefield today may notice that several of the surviving craters from the attack of 7 June 1917 – Hollandscheschuur Farm, Petit Bois, Peckham, Maedelstede Farm and Spanbroekmolen, in the middle of the battlefront – are closely grouped, while in other parts of the line, particularly the northern sector between Hill 60 and St Eloi, there are wide gaps between blows. It was not planned thus; the intention was to neutralise as many of the myriad German strongpoints as possible along the full length of the ridge. Most authorities accept that twenty-five big charges were laid in preparation for Messines; in fact the latest research shows that at least forty-nine separate mines had been proposed; and a substantial

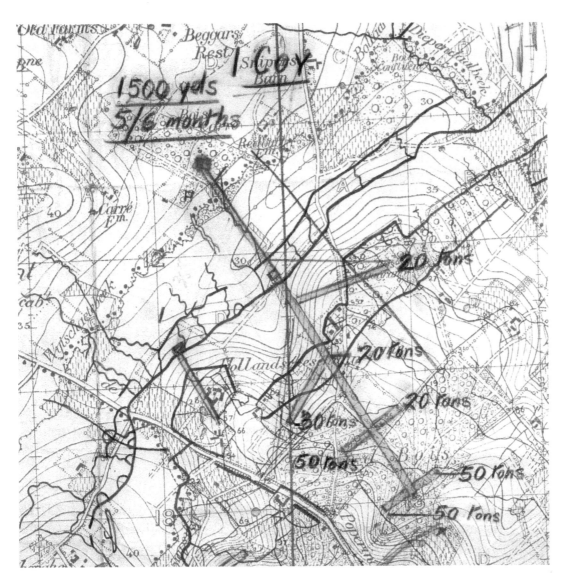

The ambitious seven-mine scheme planned for 250 TC to attack Bois Quarante and Grand Bois

number were either completed or well underway by zero day.

Just a single British charge at La Petite Douve Farm was lost to enemy countermining – an incredible feat after eighteen solid months of work on so many schemes. Apart from four other mines at 'The Birdcage' south of Ploegsteert Wood, just outside the southern edge of the theatre of battle, the nineteen mines which were detonated on 7 June 1917 were the only ones ready to fire on that date. The old adversary – geology – claimed another 'big one' at Peckham, but many more had been within a few short weeks of completion.

THE ONES AT THE TOP – HILL 60

The northernmost mines on the battlefield were at Hill 60. But beyond the Hill at Sanctuary Wood, Tor Top, Armagh Wood and Mount Sorrel lay other complex tunnel systems. Apart from

forming the upper boundary line for the 7 June surface battle, the mine systems in this sector would play no active part in the Messines scheme, and no great charges were contemplated or laid. Unlike almost everywhere else in the Salient, the tunnels here lay exclusively in the upper geological layers as the thickness of running sands had foiled both tunneller and *Mineur* in developing deep schemes. Unusually, this was a sector where both sides employed defensive laterals. During 1916 fighting with small, bored charges had been widespread and bitter until offensive ambitions on both sides waned and defence began to dominate – the stalemate that German HQ had expected to appear everywhere.

As usual, the reason lay in the geology. Work in the firm sands of the ridge was so silent that no more than simple blades were needed to 'carve' the earth directly into sandbags – the

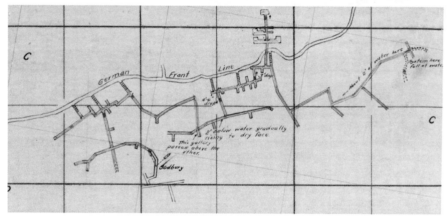

Top: Excavation at Mount Sorrel showing surface trench remains (marked by red and white pole) and shallow tunnels beneath

Above: Canadian plan of a section of captured German mine and dugout workings at Mount Sorrel, later connected to their own systems for extra infantry shelter

Right: Mine plan of deep Hill 60 and Caterpillar mines prepared for 7 June 1917

Hill 60 sector that the first major British underground attack in the Salient had taken place. Here, on the evening of 17 April 1915, 171 Tunnelling Company blew five small mines. Hill 60 was taken and held at enormous cost, before being lost on 5 May – not to mines, but poison gas. The British would not set foot upon '60' again for another two years, during which time underground warfare in the sector was to expand enormously, gaining the hill a gruesome reputation as one of the bloodiest corners of the whole of the British Western Front.

I went to Hill 60 about August 1916 having had two years in a Field Company. It was my first job tunnelling. It was absolutely dreadful – lice, bugs, every darned thing you could think of. If you cut your hand it was a criminal offence not to go and be injected against tetanus. Jaundice, boils and tetanus were rife. We were underground all the time and hardly ever saw daylight except from deep dugouts, and we were bombarded to blazes the whole time, and there were shots going off every week – either the Germans blowing us, or us blowing them. And it was terribly wet.
Lieutenant B C Hall, 3rd Canadian TC

The sheer extent of the 1915 and 1916 tunnelling, the closeness of the enemy in the trenches (in places both sides could easily toss pebbles at each other), and the difficult geology dictated that achieving deep underground success was considerably more challenging here than in many other sectors. In places the Hill 60

Germans employed heat-softened, bent bayonets. As a result in several places both sides had managed to secretly penetrate the opposing defensive shield and install advanced listening 'pockets' beneath the enemy's support lines. After the capture of Mount Sorrel in 1917, the 2nd Canadian Tunnelling Company carried out a complete reconnaissance of enemy workings. As well as evidence of several failed attempts at deep mining, they found that the Germans had given up all offensive work and settled into an entirely defensive mode.

The Hill 60 sector lies immediately south of Mount Sorrel, but could not have been more different in nature. The hill itself was a small but prominent man-made knoll just sixty metres above sea level, formed by spoil derived from the construction of the Ypres–Comines railway cutting, which runs along its west flank. On the other side of the tracks a second spoil heap created another more sinuous feature, known to the British as the 'Caterpillar'. It had been in the

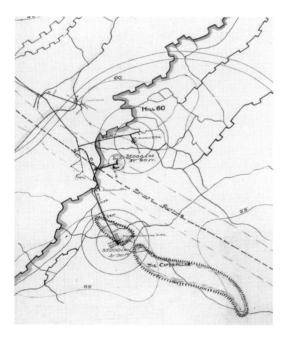

tunnels were so damp – one was actually called 'The Wet Sap' – that candles would not burn and acetylene lamps were required.

Only at St Eloi and the Bluff did both *Mineur* and tunneller face similar thicknesses of wet Kemmel Sands that existed at Hill 60; elsewhere the British enjoyed the advantage of lower sites and a thinner overburden of saturated strata. Significantly, in late 1915 175 TC had managed to reach the blue clay by sinking an angled incline – a stairway – and in timber. The offensive gallery it was to serve, the future Berlin Tunnel – so called because tunnellers half expected it to end up beneath the German capital – was driven at a depth of twenty-eight metres. The whole project which the tunnel was to serve would be a truly Commonwealth effort.

In the spring of 1916 the 3rd Canadian TC relieved 175 TC, inherited the wooden incline, and continued the deep work; branching the Berlin Tunnel, and driving left beneath Hill 60 itself and right, under the railway line, to the 'Caterpillar'. But the old incline was struggling under the strain of the running sands. As the ground shuddered from shelling on the surface and trembled through mine explosions underground, it became less and less stable, and grew more fragile every day. Water poured between the timbers as it passed through the wet sand level, and pumps had to be worked day and night to keep floods at a manageable level. The structure was clearly vulnerable to a well-placed enemy *camouflet*, and the tunnellers had to face the fact that it was liable to collapse at any moment; if it did fail all the deep workings would fill with water and quicksand, putting the new galleries and the two projected mines beyond both recovery and completion, and drowning or entombing all those working in the deep extremities of the system without any hope of escape.

There was no time to begin a new approach tunnel back on lower and better ground to connect with the existing deep galleries, so the 1st Australian TC, taking over during the first week of November 1916, were to continue a project which the Canadians had recently begun. By this time the two big mines had already been laid by the Canadians; the success of the whole scheme was now under threat from the ever weakening incline. In response, the Australians sank a new shaft from a support line position which would connect to a new gallery designed to by-pass the timber incline completely, making it redundant. For safety, the new shaft house was installed well underground, at the six-metre level.

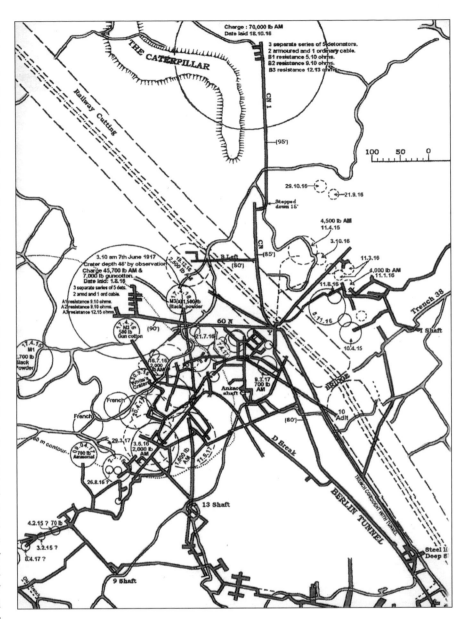

I took a small forward party up to investigate the geography and underground system. 171 Coy, consisting of clay-kickers, Durham and Welsh miners, had been instructed to put in a mine. Quite a job. It had to be quiet, and had to go through 40 feet of waterlogged quicksand under a layer of yellow sandy clay. They had decided to put in a timbered incline through the quicksand, water poured in through every joint and they had a system of pumps with a sapper on each one. This was the Berlin sap. 171 started it, and the Canadians finally got it down. When we arrived they had got down to the blue clay and had driven out a long cross cut to the German line. They put a Y in – the left hand

Plan showing tangled mass of underground galleries at Hill 60, colours indicating different depths. Note no German workings are shown. Trenches are shown in green and blue

branch went to the Honey Snout, the highest point of Hill 60, and the right hand branch went under the railway cutting.

We had to put in a more elaborate listening system in the upper branches to stop a high level approach by the Germans; this was in sandy clay – we couldn't put listening posts in the quicksand. We put a cylindrical steel shaft down vertical, and six feet in diameter and forced the cutting edge of the shaft down with four hydraulic jacks: the ANZAC shaft. But first we had to approach from Larch Wood, the forward battalion HQ, and put a tunnel in with about 30 feet of headcover, dig dug-outs to house our shift men and excavate a chamber for the top of the shaft with enough cover on top to take the back pressure of the hydraulic jacks. It was a race between the amount of water and sand coming in, and getting down to the blue clay to seal it off. You couldn't touch the steel shaft because the Germans would pick up the sound on their geophones miles away.

We put the cutting edge down first, then took the jacks off and bolted on another 2 foot section, put the jacks back on again and pressed them against the roof – and down again. There was a team of stalwarts inside hooking out the sand as fast as they could. We were wet all the time until we got through to the blue clay. Men passing from the top of the shaft down the cross cut to their dugouts passed a cubby hole in the side where there

was a sergeant, an officer and a man with a rum barrel. The rum ration was served out with a 2-ounce Capstan tobacco tin, and men coming up the shaft got two dips. Some of the young Tommies helping in bag-shifting had never drunk 2 ounces of rum before – they were roaring before they got to their dugouts.

Lieutenant William J McBride, OC No. 1 Section, 1st Australian TC

McBride's men further strengthened the shaft with internal timbering. It still leaked a little, but whereas the old workings had demanded eight pumps in series on the incline alone, now only one was necessary for the complete system. Progress was good, and flushed with enthusiasm McBride even suggested the installation of electrically driven conveyor belts in the deeps. He was overruled by Major R S G Stokes, Assistant Inspector of Mines; it would be too noisy – and much less reliable than musclepower.

Meanwhile, in the upper levels the Australians were being deliberately noisy and fighting as many *camouflet* battles as possible in an effort to distract German attention from the deeps, just as Hickling had done at St Eloi the year before. 'Dummy' picks and shovels operated remotely by ropes made noises to draw unwelcome attentions away from more sensitive spots, whilst British artillery harassed suspected shaft sites on the surface. But despite the diversionary tactics, listening reports made it clear that the *Pioniere* were tenaciously attempting to

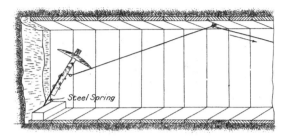

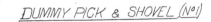

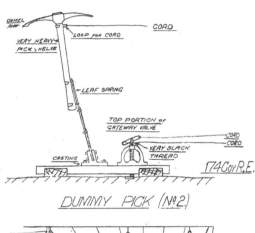

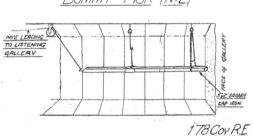

beat the *Schwimmsande* in search of the big mines. It was not the first time they had been suspected of trying to go deep.

Early in 1916 we had a raid at Hill 60 because we were worried about the Bosche doing deep mining. We thought they had a tunnel along the railway cutting. Didn't find out much on the raid but captured a young tunnelling officer, nice young chap. They softened him up by telling him he had been taken prisoner in a vast offensive by the British which would go on for another ten miles, taking in a large town. Any information he gave therefore would not be revealing anything we didn't already know. He was very loyal, but very anxious too about his men who we asserted were buried down below the

railway cutting. As I had been involved in the Hill 60 warfare, I was brought up to Army HQ to interview this chap through an interpreter. Fortunately I am an interpreter in German so could hear and understand what was going on although I pretended I couldn't understand a word.

I brought up my maps of the old show and we had our current maps which I showed to him, and we talked like old buddies of how we had fought underground in 1915. He cottoned on to it splendidly and pinpointed for us on the map where the shaft was and where they were driving. It was deep, as we had thought. He was most anxious about his comrades, and asked us please to get on to it at once before they suffocated. We immediately telephoned HQ and they got onto it and blew the place up. I feel I wouldn't like to meet him again because it was a rather dirty trick.

Major-General F Gordon Hyland,
Controller of Mines 3rd Army, ex-OC 171 TC

Hill 60 was the first major offensive project entrusted to the Australians. As experienced and professional engineers and miners, they were determined to make their mark. Nevertheless, the possibility of German countermining opened a period of extreme tension for the 'diggers'.

We blew the Germans up a couple of times. On one occasion a listener in a 'snout', an offshoot from a cross-cut – it looked like a hooked nose on the contour of the German front line. An officer, Ronald Hinder, went down to listen. He said he thought it was a windlass. Further listening seemed to confirm this, you could count the noise increasing at

Left above: British tricks of the trade. A dummy pick to attract or distract German attention

Left below: More complex ruses. The listener activates these contraptions remotely by pulling a cord. The dummy shovel was worked by pulling the two strings alternately forcing a steel shoe on the end of the coarse thread to rub on the ground below, mimicking the scrape of a shovel

The Australian Hill 60 firing party. L-R rear: Lieutenants John Royle, James Bowry and Bert Carroll; front row: Captain Oliver Woodward, Major James 'Lollylegs' Henry, Captain Robert Clinton

about the rate it would each day by the windlass having to sink that much lower. Our Major, J D Henry, nicknamed Lollylegs, was not noted for coming down into the deep saps, but the officer in charge couldn't do anything without his permission. He [Henry] wouldn't do anything without going down to HQ 2nd Army to see the Controller of Mines. The chaps underground, 100 feet down in the blue clay, were not too keen on waiting for HQ – they might be blown at any moment.

We had to blow, otherwise the chaps wouldn't go down there. We got the Major underground, lying on the ground with geophones fixed. His heart must have been going like a sledgehammer. Lt H S Carroll took a handful of clay, held it over the Major's head, and trickled it onto the geophone. This, plus the Major's pulse, convinced him that the Hun was about to break through at any moment. He scuttled back out of the tunnel, rushed to the bottom of the steel shaft shouting 'We must blow, we must blow'. We got back into our top level dugout where the charges were prepared. Carroll looked at me and said 'What are we going to do?' I said 'We're not going to wait to be blown up!' So we went down and blew. That was the last we heard of the windlass – we must have blown right into their shaft. It was only a small charge – enough to shake the ground and fill it with gas to prevent them working there. We always blew whenever we detected enemy mining. The idea was to blow hard enough to shatter the blue clay, but not hard enough to let in water from the quicksand. When we sent a message back to HQ to say the charge had been blown successfully, we got rapped over the knuckles. We could all have been court martialled.

Lieutenant William J McBride, OC
No. 1 Section, 1st Australian TC

As time passed, the scheme progressed and the mines remained safe. The fundamental problem faced by the Australians now was common to all the other Allied miners in and around the curve of the Messines Ridge: how to preserve their tunnels and keep their charges intact until the day of battle – whenever that might be. A universal complication was that the Messines offensive had been meant to take place in 1916; the original galleries had not been constructed to last the extra year that was now required. Successive German blows, even distant ones,

had been weakening and threatening workings with the inrush of quicksand through fissures from the shattered ground above, at the same time increasing the water levels. It was essential to keep the galleries open, firstly for drainage to keep the charges dry, but also to make sure that leads were not broken or pinched by collapsing timbers. The tunnellers had no choice but to 'nurse' their mines until zero hour – for some charges this meant more than twelve months of guardianship. In the meantime every listening post in the upper galleries was manned around the clock, and each had one or two torpedoes to hand ready to blow at a moment's notice, should German activity be heard.

As a further precaution at Hill 60 the Australians installed a new lower level listening and fighting system. The Germans heard them building it – and blew a heavy *camouflet*.

The listener in 'B' was recovered in a few hours, but the entrance to 'A' being crushed, it was thought that the man in 'A' was done in. But when reopening and 15 feet in, his signals were heard and he was recovered at 52 feet from the junction – quite fit. This man reports that after the blow he went back to listen at the face and heard the enemy winch again at work. Also that he heard the man who was caught in 'B', signalling to the helpers.

The site of the blow appears to have been rather to the left of the junction of Berlin and 'B', and it must have been shallow to have blown out into craters. The situation of the blow was dangerously correct, and it is probable that the vertical RR [radius of rupture] or downward kick was overestimated by the enemy. The third lead to 'B' has now been picked up and the circuit is OK. So that the most serious result has been the wrecking of these galleries and their greater liability for them to come in under another blow.

The most satisfactory result: the false confidence probably given to the enemy as to the 'clearing' of this area, by our three blows in the D's [deeps], and his own, about that level. A lot of noise was made by the entombed listener in 'B' and in the reopening work.

Diary of Major R S G Stokes, Assistant
Inspector of Mines, 28 March 1917

The date of this diary entry, just over eight weeks before zero day, 7 June 1917, shows how the fortunes of the two mines at Hill 60 and the Caterpillar were still frighteningly uncertain. One of the trapped listeners had the extraordinary self-control to overcome his fears during entombment to report hearing a winch – a sure sign of an enemy shaft nearby. The warning was unambiguous: the German *Mineure* were still trying to comb the deeps.

Two specialist listeners were drafted in from the 2nd Army Mine School. Captain Pollock and Lieutenant Clarke both agreed that the German shaft was deep and was being sunk for only one reason – to find and destroy the Hill 60 and Caterpillar workings. But they also predicted that even if the direction of the enemy tunnel was accurate, at the normal German rate of progress in this geology, the two British mines which had been laid and tamped since August and October 1916, should be safe until zero day. The mines must therefore be made totally silent. All work in the deep galleries stopped and seismomicrophones were installed in the two chambers.

As zero day approached, the Germans drew ever closer. Pollock and Clarke had calculated that the *Mineure* would be well within range of being able to destroy at least charge 'A' beneath Hill 60; however, they concluded that it was unlikely that they would actually find the chambers without having any noise to detect, and therefore the mines should be safe as long as the Germans did not blow 'speculatively'. The Australians were forced to hold their breath until the last moment. The AEMMBC had replaced and maintained the cabling for the mines, tamping was complete, and firing mechanisms prepared. There was now nothing left to do in the deeps, so the tunnellers busied themselves in other work.

On 2nd June we reached Hill 60 at 10.30pm and immediately commenced the work of reinforcing our dugout and mine system. This consisted of putting struts in all galleries, in order that these sections would more effectively withstand the force of the explosion. In war nothing could be taken for granted and this measure was adopted in order to guard against a failure in the attack.

Lieutenant O H Woodward,
1st Australian TC

The Hill was a critical part of the Messines plan. It was essential that even if attacks failed in other sectors on the day, the assault on '60' must succeed; capturing the hated 'carbuncle' would at least constitute a symbolic victory. So determined were the engineers to make this happen that they simulated the entire Hill on a site near

RE HQ at Chatham, Kent, complete with trenches, railway cutting, roads – and mines, which were blown to gauge potential destruction and throw of debris.

THE WAITING GAME: MINES AND COUNTERMINES

Seventeen mines had been laid, charged and tamped by the close of 1916. Four had been completed during April and May of that year at Trench 127 and Trench 122 at the southern end of the ridge, in front of Ploegsteert Wood. Those laid during the lead up to battle in 1917 were either started later or had been damaged, either by enemy action or simple degradation. Apart from the troublesome necessity of having to tend so many 'dormant' mines, the postponement of the Messines attack from 1916 to 1917 also had a genuinely beneficial effect for the tunnellers hopes: it gave them the time for a second stab at sinking shafts in places where they had earlier failed either through lack of manpower, time or materials.

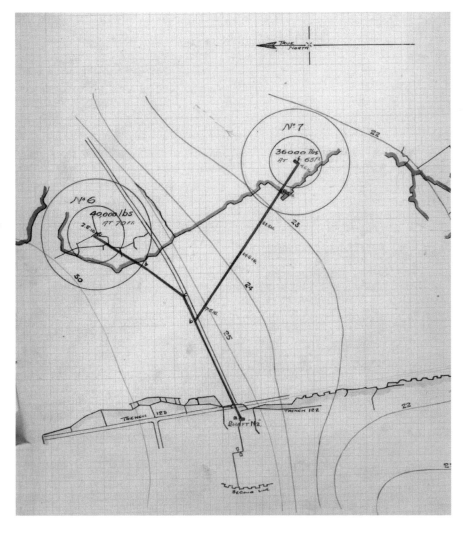

The Factory Farm mines planted from Trench 122 in front of Ploegsteert Wood. Both craters can still be seen today

Reciprocating hoisting arrangement in a German shaft for men and materials

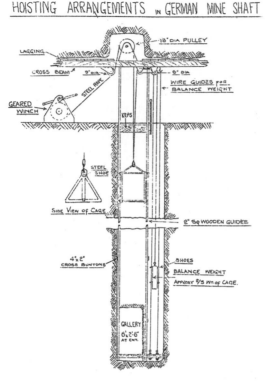

Schemes that had been abandoned were reinstated, and new ones begun. The fresh work was no less arduous, and with the Germans now on the alert, it was certainly more dangerous. However, the tunnellers knew that the more schemes they could put into action, the more disturbed the enemy would become; being so far behind and overwhelmed with work piercing the *Schwimmsande*, the enemy could also only challenge on a limited number of sites. In

Vertical view down a timber German mine shaft at Bois Quarante identical to the above plan

addition, by the autumn of 1916, the British had access to much more specialised mining equipment at the front. GHQ had recognised the tremendous endeavour and dedication required to pursue the great scheme, and had ordered that tunnelling company indents for stores should be prioritised over those of the infantry and artillery. Although timber supply continued to be intermittent, steel shaft sections, steel girders, and powered ventilators, pumps, lighting and winches were now mostly available 'from stock'.

Despite being assured of an unassailable lead in the 'mining game' the British, Australian and Canadian tunnellers feared that the *Mineure* might be sinking more and more shafts, probing all around the arc of the ridge in search of their galleries.

As summer [1916] approached we unmistakably heard sounds of enemy working. To our relief he turned out to be well above us, so would be unlikely to hear us, though we could hear him plainly. He appeared to be just in front of his own line – a point we were well past by this time – and was obviously searching for us. In three places he drove clean across our gallery; we could mark his daily progress, and would have dearly loved to have delivered him a surprise packet, as we felt we owed him a few, but this of course was out of the question as it would have given our own position away. We could only hope he had not heard us, and would remain content to search for us at his own level, but it was nervy work. It was not so bad when you could hear him working – it was when you could not hear him that it was unpleasant. You knew he was there but could not tell what he was up to.

After hunting in vain for some time he gave up and changed his tactics. He must have concluded we were deeper, so apparently worked out the most likely places for us to be going under his line, then proceeded to blow heavy charges at 50 feet depth all around these points, in the hope of catching us beneath. He blew his craters just in front of his own line, which he then consolidated. This was one of the worst phases we had to endure; each night he blew two or three charges, and all our galleries were getting badly shaken. Finally, he got us properly: one gallery was about 250 feet beyond his line, at about 90 feet below, when he blew a charge estimated at 4,000 lbs, at 40 feet clean over it. He destroyed just over 300 feet of our gallery, entombing thirteen men. We drove round the break and reopened the gallery in 6½ days – record driving – and got one man out alive. The tales of that rescue would almost form an epic on its own. We noticed however, that Fritz – methodical person – always blew between 1am and 5am, so after that we cleared all galleries during those hours and, although we were blown in twice again, avoided further casualties.

Anonymous tunneller 250 TC, 1927

The sole surviving miner from this blow at Petit Bois on 10 June 1916 was Sapper William Bedson, a miner from Cadeby Colliery near Rotherham. After the almost inconceivable horror of spending more than six days entombed sixty feet below ground in the dark surrounded by the corpses of his mates, Bedson simply spent a week in hospital and a week convalescing before being sent home. Tunnelling HQ felt he had done his bit. The grave, which had already been prepared for him, went unused. The enemy action which had precipitated Bedson's ordeal had been the first serious interruption to the Messines scheme. At the time it was not known whether the Germans had blown the heavy charge to destroy a wide area of British workings, or to create craters for better observation and defensive capability. Either way, it was

A German concrete counter-mine shaft near Petite Douve Farm, possibly serving the gallery accidentally encountered by the British in August 1916 which led to the loss of the mine

a clear warning of activity and intent. Fears would come to a head later at Petite Douve Farm near Messines – the only charge completely lost to enemy countermining.

On 24 August 1916 a spur off a deep gallery beneath the farm, one of three potential targets for this scheme, ran into an unsuspected enemy tunnel. At the time one mine, a 50,000-pound (22,727-kg) charge of Ammonal, was already in position, wired up and tamped, and a second, from a left spur off the gallery, had been chambered and was in the process of being loaded. The British had decisions to make. Concealment of their breakthrough was clearly impossible. The choice was to blow their fully charged mine immediately, or try to destroy the German counter-workings. If they blew the mine it would both give away the deep offensive scheme in the area – the Germans did not know there was a mine ready and could of course not be sure that it existed without physically finding the evidence – and also guarantee an intensification in the enemy search for more hostile mines. Blowing early would not enhance the British position tactically as the mine was planted beneath the enemy support line; the explosion would probably result in a crater that the British, as always, would suffer considerable losses in trying to capture, a skirmish they would also probably lose due to the superiority of German crater fighting. The most likely outcome was that the Germans would suffer casualties to the blow, but immediately convert the crater into an even

Perfectly preserved stepped incline to the Petit Bois mine and dugout system at Vandamme Farm

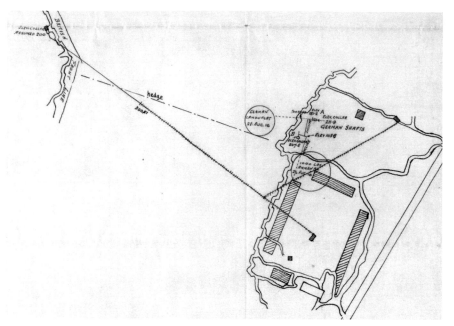

The 'lost' Petite Douve mine scheme showing German and British camouflets and destroyed (hatched) galleries. The mine beneath the courtyard was fully charged; the spur gallery can be seen to no. 2 chamber which was finished and for loading. A third mine was also planned nearby

more formidable strongpoint. Given the choices, the only course available was to try and destroy the enemy workings underground and hope the mine could be saved.

Two carefully calculated *camouflet* charges of 500 pounds (227 kg) were blown in the left spur. This size of charge was calculated to destroy the enemy shaft without damaging the big mine just seventy metres away, and at first the British thought they had succeeded – smoke was seen to rise just above the spot where the shaft was thought to originate, a normally reliable sign of damage. But the enemy workings were more robust than thought. The shaft survived. On 27 August the *Mineure* were on the offensive again blowing a heavy medium-depth mine in no man's land before draining a large area of nearby trenches into the shaft of the original countermine. The Petite Douve mine again survived the blow, but investigation showed the leads to be severed, and galleries smashed beyond repair. Abandonment of the original gallery was the only choice. A later attempt to reach and rewire the Petite Douve charge from a new drive made rapid progress but ultimately ran out of time. Although the *Pioniere* never actually knew that a mine had been planted, they had scotched the scheme.

THE GATHERING MOMENTUM

As the Battle of the Somme drew to a close in November 1916, the Germans, desperate to break the British underground offensive in the Salient, poured more trained men into the

sector. The full scale of the British mining offensive was still unknown to them, but during the coming winter – and indeed all the way up to the critical date of 7 June 1917 – the complete scheme could have been rendered totally useless, and with little tactical loss to the German forces, by the simple expedient mentioned earlier of pulling troops back from the existing front and support lines into reserve positions. Such repositioning would have caused insurmountable difficulties for the tunnellers. Mines would have had to be de-tamped, undetonated and unloaded, galleries and firing leads extended, and new chambers built, charged, detonated and re-tamped. The increased labour required to extend the workings would have forced the termination of the many fresh schemes underway, and the noise of the extra work would almost certainly have drawn hostile underground attention. Especially if left until the last moment, a German withdrawal could have rendered all the many months of effort, stress and gruelling struggle totally worthless. Just 150 metres would have been sufficient.

Such an eventuality was obviously the worst fear of all on the Staff at British GHQ. The blow to the morale of Plumer's 2nd Army – especially to the tunnelling companies – would have been crushing, and the outcome of the coming battle would certainly have been very different. However, whilst the British held their breath for month after month, they had no inkling that repeated infantry requests to pull back were being ignored at German GHQ.

All efforts to sink timber shafts at Spanbroekmolen were futile. The single timber shaft at Backhof [Ontario Farm] was almost as bad, and progressed slowly. The two at Weinachsthof, both about 20 metres deep, were constantly on the point of flooding. This meant either abandoning the old timber procedures in favour of light concrete shafts, and sinking them in the front lines, or giving up the front lines altogether. But at that time the tactical value of the Wytschaete–Mesen Ridge still appeared so great that no one wanted to abandon the positions. It was only recognised in the coming great defensive battles [Third Ypres] that the inflexible retention of high ground, which appeared to be tactically significant, was absurd.

Oberstleutnant Otto Füsslein,
Kommandeur des Mineure,
4th German Army

In seeking to hinder British, Australian and Canadian tunnellers, all of whom were playing their part beneath the ridge by the end of 1916, German efforts were not restricted to counter-mining. Low flying aircraft were sent out to examine the forward areas for any signs of tunnelling works, communicating all sightings of blue (grey-green to the Germans) clay to the artillery.

At the Weihnachtshof we had laboriously sunk two timber-lined shafts, Heinrich I and II, into the clay and were already quite well advanced with the galleries. We heard no sound from the enemy, but the grey-green sandbags around his trenches told us that he was there.

Oberstleutnant Otto Füsslein,
Kommandeur des Mineure,
4th German Army

Having been identified, suspect sites were then subjected to persistent strafes from heavy German trench mortars – *Minenwerfer* – seeking to destroy shafts and dugouts. However, the British had also foreseen this difficulty and, thanks again to the postponement of the battle, had been granted time to sink auxiliary shafts precisely to counter the 'Minnie' threat. As 1917 dawned the tunnellers were taking every conceivable precaution to protect their existing and new work. Short of a German withdrawal or an offensive overrunning the British mine systems, it began to look as if only bad luck could halt the progress of Norton-Griffiths' great 'earthquake'.

Some mines enjoyed no interruptions at all from enemy action; but they still had the vagaries of geology to cope with. In December 1915 250 Tunnelling Company had begun an offensive drive against another farm which hit every form of problem except that of enemy action, including inrushes of sand, mud, and water, and the hindrance of powerfully swelling ground.

We were going for Peckham Farm. We had camouflaged dugouts and got through the sand fairly easily, sinking the shaft down 70 or 80 feet and then drove in the direction of the front line. We used ladders to go up and down the shaft and a pulley to haul out the sandbags of excavated sand.

We drove in about 1,500 feet and then drove left and right in a Y fork. We were then beyond the enemy lines and deeper than 80 feet because although we kept level, the

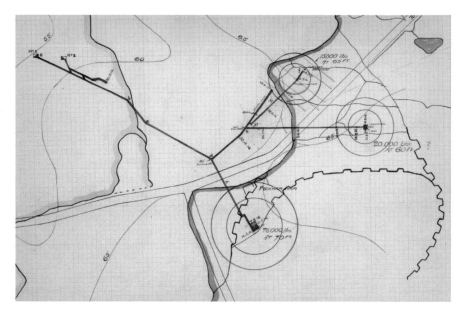

ground above rose. The walls were timber lined; it was clay and we kept fairly dry. We had electric light part of the way and then it was candles. We used the clay-kicking method; the tunnel measured 5 feet by 3 feet but got smaller towards the end, and we were digging from the end of 1915 until nearly the end of 1916. Then the charge was laid, the leads were taken to the surface and we stood by waiting for 1917. We had expected the big blow in 1916. The men all came out but we kept a guard on the entrance.

Then the tunnel collapsed and the leads were broken – we knew because the circuits failed, so we had to dig a new tunnel beside the old one to reach the charge, and take new leads to the surface. We didn't hear anything of the Germans at Peckham but always felt there was a danger of being blown and we were constantly listening with geophones.

Captain Haydn Rees, OC no. 3 Section, 250
TC, RE

What Captain Rees fails to mention is that two mines had been laid at Peckham, one in each arm of the Y, and a well advanced third offensive gallery had also been abandoned on 19 July 1916. The second charge of 20,000 pounds (9,070 kg), completed on 6 September was irretrievably lost in the great collapse; it was never recovered and today lies beneath the 'new' farm next to the vast 1917 crater.

Immediately adjacent to Peckham was Spanbroekmolen, where the story was very different. The Germans recognised the hilltop strongpoint as an obvious target for hostile

Plan of the three proposed Peckham mines. Two were planted, the 'big one' was blown on 7 June, the second (20,000-pound) charge remains, whilst the gallery for a third (top) was unfinished

attention, and several shafts were sunk in an attempt to thwart the tunnellers. But the British had made a flying start: 91,000 pounds (41,000 kg) of Ammonal had already been laid and tamped by 171 TC by the end of June 1916 – almost a full year before it would be needed. As no work was in progress there were no sounds to indicate the mine's existence. All remained quiet until February 1917.

It had been decided to place a second mine beneath another nearby redoubt known as Rag Point, and work had been going well. An underground incline off the original gallery had taken the new drive forward and deeper towards the target when the Germans blew a heavy speculative *camouflet*. It actually shook the self-assurance of the tunnellers more than it did their galleries – after eight months of progress they now knew the Germans might be on to them. From that moment strain began to escalate. A week later another blow damaged the new gallery and part of the incline; on 3 March yet another broke the leads to the main Spanbroekmolen mine. After so long without problems this was a depressing and alarming setback; 171 TC were forced to drive a 'by-pass' tunnel to make repairs, just as at neighbouring Peckham.

And then there was more unexpected misfortune. During their frenetic attempt to rescue

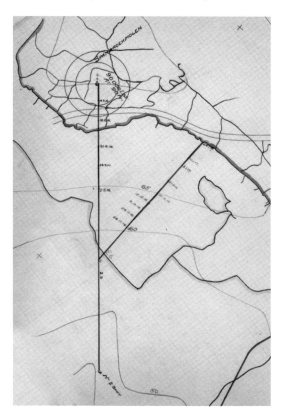

The British Spanbroekmolen mine gallery with the failed spur branching off to the right towards Rag Point

the mine, the tunnellers driving the by-pass gallery pierced a gas-suffused area of clay shattered by the German *camouflet*. The broken ground lay almost 500 metres from the shaft; rescue was too slow in arriving and the deadly carbon monoxide claimed three lives. A 'gas block' had to be built and the drive restarted to 'nip around' the deadly patch of ground. Time was now getting short at Spanbroekmolen; it would require a full five weeks' clay-kicking to reach the lost mine, and mend the damage. The work was completed just hours before zero on 7 June.

In other places the timing was almost as tight as at Spanbroekmolen: the Ontario Farm mine, deep beneath the wet alluvial soils of the Steenebeek valley, was finished with two days to spare on 5 June; in the central sector, St Eloi's huge 95,600-pound charge (about 50 tonnes – the attached infantry carried up an average of four tonnes of Ammonal per night) was completed on 28 May, whilst farther to the south, the leads to the Maedelstede Farm mine were finally connected on 2 June. The tightest timing of all was on the southernmost part of the battlefront close to Ploegsteert Wood. At Factory Farm repairs and alterations to the number six right mine from Trench 122 were completed just twenty minutes before the blow.

MAN AND MACHINE

Several attempts at mechanised tunnelling were made in 1915–16. Electric and air driven hand-held power tools devised by the Munitions Inventions Department were regularly tested at Chatham. They were not designed to drive the whole offensive gallery, but only the initial portion where the workings were still out of listening range of the enemy. None were successful and none were ever used offensively at the front; it was also found that experienced clay-kickers were able to match and often exceed the driving rate of machines – and they were considerably more reliable. However, the age of the tunnelling machine was not over; with a man like Norton-Griffiths in charge the unexpected was always to be expected, and as 1915 drew to a close he hatched another idea that raised every eyebrow at GHQ.

Early in 1916 I met Norton-Griffiths again and he became greatly interested in the work going on at our shaft position at a place known in trench language as SP 13. Our shaft was down 70 feet in the blue clay and we were 500 yards from the enemy lines, our objective being a salient position known as Petit Bois. Norton-Griffiths must have thought of a more ambitious work making use of our shaft, his objective being the village of Wytschaete on top of the ridge, estimated distance of tunnel required was 15 to 16 hundred yards. Experts were sent over from London to inspect the blue clay formation and the shaft. The machine [a tunnelling machine] was designed for our use and was made and sent over to us with a team of experts. An air compressor was installed at the shaft head for working the machine underground. All our activities at SP 13 were on the secret list and very hush-hush, certainly all mining operations were secret, but this was something of special importance. Our great worry was that the enemy would hear the exhaust from the compressor on still clear nights and begin to shell us out of our position. We drove the tunnel out with a 'head-shield' before the breakdown occurred. We couldn't go on because the clay swelled so fast it seized the machine. This condition put an end to all our hopes of ever reaching our objective within a reasonable time and the scheme had to be abandoned.

Captain Cecil Cropper, OC 250 TC, RE

The appliance was a Stanley Heading Machine. Originally designed for use in coal mines to drive roads and headings, the huge machine ran on rails, had flanged wheels like a locomotive and was powered by compressed air fed via pipes from a two-cylinder engine located remotely in a dugout about fifty metres from the shaft. A pair of rotating blades screwed their way into the clay face cutting a circular tunnel about 2.4 metres in diameter whilst the body of the machine was held in place by jacks tightened against the roof; after the blades had 'cut a ring' the jacks were slackened and the machine edged forward

whilst a timbering team installed a specially designed interlocking oak lining behind the monster – the whole contraption weighed around seven tonnes.

Being used to the harder sandstones and shales of coal-bearing rocks, the Stanley objected to the Flanders clay. Not only did the machine refuse to dig in the required direction, constantly wanting to 'dive', but each time it was stopped for maintenance or there was a delay in moving the apparatus forward for the next cut, the newly-exposed clay walls had time to swell, and gripped the whole contraption like a vice. It was no simple matter to release by hand from the cloying caress of the dense Paniselian and Ypresian clays.

Bottom left: A Whitaker tunnelling machine at work in the Folkestone cliffs in 1923. This same machine had been used beneath the trenches of the Western Front

Below: A successful looking German machine driving headings for dugouts

Bottom right: Another design for a machine capable of coping with Flanders clay. This model was never used in action

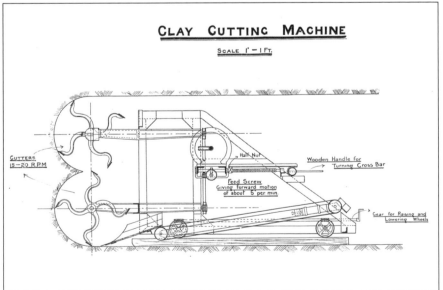

CLAY CUTTING MACHINE

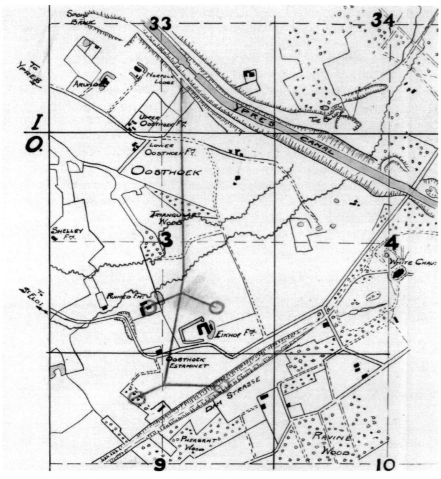

The proposed Eikhof Farm/Damstrasse mine scheme near the Bluff where the Canadians unsuccessfully employed the Whittaker tunnelling machine. German front line shown in red

June 1917. British (red) and captured German galleries at the Bluff. Closed up faces and unkempt galleries show the lack of Pioniere *mining effort in the sector at this time*

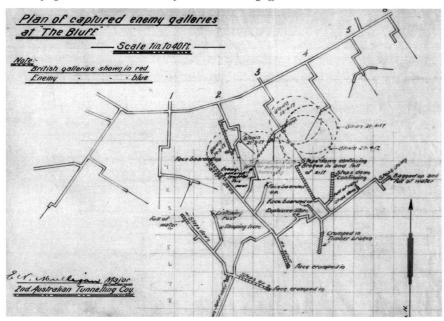

The tunnellers persevered, sweating and cursing, but after driving around thirty-six metres, both time and patience ran out. The machine had broken down three times, and enough was enough. It was abandoned where it had last come to grief, pinned in place by the blue clay. The two Petit Bois mines were successfully completed by Cropper's reliable West Country clay-kickers. The Stanley Heading Machine still lies where it stubbornly gave out – thirty-six metres beneath the Messines Ridge, almost directly beneath the road running past Vandamme Farm today.

The Stanley was not the only tunnelling machine to be tried at Messines. Since the spring of 1915 the Bluff sector, adjacent to the Ypres–Comines canal midway between Hill 60 and St Eloi, had been the scene of some of the most intensive mine and surface warfare in the Salient. Today's visitor will see many a crater at the Bluff, but none that can be attributed to 7 June 1917. A glance at the post-Messines mine map shows the sector to form a distinct and perplexing gap in the great British mine scheme. The gap should not have existed, and was to have been plugged with not one or two mines, but five 'big ones', four grouped around Eikhof Farm and the long, straight sunken lane known as the Damstrasse – the driveway to the infamous White Château, and the fifth in adjacent Ravine Wood. The latter scheme, which Haig was keen to pursue, was dropped by consensus at HQ, but the White Château sector which was recognised as being one of the toughest nuts to crack, being heavily defended with many ridge-top concrete emplacements and machine gun positions, was critical. Four big mines would create the perfect launch for the attack, and a tunnelling machine would be deployed to help plant them.

The Whittaker was a machine devised for softer ground than the Stanley. It was installed in a wave of optimism in early March 1917 to swiftly cut an offensive tunnel from the safety of 'Lock Hospital' located at Lock 6 on the Ypres–Comines canal, to a point beneath the British lines some 400 metres away; the final approach gallery beneath no man's land to the German support and reserve trenches was to be left to the silent skills of the clay-kickers. But the geological gremlins intervened once more. By 21 March only six metres of circular gallery had been cut and timbered by the Canadian tunnellers.

The borer is still standing, while the gallery is being carried on to find easier clay. The ground below about 80 or 90 feet has been very heavy – although normally hard, it is full of small slips with polished surfaces, dipping in all directions. The blades of the cutter... disintegrate the clay in blocks so rapidly that the necessary steady slicing action is impossible, and the face breaks away in lumps (up to several hundred pounds) and rotation is checked. There is no trouble with the gallery behind the cutter before the lining is put in. It is smooth and regular. When the ground was good at the beginning of the run, the progress was excellent – one ring being cut in 8 minutes, though of course any unit of time of less than a month may give a false impression of a continuous running machine.

Maxwell [Major M W Maxwell, OC 1st Canadian TC] says the machine could not now be run out of the gallery, although there is only 20 feet of it completed. He considers he has proved the machine capable of doing all that was expected of it in suitable ground, and is a little more hopeful than North and Spencer [both also 1st Canadian TC officers] of making it succeed in the Lock Hospital job. North is beginning to feel the expenditure of officers and men on work not helping probable operations. There is indeed no real optimist on the job and this is a serious factor with a new plant like this. The...borer needs a Norton-Griffiths behind it – all the time.

Diary of Major R S G Stokes,
Assistant Inspector of Mines.

The mines were never completed, with tragic consequences. It was in this sector especially that the attacking troops proved the efficacy of the preliminary mine attacks elsewhere on the battlefront. On 7 June casualties amongst the 47th (London) Division charged with taking the Damstrasse and White Château, were considerably greater than in those units who had attacked in sectors where mines were used. The post-battle examination of German workings in the area must have infuriated the Canadians; it showed that underground opposition would have been very weak if not entirely non-existent throughout the intended area of mine attack; they could probably have ignored the Whittaker altogether and clay-kicked their way to the target with impunity – and with time to spare.

TENSION – THE LONG WAIT

As weeks turned to months in 1917, a clear defensive atmosphere was growing throughout the tunnelling companies of the 2nd Army. It had been a long haul – something was bound to go wrong right at the last minute: a German withdrawal? An attack? Perhaps the enemy had known the plans all along and was deliberately waiting until the last moment to pull back, advance, or blow something big themselves?

In the run up to zero day British trench raids were carried out to destroy potential German countermines and gather information from prisoners. All reported complete success, which comforted the tunnellers, although later comparison of British reports with captured German ones describing the same raids revealed how, in war, the attacking force tends to overestimate their accomplishments. The tunnellers were no different.

Major Hutchison, a New Zealander and OC of 174 Coy, was always boasting of the damage

A top secret German map showing locations of countermine shafts along the Messines battlefront

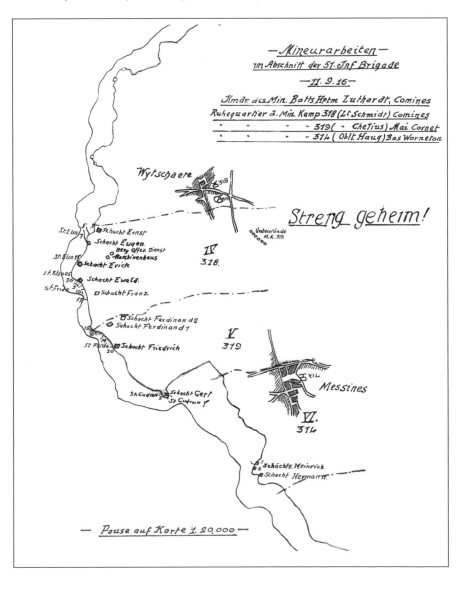

his mines had done to the Boche. A couple of months later we captured the German diaries; they said that the only casualty they suffered was one man accidentally shot through the penis by a soldier in the trenches!

Captain Alan Reid, 176 TC, RE

In the weeks before zero the German Army were fully aware that something grand and significant was afoot beneath the ridge, but still had no inkling of the full scale of the scheme. Trench raids to capture British prisoners, collect information and destroy anything resembling mines and dugouts were made on several occasions, but long experience had taught the British another curious German habit: they noticed that such raids were always preceded by a 'dose of hate' by field guns and *Minenwerfer*. This disagreeable but helpful sign gave the tunnellers the opportunity to camouflage entrances to shaft chambers, deliberately kept small and unobtrusive anyway, with sandbags. A small store of bags was kept near each opening especially for this purpose, and teams of men were always on hand to make the entrances look like just another section of trench wall. But the German trench raids were still a worry. If deep mining was suspected, the enemy could easily damage the scheme by blowing some medium-depth heavy charges in no man's land. Every ruse was employed to put them off the scent. In some places new camouflaged stepped inclines were connected to the workings and the original shaft heads made to look derelict and decayed. At the head of every incline was an explosive charge which could be blown in an emergency, sealing off the tunnel below, and hand bells were conveniently kept in shafts and stairways to warn those below of an enemy incursion.

But there were some things which were entirely beyond the control of the tunnellers. On 28 November 1916 a British deserter in the Ploegsteert Wood sector might have almost caused the loss of one system.

Someone's batman, I think George Dickson's, got too familiar with the jug containing the rum issue in the dugouts at the mine at Trench 123. He was put under open arrest, and sometime during the night disappeared, and the next thing we heard of him was when the Germans reported him as wounded and prisoner of war. He evidently spilled all he knew, as not long after, one afternoon, the Germans put down a terrific box barrage on that part of the front. I was off shift back at the dugout in Plugstreet Wood but I didn't like the sound of it, so I decided to go up the line. I got up to the mine in Trench 121, which was on the edge of the barrage, and tried to work my way along the front line to the mine at 123; but the barrage was so intense that there wasn't a chance of getting through alive, so I came back to 121.

Soon we could see the Germans coming over the ridge at 12, about half a mile away, too far for us to do anything about it. They didn't stay long, and then the barrage stopped, and I hiked up to 123. There wasn't a man left alive in the trench, and I was expecting the worst when I got to the mine, and I was very pleasantly surprised to find all the men who were on shift huddled in the shaft house, scared to death, but safe. We found remnants of potato masher bombs within 10 feet of the shaft, and the explosive they had brought over to blow the shaft.

Captain Harry R Urie, 3rd Canadian TC

Had Dickson's batman, Sapper Bromley, spilled the beans? Tension mounted. There was little more that tunnelling commanders could do to ensure success; every possible precaution had been taken, even to the point of toasting the brooding mines – underground.

We drank champagne in the chambers under the German line – in the mine chambers just before we closed them up [with tamping]. General Harvey was in on one to drink success to the mine. We would sit in a little passage which was empty of explosive and drink champagne from glasses from Company HQ. We were four section commanders, used to get through four bottles of champagne, 3 francs a bottle.

Captain H M Hudspeth, 171 TC, RE

A tour of duty in the tunnels was normally four days in and four days out; as time went by, with casualties and increased demands to expand mining activities, this was increased to six in and two out. Tunnelling company OCs and section commanders were given as much leave as possible to help them cope with the endless and mounting strain of responsibility, work and incessant danger. They already received more leave than their infantry colleagues – a fortnight at least every three months was the aim – and by mid-March 1917 many had enjoyed an extended break: a whole month away from their shafts and tunnels.

According to Stokes it was still not enough. Many officers, such as Lieutenant John Westacott at Mount Sorrel, had turned to drink to control their nerves; a mug of rum was required before Westacott could rouse himself each morning and face the stresses of the day underground. The problem was far from uncommon. Drunkenness was to be the most frequent cause of field punishment in the tunnelling companies. The tension created by the huge scheme at Messines was crushing and inescapable, and particularly after the postponement of the attack from 1916 to 1917, it seemed to go on and on. Most men returning from leave looked, in the words of the day, 'no better for it'. After a full thirty-five days away from the front Major A W Davis, OC 3rd Canadian TC, was noticeably still affected.

[Davis is] not fresh. Seems to have lost all his push and interest – now only waiting for the end of the war. His thoughts are thoroughly jumpy.

War Diary, Major R S G Stokes, RE, Assistant Inspector of Mines

Eighteen months of toil on the same mission – a mission which would be over in a matter of moments on the push of a plunger or flick of a switch, and upon whose success so many lives depended, left the nerves of every tunneller ragged. Davis may have had more reason for exhaustion than most, having been with 177 TC in the early days before the Canadian tunnellers were formed, but his nervous condition was clearly evident in the orders he gave for the blowing of the Factory Farm mine on the southern boundary of the Messines battlefield.

None of us blew our own mines. We were switched around, I don't know why. I blew the Factory Farm mine but I had been working on this mine for months before. Before the Messines blow I had been working on preparing the mine for a year to eighteen months. Everyone was champing to get the job. There were 26 officers in the company, all anxious to do the blow. It was quite a suicide job – we had to blow from the bottom of the shaft, which was probably 75 feet deep. One day the OC sent for us in pairs. Myself and Dickson on our mine and two others on our left. He didn't ask us if we were prepared to do it – he just told us. He then drew a map showing how they had put an inclined way 30 feet down, where the dugout was, and how the main tunnel went out under the German second line.

Lieutenant B C Hall, 3rd Canadian TC

Fortunately for Hall and Dickson, Davis' suicidal directive to blow from the shaft bottom was amended by another officer during the afternoon before the attack. The two men must have gasped with relief, but the alterations meant a race against time.

A day or two before they put a 6-inch armour-piercing shell clean through our escape gallery. There was nobody in the tunnel at the time. It was an exit from 30 feet down the shaft to the trench – just an extra escape. [Sergeant] Beer was trumps there. He and I got some timber down and got in and stopped it. We had a hell of a job. If we had left it, it [running sand] would have filled up the shaft and we wouldn't have been able to get to the leads at the bottom.

At 4.0 pm in the afternoon before the blow Captain Urie [Second in Command, 3rd Canadian TC] came up and gave us our sealed orders. They said 'To lengthen all leads, test with a Wheatstone Bridge and blow from the top of the shaft in the trench at 3.10'. The change of orders was because of the risk that everything would fall in on me at the bottom of the shaft – which it did. Everything collapsed – filled up to the top with running sand. At 4 in the afternoon I started work on the leads, branching them all and bringing them up to the top of the shaft. It was 2.50 am when I got everything tested up and finished. I had the sergeant with a watch to warn me, but I told him not to keep nagging me.

Lieutenant B C Hall, 3rd Canadian TC

Finishing at 2.50 am gave Hall and Beer exactly twenty minutes to catch their breath. Soon the waiting game would be over, and the aspirations of thousands of dog-tired tunnellers to blow the enemy to kingdom come would be realised at 03.10 hours, 7 June 1917 – zero hour for the opening of the Battle of Messines.

Chapter X

MOUNTAINS IN THE SKY: MESSINES AND AFTER

It was now becoming increasingly evident that the day was at hand, guns were massing on a scale never before dreamed... We knew that this attack was but the first move in an offensive on a very large scale, and was vital to its success. But we also knew that the higher command considered the taking of the ridge to be an extremely hard nut to crack, and, therefore, were placing great hopes in the value of our mines. More than we dared do ourselves, for many of our leads were rapidly deteriorating, each day showed a fainter response to our testing sets, also it was possible that our chambers had completely collapsed... allowing water into the explosive, rendering it useless. However, we had done our best. We felt that our much dreamed of mine offensive would be a fiasco, and our long months of effort end but in failure. Had that happened there could have been no disappointment so bitter.

Anonymous 250 TC officer, 1927

The opening crescendo in the early hours of 7 June 1917 with the eruption of the great mines promised to be a spectacular 'show'. High-ranking guests, including the Commmander-in-Chief, Field Marshal Sir Douglas Haig, and the press had been invited to witness the moment from the safety of specially-built dugouts on Kemmel Hill. Expectation of great things of the tunnellers by GHQ had been almost tyrannical, and they were not to be disappointed. German defences had been 'softened-up' by artillery for several days before the assault. For the moment of attack itself the greatest artillery concentration of the war to date had been drawn up and was ready to blaze. The mines were to be the signal for the guns. As the hands crept slowly round the clock on the eve of battle, final arrangements were being made.

6.6.17. 6pm. Went to 171 Coy HQ and picked up Major Hudspeth, proceeding to HQ 36th Div. Kemmel Dugouts, to arrange about synchronising watches. Were stopped at IX Corps boundary by sentry. My pass satisfactory, but sentry stated it would not cover Major Hudspeth (who knew nothing of the matter and had no pass). I pointed out urgency of Major H. proceeding – road control firm – Major H. could not proceed. Orders were definite. Found out in course of discussion that anyone could walk in. Hudspeth alighted, walked past the post, and got into car again 20 yards further along. The restrictions related simply and solely to vehicles and not persons, who could walk in anywhere.

War Diary, Major R S G Stokes,
Assistant Inspector of Mines, 6 June 1917

The preparation for the attack, coordinating the blows with the movements of the infantry and the artillery barrage, had been considered countless times during the preceding months. It was a knotty problem; the British Army – indeed no army in history – had ever carried out a mine attack like this, and the results were simply a matter of educated guesswork.

Prior to the firing of the mines it was necessary to frame such instructions to the assaulting troops as would obviate casualties resulting from the effect of the enormous concentration of high explosive at the depth of 70 to 100 feet below the surface. There was no information to be obtained from history as no military mining had ever dealt with so many large charges for one operation. Our own experience was limited to the effect of the mines at St Eloi in [March] 1916 and to the few isolated mines on the front of the Battle of the Somme. The following regulations were drawn up:

No man to be within 200 yards of the charge until 20 seconds after the mine was sprung.

All trenches and surface dugouts within 300 yards of the charge to be vacated at the moment of firing, and all men to be well down behind the parados, and well clear of any parapets which might collapse.

All tunnelled dugouts and subways within a radius of 400 yards to be vacated at the moment of firing.

All old brick buildings, walls and damaged trees within 500 yards to be avoided at the moment of firing.

The bottom of craters to be avoided by the assaulting troops. Any work of consolidation to be confined to the top 10 feet of the lip to avoid poisoning from mine gas.

> Brigadier General R N Harvey,
> Inspector of Mines

On the day before the 'blow' all but the Factory Farm mines were ready. The tunnellers spent their time checking and double-checking that leads were still sound, keeping every pump going until the last possible moment. By now all of them knew the precise time of zero hour.

Wednesday 6th June seemed to be a day during which one's nerves seemed to be strained to the breaking point. The chief task of the day was to extend the mine leads to the firing dugout, which was located in Bensham Road support trench, distant about 375 yards from the Hill 60 mine and 462 yards from the Caterpillar Mine. At about 12.30 am on the morning of 7th June the extension of the leads was completed. I approached the task of final testing with a feeling of intense excitement. With the Wheatstone Bridge [a device used to test resistance of cables and confirm continuity of electrical current] on an improvised table, I set out to check the leads and as each one in turn proved correct I felt greatly relieved. At 1.15 am all was correct, and as there was still about 2 hours to go before Zero it was essential to keep taking resistance tests as rapidly as possible in order to insure that nothing happened in the closing stages of the drama about to be enacted.

> Captain O H Woodward, 1st Australian TC

Inspected firing arrangements at Spanbroekmolen and Kruistraat, which were

Sapper officer and NCO using a galvanometer to test continuity and resistivity of current in mine leads before blowing

excellent. Satisfied myself that in case of failure of power (owing to effects of earth tremor of other mines), the exploder could be used within 10 or 15 seconds.

Went out to point of observation (at head of incline above firing point) in support line at 2.45am. From that time up zero minus one minute, there was no trench sound to suggest any unusual condition, very few lights going up – a few machine guns for two minutes at minus five – normal occasional shelling. At about 3 minus 9 a plane came up fairly close to our line.

War Diary, Major R S G Stokes,
Assistant Inspector of Mines, 7 June 1917

The attack had been planned to coincide with daybreak so that attacking troops would not be moving forward in darkness. Over one hundred infantry battalions from ten divisions – English, Irish, Scottish, Australian and Kiwi – were waiting to play their part.

Daybreak on the morning of the 7 June was beautiful, and at 2 am everything assumed an atmosphere of peace and quietness as our guns eased down, in order to lure the enemy to keep quiet. As all the attacking infantry were lying out on the surface, shelling by the enemy was not desired. The enemy proved obliging, and during the last hour before zero a deathly stillness reigned, broken only by the dull, sleepy drone of heavy shells going across to the back areas. At 2 am all troops were withdrawn from the dugout and mine systems and posted in their position for the attack.

At last, when hope was almost dead, orders came to stand to. About midnight on the 6 June we assembled, were given the zero hour, synchronised our watches and departed to our posts. The hours to 3.10 am, the appointed time, seemed interminable. The artillery preparation which, for days, had been intense, had died down and the night was comparatively quiet – strangely so, it seemed, after the continued heavy bombardment of the previous days. How those hours dragged till 3 o'clock came; breathlessly we watched the minute hand crawl towards the ten minutes, then, with white faces, we strained our eyes towards the enemy line, which had become visible in the grey dawn. It was zero hour.

Yet in all this quietness there was wave upon wave of infantry ready to leap into action at the moment the mines exploded. Thousands

of artillerymen stood at attention, lanyard in hand ready to pull. Just before zero there shot up from the enemy lines a few star shells which illuminated no man's land, and the German sentry probably felt relieved that his searching gaze discovered nothing out of the ordinary.

Lieutenant O H Woodward,
1st Australian TC

At 3.00 am Major Stokes was in precisely the location that another officer had wished to be – supervising the Spanbroekmolen mine.

I had the very good fortune to see the whole of the mines go up that night on the Messines–Wytschaete Ridge. I had hoped very, very much that I would push the switch in the mine that blew up Spanbroekmolen in which I had been concerned with the chambering, loading and detonating. Instead I was ordered to get up on Kemmel Hill that night and act as official observer for all the Tunnelling Companies. When zero came my anxiety was that some of the mines had been sitting in extremely wet ground for nearly a year, and the explosive was ammonal which doesn't go off when its wet; it was in soldered waterproof tins – but we wondered how they'd fared.

Lieutenant Brian Frayling, 171 TC, RE

South of Spanbroekmolen, and close to Ploegsteert Wood at Factory Farm, Lieutenants Hall and Dickson of the 3rd Canadian Tunnelling Company, together with Sergeant Beer, had finally completed the extension of leads to the surface – but it had been touch and go.

A Lt Dickson was with me – he was very ill, I think he had got gassed, and was unable to do anything. We had each worn a gas mask out by eating through the sides. There was gas all day every day. All we could do was lift our masks up and poke bits of boiled egg in for meals and the same for drink. We had a watch which was used in blowing the mine. It had an artillery number, 40275. All 19 mines had watches; they were synchronised and we were given corrections. Mine was 3.10 and 13 seconds – meaning the time was 3.10 in the morning and I had to wait 13 seconds after this time before I blew. They all had different corrections. The weather was normal – no rain. We were all on our own. The infantry were back 400 yards. I had no protection over my head, we just blew from the open trench.

I connected one small battery up which I knew wouldn't blow – it was a 60 volt battery – for the sergeant, a wonderful little chap. I said 'You can have a go sergeant, when I do'. There were two wires, making one circuit, going into my exploder. If they had failed I would have put on another set of two. I had twelve sets altogether, which gave me plenty of spares in case the first set failed.

Lieutenant B C Hall, 3rd Canadian TC

1ST SAPPER: "Hello! Is that you, Jim?"
2ND SAPPER: "No! Is that Dick?"
1ST SAPPER: "No!"
2ND SAPPER: "Well, I'm blowed! It's neither of us, then!!"

At the opposite end of the battlefield to Plugstreet, at the long detested Hill 60, it was Australians who nervously contemplated the scene.

It is difficult to describe that last half hour. A beautiful clear starlit night – as calm a night from a bombardment point of view as had ever existed on that much contested front. An occasional Verey light falling like a bright meteorite and a less occasional crack of a rifle.

'How are you feeling?'
'Fine, thank you, Sir.'
'This is our great occasion!'
'Yes, Sir.'
Still eight minutes, still clear outside. One gun fires and then silence.
'When do you get leave?'
'Next week with luck.'

Only five minutes now. All quiet. Wonder what Fritz is doing? Will he beat us to it? Has he heard about it and withdrawn?

'Get ready boys. One minute only.'
Someone asks: 'Can I have this switch Major, when its over, for a souvenir?' 40 seconds 'Yes, you can and you other two can have the others.'
'What about the watch, Major?'
20 seconds to go
'That is mine'
10 seconds…

Lieutenant J MacD Royle,
1st Australian TC

At 2.25 am I made the last resistance test, and then made the final connections for firing the mines. This was rather a nerve-wracking task as one began to feel the strain, and wonder whether the leads were correctly connected up. Just before 3 am General Lambert took up his position in the firing dugout. It was his responsibility to give the order 'FIRE'. Watch in hand he stood there, and in a silence that could almost be felt he said 'Five minutes to go'. I again finally checked up the leads, and Lieutenants Royle and Bowry stood with an exploder at their feet ready to fire should the dynamo fail. Then the General, in what seemed interminable periods, called out, 'Three minutes to go, Two to go – one to go – 45 seconds to go – 20 seconds to go – 10 seconds to go – and then 9, 8, 7, 6, 5, 4, 3, 2, 1, – FIRE!'

Lieutenant O H Woodward,
1st Australian TC

Left: The minor hazards of gas

Standard RE exploder (large size)

The three Kruistraat mines which were planned to neutralise German opposition in front, support and reserve lines

I told the sergeant not to do anything until he saw me pump, then he could do what he liked. We were standing up, I had my exploder between my legs and my watch in my hand on a strap. I had one hand on the plunger and the other holding my watch. The sergeant was behind me – out of the way for safety. I gave him a warning when the time was coming up: 'We've only a minute to go!' I had my eyes on the small second hand – had to count those thirteen seconds after 3.10. It was a very tense 13 seconds. I was too busy to be scared but conscious that this was a big moment. No rats in the dugout – the gas had got them all. I had great difficulty in keeping my gasmask eyepieces clean to see the watch. When the watch came round I said 'DOWN!' and we both flew clean up in the air. The wind came up the shaft and corrugated iron came out from everywhere. We were blown about 20 feet along the trench and ended up in a communication trench. The sergeant was still behind me, dazed – he was still pumping and saying something like 'Have mercy on me'. He still had the whole little box with him; mine, a big job, was where I left it.

Lieutenant B C Hall,
3rd Canadian TC at Trench 127.

Suddenly, all hell broke loose. It was indescribable. In the pale light it appeared as if the whole enemy line had begun to dance, then, one after another, huge tongues of flame shot hundreds of feet into the air, followed by dense columns of smoke, which flattened out at the top like gigantic mushrooms. From some craters were discharged tremendous showers of sparks rivalling anything ever conceived in the way of fireworks. The whole scene was majestic in its awfulness. At the same moment, every gun opened up, the din became deafening and then nothing could be seen of the front, but the bursting of our barrage and the distress flares of the enemy.

Anonymous tunneller, 250 TC, 1927

At about 03-9.30 Peckham was fired; 20 seconds later, Spanbroekmolen, and 2 seconds later, Kruistraat. We only saw these five mines – fumes screening the rest. Kruistraat's 3 mines, broadside on to us, were the most spectacular, but more picturesque than alarming at this distance. The tremors were confused – evidently we received the effects from other mines not seen. At the

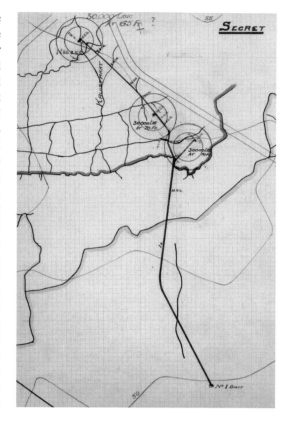

firing place

O i/c [Officer in charge] firing felt:

Distant tremor

Heavy tremor – Peckham at minus 20 seconds

Distant tremor

before firing Spanbroekmolen, which shifted the petrol lighting set off its bed, cracked a few sets near the officers dugout, upset everything in the dugout such as jam pots, crockery etc.

War Diary, Major R S G Stokes, RE,
Assistant Inspector of Mines

The vast Peckham crater today occupies the site of the original farm

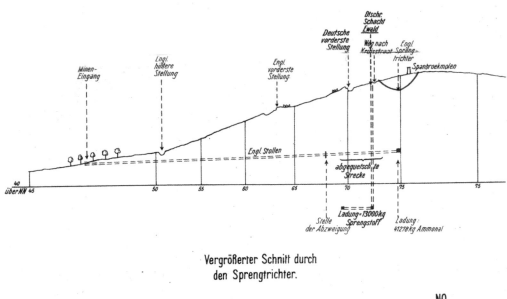

Left: German plan of Spanbroekmolen showing the deep countermine driven from Schacht Ewald which damaged the British gallery.

Below left: the 7 June crater in relation to the geology

Vergrößerter Schnitt durch
den Sprengtrichter.

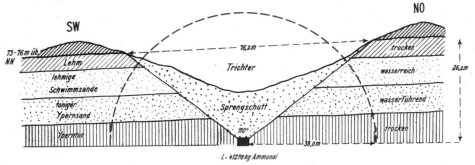

The first thing we knew was a terrific tremor of the ground. It was quite fantastic. Further down the hill the Commander-in-Chief was in a dugout with lots of steel girders on top of him for safety, and so were some war correspondents in another, and I remember we remarked that they must be like dice in a pot being shaken. It [Spanbroekmolen] was a sheet of flame that tongued in the end. It went up as high as St Paul's – I estimated about 800 feet. It was a white incandescent light. We knew the temperature was about 3000 degrees centigrade. The biggest bit of German I found afterwards was one foot in a boot.

Lieutenant Brian Frayling, 171 TC, RE

I can see the tunnelling officer with his torch flashed on to his watch, he and the General, their heads close together, waiting for that hand to move round to that second which seemed years distant. Then we saw him turn towards the officers with the firing apparatus, his eyes still on his watch. Suddenly he straightened up and said one word, 'Fire'. Nothing seemed to happen. My impression was that the mines had failed to go off. I looked at the tunnelling commander: he was again looking at his watch. Then there was a dull thud, as if a dud shell had landed some distance away, and then a peculiar earth tremor, another and another, stronger and stronger, seeming to come in waves from beneath one. A faint tinge of light began to creep up from the horizon; it was the first streak of dawn. It caught my eye and, as I looked, I suddenly became aware that Hill 60 was rising. Up and up, slowly and ever up, the whole crest of the ridge appeared to rise, while the earthquake became more pronounced. Then I saw the crest of the hill, standing boldly out against the sky, crack, and still more upward; the crack grew wider and wider, and then a beam of yellow light, as if emanating from 10,000 searchlights, leapt to the heavens. With one resounding crash the barrage fell. A great flame of burning gas drifted towards the British lines, suddenly going out just before it reached them.

Anonymous Australian tunneller,
1st Australian TC

When the tunnellers emerged above ground they could easily be distinguished by their poor pallid faces. We who lived, or died, at sap head or observation post, daily subject to bombing, shelling or sniping, pitied them from the bottom of our hearts. One night I retired to rest in my bunk in the tunnels and was made aware of the imminence of 'the event' but unaware of Zero. Suddenly, I believe about 3 or 4 in the morning my little crib in the bowels of the earth just rolled. All the electric lights went out and as far as I was concerned I might have been in the dark cabin of a ship at sea. I knew 'it' had started.

Gunner Charles H Brett, No. 15 Battery, 15th Brigade, 47th London Division

Brigadier General Harvey, who had seen the gestation of the scheme from the day Norton-Griffiths first 'blew in' with the idea, also watched from the dugouts at Kemmel. Norton-Griffiths himself, busy with his Romanian devastation, would be invited to inspect the handiwork of his moles later. It is not hard to imagine that he would have been thrilled and contented had he witnessed the moment.

3.10am. A violent earth tremor, then a gorgeous sheet of flame from Spanbroekmolen, and at the same moment every gun opened fire. At short intervals of seconds the mines continued to explode; period which elapsed between first and last mine, about 30 seconds. I found it difficult to concentrate on looking for the mines, there was so much going on, and the scene, which baffles description, developed so quickly that my attention was distracted. The majority of the mines showed up well with a fine flame. Others merely showed a red glow; this may have been due to their being blotted out by the smoke of the bombardment. The earth shake was remarkable and was felt as far as Cassel.

Brigadier General R N Harvey, Inspector of Mines.

I don't remember being hurt, but wouldn't have noticed if I had. We picked ourselves up, but didn't see anything of the explosion. There was a lot of dust and we could hear the pillboxes and earth dropping but nothing fell on me. We collected our exploders and stuff and put them back in the store in the communication trench, then went up and had a look at the craters.

Lieutenant B C Hall, 3rd Canadian TC

I dream about sapping more than anything. More than the firing squad. You can't forget explosions like that – I'd never seen anything like it. Arms, legs, trees, bricks coming down all over the place. I don't remember the noise from it but I think the barrage started at the same time. But there was this damn great flame – white it was, which made me think, I'd never seen a white flame... I can't really

A German pillbox upturned by the blast of a British mine on 7 June 1917

describe it... it was like a mountain standing in the sky, a mountain. I'll never forget it as long as I live. I thought, 'I wonder how many poor buggers have gone up with that lot'.

Private John Rea Laister,
attached to 171 TC, RE

AFTER THE 'BIG BANG'

All nineteen mines had detonated, an astonishing feat of engineering, patience and perseverance by the tunnellers. By midday on 7 June the Wyschaete Bogen, a rigid and despised barrier for so long, no longer existed, and along almost the full length of the battlefront the fighting had already moved well beyond the ridge crest towards the final target, the Oosttaverne Line on the eastern slopes. The British post-mortem began after lunch.

The scene of desolation along that front beggars all attempt at description by me. What comes back to me as vividly as anything else was our lunch on that bright summer morning [7 June] in the middle of what had been Wytschaete village. The General picked up some tins of German Bully beef, and we found some of their biscuits too. After a hard morning's tramp they went down very well, until the General remarked that he hoped the biscuits were not made from 'Kadaver' meal! Away in the distance, three miles beyond the ridge, the battle was still going on, but up there it seemed a place forgotten by war.

Captain H R Dixon, RE,
Assistant Inspector of Mines

Six months previously I had viewed below a picturesque cluster of buildings in a fair state of preservation, on either side of which were green fields and many farmsteads. Now there was scarcely a foot of soil in its natural condition, and what remnants of houses stood were difficult to recognise as such. Nothing remained over the mutilated surface but desolation and chaos. In the full light of day we saw many grim scenes, but I believe the strangest sight of all was in the crater. Deep down here on a ledge, were a lot of dead Germans around a table, one of whom stood upright against the wall, wearing still a smile upon his face. The rest of the group were seated and also wore a grin just as if a good joke had been cracked when the mine went up, leaving them on the outer fringe of the chasm. The concussion had killed them all, but the last living expression had remained on their faces in death.

Sapper Thomas Lloyd, RE

One can readily excuse the enemy breaking down under the strain of this Hell on earth, as even to our own men, who anticipated the explosions, the sight was absolutely awe-inspiring. A careful inspection of the area surrounding the mines showed how thoroughly the mines had done their work. Trenches were squeezed together so quickly and thoroughly that enemy dead were seen in a standing position. Relatively few prisoners were captured from Hill 60 proper, and those of the enemy who were alive were nervous wrecks, a great number of them actually crying with fear.

Lieutenant O H Woodward,
1st Australian TC

Desolation around the Hill 60 crater. Zillebeke Lake is just visible in the distance

Just like a great big black mushroom, all shot with flame, and it seemed to rise slowly into the air, and then it just collapsed. We were told not go anywhere into it because of the gases, and the infantry had to avoid it too.

It was a tremendous crater. There was very little noise, it was just like a great big woooof, it seemed to rise slowly up into the air and then just sank back again. Our job was to get into Messines. We were to go over with the second line of infantry, go into Messines and get all the dugouts cleared for the infantry. The whole of my section – we were extraordinarily lucky. The Germans were so thoroughly disorganised. Both objectives were taken straight away. It was one of the few times when you could have practically gone anywhere.

Lieutenant Martin Greener, 175 TC, RE

The craters were a great success. They had a very big lip on them, then straight down and up the other side. They were about 70 feet deep. I then had to go and inspect the other mines which weren't blown [the four

'Birdcage' mines] and send a report down as to whether the leads were alright and so on. The leads were alright but the tunnels were hour-glassing – all the timbers were broken. As far as I remember there were two other mines. There was another mine left in case the Germans counter-attacked further on the right, which was left to blow for many days, but it wasn't blown.

Lieutenant B C Hall, 3rd Canadian TC

On 8 June all the commanding officers of each of the participating Tunnelling Companies were paraded to receive the personal congratulations from General Plumer. Within days the first official post-battle reports of their achievements were arriving at Mines HQ.

CONDITION OF THE BRITISH LINE. Passing along no man's land back to Hollandscheschuur the British front line appears quite untouched. The parapet looks strong and in good condition, and much of the wire, opposite Bois Carre in particular, might have been made for demonstration purposes at home.

BRITISH ARTILLERY FIRE. Our shelling of all enemy positions seems to have been entirely complete and satisfactory, while it appears that all enemy ammunition must have been kept for back areas and counter battery work.

GOC 58TH INFANTRY BRIGADE. Met GOC 58th Inf. Bde. who was on the right of the 19th Div. sector for the attack. He said he had applied for the Hollandscheschuur mines not to be blown. His men had started to get over the parapet before the mines in front of them had gone up. Consequently they were somewhat shaken but got over with practically no opposition.

GERMAN CASUALTIES. One of the most striking features of the visit was the absence of indications of dead Germans. The burial parties had either been remarkably quick about their work, or else the actual number of killed was very low. In the neighbourhood of the craters the air appeared very tainted – it is possible that the mines accounted for considerable numbers who would be completely buried. Subsequent prisoners reports have indicated that the enemy had withdrawn a large number of guns to the flanks without giving warning to his front line infantry.

Captain H R Dixon, RE
Assistant Inspector of Mines, 10 June 1917

The Trench 121 or 'Birdcage' mines which, lying just outside the Messines battlefield to the south, were not used on 7 June 1917. Five were planned, and four laid. The mine marked here as Number 3 exploded in 1955

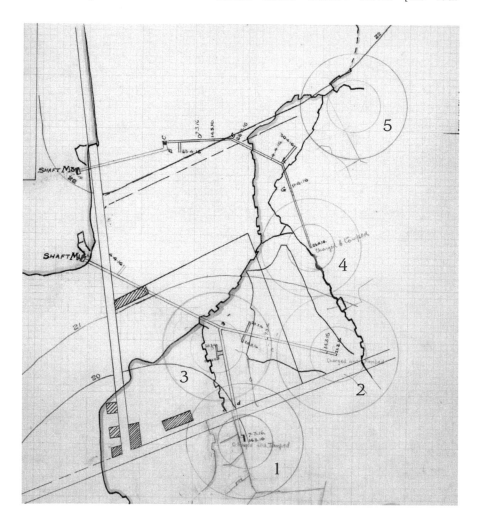

After experiencing the blow at Spanbroekmolen, Major Stokes had gone over the top with the fourth wave of infantry at 5.10 am. Later that day he produced his first summary.

> Owing to the circumstances it was little more than a day of impressions, the strongest being:
> Timing arrangements poor
> Enemy actually killed by mines small – but probably 10–20 men per crater (less than anticipated)
> Indirect effect of mine upon enemy morale in throwing out of gear all early defence, in giving the attack an overwhelming 'send off' – of inestimable importance (greater than anticipated)
> Limited range of surface rupture of trenches and dugouts outside rim of craters
>
> War Diary, Major R S G Stokes, RE,
> Assistant Inspector of Mines, 7 June 1917

COUNTING THE COST

It was later revealed by Army Intelligence, from German prisoners taken in the battle, that the supreme negative psychological effect of the mines had been the fact that they had not been fired simultaneously – as had been so carefully planned. Although a synchronous blow had been attempted, due to variations in the watches, the timing had in fact been fractured. It was an involuntary act of military genius. As blow succeeded blow to left then right, in front and behind, there was no telling how many more mines had been planted, or where the next one would go up. For the German front line infantry there was nowhere to run. Morale was shattered and abject terror ensued.

The true number of men killed and missing by the mines has never been calculated with any degree of accuracy and probably never will, but it is today clear that Major Stokes was mistaken in his initial estimations. Of a total of around 20,000 German casualties at the end of the first day, ten officers and 679 men were known to have died when the Hill 60 and Caterpillar mines went up, and a further 400 souls simply ceased to exist in the St Eloi blast. Here, a German force had been unlucky; it was forming up in Hickling's old 1916 craters in preparation for a trench raid of its own, entirely unaware that the great mine lurked directly beneath their feet. Even an approximate final number for all the mines cannot be extrapolated from these two examples as the sectors in question were known to be heavily manned; by

contrast, the trenches which were obliterated by the five mines at Petit Bois and Hollandscheschuur were understood to have been lightly held, and farther south opposite Trench 121 the greatest fear of the British high command, a limited withdrawal, had been independently effected by order of the local commander.

The Caterpillar Crater opposite Hill 60. Still a mass grave, it is today the most memorable of all the Messines craters, a haven of peace and tranquillity in all seasons

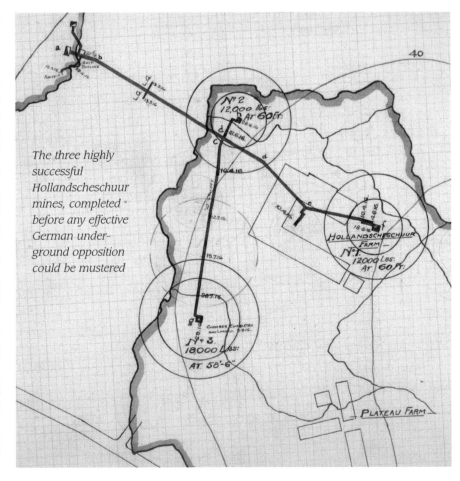

The three highly successful Hollandscheschuur mines, completed before any effective German underground opposition could be mustered

One of the Petit Bois craters today, with the raised lip of the No. 2 visible on the right

Petit Bois, showing the damaged section of gallery in which twelve men died and one, Sapper William Bedson, survived, in the summer of 1916

The ground trembled as in a natural earthquake, heavy concrete shelters rocked, a hurricane of hot air from the explosions swept back for many kilometres, dropping fragments of wood, iron and earth; and gigantic black clouds of smoke and dust spread over the country. The effect on the troops was overpowering and crushing.

Anonymous Report,
204 Reserve Infantry Division

What achieved victory at Messines for the British was Plumer's careful planning – and shock, contrasting greatly with many other battles of the Great War, where attrition was the watchword.

One of the points that commentators on this action do not seem to have emphasised in diaries, notes, etc., has been the planned erosion and resulting collapse of enemy defence. There is something about a mine explosion that shocks the soul no less than the body, exceeding the effect of any shell, mortar or bomb. To this effect at St Eloi [on 7 June 1917] was added the creeping horror of the steadily advancing, sky-shaking blasts from Hell, which could only have one end in their march closer and closer, like footfalls of doom.

Captain Marvin Maxwell, 1st Canadian TC

Almost every German report was the same, that of the 204 Reserve Infantry Division being typical.

On 23 August 1917, ten weeks after the blows, Frank Hurley, Australia's official war photographer, arrived from London to record the next stage of the summer offensive. After two days setting up a billet and dark room at Steenvoorde, his first visit to the front lines was destined to be at Hill 60.

After, we climbed to the crest of Hill 60, where we had an awesome view over the battlefield to the German lines. What an awful scene of desolation. Everything has been swept away – only stumps of trees stick up here and there and the whole field has the appearance of having been recently ploughed. Hill 60 long delayed our infantry advance, owing to its commanding position and the almost impregnable concrete emplacements and shelters constructed by the Boche. We eventually won it by tunnelling underground, and then exploding three [sic] enormous mines, which practically blew the whole hill away and killed all the enemy on it. It's the most appalling sight I have ever seen. The exaggerated machinations of hell are here typified. Everywhere the ground is littered with bits of guns, bayonets, shells and men. Way down in

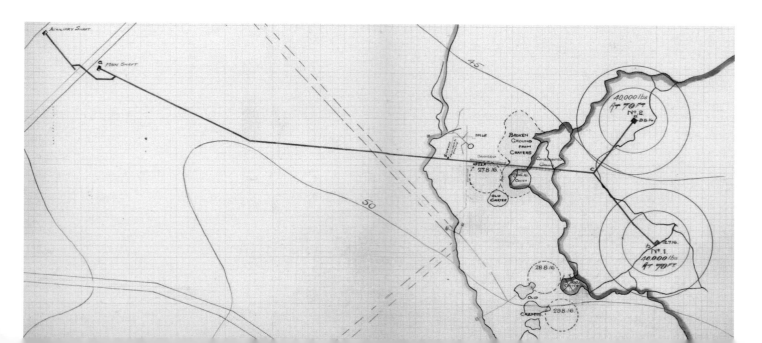

one of these mine craters was an awful sight. There lay three hideous, almost skeleton, decomposed fragments of corpses of German gunners. Oh, the frightfulness of it all. To think that these fragments were once sweethearts, maybe, or husbands or loved sons, and this was their end. Almost back again to their native element, but terrible. Until my dying day I shall never forget this haunting glimpse down into the mine crater on Hill 60 – and this is but one tragedy of similar thousands. Around this small mound on which we stood, hundreds, nay thousands of lives have been lost. What was it worth before the war? Just a pound or two; and after the war probably less.

Captain F Hurley, Australian photographer, 23 August 1917

OTTO FÜSSLEIN AND THE GERMAN OPPOSITION

I had to make a plan of all the undamaged pillboxes and concrete machine-gun emplacements on the slope of the ridge, and by the time I had finished there was room for little else on the plan and very few of these had been even slightly damaged, in spite of the intensity of our bombardment. These had been sites chosen with great care and it is inconceivable that any troops could have advanced up that slope, had there not been a complete panic on the part of the enemy.

Anonymous 250 TC officer, 1927

As soon as it was safe to do so, the British tunnellers began a survey of all the German mine workings which remained accessible after the blows. It must have been a fascinating task for the men who had for so long wondered just exactly what their opposite numbers, the *Mineure*, had been up to. Maps marking shaft positions had been found after the battle, but these were discovered not to be fully up to date, leaving many tunnels unmarked. It was found that almost all enemy galleries around the crater sites had been totally destroyed up to an extraordinary 260 metres from the mines.

The investigations confirmed that which had long been suspected, that only shallow mining had been fully developed in most places, and that laterals were few. It was particularly gratifying that many mine systems corresponded very favourably with the imagined plans drawn from British listening reports. Several failed attempts

at sinking deep countermines in timber were also discovered. In these, the shafts were either swamped by the running sand or tilted so far out of true by the shifting geology that abandonment had become obligatory. The successful shafts, more than had been thought, were mainly of concrete and steel.

Our job had to be the defence of our own positions, and that meant driving down through the quicksand into the clay. That was virtually impossible with timber-lined shafts, due to the immense pressure of water. We therefore sank concrete shafts, using a circular steel 'shoe' with a cutting edge, building up the lining of the shaft with iron rods and concrete inside metal shuttering. We then excavated the earth inside the shaft and beneath the shoe, allowing the shaft lining to sink under its own weight, while we continued to build from the top. It sounds easy, doesn't it? But when you consider that everything – iron rings, metal rods, sand, cement, aggregate and all our equipment had to be brought forward first on rail trucks, then by narrow-gauge railway behind the lines, and then finally manhandled into position through muddy, cratered trenches under enemy fire; that we could not work in peace and safety, as we might have done at home, for here the enemy observed every movement; that we constructed the shafts in open trenches which offered little shelter, with enemy shellfire scattering our materials, killing our miners and on many occasions destroying our workings – then you will understand what effort went into the construction of those shafts.

Oberstleutnant Otto Füsslein, Kommandeur des Mineure, 4th German Army

Some shafts were found to have been cast *in situ* using steel tubbing as a mould, which was removed as soon as the concrete was firm enough to be self-supporting. Most of the workings were electrically lit and ventilated, and unlike the British the Germans employed powered winding gear for hoisting spoil. Construction techniques in galleries had been almost identical, with an average three-inch (7.5-cm) spacing between morticed timbers in normal clay. Progress marks on the timbers finally confirmed the studies of Pollock and Clarke; German driving rates were vastly inferior to those of the British clay-kickers. This further accentuated the accuracy of listeners' reports, and finally illuminated how the early German underground superiority was so quickly turned on its head by the speed and efficiency of the British tunnellers; no German records showed more than an average of two metres per day, compared to eight metres by the clay-kickers.

One of the greatest surprises was that tunnelled dugouts attached to mine systems were few in number and built on a relatively small scale compared with British examples. It had always been imagined that entrances reported as being destroyed following British trench raids were evidence of large underground accommodation complexes, as had been seen in so many other places along the Western Front, and as they themselves had been building. Nevertheless, the workings were most useful and welcome to British troops short of a safe haven after the battle.

THE BLAME GAME

Oberstleutnant Otto Füsslein, the Kommandeur des Mineure for the 4th German Army, laid the blame for the Messines disaster squarely at the door of the infantry and German High Command. Discounting the slow, often noisy, and relatively inefficient excavation methods of his *Mineure*, Füsslein was of the opinion that he had never had sufficient support and encouragement from his superiors, not because of a lack of understanding, but a lack of the will to understand. The German military geologist Walter Kranz, writing after the war, also supported Füsslein's position. Until the St Eloi debacle in March 1916, German orders had been to concentrate on shallow mining. This exhausted the *Pioniere*, he said, worried the infantry in the trenches, and frustrated the mining officers.

Füsslein had indeed reported at Christmas 1916 that the British were stepping up their tunnelling offensive and he would require more men to counter the threat. Three more mining units had been deployed. But after this confident start, his messages then began to appear mixed. At the beginning of February 1917 in a note to all troops, he further drew attention to the possibility of a massive British undermining of the complete ridge, explicitly suggesting the precautionary evacuation of certain frontline positions. By March the ground had shifted. His view was that the enemy mining situation was still dangerous at several locations, but from the decreasing British activity underground he

believed that either the majority of their major charges had already been laid, or the countermining of his *Mineure* had been successful. He now suggested that an imminent attack was not to be expected, although again adding that the clearing of a number of forward positions was still appropriate. He was hedging his bets. In fact, by this time so many projects had reached completion that less and less noise was available for his listeners to pick up.

Füsslein's confidence that his *Mineure* were effectively dealing with the Commonwealth mine threat was evident throughout May. On the 10th he was able, falsely, to 'boast success' at several key points.

> Everywhere he [the British Tunneller] is repulsed he merely consolidates his position and only attacks where he hopes to approach us without being noticed. We must still watch out for enemy attacks in great depth at both sides of the Ypres–Comines railway [Hill 60 and Caterpillar], at the canal [The Bluff – no mines laid] at the Eickhof Heights [Lock Hospital – Whittaker tunnelling machine sector – objective not reached in time], near Hill 73 [Spanbroekmolen – one mine] and south of the Fransecky Farm [Kruisstraat – three mines]. If a large British attack materialises they could initiate this by large explosions at any of these locations in front of or in our lines.

> Oberstleutnant Otto Füsslein,
> Kommandeur des Mineure,
> 4th German Army, May 1917

On 24 May another report from Füsslein stated that the risk at Spanbroekmolen was also now reduced. In the same month, General Erich von Ludendorff, one of Germany's most powerful and influential leaders, urged the XIX Korps Generalkommando to clear their forward positions as soon as any threat from mines was perceived. He was not only assured by his line commanders that any threat was extremely limited but that the troops preferred to remain in their original positions.

Füsslein and his men may have failed to locate the existence of thirteen of the British mines, but much of the blame seems to be applicable to German GHQ, who materially neglected to offer sufficient backing to the *Mineure*, despite countless pleas over a period of a full year. An illustration of this can be found in the German HQ communiques for 1917; in the six months leading

up to 7 June not a single one makes a mention of mining.

The German 4th Army commanders had been assured that their artillery was excellently organised and commanded and would be able to master the British guns in the event of an attack, and that the infantry were capable of a mobile defence and had few concerns over holding the ridge. Yet a further report was about to be received at headquarters which would crown their confidence and sooth their troubled minds. It came from Füsslein himself and was delivered just two days before the attack. No missive could have been more comforting. Füsslein stated that during April the countermining efforts of his *Mineure* had been so triumphant that a British mine attack preceding a large scale infantry assault on the Messines Ridge was no longer possible.

Acting as if he had never warned them of any risk, the German High Command characteristically placed the blame firmly upon Füsslein and his *Mineure*. As did the official historians after the war.

The *Mineur* was of the opinion that any danger to the forward positions on the Wytschaete Salient from underground enemy attack was no longer prevalent and that we were secure everywhere. Had there been any possible doubt in this respect the natural reaction would of course have been the early clearing of the whole of the frontal positions.
Post-war letter to Brigadier General J E Edmonds, Official British Historian

The official German history of the Battle of Messines Ridge is slightly more supportive, but still lays part of the blame at Füsslein's door.

The Kommandeur des Mineure of the 4th Army certainly took into account that the British would accompany the great battle in Flanders by an underground attack. He had reported to this effect and had taken great pains to keep the command informed about the situation, but had not realised the full extent of his opponent's underground activities. This was caused by the following circumstances: when he took over command of the mining operations, the British had already charged five deep mines and had driven other galleries a great distance forward. He could not establish the full extent of their operations, particularly those south of the Douve because the Lille Group did not form a part of the 4th Army until May 1917.
Anon., *Der Weltkrieg 1914–18*, 1939

Records show that the Germans were confident that twenty British mining schemes had been definitely underway with a further nineteen possible problem areas, all lying north of the Douve river. When push came to shove it was all semantics. Put simply, the overwhelming problem for the Germans was to find an enemy with a head start in a geological medium which did not readily transmit noise – clay – and without having any firm evidence as to where that enemy might be, at what depth, and in what numbers. The task was gargantuan – and frankly impossible.

Otto Füsslein survived the 'shame' of Messines and the war. He was tragically killed in a civilian mining accident in Germany on 29 September 1923.

LEGACY OF BATTLE

From the present day perspective, perhaps the most important comment on Messines was made by Lieutenant B Cecil Hall in an interview with Alexander Barrie in 1960. He recalled that

The continued use of noisy picks and mattocks in German mines – one of the greatest advantages to British tunnellers – at 'Flora' workings, near the Bluff

June 1918; Spanbroekmolen crater recaptured and consolidated by the Germans

KEMMELBERG. LETTEBERG. SCHERPENBERG.

SPANNBROEK-Sprengtrichter

The crater of No. 3 Birdcage Mine in spring 1955. It is today filled in

after the Messines success the leads to the unused mines at the Birdcage, in the southern-most part of the line, were sound, but that the shafts were 'hourglassing' – slowly filling with sand due to fracturing of the shaft lining passing through the running sand layer. When it was made known during the war that at least four mines were still in position here, the Belgian Government asked that all efforts be made to recover the charges, which totalled a vast fifty-five tonnes of explosive. A start was made on the task. First, the firing leads were cut. As the shafts and galleries were suspected to have collapsed, the simplest way to reach and remove the mines was to ignore the original site and sink new steel shafts adjacent to the mine chambers. This action may well have been contemplated but was not acted upon before the German offensive of April 1918 retrieved all the ground lost the previous year, and more, in a matter of hours. The advance finally sealed the fate of the Birdcage mines; they were there to stay.

Apart from the big La Petite Douve and Peckham mines – a total of about thirty-three tonnes of Ammonal explosive – the contemporary records of both sides make it clear that a great many smaller mines and *camouflets*, placed in the years and months before June 1917, were also abandoned, either forcibly by enemy action, or by choice. The official post-Messines reports concluded that the destructive force of most of the British mines had made reconnaissance of German workings impossible, and it was therefore equally impossible to assess how much explosive had been stored underground for use in countermining from their own deep systems or in position as mines or *camouflets* awaiting use. Finally, as a gentle reminder, on 17 July 1955 the Number 3 Birdcage mine exploded – thirty-eight years after its completion – possibly as a result of a lightning strike carrying a massive burst of electrical energy along Lieutenant B C Hall's armoured firing leads; a testament to the care the Canadians had taken in preparing their scheme. In reality, it is likely that only charges such as this

– to which firing leads are still attached – have any possibility of causing future problems. This time no one was hurt, but the milk yield of several dozen dairy cows took a sharp downward turn. That the detonators had still been effective was no surprise – they still are highly dangerous today, but what startled most experts was that the Ammonal, an explosive known to be prone to degradation in damp environments, had survived almost forty years under water (for the tunnels are totally flooded) in such an unspoiled and dangerous condition.

As a footnote to this section it may be useful to attempt to put into perspective the explosive scale of the mine attack at Messines on the morning of 7 June 1917. When expressed in pounds and tonnes, the huge quantities of explosives involved becomes difficult to grasp, indeed meaningless to those of us who have been fortunate enough not to have experienced warfare. If one considers that a Mills hand grenade contains a quarter of a pound of explosive, elementary multiplication provides the equivalent of 382,400 grenades for the mine at St Eloi alone. If the figure is extrapolated to embrace all the Messines mines the total reaches a staggering 3,612,800 hand grenade equivalents.

AFTERMATH OF DEFEAT

German defensive policy after the 'black day' of Messines had to be radically re-thought. It had been the first major allied assault in the Salient for over two years, and was therefore the first test for their extensive defence systems. The results fell far short of what had been hoped for, and indeed expected. The rows of fixed continuous lines of trenches with integral pillboxes of the *Flanderen Stellung*, in which so much confidence had been placed for so long, had clearly failed. After the shock effect of the mines, the British advance had proceeded so swiftly up the ridge behind an almost perfect creeping barrage, that it soon overran those defences which had not already been destroyed by artillery fire. And in the dry summer conditions the accompanying tank attacks achieved almost all their objectives. The defeat was as near complete as could be imagined. The Germans knew that it was only the limited objectives of the British offensive which had avoided a potential breakthrough. In the knowledge that major hostilities were far from over in the Salient for 1917, the battle triggered serious thought amongst senior German commanders. But where to start?

The dugouts [pillboxes] situated in old trenches, principally in the first and second lines, were man-traps and often led to the loss of a large number of prisoners. These circumstances prove the weakness of the rigid methods of defence practised hitherto.
    General Sixt Von Arnim,
    Commander, German 4th Army

British reports produced after the battle also noted that many German dead found inside pillboxes were killed by the concussion of heavy shells striking the rigid structures – the men were unmarked. For the Germans, the lessons of Messines dictated that a new approach to defence had to be found.

Von Arnim's revised orders to all his troops in the Salient were that they were to concentrate on concealment to escape the eyes of British airmen and the wrath of the guns they directed. This meant that everything – trenches, dugouts and battery positions – was to be hidden or camouflaged. He also maintained that the constant effort to repair smashed trenches exhausted the fighting strength of the troops. Under persistent artillery attention, they were simply unable to keep up with the rate of destruction. Von Arnim's preferred option was an adaptation of the existing defence-in-depth initiative, with well-concealed zones of defence to allow for counter-attacks, and lines manned lightly up front and ever more strongly towards the rear. The old positions were to be ignored, and all conspicuous works under construction such as new concrete emplacements, discontinued.

Shell hole nests occupied by squads of troops with single machine guns would replace trench strongpoints, and all positions were to be arranged in a checkerboard pattern to give crossfire support. After camouflaging, these positions should be undetectable from the air. All shell holes forward of the front line were be filled with thickets of barbed wire so that attacking troops were unable to use them as cover. Close behind the shell hole defence line strongpoints were to be built each containing several machine guns, a party of assault troops for counter-attack, and support troops who were to be brought forward at the moment of first warning of enemy movement. Behind these, more shell hole posts, lightly wired, each containing a *gruppe* of nine men, were to be built.

And there was another radical alteration: in the second and third positions *minierte unterstand*, or mined (deep) dugouts, were to be constructed in preference to concrete emplace-ments. Driven from shell holes in the front line smaller dugouts should accommodate one sixth of the forward garrison; in the second line this figure should rise to one third, and farther to the rear, one half. If concrete dugouts were necessary they must no longer be of the tall blockhouse variety but, in an ironic throwback to Vauban's eighteenth–century designs, kept low with a flat roof.

Forward line tunnelled dugouts were to be deep enough to be shellproof, but if due to geo-logical position and groundwater level it was not possible to obtain sufficient head cover through depth, then extra surface protection was to be added with concrete, logs or steel beams – all camouflaged. Dugout exits were to be sufficient-ly wide and high for rapid movement of men in an emergency, and close to all of them splinter-proof look out posts were to be built. Sprinkled amongst all these positions there should also be large numbers of dummy posts to confuse attacking troops.

A unique feature of the tunnelled dugouts was to have been a staggered entrance system. The idea was to leave a rear exit for men who were underground when entrances in the front posts were overrun by the enemy. The idea was not to offer an escape route enabling troops to retire to defend the next line, but to allow men to come back over the top and retake the forward positions. In the front dugout entrances specially built niches were to be manned by sentries who would engage the enemy directly he entered the trench, and by keeping the entrance free to enable the full underground garrison to turn out.

Von Arnim directed that this new work be started immediately and urgently. However, like the response to the deep mines of Messines, by the time the order was issued it was already too late – the beginning of the Third Battle of Ypres was just days away. On 31 July 1917, after two and a half years of struggle, one of the bloodiest battles in world history began.

The miner's unseen and largely unsung offensive campaigns were now more or less over in the Salient. But only the British knew this, of course – after the shock of Messines the nervous German commanders still suspected further huge deep schemes to be present everywhere where tunnelling of any kind had been known to be taking place. As Third Ypres loomed the Germans panicked and blew a substantial series of heavy, medium-depth mines at Railway Wood and Tor Top hoping to destroy any 'hibernating' deep

British mines which might be used at the beginning of the offensive they were expecting. There were none.

Such was the nervousness of the Germans that any sign of blue clay anywhere, be it in front, reserve or support lines, was sure to bring on a bombardment. At the far northern end of the Salient at Boesinghe, the tunnellers, in advance of Third Ypres, had dug eighteen tunnels for storing bridging material in preparation for crossing the Yperlee Canal on the opening day of battle. An enemy trench raid assumed the tunnel entrances to be mine shafts, and on the basis of their report German GHQ evacuated the forward trenches opposite, pulling back almost 500 metres. A similar event took place a little farther north at Lancashire Farm. Here, the tunnellers had driven a deep subway connecting reserve and front lines, built so that British troops could move forward unmolested on zero day. The ubiq-uitous blue clay was spotted near the shaft – and another German withdrawal was made.

It may be thought that with the Third Battle of Ypres and the advent of a more mobile phase of the war the tunnellers work below ground was over. Indeed, for a while half companies were put onto reconnaissance, repair and gas-proofing of captured German dugouts, both the concrete and mined varieties, and essential road-making and tank crossing duties. But subterranean enterpris-es were very far from finished for the tunnellers; the impending battle for the Passchendaele brought with it conditions such as had never before been experienced in warfare. On the surface the shell torn and shrapnel swept landscape would soon become a vast charnel house where human life would become almost untenable – and expendable. The final sequences of the battle were of such horror that the word Passchendaele – the name of the village ulti-mately designated as the final objective – was destined to pass into the English language as a descriptive noun denoting desolation and human suffering. Generations later the events of those months of misery continue to occupy a place in the consciousness of nations the world over.

Two mornings later we sat on Tower Hamlets Ridge and surveyed desolation. Many months hence, I was standing at this point with a Major in the Bedfords. 'I was here in nineteen-fourteen,' he said; ' then you could not see half a mile for the woods.' It was scarcely credible. In nineteen-seventeen it was as bare as a man's hand. It could not, one

A sign of things to come following the victory of Messines

thought, ever have been otherwise...The soil has been churned and furrowed until no two paces are level. In this belt, perhaps four miles wide, there are no seasons. The air grows colder or warmer; the days contract or lengthen, but the earth makes no response. To our eyes, its life has ceased. There is not a blade of grass, not a leaf. Only man by his superior agility, has survived: but not often if the sallow death-masks near the line – to bury them at this season demands greater leisure and fortitude than the infantry can command – are to be believed.

Lieutenant Guy Chapman, Royal Fusiliers

In such a location true safety was to be found only in one place: deep beneath the battlefield. It might have been too late for the German Army to put General Von Arnim's plans into action, but the British decision to use dugouts rather than blockhouses had, like Messines and the mines, been made standard policy much earlier. The tunnellers were now masters of the earth – in the Salient at least – and more than capable of delivering the massive number of shelters which would be required during the coming months of carnage. The British therefore did what they knew best – they went underground. And on a grander scale than ever before.

Chapter XI
'A HOLE IN THE GROUND WITH A LID ON'

D UG-OUT. – A hole in the ground with a lid on. There are three kinds of dugouts at the front. The 'Bungalow' for officers, the 'Love in a Cottage' for sergeants, and the 'Noah's Ark' for privates. They are built for men, mice, rats, and cats to sleep in. A dug-out is decorated with jam, cheese, photographs and fleas.

Anon., *Made in the Trenches*, 1916

Where the British learned the value of depth: German deep dugouts near Mametz on the Somme

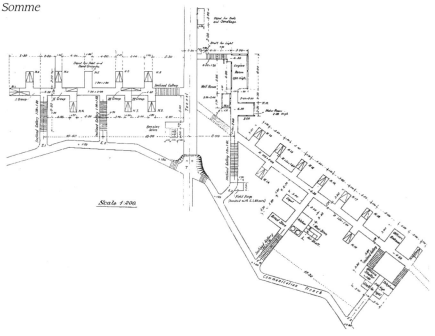

With the end of offensive mining in the Salient following the Battle of Messines Ridge, the life of the British tunneller changed completely. After a brief 'rest cure' his full attention was turned to what would become one of the greatest military engineering endeavours of the whole war – the creation of underground cities in the Salient. These cities were conurbations of dugouts, subways, shelters and subterranean posts of all kinds; the logical expression of a desire to get to earth, deep enough to escape the searching of bombs, naval guns, howitzers and mortars.

The British had first come to understand the true value of the deep dugout during the Somme offensive of the summer and autumn 1916. Now enshrined in the popular mythology of the Great War, it is nevertheless accepted that having escaped the wrath of a devastating bombardment by sheltering deep underground, German troops had emerged to inflict 56,000 British casualties on the first day of battle alone. Later, when the British were able to explore some of these deep enemy workings for the first time, they found a vast maze of connecting tunnels and chambers cut into the solid chalk of Picardy.

In the Y Ravine he [the German] dug himself shelters of unusual strength and size. He sank shafts into the banks, tunnelled long living rooms, both above and below the gully-bottom, linked the rooms together with galleries, and cut hatchways and bolting holes to lead to the surface as well as to the gully. All this work was securely done, with baulks of seasoned wood, iron girders, and concreting. In this gully barracks, and in similar shelters cut in the chalk of the steeper banks near Beaumont Hamel, the enemy

202

could hold ready large numbers of men to repel an attack or to make a counter-attack. They lived in these dugouts in comparative safety.

John Masefield, *The Old Front Line*, 1917

Although the dry chalk geology of Artois and Picardy was almost universally suitable for deep dugouts, it was very different in the Salient. Here the complexities of strata, groundwater and topography meant that while some areas were suitable for deep dugouts, others were quite hopeless. But after two years of offensive mining the British had acquired the knowledge and experience that would allow them to quickly and accurately identify geological vagaries and continue to hold sway deep underground.

FIRST IN THE SALIENT

For several months after war first came to Ypres in 1914, fighting continued to be fluid. The British doctrine of the offensive was ubiquitous and its perpetuation meant that well-designed, safe shelters for troops – which required time and substantial manpower to construct – were deemed unnecessary. As official policy on security in the line remained practically non-existent until well into 1915, protection against shell-fire and the grim Flemish winter weather was left to the discretion of the individual.

November 13th 1914. Reveille 4am. Move off after a hasty breakfast to our quagmire near Ypres. We go off mounted after many delays – and take over trenches in Zillebeke Wood – facing inwards – the Germans 100 yards away. The Munsters [Royal Munster Fusiliers] are overjoyed to be relieved and leave lots of excellent things behind as they are in such a hurry to leave. We arrive at 12. We live in little holes, holding from two to five men in each. The trees broken by shells form a natural obstacle in front – so sleep quite comfortably, tho' the A Squadron shoots for fun most of the night. Snowing!

Second Lieutenant B J 'Biffko' Marden, 'C' Squadron, 9th Lancers

German officer's dugout on the Somme, whitewashed and electrically lit

Below left: An early British shelter built against a breast-work. Using scrap timber and old doors was a common practice everywhere

Below: German troops inspecting primitive captured French trench shelters in Polygon Wood

The simplest cover. A line of British rifle pits on the edge of a road near Ypres, 1914

Three months later, little had changed.

By dawn they were up and away and led to so-called dug-outs [on the Kemmel–Kruistraathoek road]. Dug-outs, as they were known later, well constructed and well protected, did not exist in those days. These, for example, were simply formed by occupying a ditch by the side of the road, putting some twigs or branches across it and covering as might best be accomplished with straw, grass and, where available, odds and ends of boards in an attempt to gain some protection from the weather. How inadequate this was soon became evident. A steady downpour set in. Wet already, the men found, with disgust, that the rain soon penetrated their make-shift head-covering, and, in addition, the ditch was filling with water. Their condition got wetter and more miserable as the day went on. Then at night back to the ruins where they had spent the previous night. Again the next morning to their dug-outs. Sodden with wet, the men gladly believed the rumour that by nightfall they would at least have the comparative comfort of farm billets. It was not to be.

Private Walter Gardner, 1st Battalion,
Honourable Artillery Company

Scenes like this were a powerful incentive for infantry commanders to actively promote self-preservation amongst their men, to ensure the continuity of group cohesion, and to ward off sickness. To endure such conditions and perform the duties of active service demanded a high degree of morale and iron self-discipline. Although extreme fatigue in war is unavoidable, no one could be expected to be able to fight unless cover was provided, and not only against enemy action, but also from the elements. The Germans, higher and considerably drier on their ridge tops, were thinking long term – they were there to stay, and their fortifications were built not only to withstand attack, but also to provide some degree of comfort; for the time being, these positions were the new boundaries of Germany. For the British, overlooked everywhere whilst on the wet Flanders plain, the choices were limited, but the idea of moving to more comfortable positions by withdrawal was abhorrent.

The word 'retirement' during training in the

German 'wigwam' style shelters in woods in the Salient

BATTALION	2nd KINGS	1st R. BERKS	2nd K.R.R.	2nd H.L.I.	2nd OXFORDS	2nd WORCESTERS
POSITION OF 5th & 6th INFY BDES ON 9th Oct. 1914.						
DISPOSITIONS	2 Coys Firing Line Bois des Boules / 2 Coys & H.Q. at Moussy / At night 1 platoon sent forward into Adv'd Trench.	2 Coys Firing Line / 2 Coys & H.Q. Metz Farm. (1 platoon pushed by night) / After 9th: 1 Coy in trenches by day / 1 Coy H.Q. Platz Farm / 1 Coy Englefield Farm / 1 Coy SOUPIR / 1 Platoon forward	3 Coys + H.Q. Firing Line portions of these Coys in pits cut into side of ravine / 1 Coy in Shelters on rear slope of hill / 1 Fd Gun in Firing Line	4 Coys + H.Q. in Firing Line Com'd path cut in wood in rear of 3 Coys on right Com'd trench for Coy on left with Shelters at intervals.	2 Coys in Firing Line / H.Q. in la Cour Soupir Farm / 2 Coys in Shelter in rear / 1 Fd Gun in Firing Line	2 Coys in Firing Line / 2 Coys + H.Q. in Carts near road.
TYPES OF TRENCHES	Recesses under both sides of trench / Scale for Sections 1 Sq. = 1 Ft.	Notches 4' to 6' wide Roofed with brushwood / 1 Man Recesses 1'6" to 2' wide	Steps up at intervals / Shelters at foot of slope	Traverses 6' to 16' wide Turfs leading back between Traverses / Rough hurdle with brambles + leaves on / Loopholes 3' apart. Cover 15 cm'r / Recesses for 1 or 2 men cut under parapet	Sacks arranged to give cover from back slant of shell. Small opening left between sacks for men to crawl through. / Second Comm' Trench – Cross trenches Cut at intervals / Recesses cut under parapet. Entrance arranged between sacks	Mostly single men recesses 2'6" to 3' wide – Had Cover provided for lookout posts – No overhead.
OBSTACLES	1000' 4 strand Fence along the front. / 500' Entanglement running sites in wood / 450' H.W.E. in front of wood / Trip wire throughout.	300' L.W.E. 15' wide on right / 900' 2-row 5-strand fence with coils of barbed wire in centre / 400' high row 5-strand fence on left.	Lane cut in wood near edge to lengths on right / 275' double 4-strand fence at centre / 300' H.W.E. on left centre Trip wire throughout. / 250' double tripods with coils on left.	50' double 4-strand fence with coils between K.R.R. + H.L.I. / 500' Single 4-strand fence with coils between it + Trip wire from Right to Re-entrant angle. / 250' L.W.E. at Re-entrant / 200' double 4-strand fence with coils / 70' Single 4-strand fence on left / Trip wire throughout	150' double 4-strand fence with coils on right / 250' double 4-strand fence with apron on left / 300' double 4-strand fence on left / Trip wire throughout / Some L.W.E. stakes + bayonets erected by Inf'y at intervals.	250' double 4-strand fence on right / 200' H.W.E. on left with gaps at intervals / Trip wire throughout.
Note	The barbed wire fences were made up in 25' lengths, 6 posts per length + carried out in bundles – Stay wires + posts carried separately. Wire was rolled on sticks for passing over + under the fence + round the posts to form loose coils. Tripods were made for use in positions where it was too dangerous to hammer in posts. They were carried out with 3 strands of wire joining the apices + in lengths of 150' to 200'. One 1 man for each tripod. The ends of the lengths were anchored –					

decade 1904 to 1914, was whispered about. It had been almost a crime to mention the word. The first winter in trenches was a trial; battalion boxers and tough navvies just sat down and cried like children. They were whacked to the wide world – by nature – the weather. Then, almost for the first time so far as the infantry was concerned, we were shown by the sappers how to dig trenches, with traverses, parapet, parados, berm and all. How thankful we were for that first lesson.

Second Lieutenant Robin Skeggs,
3rd Battalion, Rifle Brigade

Living conditions for the British throughout the first winter were appalling, with sickness, frost-bite and trench-foot being rife. It was up to the troops and their commanders in the field to overcome any tactical weaknesses and 'make do' until the spring offensive began: an offensive which would surely end the war.

By March 1915 the defence of Ypres was slowly becoming a wholly British affair as French troops were withdrawn to other hard-pressed sectors of the Western Front to the south. British reinforcements arrived daily, but their accommodation in the front line trenches continued to be rudimentary. There were certainly more peaceful sectors to have one's baptism of fire than in the Salient.

The journey to Hooge the next night with a dozen men untrained in soldiery, let alone warfare, was a nightmare. Our route lay from Hellfire Corner through the remains of Zillebeke, a part of which was covered by 'whizz-bang and pip-squeek' [German high-velocity shell] fire. Every time a whizz-bang arrived anywhere near us I lost all my men. The only training they had ever had it seemed was in taking cover. Just before reaching our destination in Sanctuary Wood, the ground rises and then descends to the wood. At this point rifle bullets passed just over one's head – there was no need even to duck. My men lay flat and it took an incredible time to get them to proceed crawling on their stomachs to the jeers of old soldiers passing by. In Sanctuary Wood we built dugouts half below and half above ground for the men and made them as comfortable as possible as materials, mud, rifle bullets, enfilading machine gun fire and flies would allow. The men were in a sheltered hollow, but my own dugout had to be found easily by signallers, messengers, and other units, so was in a more open spot

The earliest known sketch of British trench shelters. Simple cover used by troops of 5th and 6th Infantry Brigades in October 1914

Dugout frame in use. Frames were designed for infantry to be able to fit them together without the need for hammer and nails. This one has been named 'The Casino'

and not so safe. Later on I built myself a really good sandbag and timber shelter with extremely thick walls, mainly above ground. As trees, the branches of which gave some protection against bullets, were felled by shell and machine gun fire, the position became more exposed and the noise of bullets hitting the sandbags interfered with sleep. I therefore had a hammock sent out from Harrods which I slung between two posts driven in the ground, and so obtained some insulation from sound.

Lieutenant G R Cassels, 175 TC, RE,
June 1915

Privately perhaps, the British were now beginning to acknowledge that the war might drag on for much longer than originally envisaged. A revolution in warfare was indeed beginning. By midsummer 1915 there were still no established regulations regarding cover in the line, although many infantry officers recognised the inherent laziness and disinclination to expend unnecessary energy of the British Tommy, and enforced their own rules regarding shelter.

Our dugouts are supported by enormous

Location of a dugout frame within the trench parapet, showing front and rear 'borrow pits', the earth from which was used to build the parapet and parados

beams – about 8" x 8" – sometimes we cut down huge trees to support the roof. I make all my own men build their own dugouts of huge thick beams too, much to their surprise

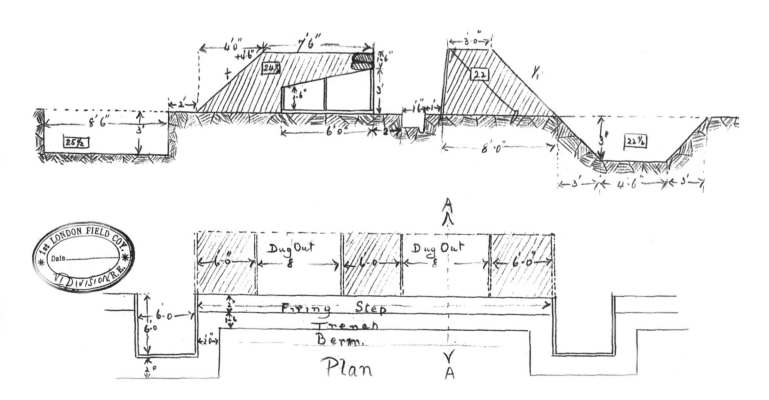

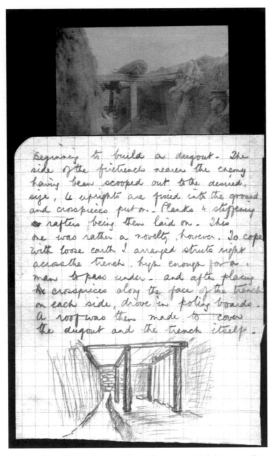

and indignation – but they would know the advantage of it if they had a Black Maria [German heavy shell emitting black smoke] pitch on top! They love to rig up a pretty little villa of matchsticks which merely keeps out the weather. I was much amused the other day in going round my platoons dugouts to see in one of them some sort of pictures hanging on the earth wall. They were nicely framed and I was afraid the men must have brought them from the billets. However, on closer scrutiny I discovered they were cigarette pictures mounted on ration biscuits!

Second Lieutenant Robin Skeggs,
3rd Battalion, Rifle Brigade, December 1914

Alongside trench mortars, German howitzer shells like the Black Maria were the sole reason for the British Army being gradually driven deeper and deeper underground. There was to be a direct correlation between the growth in numbers of artillery and their calibres, the frequency and intensity of bombardments, and the adoption of a troglodyte lifestyle in forward areas. Only a few weeks after stringing up his hammock in Sanctuary Wood, Lieutenant Cassels had been forced to move into a more

substantial and secure abode, offering much more than just sound insulation. But this too became obsolete almost as soon as it was completed.

The Germans started shelling our support trenches methodically. These trenches were in ground sloping away from the front line, and my own dugout, an exceedingly strong timber and corrugated iron one, was well dug in. It consisted of two compartments, the outer one was an office and living accommodation, and the other tunnelled deep into the hillside as my bedroom. My batman and I took shelter in the outer one. The guns fired two rounds in one place, then altered direction about one degree and fired again, and so on, thereby traversing the whole trench. Our turn came. The first shell fell beyond us, downhill. The second pierced through the inner dugout wall, and hung protruding between the timbers like someone putting out his tongue at you. It was a dud. It might have had a delayed action though and go off later, but we daren't go out into the open so we both took what shelter we could near the entrance to the outer chamber.

Now, usually the Germans when traversing a trench with this kind of shooting covered the trenches once, then reversed and shot them over a second time but altering direction slightly so that the second lot of shells fell between the spots the first lot had

A simple splinter-proof trench dugout built by Lieutenant Robin Skeggs of 3rd Rifle Brigade in the Wez Macquart sector during the winter of 1914/15

Robin Skeggs stands proudly outside his finished dugout, 'Virtue Villa'

Captain Bruce Bairnsfather's appreciation of dugout life in 1915

hit. We therefore thought we were safe, except for the dud. The shells came nearer and nearer along the line of the trench, and then suddenly the whole place exploded. Something hit me so hard that the sensation, though extraordinary, was by no means painful. At the same time the roof and sides collapsed, the floor rose, and I was almost buried. I had been blown into the inner chamber. What had happened was that the second shell had hit the dud and the two had exploded together. How long I lay there I don't know, but I managed to struggle out and when I looked for my batman he was nowhere to be seen. I thought he had run away, but that was the last thing he would do. Eventually he turned up. He had been for a pick and shovel to extricate me after he himself had been blown completely out of the dugout down the open slope. He was unhurt, but I was in a sorry mess. My canary-coloured tunic and new suede weskit and britches were soaked with blood and full of holes. I had three minor chest wounds and a cracked jaw; my left ear was hanging on by only the lobe; my head swelled like a misshapen turnip.

Lieutenant G R Cassels, 175 TC, RE,
June 1915

The ideal home. A cosy, clean, strong and simple structure with brick floor - and rum.

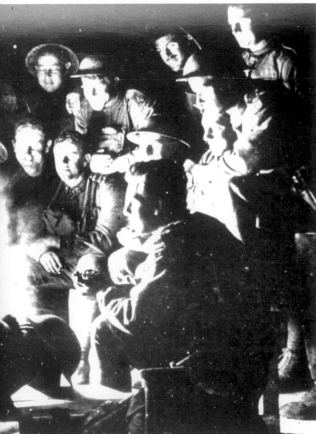

Until the autumn of 1915 dugouts, if not in house cellars, remained either surface or semi-buried structures. When shells landed nearby they collapsed; when it rained, they collapsed; when it froze and thawed, they collapsed again. The troops lived with it, there was no choice – and exercised their supreme talent for cursing. Risks from shelling were simply accepted, everyone was 'in the same boat' after all, and direct hits were simply put down to bad luck. But in August 1915 two apparently mundane but significant events occurred on consecutive days. The repercussions of both were to save tens of thousands of lives, and although the first is not related to shelter it is unusual, and worth mentioning here.

On 18 August the Indian Corps 'captured' the first metal screw picket, a simple but ingenious German device for suspending barbed wire entanglements. Up until then wooden posts had been used, but these had to be hammered into the ground with a maul, under cover of darkness – a noisy indication of nocturnal activity to an enemy who were wont to 'spray' any area of commotion with machine gun fire. Hammering was therefore the cause of large numbers of unnecessary casualties; with a screw picket barbed wire entanglements could be erected almost silently: by sliding the handle of an entrenching tool (the 'piggy stick') through one of the eyes of the picket, and twisting, it could be screwed into most kinds of ground with minimal effort. On the day of the valiant capture of the first picket, 19 August, Lieutenant Colonel C H Harington, Commander, Royal Engineers for the Territorial 49th (West Riding) Division, reported on a visit to some newly finished French field works.

Australian soldiers billeted in a vaulted cellar, 'strutted' for extra strength with pit props

Tall tales told around a glowing brazier in a spacious dugout, a house cellar in Ypres. Moments such as this formed some of the most powerful memories for veterans

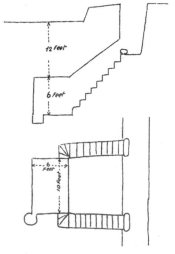

These dug-outs are made by Infantry and are tunnelled out under the parapet to a depth of 12 feet solid earth over the roof. They had two entrances in case one should be blocked. They were drained and served as good stores for spare ammunition and parts. Sandbags were placed at top of steps to prevent surface water getting in.

Sketch from the earliest known proposal for deep dugout schemes drawn by the CRE 49th Division. August 1915

Note 11. Dug-outs. These were the great feature. On the way from Fouquevillers to the front trench there were a row of dug-outs behind a bank. These were entered by a flight of steps leading into a sort of area in front of the actual dug-out. They were very roomy with plenty of room to stand up. Some were made with the covered iron sheets, but most were made with timber and sandbags and had at least 12 feet of material on the roof.

Later on in the village we saw a dug-out which had been made by an infantry company composed of miners, who had not disturbed the top soil at all but had tunnelled down to a chamber whose roof was 4 metres below the surface, and in addition had the soil which had been brought from below put on top to a height of a further 2 metres. The chamber was a large cross-shape chamber and had a stove and chimney in one corner. All the dug-outs were connected by drains to deep sumps, and were very dry. Beds were made by stretching sheep netting across a wooden framework down one side of the dug-outs. This makes a very clean and sanitary form of bedstead.

Lieutenant Colonel C H Harington, CRE
49th Division, 19 August 1915

Harington also observed that the French machine gunners had their own separate shelters.

Note 23. The guns are used in the 'Jack in the Box' system. Deep dug-outs are constructed near the gun emplacement into which the detachments and guns retire during bombardment, coming out as soon as required. These dug-outs are made by infantry and are tunnelled out under the parapet to a depth of 12 feet solid earth over the roof. They had two entrances in case one should be blocked. They were drained and served as good stores for spare ammunition and parts. Sandbags were placed at the top of steps to prevent surface water getting in.

Lieutenant Colonel C H Harington, CRE
49th Division, 19 August 1915

Harington's notes foretold the future for all protective accommodation in the Salient, and by the end of August 1915 the British had followed the French lead and had begun developing their own deep shelters.

THE WAR OF THE GUNS

Different British commanding officers had conflicting ideas about dugouts just as they had about the use of mines. Controlled by an almost religious adherence to the doctrine of the offensive and confident in the strictly 'temporary' nature of trench warfare, some believed dugouts should be universally encouraged as an essential defensive and protective component; others saw them as bad for morale, that they would make the troops 'soft', and that men should take their chances in the open.

[Vermelles sector, French Flanders] August 1915. 23 Field Company RE. Tunnelled dug-outs, looked upon with great suspicion by the staff, were commenced. They were not allowed in the front line, and entrances had to be made under the parados [mound at rear of trench lip] of the second line. They had but 6 to 8 feet of cover at first, but, in a test carried out by burying a 6-inch howitzer shell 18 inches deep over the top and firing electrically, this was found to be insufficient and was increased to 8 to 10 feet. 3-inch timbering was used instead of 1.5 inch and these dug-outs were then pronounced proof against 5.9 inch [shells].

Major H W R Hamilton,
23rd Bombay Sappers and Miners

Shell calibre was the key to construction. Until 1916 larger calibre guns were used to harass troops and transport, concentrating on hotspots such as Hooge and Hill 60, and largely ignoring all but the most tempting or important targets behind the lines, but after the Somme there was a marked change in artillery intentions along the full length of the front. Artillery numbers and the supply of ordnance had increased to the point where heavier guns could begin to fight each other (counter-battery fire) on a regular basis and also harass many places previously regarded as relatively 'safe'. The result was a widening of the thin ribbon of destruction in the Salient through 'area shoots' where large numbers of guns targeting a relatively small patch of ground could create a miniature version of the 'obliteration' conditions of the great battles that constituted Third Ypres in 1917. The targets were usually enemy battery positions, but camps, rail, tram and road junctions, engineers dumps and trench redoubts were also bombarded if ordnance was available.

During 1916 the Germans also vastly

HAVE YOU COMFORTABLE

WINTER QUARTERS ?

—o—o—o—

IF NOT, THEN DROP A P.C. AT
ONCE WHEN OUR MR BLEWES
WILL CALL ON YOU.

—o—o—o—

TRY ONE OF OUR NEW AIRY 17in.
PROOF DUG-OUTS. THESE ARE

Guaranteed Rat-proof

—o—o—o—

DON'T DELAY PLACE YOUR

CONTRACT AT ONCE.

—o—o—o—

THESE ARE NOT

Jerry-built Residences.

—o—o—o—

If you're really nice and deep,
Minnie rocks you off to sleep.

—o—o—o—

WRITE :—

SHERWOOD, FORESTER & Co.
Contractors to H.M. Government.
Telegrams : '' KNOTTS,''

expanded a specialist arm of their services – an arm arguably more feared than any other – the trench mortar companies. The 'minnie', short for *Minenwerfer* – literally 'mine thrower' – fired high-trajectory, low velocity missiles containing high explosive, gas or incendiary charges accurately over short distances. There were three sizes of projectile: 76 millimetre, light; 170 millimetre, medium; and the dreaded 245 millimetre, heavy, the latter with a range of about 1,000 metres. Big 'minnies' exploded with devastating effect. Trenches were simply shaken apart by the immense blast, and shaft chambers, inclines, stairways and mine shafts could be completely demolished by a single shot even if it was not a direct hit. The use of such mortars, in conjunction with the growth in other artillery pieces, led to British forward areas becoming ever more lightly manned. Yet it was still critical to have troops in place in case of emergency. There were just two choices available: to inhabit surface shelters constructed from reinforced concrete as the Germans had chosen to do, or to go deep underground, where timber was the dominant material. The German *Pionier* had had little alternative: in most places the positions of his infantry were on ridges, so digging deep dugouts would inevitably intercept the dreaded *Schwimmsand* layer. The British, however, did have a choice.

CONCRETE OR TIMBER?

Concrete is an ancient material, and its military use dates back to at least Roman times, when, amongst other things, it was used in the core of the otherwise stone-built Hadrian's Wall. The use of steel-reinforced concrete has a more recent history, and it found application in military defensive works in the latter part of the nineteenth century when its properties in the face of artillery attack were shown to be superior to those of more traditional building materials. Keeping pace with progress, countries throughout Europe redesigned and improved their older stone and brick built defences using the new material. As we have heard, in the opening campaigns of the war, the Germans had easily reduced the fortresses on the Belgian frontier with super-heavy artillery. Yet despite this experience, in occupying the geologically troublesome Passchendaele Ridge system the Germans had little choice but to opt for concrete shelters in most cases.

Following the Second Battle of Ypres in May 1915 a period of relative quiet descended upon the Salient. During this time the Germans constructed three main defensive trench lines, the *Flandern Stellung*, consisting of thousands of concrete *Mannschafts Eisenbeton Understände* (MEBU), soon to be labelled 'pillboxes' by the British. They stretched across the Flemish fields in ranks, checkerboard clusters and echelons, forming an integral part of a defence-in-depth trench system which was intended to be impregnable. This formidable barrier was entirely reliant upon steel reinforced concrete for everything: protection against shelling, defensive gun

Another delightful 'Wipers Times' advertisement

Belgian civilian labour assisting in the construction of one of the monolithic concrete emplacements in the Flandern Stellung

positions, machine gun emplacements and accommodation. Dugouts were installed wherever geological conditions permitted, and because of the problem with the water bearing sands, this often meant shelters with limited headcover.

The RE fully understood the advantages of finished concrete works: easy and swift access for troops, guaranteed waterproofing, and far less thickness of material needed for protection against heavy shells – a metre of reinforced

A well-populated German dugout in the Salient. The sign reads 'Officer's dugout'

concrete provided a similar degree of protection against an eight-inch shell as around seven metres of soil – but the logistical difficulties for the British were manifold. Unmolested transport of costly material to the site, the preservation of that material in dumps, concealment of those dumps, the amount of valuable time and timber required to 'shutter' the structure before concrete could be poured, concealment of the work during construction, and camouflage against aerial observation afterwards were colossal challenges for a force under the constant gaze of the enemy. These conditions were partly faced by the Germans too, but to a far lesser extent. The British, trapped in the narrow pocket of the Salient and reliant upon few transport routes, were in a far more invidious and difficult position. For the moment, a protective scheme based upon concrete was out of the question – there were simply too many technical and logistical difficulties to overcome. The yardstick by which protection was measured was the most commonly used enemy howitzer shell, the 15 cm, or to the British, the 5.9".

Protection with concrete against anything over 5.9 was not possible, and nothing less than 3 feet of concrete or double two-feet walls will stop even a 5.9. This means that a dugout or emplacement will be 7 feet high above the floor and therefore a site must be chosen where the amount of cover can be obtained. The smallest dugout possible, strong enough to stop a 5.9 shell will contain

This unfinished pillbox shows the time, complex construction and variety of materials required to build steel reinforced concrete emplacements

Excavation of a buried German pillbox near Gheluvelt. The structure had no windows and would have been entirely covered in earth for camouflage. Periscope holes can just be seen in the roof

70 wagon loads of material and therefore it is not practicable to construct anything of this kind unless there is a tramway or road within 100 yards of the site. Any concrete work will not set hard enough to withstand a 5.9 shell in less than two months at the earliest.

CRE 39th Division (New Army)

This latter point – the delay before the concrete hardened and the emplacement could be opera-

tional – was critical. Pillboxes simply could not be safely used before they were completed, and this was an unacceptable matter of months. The problem could be overcome to a point by the use of block-built pillboxes rather than the monolithic variety which were cast *in situ*, but once again the perennial British bugbear of reliability and security of transport under German observation and fire thwarted any ideas in this direction.

As with offensive mining, the British again

Construction of a German concrete aid post

enjoyed the geological advantage: their lower lying positions were closer to the blue Ypres Clay. The Germans therefore geared up the construction of MEBU, using ingenious precast concrete blocks – the aggregate constituents of which were sourced from the homeland. The transport of raw materials for pillboxes by barge along the Rhine and into the waterways of Holland was to threaten Dutch neutrality. This particular German military engineering exercise had a long and complex supply chain, which was expensive in manpower and materiel. The British had more opportunity to be inventive, using the available local resources.

One of the major advantages of dugouts was that a degree of useful protection was created almost immediately the sappers pierced the surface, and it increased at every stage of development as they drove deeper; although the initial work was dangerous and exposed, it offered quick cover. Due to the problems with enemy observation, any concrete scheme in British forward areas would be restricted to night work only, perhaps throughout the whole of its construction period, yet once a tunnelled dugout had sunk its first shaft or incline, work could continue around the clock, with the spoil being stored for removal at night. And pillboxes demanded sand, gravel, steel, timber and water to be on site during the entire building process. Although many systems were also to use a proportion of steel in their construction, the main ingredient of a dugout was wood. A great deal of wood. In

1917 alone the RE Stores issued over one and a quarter million tonnes of cut timber.

Having had to wait for the concrete to harden sufficiently to become protective against shells, once it was 'cured' a pillbox posed an inversed threat to its occupants. Investigations into the effects of shell-fire upon German concrete structures had been carried out after the Battle of the Ancre on the Somme in November 1916, with a further major review after Messines the following year. Tests showed that the British 'distrust' of concrete was well founded, and

COST OF ENGINEER STORES.

Article.	Price.
10′ pit props	4 francs each.
1 sheet C.I.	3s. 3d. each.
1 crate X.P.M.	£2 10s. 0d.
1 sandbag	3d.
1 steel joist 9′ × 3″ × 5″	1s. 7½d. per ft. run.
1 steel rail	£15 10s. 0d. per ton.
1 pick and handle	3s. 3d. A.O.D. supply.
1 shovel	1s. 6d. A.O.D. supply.
1 cubic yard concrete	(about) 25s. per cubic yard.
100 lbs. cement	(about) 7s. 0d. per cask of about 400 lbs. 4s. 6d. for each cask.
1 piece timber 12′ × 9″ × 3″	4s. 2d. per length.
1 piece timber 10′ × 6″ × 6″	3s. 10d. per length.
1 roll wire netting	£1 4s. 0s. per roll.
1 roll green canvas	1s. 3d. per sq. yard.
1 set (4 pieces) mining timber	4s. 6d.
1 angle iron picket 5′ × 2¼″ × 2¼″	5d. per foot run.
1 length Decauville Track	£3 per yard.
1 roll tarred felt	6s. 3d. per roll.
Long screw pickets	1s. 6d. each.

Segment of British panoramic photograph taken near St Julien showing German pillboxes captured and numbered, and entrances reversed by RE, Autumn 1917. Note several rows of camouflage netting stretching across the complete battlefield in the background

matched Von Arnim's findings; not only were men in captured pillboxes often found to have been killed or wounded by flying fragments blasted off the inner skin by the force of direct hits, but a large number of deaths were caused, as by the Messines mines themselves, from the concussion created by the massive shock waves reverberating inside a confined space.

We had been up for two days. I don't think we had advanced much more than a couple of hundred yards or so. There was no line, just shell-holes which we were ordered to try to join up; but that was impossible after the march up there and the fighting – we were exhausted. In the evening they [the Germans] counter-attacked. I was in a cemetery on the edge of the railway cutting; just shooting as fast as I could into this dark mass of men coming down the ridge. There were no targets; they were just a dark shape moving towards us – you couldn't know if you'd hit anyone. Anyway, we drove them off. After this and the previous day's attack I was so tired I don't believe I actually cared whether I lived or died. Anyway, I crept into a German pillbox. A filthy dark place, you couldn't stand up – I never understood why they built them like that – and couldn't see much, but there were men already in there, all exhausted. I dropped down next to another chap and was asleep in no time. When I woke up I had my head on his shoulder: it wasn't another LF, it was a dead German officer! He hadn't a mark on him – we all looked – he had been killed by concussion. There were three others in the same state. The Australians relieved us that night: 'You the LF's? Well, piss off!' We needed no second bidding; I slid down a bank into the cutting and tried to follow the railway back to Ypres.

Private Bert Fearns, D Company, 2/6 Battalion, Lancashire Fusiliers, 9–11 October 1917

The British did not drop the idea of pillboxes completely however; indeed, many examples were built in French Flanders, especially in 1916, and a large scheme of small concrete shelters was put into production in the Salient in 1918, but it cannot be said they were ever fully embraced. Ultimately, there was little choice for the British but to go underground. The benefits were clear:

Their construction involved less labour in proportion to the accommodation given, and afforded more immediate results;
1. They gave complete protection, both from actual (shell) penetration and serious concussion effects; and
2. Their exact position could, as a rule, be better concealed, although the spoil removed from them might indicate their existence in a particular locality.

As were the disadvantages:
1. Difficulty of exit, owing to the depth to which they have to be taken;

A substantial trench shelter at St Eloi occupied by Lieutenant Horace Hickling 172 TC

After Third Ypres, individual posts with elephant shelters were used by the British instead of continuous front trench lines. This cartoon-like 66th Division drawing offers construction details

2. Ventilation, lighting, and drainage were often very difficult problems; and
3. The nature of the local geology could prevent the siting of the dugout in the best tactical position.

Dugouts were the only option. Throughout 1915 they were few in number and usually consisted of reinforced house cellars. When built as an adjunct to military mining they were still seldom more than two or three metres below ground, and attached to tunnel systems as temporary accommodation for miners and storage for kit. Hickling's 172 TC in the fiery St Eloi sector were some of the first to install a small group of tunnelled chambers off a shaft. To become as numerous as they eventually did showed that certain attitudes at HQ had changed; dugouts had to fulfil a purpose, and they must be built to last as long as the war itself. The adoption of extensive dugout schemes loudly broadcast to the troops that there was no end to the war in sight.

INTO THE DUGOUT PHASE

The first tunnelled dugouts in the Salient were begun by 177 Tunnelling Company in Ypres itself, adjacent to the Menin Gate.

> Bliss took me to see some dugouts his Coy. [Company] are making in the old ramparts of Ypres. They are very good indeed with I suppose 15 or 20 feet of earth cover. The officer in charge [A W Davis, later OC, 3rd Canadian TC] explained that anyone in there would be 'as safe as in Gawd's own pocket'. And I'm almost inclined to agree. Still, all the same it is hardly 'Offensive Mining'.
> Major S Hunter Cowan, OC 175 TC, RE,
> 12 September 1915

It infuriated John Norton-Griffiths that his moles had been taken away from the mines and given such ineffective work.

> While dugouts have been made by miners brought out for mining, the Germans have been mining – OC 177 not very popular. I think if things do not mend in this company an official growl will come through. It appears that dugout work was given to 177 because they would not mine. This northern side of Ypres is very important and unless a live mining OC is put in quickly I fear we shall suffer here.
> Lieutenant Colonel John Norton-Griffiths, RE,
> 2 November 1915

Nevertheless, even 'Empire Jack' could no longer deny that safe shelter was becoming an increasingly important aspect of the war, especially in active mining sectors regularly and intensely targeted by mortar, shell and bomb. The enemy also knew when the tunnellers changed shift, and casualties getting to and from the mines had been gradually increasing. The answer was elementary – move the dugouts closer to the action. Soon after the Menin Gate dugouts had got underway, 177 TC began a forward accommodation scheme at Cambridge Road along the rear edge of Railway Wood – within a hundred metres of the front line.

10.2.16 … there was a wire from the North saying that a heavy charge had been fired by the Hun bringing down a lot of roof and most unfortunately killing three good men. No gas so it must have been far away. Hannay and I went up to investigate. It was a beastly raw day so the walks both ways were quiet enough. We found the necessary work had already been started to make good the damage and recover the bodies for decent burial. Naturally it all took time so we were glad to stay to a most sumptuous three-course lunch in our dug-out less than fifty yards away from the German line but fitted with three bed chambers and a living room with a real fireplace – the whole panelled with wood and lined with canvas! I've never seen a palace quite like it.

Major S Hunter Cowan, OC 175 TC, RE

The subterranean war was evolving in different directions. During 1916 the British, learning from the geological conditions experienced during mining work, burrowed ever farther into the earth everywhere inside the arc of the Salient. As artillery firepower increased, the significance of deep dugouts grew, and many more

Above left: Lille Gate dugouts lie beneath the Ramparts Cemetery

Above: 177 TC dugouts in the Ypres Ramparts near the Menin Gate, the first British tunnelled dugouts in the Salient

Below: Plan of the Ramparts dugout system. 'Borrowed' fireplaces and wood panelling were fitted in officer's quarters

Below left: Lille Gate dugouts, home to some of the tunnellers working at Hill 60. Note the annotation 'Graveyard on surface'

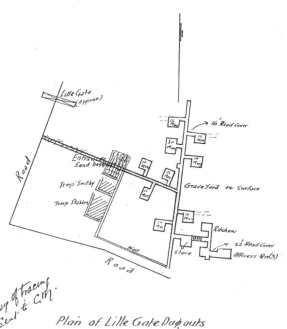

Plan of Lille Gate Dugouts
Scale 40ft = 1in.

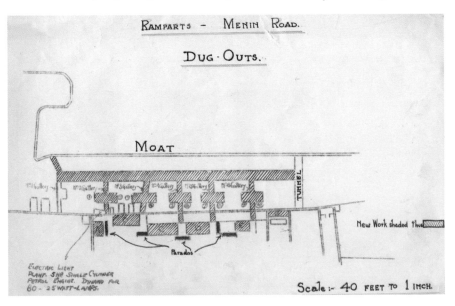

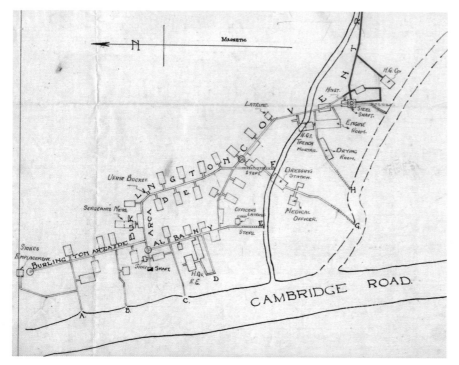

Above: Lower section of the Cambridge Road (Railway Wood) dugouts. The system was connected to the mining scheme, and became one of the most complex in the Salient. Note galleries named after London streets

were 'officially' requested. Indeed, after the 1916 Flanders offensive was postponed until the following year, tunnelled dugouts played a significant role in preparations for the Messines battle. By 7 June 1917, in addition to their great offensive mine scheme, the British tunnellers had completed, with the invaluable assistance of Royal Engineer Field Companies, Pioneer Battalions and thousands of attached infantry, twenty-four shell-proof Brigade headquarters, twenty-eight shellproof Battalion headquarters and further underground accommodation for 200 officers and 10,000 men.

The tactics employed at Messines, especially the success of the British creeping artillery barrage upon surface fieldworks, only served to reinforce the importance of dugouts. The battle had signalled the beginning of an era of total destruction in the Salient. Now, the artillery was required to demolish successive ribbons of territory before it could even be approached by the infantry. The intensity and destructive capa-

Left: Cambridge Road dugouts were not quite as organised and neat on the surface as below ground

Below left: A cookhouse dugout system (note chimney) protected by a 'scrounged' Madonna

Below: Gott Mit Uns. Churches were almost universally undermined for the extra protection afforded by strong masonry and vaulting

bility of the guns increased daily, and as the Third Battle of Ypres burst across the fields of Flanders at the end of July 1917, life on the surface during daylight hours was about to become almost untenable.

Safe shell-proof accommodation was therefore now as fundamental to the military tacticians as any aspect of battle. The need for deep cover extended the full length of the line – and in other sectors, it was the same on both sides of no man's land.

4.11.17 Caudry Group. (German) XIII Corps Staff
The work of this detachment (Catacombs) must be supported and encouraged in every possible way. It is most important that all discoveries of underground passages and also of suspicious places, e.g. cellars bricked up, excavations in well shafts, should be immediately brought to the notice of the Catacomb Detachment. Any books on the subject, village registers, etc., should also be sent in at once. A reward of 30–50 Marks is offered for the discovery of catacombs with at least 9 metres of cover, which can be made use of. For the discovery of catacombs in the country in rear of the Siegfried Line smaller rewards may be paid according to the importance of the catacombs.

Captured German document,
49th Division CRE

Dry and bright thanks to the chalk geology, the catacombs of Picardy which were so keenly sought by German commanders were spacious and airy. It was a different story in Flanders.

Now I am in the trenches again at a different place. It is a lonely desolate place like the middle of Ilkley Moors, we have not to show a sign of life during the day, only come out at nights. Fritz is sending over his big shells but we are quite safe. This is a big dugout 70 or 80 feet down in the ground, room for 50 men, and room to stand straight up and lie down full length, with a wire mattress for a bed. It is like being on an old slave ship in the days of

British troops in part of the huge complex of deep chalk caverns outside Arras. The New Zealand Tunnelling Company connected the caverns with subways

German soldiers in chalk catacombs near Cambrai. The wide expanse of unsupported roof denotes very solid geology

Old Benbow. It is pitch dark, except for a candle here and there, and one sees dark shadowy forms moving about, and little bits of flickering fires when men are struggling to make a brewing of tea. The place is full of smoke, a mixture of tobacco, candles and wood. The shells bursting, although we are so far down, makes the place tremble. We are quite safe, and go calmly on doing whatever we are on with; I shall have to stop now to drum up: 'drum up' means to make some sort of fire, to boil water for tea.

Corporal Frank Williams, 4th Battalion, North Staffordshire Regiment, 2 November 1917

THE SUBTERRANEAN LIFE

For the infantry, soldiers would go in and come out of dugouts following a strict cycle of rotation. After Third Ypres, it was typical for British troops to spend three days in the front line, three in support trenches, and three in dugouts near reserve positions, before going back 'up front' once more. After the 'tour of duty' was finished, perhaps after a month or so, a battalion would be relieved and drop back into billets behind the line for a rest period. It was typical that during the tour, those not holding the front and support positions stayed underground during the day, emerging at dusk to form carrying parties for ammunition, timber, corrugated iron, rations, water and so on, before becoming troglodytes once more at dawn.

Pencillings from Our War Artist's Sketch-Book.

This romanticised sketch from 'War Illustrated' depicts scenes which are not far from the truth

Dugouts were the only places where you knew you were safe. The deep ones were safe and warm – sometimes too warm – fuggy and sometimes damp. If they were badly ventilated we called them 'fruity'. If you can imagine a couple of hundred men or more in a small space, two men to a bunk, three bunks high. No one was able to have a proper wash; I think I went six months without a bath once. But some [dugouts] were good and dry. You could curl up on your bunk, pull your blanket over your head, light a cigarette – and you were at peace with the world. The dugouts I was in were all candlelit except one on the Somme – I remember that one because one of our blokes accidentally killed one man and wounded a sergeant when he was sitting on a bunk cleaning his rifle. Just one bullet; went through the first man.

Anyhow, that one had electric. I preferred candles because – if you could get them – you could use them on the lice! We never talked about how the war was going on because we didn't know – nobody told us. You didn't know why you were doing something, you just did it. There was no point in thinking about the future or the past in that way. We just chatted and pulled each others legs – that, and swearing, is what kept us going. Food was a big subject – everyone had their favourite dishes; we talked about what our mothers were going to make us when we got home; whose mother made the best Lancashire hotpot and so on. And women of course. Being only eighteen I hadn't a lot to say about that! There was always a lot of teasing of us youngsters by the older men – we'll get you fixed up next time we're out of the line, lad, that sort of thing. The tales they used to tell about sex – frightened us to death! All the talk and teasing kept you going, but at the same time it just made you want to go home even more. I never got a day's leave in over a year – then I was captured.

Private Bert Fearns,
2/6 Battalion, Lancashire Fusiliers

Officers were more fortunate when it came to leave, especially tunnelling officers, but for some it was never enough.

In early 1915 there was no organised leave. Leave was granted on urgent compassionate grounds. Application was made on a form and one of our regular officers filled in his:

Q. Who do you wish to see?

A. My wife

Q. Why is this urgent?

A. Acute sexual starvation.

This created quite a stir. It smacked of impertinence to his superiors. If granted, a precedent would be created which could have emptied the front line.

Lieutenant Brian Frayling, 171 TC, RE

At the height of the mine war, tunnelling company personnel had a different dugout lifestyle. A few were so heartily sickened by the permanent troglodytic routine that they rested and slept on the surface despite the enhanced danger, and much to the disgust of the infantry. Being engaged twenty-four hours a day, some lived permanently underground close to their mines. For these dugout 'residents' it was important to make the abode as comfortable as possible.

The new dugout we named Lily Elsie, and it was quite an ideal home. We whitewashed it throughout, drove a chimney with a wombat machine directly through to the surface, and annexed a stove, a form of looting at which Rount was an expert. We were always warm, and the whole dug-out was as dry and snug as ever it was our lot to live in. The men of the section were quartered in some German dug-outs, which were made nice and habitable.

I suppose it will remain a mystery to our dying day, how each one of us spent the hours in a dug-out. Hour after hour would slip by in an aimless manner, and, of the twenty-four hours, perhaps eight would be passed in sleep, four in strolling around the work, and two in eating, leaving ten unaccounted for. Although some of us were keen readers, we could not concentrate our thoughts for long on anything but the lightest of literature. And yet we'd be stuck for the major portion of twenty-four hours in the dug-out. How we eked out the time with perhaps a single companion I cannot now imagine. I fear our minds were often blank, and much more of that kind of life would have left our brains a perfect wilderness. No doubt the constant strain of the last three years was beginning to tell on all of us – constant touch with danger, with death jogging at one's elbows, was apt to put our nerves on edge.

Our afternoons were usually quietly spent in the dug-out, unless the work specially required our attention. It was always a favourite time of mine to stroll around the work leisurely about 4pm during the winter months or at 5.30 in the summer. It was a quiet time and it was nice to get some air, and, if there was some shelling going on, it was interesting to watch it. One could find an elevated position and let one's thoughts play full. As dusk set in, observation was poor, and we could take greater risks of exposure. At 5.30 I would return for tea, and then prepare my daily reports, giving footage, number of men employed and demands for material etc., after which I would wait as patiently as possible for the arrival of the rations and material. This was the most important event

Above: Martha House dugout near Zonnebeke in 1996 still complete with wire, blankets, bottles and groundsheets after eighty years

Below: A similar view in 1918

of the day. The scurry of new shifts, orders to be given, batches of letters brought in by the Transport NCO etc., gave us something to think about. The letters, indeed, were the chief item, and, after that, the rum.

Captain H W Graham MC, 185 TC, RE

The situation was very different in forward accommodation during the long grind of Third Ypres. Here, the inmates were most definitely transitory, and little or no pride was taken in the condition of dugouts unless an officer was on duty to enforce hygiene rules.

There was put at our disposal a tiny chamber next door to Brigade Headquarters in Canada Street Tunnels. It was perhaps ten by five, filled with fetid air, impregnated with the reek of burning fat from the Tommies' cookers, on which the men in the passage brewed endless tea. To me that cell has fixed itself as the portrait of any battalion headquarters in this dirty war. The walls were of pit-props, covered with stained and ragged canvas. At the end a previous tenant had pinned a *Vie Parisienne* picture of a naked girl. The pins had fallen out and it now hung awkwardly

Dugout life in the 'Wipers Times'

neglected, a great smudge of black across the face. Below a rough shelf was hooked a sheaf of pink telegraph forms, relics of earlier guests at this road-house. A two-tiered bunk of rabbit wire occupied a third of the room. There was one double stool and an upturned SAA [small arms ammunition] box. A narrow table ran along one wall. On it lay a nature morte, a scrawled map, a whisky flask, a packet of Goldflake, a steel helmet, a couple of Mills bombs, a half-pint enamelled mug full of thick tea, lighted by three inches of candle stuck in a bottle neck down which the grease of countless forerunners had spilled and congealed.

Beneath the table a petrol tin of chlorinated water clanked when it was kicked. From nails hung two panoplies, tangles of equipment, helmets, haversacks, water-bottles, and revolver cases. Outside in the darkness there was the never-ending tump-tump of pumps keeping the water back: and every now and then the muted explosion of a heavy shell near the top of the staircase. When a barrage was fired one's brain was assailed by a series of countless small pressures. For the rest, it was waiting for something to occur, the next meal, the next orders, the end of the war, or the end of the world.

Lieutenant Guy Chapman, Royal Fusiliers

Adjacent to Canada Street Tunnels were the several other large dugout systems of the Observatory Ridge sector: Tor Top, Hedge Street, Krab Krawl, St Peter Street. Most systems were connected by galleries to their neighbours, and together they incorporated over eighty entrances. Here, it was possible to enter the line near the top of Observatory Ridge and travel safely unobserved via a 400-metre subway to the support and front lines without coming within eight metres of the surface.

Before that I had a special duty to do. It was to act as 'Tunnel Major' in Hedge Street Tunnels – to regulate the very limited and fiercely coveted accommodation there, and the traffic in and out. This appointment took me back to the accursed area again [Observatory Ridge sector]. For a week, I think, I patrolled this dirty but precious underworld, and fancied I improved the conditions. Not the actual state of the works. It was the business of the tunnellers to pump out the foul water which stank along the passages, the light of the electric lamps falling on it doubtfully through the black lattice of flies which hung to the warm bulb, swarming and droning round the head of the passer-by.

The space available became hourly more important. Once, a machine-gun major threatened to destroy my labours, which had cleared a chamber or two for some officially incoming troops, by sending his men in and telling me to go to hell. I had to call for aid to General Hornby, who was in Canada Street Tunnels, and returned to eject my pirate with a signed paper proclaiming that 'in the Tunnels, the word of the Tunnel-Major is law'.

Lieutenant Edmund Blunden, 11th Battalion, Royal Sussex Regiment

By a curious quirk of fate Chapman and Blunden, destined to be two of the finest chroniclers of the war, later met in the Hedge Street Tunnels. By this time the dugout had taken over from the trench as the focus of 'social' life.

With the increasing pressure for more and more accommodation space attention was turned to a systematic approach to dugout construction. The lessons learned from the mine warfare phase would now be turned to improving the lot of the average soldier in the Salient, improving the degree of their protection, and providing the security to get the final job done.

Chapter XII

DEGREES OF PROTECTION, 1917–1918

Australian troops relax in the safety of a mined dugout

I was a scout. I'd volunteered for the job thinking it sounded glamorous. It was a hell of a job, crawling about in no man's land every night expecting trouble every second. Bloody fool I was, but you didn't know any better, and it was too late afterwards. We went out when and where we were told to during the night and came back before dawn, then after we had reported what we had done and seen and found – which was usually nothing but a lot of wire and holes – we spent the rest of the day in dugouts. Not in funkholes in the trench, but proper sapped [tunnelled] dugouts underground. It was a wonderful feeling to stagger down the stairs and get a brew on. They had soup kitchens in there too, you know. You'd get something to eat and lie down and stretch out. You'd left the bombs and shells behind you see. You were safe in there. You couldn't hear anything inside unless one landed near a doorway, then it made the candles jump, but otherwise it just shivered a bit when there was a barrage on. That was home for us.

Private Ted Rimmer, 2/6 Battalion,
King's Liverpool Regiment

For the British and Commonwealth troops the arrival of the dugout as an integral component of the trench war was a saviour, offering degrees of protection previously unknown in earlier forms of shelter surrounding Ypres. Protection was all about escaping the attentions of artillery, pitting the ingenuity of the engineer against the skill of the artilleryman. At the close of 1917 the British, at last with some hills of their own behind which to work, were in a position to exploit the geology of Passchendaele Ridge complex itself, and the Royal

Engineers and their Commonwealth colleagues were to make the most of the opportunities.

NUMBERS AND DEGREES OF PROTECTION

Before work began it was necessary to first prepare a scheme by calculating how many men needed to be accommodated in a chosen sector, so that the size and design of the dugout could be gauged and material needs calculated. Next came a consideration of the degree of protection required from artillery and mortar fire, something that evolved as the war progressed.

Elephant sections used to make a well-built splinter-proof shelter in a forward trench

It was again the German 5.9 which was used as a guide. A 5.9's average penetration in 'ordinary' topsoils was recognised as being 13' 6". Using this as a control the RE identified three basic categories of cover: splinter-proof, medium shell-proof and shell-proof.

Splinter-proof shelters offered a shield against the penetration of shell fragments of all calibres, and shrapnel balls. They were widely used for temporary emergency use in forward areas even where bombardments were regular, but were most numerous behind the lines. Here they protected troops working on communica-tions, roads and transport from desultory shelling, particularly with shrapnel. Simple to erect and quick and easy to build, splinter-proofs were usually based upon prefabricated corrugat-ed heavy steel 'elephant' shelter sections, usually with added protective material such as timber and sandbags piled on top. During Third Ypres, and prior to the construction of deep dugouts in the forward areas, thousands of splinter proofs provided limited but almost immediate cover the moment ground was occupied. Indeed, at the commencement of dugout works the tunnellers themselves sheltered in splinter-proofs until

Below left: Life inside an elephant. Australian artillerymen at Hill 60 in a shellproof, buried elephant shelter

Below right: A comfortable German elephant shelter occupied by evidently warm and well fed artillery signallers

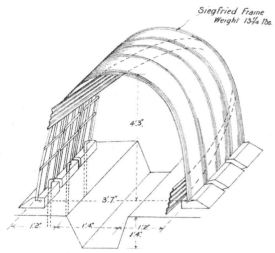

Above left: Small Siegfried type shelters in the ruins of Passchendaele village after German reoccupation in spring 1918

Above right: The Siegfried shelter, German equivalent to the British baby elephant

sufficient habitable accommodation was obtained underground. Large numbers of elephant sections can still be seen today, used as sheds and shelters by farmers and gardeners throughout Flanders.

I don't suppose you have ever carried an elephant section? I hated those bloody things – it would have been easier to carry a mule! I was always good at falling over anyway, but imagine four men on an eighteen-inch duck walk trying to manoeuvre those damned great lumps – you could only have one man on the track at a time; the others were in the mud. They were so heavy, you'd sink up to your knees under the weight. And if you dropped it, IT sank and you had to fumble about up to your elbows in muck to find an edge to lift, pull it out, which pushed you in further, so then your mates had to pull YOU out. Mind you, they were a lifesaver up front [in the forward areas]. There were small ones too, just for one man to crawl inside, babies we called them, but they were not so handy as you had no space to do anything or store anything. The sappers put in thousands of babies in the banks of streams and sunken roads.

Private Wilf Wallworth,
South Lancashire Regiment

Recycling the past: elephant shelter sections still in use today in Flanders

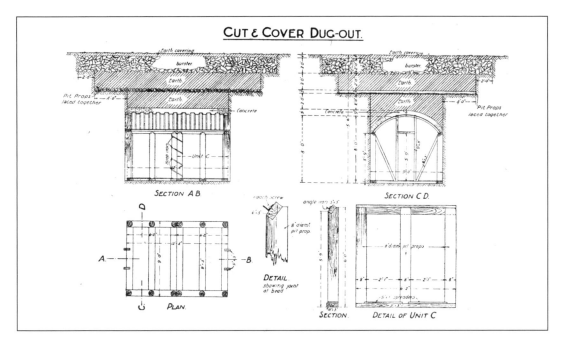

A cut-and-cover shelter showing arrangement of 'burster courses' above roof

Medium shell-proofs were 'safe' against direct hits of shells up to 5.9 calibre. These were often of the 'cut-and-cover' dugout variety, where a deep trench was dug, strongly revetted, then roofed over with elephant sections. On top of the elephants were arranged rows of heavy timbers, steel rails and girders, capped off with bonded layers of sandbags. Between the layers one or more air gaps were left to further cushion the impact of an explosion. A substantial depth of rubble was then piled on top of the bags to

Shallow, splinter proof cut-and-covers for accommodation in rear areas

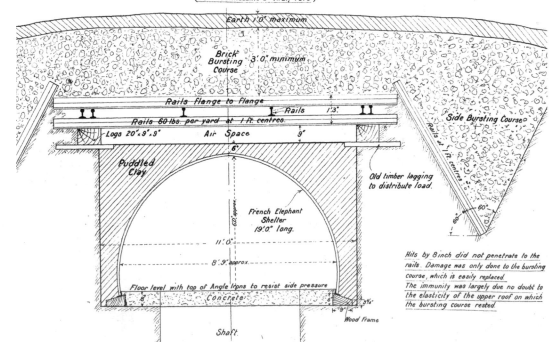

A cut-and-cover (shaft) dugout designed by 251 TC to be proof against 8-inch shells

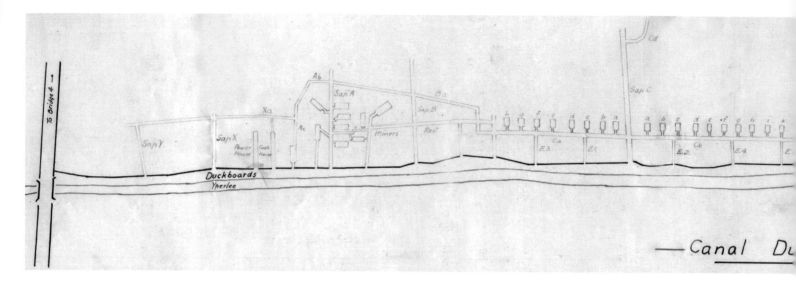

177 company's plans of the Canal Dugouts (sometimes called 'Shell-Out')

either deflect a shell from its trajectory before it burst, or cause it to explode before penetrating the protective barriers – 'deflector' and 'burster' courses. Without these added shielding layers, the shelter was decidedly still unsafe.

Whereas splinter- and medium shell-proofs were located either on or near the surface, shell-proofs were required to protect against direct hits of all sizes of shell, mortar and bomb, and had to be deep. It was impossible to be safe from every kind of projectile, but direct hits from super-heavy calibre weapons capable of driving a shell far enough into the ground to destroy mined dugouts were relatively unlikely. It could

certainly be a risk if a dugout was deliberately targeted, but such guns in German service in the Salient fired limited numbers of shells and had literally hundreds of alternative and more important targets to attend to. The engineers therefore settled upon a 'threshold' shell size for deep dugouts based on the two most common heavy troublemakers in the German armoury: the eight-inch howitzer and the heavy trench mortar, both fitted with delayed action fuse. The safe head cover against these depended upon the nature of the geology. The weakest material was 'made ground', a term encompassing the build up of soils, aggregates and waste materials by

The immaculately built British linear dugout system in the banks of the Yser Canal, courtesy of 177 TC

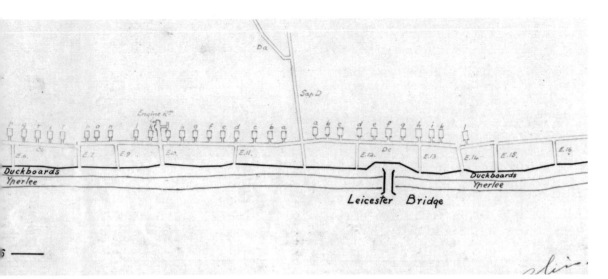

human activity – railway and canal embankments, for instance. However, certain man-made features such old pavé roads built from cobbles of hard sandstone offered excellent instant 'burster' protection and many dugouts were built in linear fashion beneath them. In this way entire villages on the surface were mirrored below ground. Wieltje, north of Ypres, is an excellent example.

The best natural head cover was provided by undisturbed geology, from hard rock and chalk to clay and sand. Only the latter two were present in the Salient. The 'safe' depth for each medium varied considerably.

Made Earth.....35 feet [10.6 metres]
Clay...............30 feet [9.1 metres]
Gravel...........25 feet [7.6 metres]
Chalk............25 to 20 feet [7.6-6.1 metres]
Hard Rock......15 feet [4.5 metres]

Military Engineering Part IV,
Military Mining and Demolitions, 1923

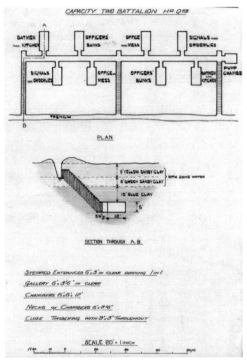

Contemporary plan showing relationship between dugouts and geology

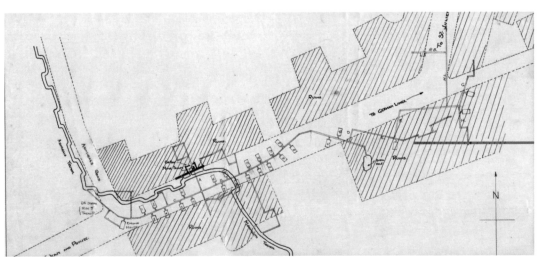

British workings undermining the village of Wieltje near Ypres. Note entrances from house cellars

Sand was by far the most arresting material, and in this soil type safe depths could be almost halved by comparison to clay. Massive shells could of course be escaped by going ever deeper, but this only meant that both construction and access and egress was a more lengthy and difficult process. It was, of course, not always geologically possible to go as deep as recommended, and tests were carried out using combinations of materials to produce an enhanced degree of cover by other means. Protecting even a small HQ dugout with the kind of complex timber and steel arrangement designed to burst shells before they penetrated deeply (as employed with cut-and-covers) was impractical as the deep works, even average-sized ones to house a company, simply extended over too

A section of Edgeworth David's dugout suitability map, drawn up from borehole information. Black dots denote good locations; red shading, dry; blue shades, wet

GENERAL CLASSIFICATION OF GROUND

ACCORDING TO

ITS SUITABILITY FOR DUG-OUTS, &c.

large an area; adding extra surface protection was therefore out of the question not only because of the huge amount of protective material required but also because enemy airmen might easily spot the work, both in preparation and after completion. The simplest method was to add headcover by placing the bags of excavated spoil over only the most vulnerable parts of the dugout – and making sure it was camouflaged. Galleries, being on the deepest contour of a dugout, were in fact relatively secure from shelling; it was inclines that were most at risk, particularly the five metres or so nearest the surface – another reason for installing multiple entrances. A company size dugout accommodating around 250 men might therefore have up to eight inclines. Protecting their upper sections could be done in several ways: by either doubling or even trebling the thickness of timber used – an expensive exercise in scarce material, or by building a brick or rubble burster course over the incline, with the addition of extra earth headcover.

LOCATION, LOCATION, LOCATION

The positioning of dugouts was of prime importance. When choosing a site the first consideration had of course to be tactical; there was no point building a system in a place where it would not fully benefit the sector it served. Access by roads or tracks should also be good enough to fulfil the transport and stores needs of the personnel engaged in construction of the dugout, those who would eventually be quartered inside, and for reliefs of the garrison to take place without undue congestion. This meant that the nearer the dugout was to a road, trench tramway or duckboard track, the better. As the construction itself drew upon vast quantities of materiel, an equally accessible dump was also required nearby which, if possible, should also be concealable from enemy observation.

After potential dugout sites had been selected, a geological investigation was usually made by boring a core sample to ascertain the suitability of the ground at depth. Beginning in May 1916, the tunnelling companies themselves carried out this work, with most of the post-Messines investigations being done by the AEMMBC – the Australian Electrical and Mechanical Mining and Boring Company. Their arrival in Flanders had coincided with the zenith of the great mining effort against the Messines Ridge and invaluable investigative work had been done to assist mining schemes, particularly where tunnellers had struck unexpectedly troublesome strata and required advice on which way to tunnel to avoid water, shattered ground, running sands, etc. Bores, quick and easy to execute, supplied immediate answers in places where the geology was not uniform or predictable. The systematic boring programmes of 1917 gave Edgeworth David at Mines HQ all the information he needed to construct his series of dugout suitability maps for the Salient. David was also to draw up geological sections of the ground 1,000 metres behind the German front lines, to gauge where the enemy were most likely to be installing dugouts, so they too might be targeted by British guns after photographic aerial investigation by the Royal Flying Corps.

Whilst three-quarters of the AEMMBC were employed on installation and maintenance of power plants and electric lighting systems in tunnels, dugouts and subways, the fifty-one-man Boring Section was the army's geological problem solving unit, investigating hundreds of sites for dugout suitability, and also locating another all important constituent of warfare, clean drinking water.

With the slacking off of active mining operations we had orders to drive our main galleries still further back and enlarge them for the passage of infantry. In this way was started the system of infantry 'subways'. Careful surveys were necessary as we had to provide not only access for the troops but construct concealed MG [machine gun] pits and 'secret outlets'. We were in fact making an underground fortress. A little later came a great innovation. An electric lighting plant was installed. Infantry dugouts leading off the main galleries were constructed. We even made underground wells. The water was pumped up and flowed through galvanised settling tanks before it was passed fit for drinking purposes. Stringent orders were issued as to keeping the subways sanitary. One private who broke the rules had used an envelope for his purpose. On it his name was clearly written, and he was sufficiently punished!

Lieutenant F Howkins, 253 TC, RE

After Third Ypres it was the British who held the ridge tops throughout the Salient. From the geo-

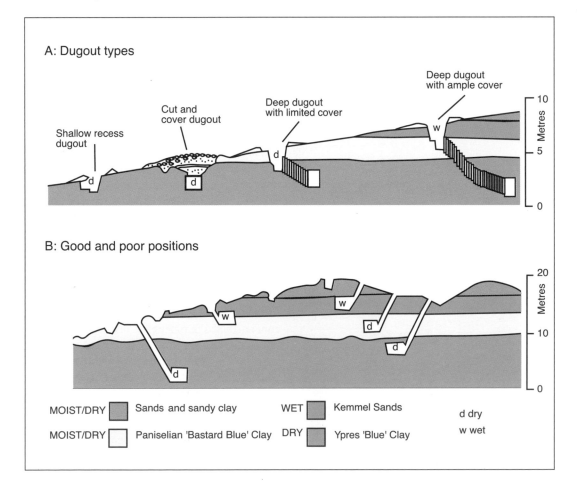

Geological influence on dugout depths along the Passchendaele Ridge

A candlelit dugout chamber used as an office at Hooge Crater

The range of timbering choices open to tunnellers when designing and building inclines up to slopes of 1:3 in differing geologies

logical viewpoint dugout construction here faced the same problems as military mining, except that one was no longer required to fight or retaliate in geologically unsuitable ground, and could choose the most favourable site. The overriding imperative was to get as deep as was necessary to be safe from shelling, preferably in the driest and most stable strata. Disregarding local variations, the geological separation and variation was of course still the same: dryish top, wet middle and comfortably dry lower strata. The upper layers of the Passchendaele Ridge complex were tantalising, but the drier sands that capped the top were generally found to act as a drain, filtering surface water to the wet Kemmel Sands beneath – the troublesome *Schwimmsande* again. Several dugouts were located in this upper layer simply because it was essential tactically, but most were installed in more hospitable geology. Just as with deep mines, deep British dugouts would have to penetrate the awkward saturated layer to exploit the 'bastard', and if possible, the 'blue', clays at greater depth. The Germans had attempted this in few places, choosing the valleys

between the spurs for their deeper work. In any case, on the ridge tops they had their massive concrete *Flandern Stellung* to rely upon. The British attacked the problem in the same way as at Messines, by studying the ground with bores and dropping back onto the lower flanks of the ridges where the Kemmel Sands were less troublesome.

Having ascertained the depth and thickness of the water-bearing layers, they were negotiated using the standard military mining methods which had by now become second nature to the tunnellers. However, for dugouts it was also equally critical to know the thickness of the deep clay bed beneath the sand layers, so that the workings could be sure of staying entirely within its impervious seam. Accidental piercing of the upper saturated layer (the *Schwimmsande*) was not the only risk: dugouts were considerably larger constructions than a tiny mine gallery, and penetration through the base of the clay bed into the fine water-bearing sands beneath would release vast quantities of water under high pressure; such a 'leak' could not be plugged.

CONSTRUCTION AND ACCOMMODATION

The most common way of getting underground was via stepped inclines (stairways), particularly for smaller systems such as Brigade or Battalion HQs. The traditional shaft was also used extensively, and not only in difficult ground, as it was the quickest, simplest and safest method of starting a scheme and reaching the required depth. Many tunnelling companies began sinking from the shelter of cellars of ruined houses and farms (which were of course, normally close to transport routes), but in more exposed places a protective elephant section 'penthouse' was built over the shaft site. This was sunk to trench depth or beyond, depending upon surface water levels, protected with almost three metres of substantial extra cover on top consisting, in ascending order, of: steel rails; brickwork; earth (cushion); bags of brick (deflector); more earth; and finally a cap of concrete slabs or paving stones as a burster. The whole lot was then camouflaged with soil.

Now relatively secure, a 'pilot' shaft was sunk. This could be either timber or steel, again dependent upon geology and water table. Having reached the desired final depth, a lateral gallery was driven, and from here the first inclines, each at least twelve metres apart, were begun, working from the gallery level upwards towards the

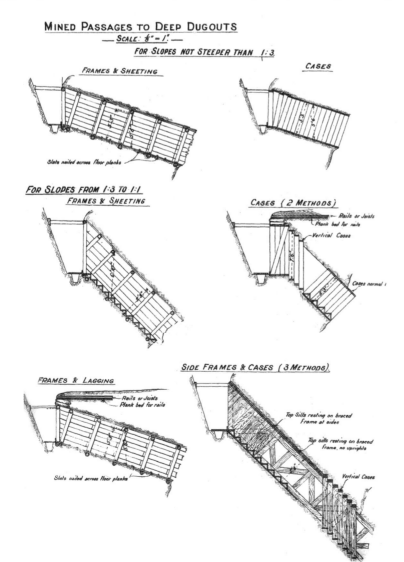

MINED PASSAGES TO DEEP DUGOUTS

— SCALE: ⅛" = 1'. —

FOR SLOPES NOT STEEPER THAN 1:3

FRAMES & SHEETING

Slats nailed across floor planks

CASES

FOR SLOPES FROM 1:3 TO 1:1

FRAMES & SHEETING

CASES (2 METHODS)

Rails or Joists
Plank bed for rails
Vertical Cases
Cases normal

FRAMES & LAGGING

Rails or Joists
Plank bed for rails

Slats nailed across floor planks

SIDE FRAMES & CASES (3 METHODS)

Top Sills resting on braced Frame at sides
Top sills resting on braced Frame, no uprights
Vertical Cases

An entrance in a well-revetted support trench. Note slope of doorway to allow gas blanket to form a firm seal by gravity

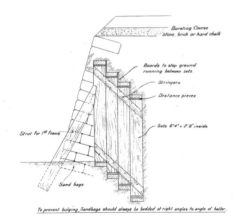

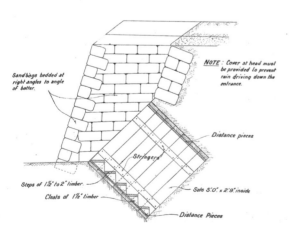

surface. When a shaft was not necessary, stepped inclines were sunk. In this case only the initial incline was driven downwards from the surface to gallery level; all subsequent work was done from below, driving each further stairway upwards, thereby using gravity as a working aid. Inclines were almost universally constructed with entrances driven either towards the enemy from

Far left: Entrance designs beneath trench parapet

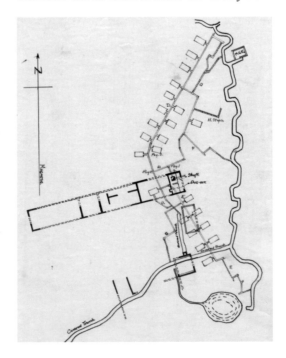

Left: Hilltop Farm dugout. A double Brigade, double Battalion and Artillery HQ in front of Pilckem Ridge. The initial shaft has been sunk from the cellar of the farm

Right: The way to the stars. View from the foot of a stepped incline.

Far right: An 'Ideal' HQ dugout plan according to RE manuals. Thanks to the wide variation in the geology of the Salient the finished article only occasionally matched the model design

Below: Martha House near Zonnebeke. An unfinished scheme. Tools and timber left behind when the dugout was abandoned during the British withdrawal of spring 1918

Below right: Grand opening of the 'Catacombs' under Hill 63 near Ploegsteert, started by British Pioneers, massively extended by the British and Canadian - and obviously completed by Australians. The dugout provided shelter for 3,000 men

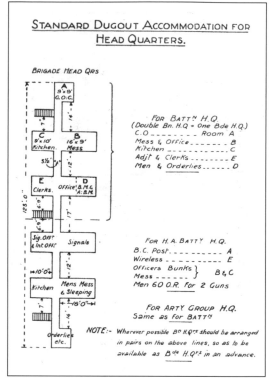

the front wall of the trench, or side on from a traverse, to avoid the possibility of incoming hostile shells falling 'down the throat' of a dugout.

Now at depth, the tunnellers had room to store timber, equipment, steel and spoil for the night-time fatigue parties, and ammunition, food, etc., for the infantry. As each entrance was completed – even the smallest of dugouts normally required at least two to create a natural flow of air just as in mine workings – so spoil removal became easier, facilitating the immediate or future extension of the dugout to whatever size was required. The ultimate design or 'shape' of a dugout was again dependent upon geological variation. Whereas the RE had drawn up 'ideal' designs for all kinds of dugouts, especially for

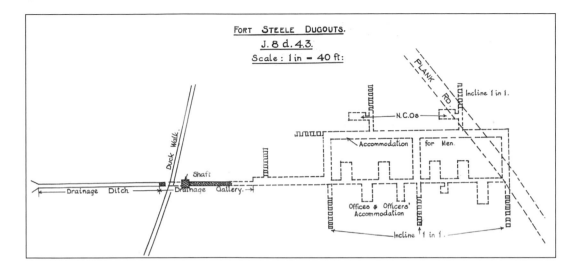

Fort Steele dugouts near Nonne Boschen follow the 'ideal' Battalion HQ design, and were therefore clearly in good tunnelling ground

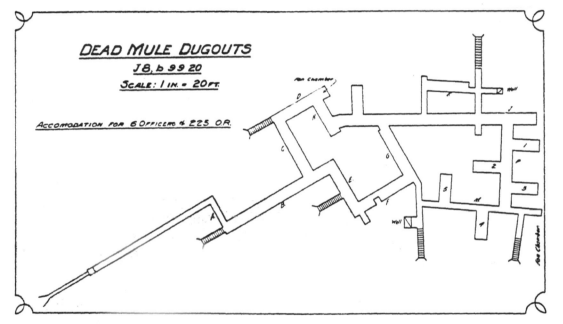

Fort Steele's neighbour: Dead Mule dugouts near Nonne Boschen where geological variation forced the tunnellers to construct an unusual box shaped design

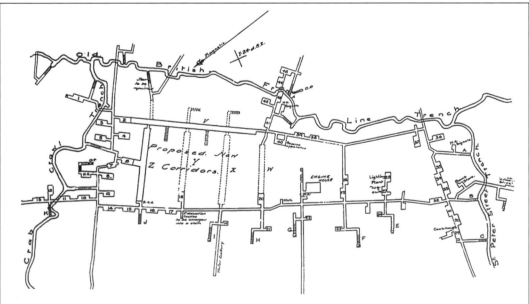

Tor Top dugout complex formed the central section of a large interconnected system joining Sanctuary Wood with Mount Sorrel. It was here that Edmund Blunden was Tunnel Major in 1917. The dugout system was connected to the tunnels; they can be seen running out under the front line. Note parallel wide bunked galleries

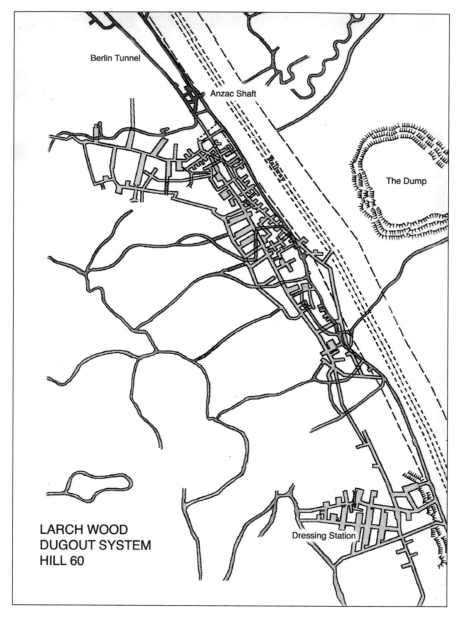

LARCH WOOD
DUGOUT SYSTEM
HILL 60

Larch Wood dugouts. A huge system connected to the Hill 60 and Caterpillar mines. The dugouts are believed to have accommodated 3,000 men

Fitting bunks in dugouts on the Belgian coast. The pressure of the sand geology in this sector restricted gallery widths to a single bunk

headquarters personnel, they could not always be followed in practice. For example, two dugouts designed for the same purpose, on the same contour and in apparently identical geology, which might have been expected to have an identical plan, could end up looking completely different due to local geological variation. Edgeworth David had consulted a wide range of information to produce his dugout suitabillty maps, but only vertical bores could give conclusive information of the geology in the precise spot where they were sunk; without sinking thousands of bores local lateral variation was impossible to gauge until one was actually underground. To assess this the tunnellers did the job themselves, using small horizontal bores called augers to test the continued suitability of ground ahead.

I was working in the Westminster Tunnel in front of Messines Ridge. One day early in 1917 a branch of a tunnel in the Westminster was being driven to connect with an officer's front line dugout so he could travel underground to the support trenches. I was using a 2" auger at the end of 35–40 foot pipe for testing the ground ahead of me. It so happened that I made a bee-line for one of the metal sheets on the wall of the officers dugout. I thought I had struck a rock. I was dragging my auger back and forth and I scared the hell out of the officers – they thought it was Fritz breaking in and I had them all on the go. They sent an SOS to the mining engineering officer and sapper. So in about 15 or 20 minutes I heard the big Major's booming voice shouting at me – had I struck sheet metal? I told him that I had hit something at about 35 feet and I had been trying to by-pass it for the last fifteen or twenty minutes. So he told me I had had the army moving from the front line! I can't recollect the Major's name but we used to call him 'Big Noise' – he was about 6' 6", 250 lbs, and his voice used to vibrate the tunnel.

Sapper James Colly, 3rd Canadian TC

Spoil disposal was just as important in dugout work as in mining: if the enemy spotted telltale blue clay, even when used in sandbags to buttress trenches, the area was guaranteed to arouse the interest of enemy gunners. Indeed, sudden additions of lots of bags on parapets or in shell holes were deliberately targeted by snipers and artillery to investigate the contents. When the Germans realised the scale of British dugout schemes, the suspected sites, with the potential to house many hundreds of troops, became important targets; heavy naval

guns drove delayed action shells deep into the earth. The results of an explosion of a big shell at depth were similar in nature to the blowing of a *camouflet*, destroying part of a dugout, gassing the occupants (carbon monoxide was of course also a by-product of artillery shells) or killing men by concussion or obliteration. No protection could be absolutely relied upon against the big guns.

The erection of bunks in dugouts was commenced as soon as galleries were completed, often with the assistance of field company or pioneer battalion personnel, so that accommodation was made available with the minimum of delay. Bunking was a topic of surprising complexity. In front-line dugouts a man could expect to own an average of two and a half square metres of floor space; in reserve lines the figure rose to a luxurious three or three and a half. Bunks were often stacked in tiers of three, often two deep, the uprights of which formed part of the roof support. Each bunk itself consisted of a timber frame, with square mesh or heavy chicken wire to support the weight of the occupants. It may have been rudimentary, but to men used to sleeping on the fire step of a front line trench, it was most acceptable.

Speed of egress in an emergency was naturally a most important aspect of dugout construction. In a normal gallery, bunked on one side, the space for men to rouse themselves, prepare kit, and exit the dugout was severely

limited. In tests it was found that dugouts with no bunking at all – with the troops sleeping on the floor – were the most efficient, as far more room was available for preparation and progress in the event of alarm. Surprisingly, a dugout like this could also accommodate the same number of men as one with two tiers of double bunks. But of course many dugouts were wet, or at least damp, and for the sake of comfort, the 'bunkless dugout' idea was not adopted.

Once the gallery network was in place and accommodation provided, shafts with specialist uses could be raised. Wherever the terrain was tactically favourable, such as on the slopes of a ridge, observation shafts were built, again driven from gallery level upwards, with the final camouflaged post at the surface being installed at night. These were key positions for Field Survey Company officers, artillery spotters and photographic reconnaissance personnel. In the most hazardous locations where the enemy were particularly attentive and minimal surface disturbance was required, telescopic submarine

Above left: Martha House. Main gallery showing bunk uprights used to strengthen roof span. Note the handles of Beck double-handed trench pump protruding from water at end of gallery

Above right: Main gallery of Martha House. The wire mesh of the bunks still retains the impression of the many soldiers who slept here in early 1918

Below: embankment on the Ypres-Comines canal with armoured OP position. Similar specialist designs were used for ridges with entrances on the sheltered rear slopes and observation posts just beyond the crest

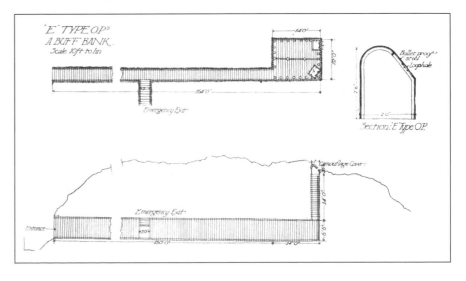

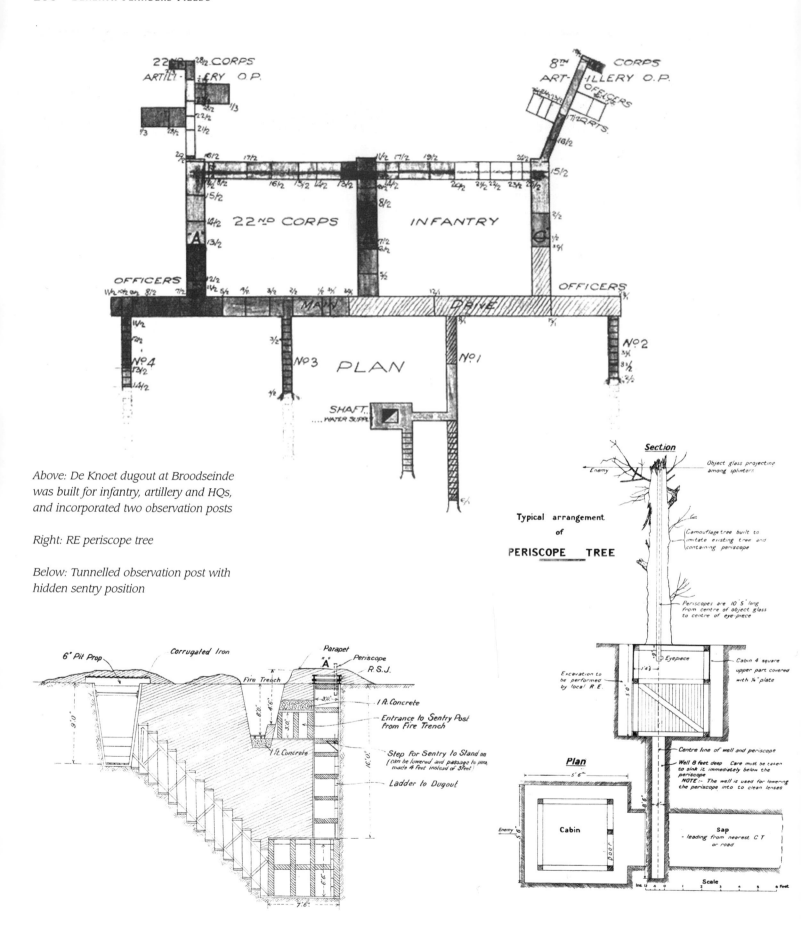

Above: De Knoet dugout at Broodseinde was built for infantry, artillery and HQs, and incorporated two observation posts

Right: RE periscope tree

Below: Tunnelled observation post with hidden sentry position

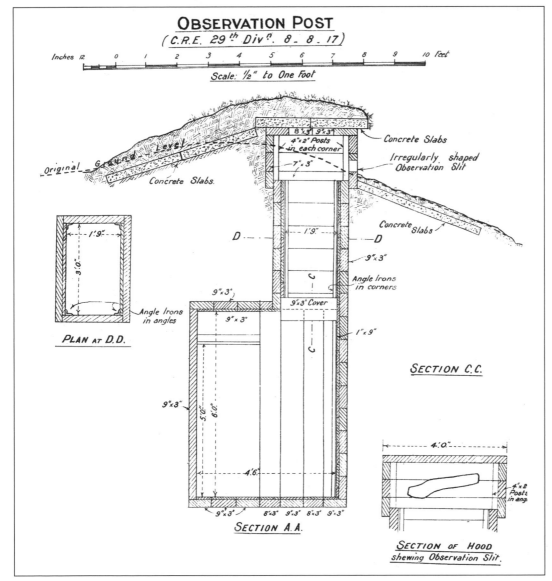

OBSERVATION POST
(C.R.E. 29ᵗʰ Divⁿ. 8 - 8 - 17)

Inches 12   0   1   2   3   4   5   6   7   8   9   10 Feet

Scale: ½" to One Foot

Concrete Slabs

Original Ground Level

Concrete Slabs.

8"×3" 9"×3"
4"×2" Posts in each corner
7"×3"

Concrete Slabs
Irregularly shaped Observation Slit

1'9"

D — — D

C

1'9"

9"×3"

Angle Irons in corners

Angle Irons in angles

3'0"

PLAN at D.D.

9"×3"

9"×3" Cover

9"×3"

9"×3"

5'0"
6'0"

1"×9"

4'6"

9"×3"   8"×3"   9"×3"   8"×3"   9"×3"

SECTION A.A.

SECTION C.C.

4'0"

4"×2 Posts in ang.

SECTION of HOOD shewing Observation Slit.

Above: British panorama reconnaissance photograph taken from Primus dugout OP on the Passchendaele Ridge in March 1918. The dugout is today in a serious state of decay and is believed to undermine two houses and the main road

Left: A design of observation post often used in ridge top dugouts. Compare the shape of the viewing aperture in the hood (bottom right) with the panorama above

Below: Submarine telescope installed beneath the lip of a mine crater at the Bluff

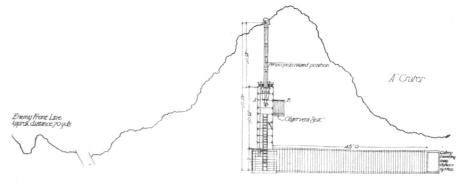

SUBMARINE PERISCOPES AT THE BLUFF
Scale 10ft to 1in

Periscope in raised position

A Crater

Enemy Front Line Apprx distance 70 yds

Observers Seat

periscopes were fitted, leaving the observers comfortable and safe deep in the bowels of the dugout.

When the dugout was finished the original pilot shaft still served an important purpose, giving extra ventilation, and being especially useful for delivery of stores, keeping the inclines free for troop movement alone. Apart from free movement within the dugout, speed of egress was also a critical feature. Laddered shafts had worked well as a means of access in mining schemes where traffic was limited to a few tun-

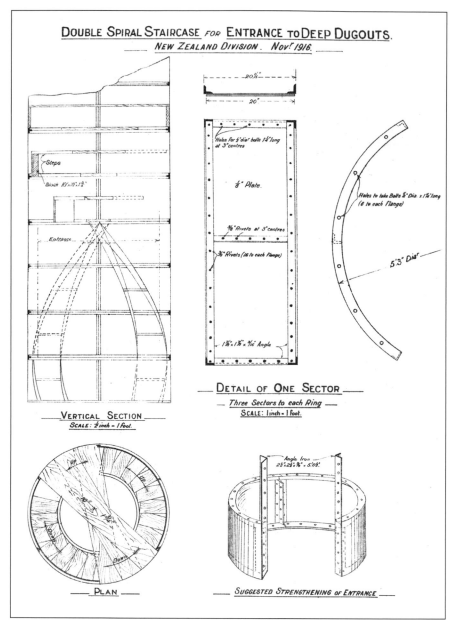

DOUBLE SPIRAL STAIRCASE for ENTRANCE to DEEP DUGOUTS.
NEW ZEALAND DIVISION. Nov.r 1916.

VERTICAL SECTION
SCALE: ½ inch - 1 Foot.

DETAIL OF ONE SECTOR
Three Sectors to each Ring
SCALE: 1 inch - 1 foot.

PLAN

SUGGESTED STRENGTHENING of ENTRANCE

nelling personnel, but were found to have flaws where large numbers of men were involved. In some sectors spiral staircases were installed, and even double spiral stairways where men could ascend and descend the same shaft. Although truly ingenious, both types were found to be slow in practice, and difficult for a man carrying rifle and full kit to negotiate. Although a few spirals were installed in the Fromelles sector of French Flanders by the Australians, they were discouraged elsewhere.

DUGOUTS FOR ALL PURPOSES
Dugouts accommodated a wide variety of troops. Command headquarters for company, battalion, brigade and divisional staffs within easy reach of the front lines were essential; signal posts, machine gun positions and observation points, all permanently manned works, also needed emplacements which incorporated deep shelters, as did trench mortar units. Aid posts and dressing stations were to be a

Above: Double spiral staircase designed by New Zealand Engineers

Right: The 'ideal' Battery HQ design for heavy artillery

Above right: A chamber in an artillery HQ dugout. Note electric lighting, telephone and typewriter.

BATTERY HEADQUARTERS for HEAVY ARTILLERY.

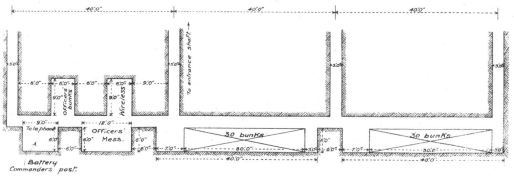

PLAN.

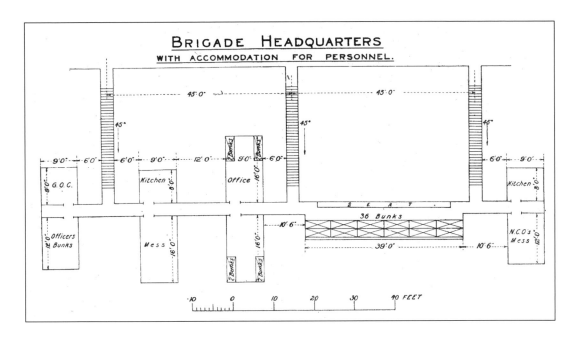

BRIGADE HEADQUARTERS
WITH ACCOMMODATION FOR PERSONNEL.

Left: Brigade HQ dugout design

Below left: Design for a 600-man dugout off a sunken road

Below right:Tunnelled machine gun emplacement

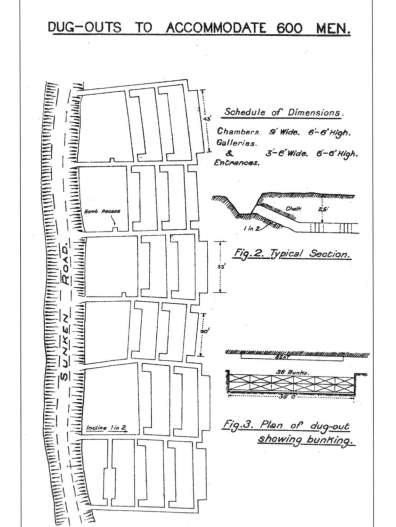

DUG-OUTS TO ACCOMMODATE 600 MEN.

Schedule of Dimensions.

Chambers. 9' Wide. 6'-6' High.
Galleries. & 3'-6' Wide. 6'-6' High.
Entrances.

Fig.2. Typical Section.

Fig.3. Plan of dug-out showing bunking.

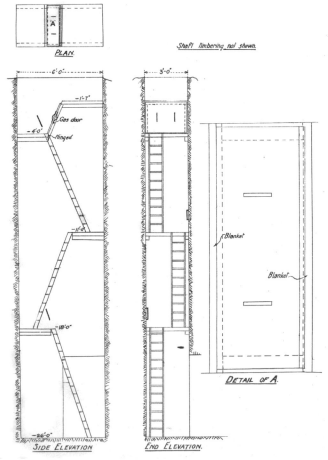

MACHINE GUN EMPLACEMENT
CHAMPAGNE TYPE
with Vertical Shaft to Dugout made by 172nd Tunnelling Co. R.E.
for Canadian Corps. Sept. 1917.

PLAN.

SIDE ELEVATION   END ELEVATION.   DETAIL OF A.

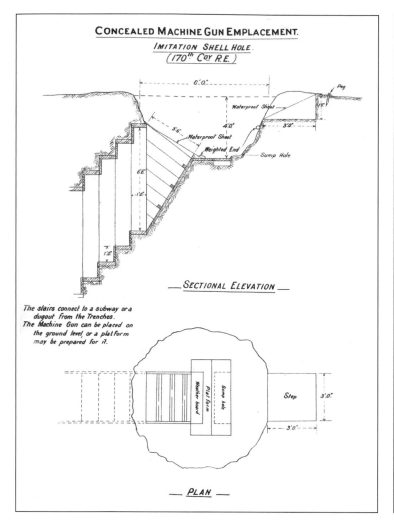

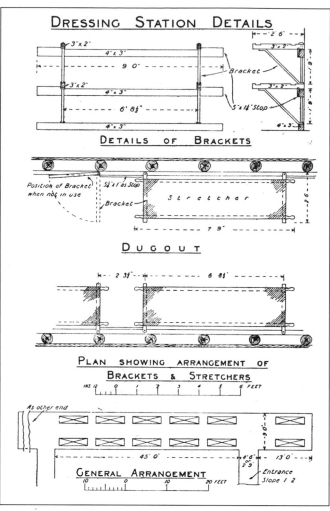

Above left: Imitation shell-hole machine gun post

Above right: Dressing station dugout

common adjunct of many systems in forward areas. Above all, there was the huge demand for a safe haven for tens of thousands of infantry and artillery troops. Although the city itself was a ruin, in Ypres every available house cellar had been converted into a shelter for troops 'at rest'.

I decided not to go into the actual fighting front but remained in Ypres. Passing over the levelled ruins, one sees here and there smoking orifices, which appear like innumerable fumaroles. There is quite a piquant odour to the smoke, which needs no telling that the occupants in the cellars are preparing grub. Large numbers are now billeted in these subterranean rooms. Even there they are not safe, for at evening Ypres is heavily bombed and shelled and even the formidable reinforcing of the roofs (the top being strengthened by piling sandbags and reinforcing with heavy beams and girders) is insufficient for safety.

Captain Frank Hurley,
Australian photographer, 31 October 1917

Section of gallery in Martha House dugout ready for installation of bunking

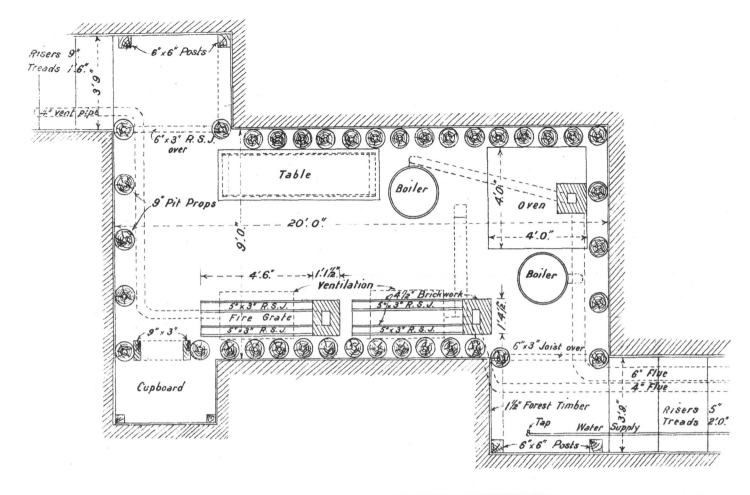

Plan of cookhouse in deep dugout

In the forward areas most if not all tunnelled systems, regardless of size, were constructed according to standard gallery and chamber dimensions, although building techniques differed according to site. Geology was once more the prime controlling factor. As in mining, close timbered setts were obligatory in the heavy Ypres Clay, whereas in the sandier, Paniselian 'bastard blue clay', frames with lagging or sheeting were used. Using a mix of setts and

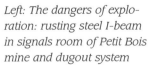

Left: The dangers of exploration: rusting steel I-beam in signals room of Petit Bois mine and dugout system

Far left: Joinery workshop in Bridge 6. Note sheeted rear wall and setted side walls

Below: The Home Front. Women foresters in the south of England felling timber for Flanders

Bottom: The Western Front. Indian forestry workers in French woodland

frames within the same dugout was not unusual, illuminating the tunnellers' encounter with geological variation as work progressed. In some cases, just as in the deep mines, pressure from swelling clays meant that rolled steel joists were required.

I visited 255 Coy when they were engaged in making dugouts near the summit of the ridge to the south-east of Houthulst Forest. Of all the examples of heavy pressure in blue clay, this was one of the very worst I ever saw. Steel elephant sections were used at first, as timber however thick was broken like matches overnight. But the elephant sections closed in like gigantic grab-dredges or nut-crackers, and it was only by using 3″ steel joists spaced at 18″ centres for top, sides and bottom, that it was possible to make a dugout at all. Of course it was necessary also to hold the girder sets together by means of special steel clips to prevent movement. The actual excavation was carried out more easily than many miners might imagine, for it was not until the clay had been exposed to the air for a little time that it seemed to develop its properties as a fluid.

Captain H R Dixon,
Assistant Inspector of Mines

Timber dimensions for all types of dugouts were deliberately standardised soon after the decision to commence large-scale dugout schemes had been made in 1916, during the latter stages of the Somme battle. Forestry companies were raised to provide the timber for the front, supplying raw materials to sawmills in France and Britain where they were cut to size ready for despatch to RE depots. With massive dugout schemes following hard on the heels of the huge mining enterprises of 1915 and 1916, shortages were not uncommon. Timber not only came from France and the UK, it had to be shipped from overseas, particularly the Baltic and Canada, for use underground in Flanders.

Much was also salvaged from dugouts which had become defunct after an advance, usually to build others in more suitable locations. This happened on a large scale after the advance at Third Ypres, with many timbered dugouts near the old front lines being dismantled by pioneers, field companies and army troops companies under RE tunneller supervision, to be moved forward by tramway to prospective new sites. During the battle itself many tunnellers had at last been allowed to emerge into daylight, albeit temporarily, to construct bridges and tank crossings over streams, and build roads across the devastated landscape of battle. Salvage was essential at this time as timber shortage was acute; vast quantities of wood were suddenly needed for hard standings for lorries, artillery platforms and 'corduroy' or plank roads to the forward areas. In the meantime dugout schemes were put on hold waiting for the new lines of battle to form.

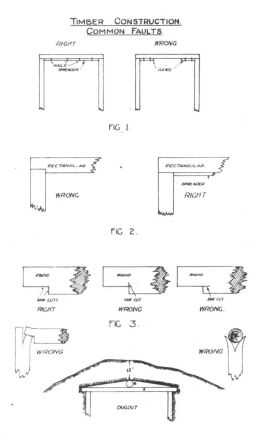

LIVING SPACE

Timber dugout setts, which were fitted *vertically*, were simply longer versions of the standard nine by three inch (23 x 8 cm) mining variety; frames on the other hand could be of sawn timber or unsawn poles or pit-props with the lagging or sheeting fitted horizontally behind them. Sheeting could be timber planking, heavy steel plates, expanded metal or corrugated iron, depending upon the geology and the availability of materials. As timber size was regulated, it follows that the dimensions of underground

spaces were also standardised. Access galleries were a standard 6' 4" (1.9 m) high by 2' 9" (0.8 m) wide, and bunked galleries and separate chambers 6' 4" (1.9 m) by 8' 6" (2.4 m) – dimensions which were calculated to be adequate for most purposes. Perhaps the most extraordinary statistic of all is the amount of timber that was consumed in dugout construction; to accommodate each soldier of the tens of thousands of men housed underground in the Salient required over 200 linear metres of wood.

Top left; Precise RE guidance for correct timber construction methods

Top right: Ravine Wood dugout, a battalion HQ and infantry accommodation, showing the use of pit props and sheeted walls. Note the corrugated roof cladding and blue clay

Bottom left: Hairpin clip used to fix steel beam to legs

Bottom right: A variety of girder clips for dugout use

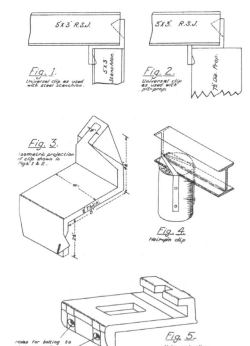

*Right: A semi-buried infantry
subway on the Belgian coast*

*Far right: Subway section
with lighting detail*

*Below: Typical arrangement
of subways, dugouts and
ancillary works between the
front-line and reserve
trenches*

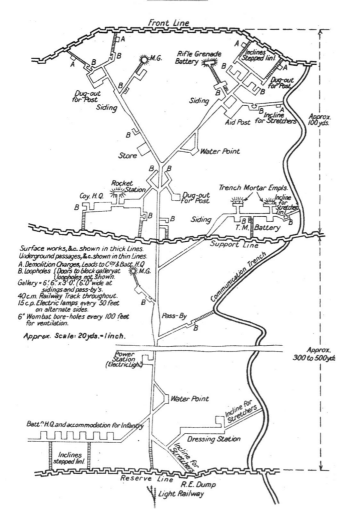

SUB-WAYS.

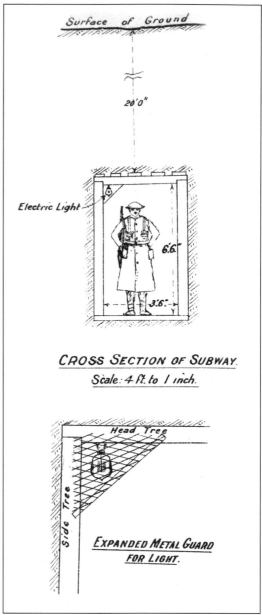

CROSS SECTION OF SUBWAY.
Scale: 4 ft. to 1 inch.

EXPANDED METAL GUARD
FOR LIGHT.

Constructing more spacious accommodation would undeniably have added to the 'luxury' of a dugout, but the non-standard, heavyweight metal and timber required to support spaces with spans of more than nine feet (2.7 m) made the proposition unfeasible. Subways, an extension of the dugout principle, were a special case. Literally serving as underground communication trenches, they were tunnelled in places where access to the front line via normal communication trenches on the surface was particularly hazardous by day and night. Often connected to front, support and reserve lines by inclines, they were subject to heavy use and required larger dimensions to accommodate men to pass each other in 'two-way traffic'; for this reason, at four feet (1.2 m) the galleries were made a little wider than normal. In several places in the Salient subways were crucial to allow reliefs and delivery of stores to take place unmolested, and in the year before the Battle of Messines over four and a half kilometres were built, most of which incorporated often extensive dugout systems along their length.

There were also 'offensive' subways such as that at Lancashire Farm in the northern part of the Salient which were designed to be used as a conduit for attacking troops to swarm out in attack by connecting the reserve trench with the front line. Such subways had already proved themselves at Vimy Ridge and Arras in 1917, in these cases driven through the chalk of Artois. Dugouts were generally not attached to this kind of subway until their offensive purposes had become defunct.

Some of the most popular dugout locations were mine craters. Throughout the war, thanks to their superiority in crater fighting, the Germans

Top: Working the pumps for the Hooge dugout system. Note the spoil being trammed out in trucks

Below: Inside Hooge crater dugouts during construction

Far left: Spiling (sheet piling). A method devised for tunnelling in poor ground, seen here in use in the sandy geology of the Belgian coast. The planking (top) was driven forward ahead of the workings to support the geology above whilst timber setts were installed

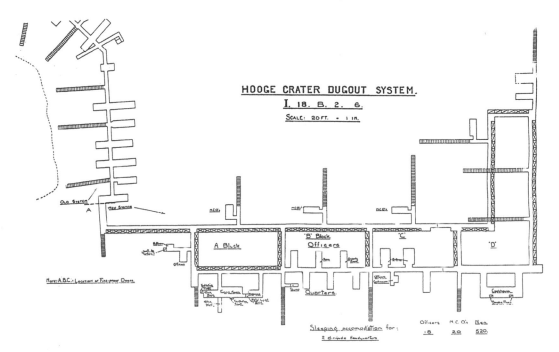

HOOGE CRATER DUGOUT SYSTEM.
I. 18. B. 2. 6.
SCALE: 20 FT. = 1 IN.

Plan of old and new Hooge dugouts. The old system was driven from Cassels' July 1915 crater seen here on the left

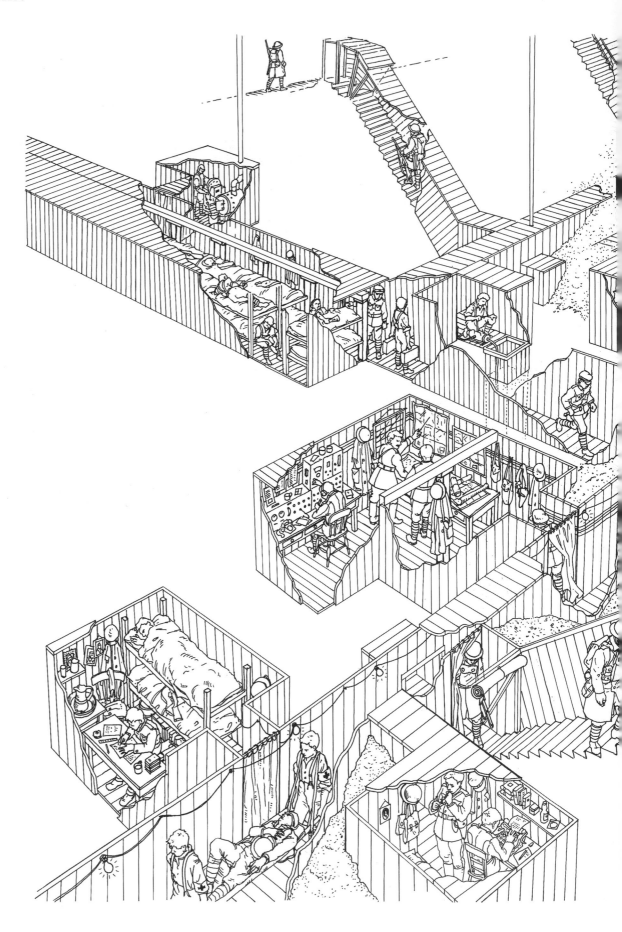

An evocation of part of a large multi-use deep dugout constructed between the support and reserve trenches. Many of the activities which took place underground can be seen here. Note the sleeved vertical holes for ventilation, and the 'mop-heads' to block the orifice in case of gas attack. Gas curtains are fitted at top and bottom of each incline.

The system is electrically lit from its own small petrol-driven generating plant. Accommodation is provided in bunked galleries for ordinary ranks, with space for NCOs situated at either end; officers have their own separate chambers. There are servants' quarters, a mess, a cookhouse, a dressing station and a pump chamber. There are offices for battalion and brigade headquarter use, and a chamber for communication

possessed most of the useful craters in the Salient and put them to immediate and good use as shelters. After the St Eloi mines of 27 March 1916, they discovered that the effect of the massive mine explosions on the surrounding geology was not to shatter it, but to compact and stabilise the earth in the vicinity of the crater; what had once been difficult soil to excavate therefore became good ground. Several of the Messines craters were also found to have these 'altered properties' and the British took advantage by installing dugout systems of all sizes. One of the most interesting sites is the Caterpillar Crater opposite Hill 60. On the surface adjacent to the crater, with its weeping willows and birdsong, a secret garden with a bloody history, the remains of the German front line pillbox defences are still visible amongst the undergrowth; under the northern lip of the crater lies Cumberland House dugout, a large Battalion and Brigade HQ system with accommodation for around 300 men.

COMFORT BELOW GROUND

Within reason, conditions underground were made to be as comfortable as possible for the troops. There were three critical aspects which affected the environment: water, light and ventilation.

No dugout was entirely waterproof. Most of those in good clay were naturally fairly dry thanks to the impervious nature of the geology, any ingress of water coming either from poorly finished entrances, or seepage through the incline timbers as they passed through the wet strata, between the clay and the surface. This was the result of rain water prevented from moving deeper into the earth by the clay itself, and the quantity of water finding its way into a system therefore varied according to the degree of saturation of the particular water-bearing strata in the immediate area. Just as in the trenches above, all dugout systems had 'sumps' – pits designed to collect excess water. In good, dry ground these might need emptying just once or twice a day, whilst in other places the occupants were almost permanently struggling and cursing on the pumps. If a dugout was found to have been built in wet ground, it was either due to unexpected encounters with water-bearing ground during construction, or the absolute tactical necessity of having deep shelter at that particular spot.

General drainage was effected, again as in mines, by planning and building the whole dugout complex on an incline of at least 1:50, which encouraged water to run away naturally over the floor and into the sumps. Sumps were always located near the foot of inclines so that evacuation hoses could be run up the stairways and into drainage systems on the surface, wherever possible carrying the water away from the system so that it did not re-percolate down into the dugout again. Concrete flooring, between three and seven-and-a-half centimetres thick and reinforced with expanded metal or chicken wire, helped drainage, kept the dugout clean, and inhibited the general wear and tear caused by thousands of cleated boots. Duckboards, universally used to keep the feet dry in trenches, were discouraged in dugouts as they collected dirt and reduced the already restricted headroom. Chambers too were built to drain, sloping towards their doors, where there was usually a small step down to the gallery to contain any fluctuating water levels in the 'corridors'. Great skill was needed for draining large dugouts. In this case the system was designed and built in separately graded sections, each having its own dedicated slope to one or more dedicated sumps.

Dugouts which had to be built in sandier strata, such as at Broodseinde, Hill 60, Hooge, Mount Sorrel or Tor Top, although satisfactory during dry periods, acted like a drain during times of heavy rain, particularly if the surface was heavily shell-pitted and fractured. Water filtered from the sandy sediments above through to the galleries below. Men descending the stairways after a spell in sodden trenches and outposts rightfully hoped for a little warmth and comfort, and a damp dugout dripping with water could be intensely aggravating.

Methods of keeping dugouts as dry as possible: sheeting the roof and preventing ingress of water at the entrances

METHOD OF USING CORRUGATED IRON SHEETS TO PREVENT ROOF LEAKAGE.

DRAINAGE SUMPS AT ENTRANCE

METHOD No. 1.

METHOD No. 2.

DOUBLED TOP SILLS OVER ENTRANCE.

ON EDGE.

We arrived at Hooge where the tunnellers are excavating a series of underground dugouts, which will be occupied by the headquarters of our infantry. It is a wretched job as they are working 25 feet below the surface level and most of the time knee deep in mud. From the roof trickles water and mud, which they jocularly term 'hero juice' on account of it percolating through tiers and tiers of buried corpses. Most of these men are miners and they are applying their knowledge to supreme advantage whilst the Boche shells whiz and burst around them.

Captain Frank Hurley,
Australian photographer, 17 September 1917

The problem of percolation from the surface was ameliorated partly by filling in the shellholes above, but underground the engineers also developed an internal system of catchment which was used universally no matter how damp the dugout. Overlapping corrugated iron sheets, known as lagging, were fitted to the ceiling to catch water dripping through the roof timbers, carrying it to a sump, from where it was pumped

Detail of remains of water-proofing in a dugout gallery. Martha House

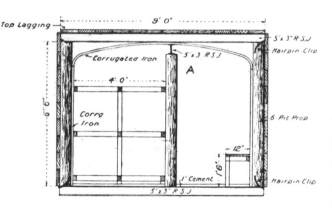

to the surface. In some geological conditions dampness through dugout walls was also a problem. A damp-resistant lining was particularly important in chambers where electrical equipment was used, such as in signals dugouts, and this was dealt with by using tarred felt to form a kind of damp-proof 'wallpaper'. Troops also added to their own comfort by tacking spare waterproof ground sheets to the walls.

In the dark recesses beneath the Salient, much consideration was given to lighting. This was important not only because darkness begets dirt – rats were a perennial

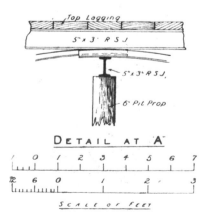

Far left: Method of water-proofing chambers with corrugated iron sheets

Left: Candlelit gallery at Yorkshire Trench dugouts

Officers of the South Staffordshire Regiment reading by candlelight

special cases, such as dressing stations and some HQs, dugout walls were painted white, and this gave a much more pleasant and bright environment in which to live and work, but these were the exception rather than the rule. Commonly, lighting was provided by oil lamps or candles. The psychological comfort of a little personal light in an otherwise murky environment led to candles becoming a form of currency, and the plea of 'Any candles, pal?' could always be heard from incoming troops. Inside, candles were fixed on small holders, occasionally with a mirror to reflect as much of the valuable radiance as possible, and placed in convenient crevices, on bunks, or just stuck to the walls using a material of which there was certainly no shortage – clay. Thanks to the AEMMBC electric lighting was not uncommon underground, especially in subways and larger dugout systems. A dugout might have its own petrol-driven lighting plant, or be fed by a single large central generator serving up to six smaller satellite systems by underground cableway. Individual sets were doubly useful, as the heat produced by both the machine and its exhaust could be used for drying clothes or warming chilled bodies as well as powering lamps, fans and pumps.

The use of powerplants could involve serious risks, however; in dugouts fire could be lethal. Not only would men become instantly disorientated in a labyrinth of small, smoke-filled galleries, the efficiency of ventilation meant that flame would spread very rapidly underground, and oxygen depleted equally rapidly. Regulating smoking was out of the question – unless the CO wished to risk a mutiny. The most striking example of this was in the tunnels of Mount Sorrel, where 2nd Canadian Tunnelling Company tried to ban smoking in their officers' mess six metres beneath the trenches. Being relatively

problem in trench warfare, and the cleaner a dugout could be kept, the fewer rodents might wish to take up residence – but also because men were sometimes required to stay underground during the hours of daylight over a period of several days. In such cramped conditions it was soon noticed how badly morale was affected if troops lived in a perennial fuggy gloom; decent lighting, at least good enough to read or play cards by, was therefore highly desirable. In

Right: Burn marks left by candles in an incline at Lancashire Farm

Far right: Gordon House machine gun dugout. The imprint of a candle in clay.

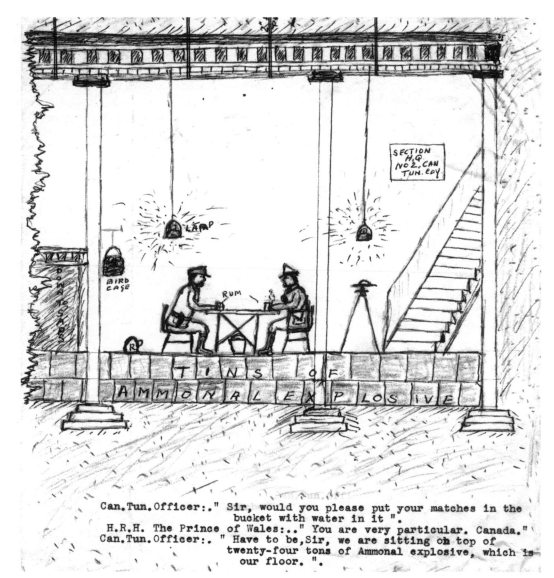

Can.Tun.Officer:." Sir, would you please put your matches in the
            bucket with water in it ".
   H.R.H. The Prince of Wales:.." You are very particular. Canada."
Can.Tun.Officer:. " Have to be,Sir, we are sitting on top of
            twenty-four tons of Ammonal explosive, which is
            our floor. ".

*John Westacott's drawing of
the visit of the Prince of
Wales to the Mount Sorrel
headquarters of the 2nd
Canadian Tunnelling
Company*

spacious the mess doubled as a useful explosive store: the floor was entirely composed of tins of Ammonal. Even here the no smoking regime lasted only a matter of days: men simply could not cope without their tobacco. This fact was acknowledged by GHQ, but stringent rules regarding fire hazards were laid down. No petrol was allowed inside a dugout except the single can needed to keep the generator going; all spare fuel had to be left under cover on the surface. The same rule applied for engine and lamp oil. All troops had heard horror stories of fires in mine tunnels and were aware of the perils; they therefore regulated themselves when cooking, making tea, or using braziers. Considering the scale of workings and the opportunities for disaster, surprisingly few fires were caused.

Not nearly so good was the look-out [observation post] at Rudkin House. It was an odd place, being actually in the mouth of an old well, the bottom of which was in a tunnelled dugout; and, as a cookhouse was installed there for battalion headquarters, the observers had domestic difficulties. Wood-smoke in dugouts already short of air was one of the war's little miseries. From Rudkin House a subway provided safe but awkward communication with the front line, and one morning early, calling there with the Brigade-Major, I was thunderstruck to see troops coming up from the emergency exit between the front and support systems and smoke rising also. The German gunners, whose opportunity filled one with horrid apprehension, stood by and no doubt preferred the information they got by watching the other action. Men crowded out and doubled and ducked back into Stafford Trench, while the Brigade-Major organised a working-party to block up the fire below with sandbags. This was the result of some machine gunner's mistaking a can of petrol for his washing water. Such fires happening in tunnelled dugouts ended a number of lives.

Lieutenant Edmund Blunden,
11th Battalion, Royal Sussex Regiment

The importance of adequate ventilation in dugouts was critical. Quite apart from the fumes produced by candles, lamps, generators, cooking fires and so on, the smell of unwashed soldiery would be, at the very least, unpleasant. Natural draughts via the multiple entrances and ventilation holes went a long way to solving these problems, but some dugout systems, such as Halfway House south of the Menin Road or Westhoek Dugouts north of Hooge, were built on more than one level. These, and some other smaller examples, needed mechanical assistance to help evacuate the foetid air and circulate a fresh supply. The AEMMBC installed powerful fans, also driven by the lighting generators, to draw in external fresh air.

British officers trying out a hand-operated ventilator in a captured German dugout

Asphyxiating gas as a weapon of war was an unrelenting problem for dugout designers and occupants. Being heavier than air, it lurked in depressions such as trenches and shellholes waiting for an unwary victim, and was equally liable to slink through unprotected dugout entrances at the bottom of trenches, and down inclines into galleries. The necessarily efficient underground ventilation system meant that any gas entering a dugout in this way would be quickly and lethally dispersed inside. To keep the

Right: Use of gas curtains at the top of inclines. A similar arrangement was fitted at the bottom

unwelcome guest at bay, every incline was fitted with two gas curtains, one at the top, the other at the bottom of the stairway, consisting of a sheet of heavy cloth impregnated with neutralising chemicals, with which it was kept constantly damp. At the first sign of gas the blankets (top and bottom) were unfurled by the simple pull of a cord, self-sealing automatically onto a sloping timber frame. Sealing the stairway effectively created an 'air lock' which, given adequate warning, allowed the residents to don respirators in good time. The equally dangerous bored ventilation shafts inside the dugout were 'plugged' with a kind of oversized mop head. With the

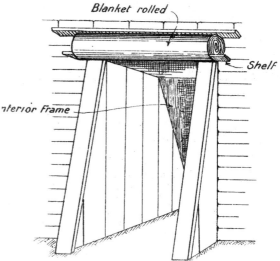

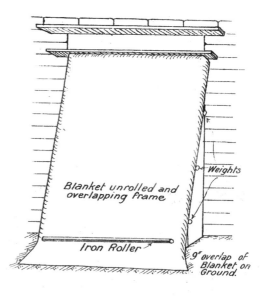

increase in use of asphyxiating gas in shell form some dugout systems were fitted with a gigantic 'gas mask' type respirator through which air was filtered before circulation by electric fans. Vaporised gas was one thing, but poison gas which was still in liquid form was an altogether different problem in dugouts.

I had only been at the front a few weeks. We were moving up to the line when the Germans shelled us with mustard gas. I think it was designed to get on to the skin when the shells burst and cause blistering. When the shells came a few of our lot were splashed with the stuff. Dreadful stuff, very painful. Anyway, I thought I was alright – I was alright – I had none on me as far as I could make out, but we all were told to take cover in a dugout until the trouble had passed. The dugout was long and narrow, not for sleeping in, with wooden benches down the middle. We almost filled it – I think we were about 100 men. What we didn't realise was that this mustard stuff changed from liquid to gas when it got warm. Well, the dugout warmed up pretty soon with all of us in there, and we must have had some on our clothes because we all got gassed. I believe I was one of 6 survivors. That was the end of the war for me. I had breathed some of the gas in. My right lung was alright; but it was worse in my left lung. Over the next few months the stuff ate its way through my chest from the inside out until there was a hole. The nurses were wonderful but they couldn't keep it from going bad. I went into a coma for a while – I don't think I was expected to live. But

I woke up again. After that my lung was drained every day and there was all this rotting flesh around the wound which the nurses carved away before flushing it out with saline solution – which put more liquid back into the lung to be drained off.

Private Harry Wells, Royal Fusiliers

DUGOUT ATTACK

Difficulties in 'mopping up' German deep dugouts during the Battle of the Somme posed problems for the British when planning dugout designs of their own. The first reports had come from the 49th Divisional Engineers just a few weeks after the battle had started on 1 July 1916.

German dug-outs, especially those under the front line parapet, are usually a complete system joined by passages. This enables the enemy

To escape to a flank by underground passage

To counter-attack from a flank by the same route unless all exits are guarded.

It is, therefore, necessary to clear all dug-outs in the occupied area; to block all underground passages leading into dug-outs under the occupied area; to make a very thorough search for entrances to dug-outs and place guards over them. It is no easy matter to find all the entrances in a newly captured area.

It is desirable to bomb dug-outs which are known to be occupied. A Stokes mortar bomb rolled down the entrance is recommended. But the fact that no sounds can be heard after bombs have been exploded in a dug-out does not prove that all occupants have been killed. They may have withdrawn by underground passage to another at a safe distance. It is necessary to detail a garrison to clear dug-outs and to prevent the arrival of fresh troops by this practice.

War Diary, CRE 49th Division, 17 August 1916

This was a fresh aspect of trench warfare for the RE to look into. The lessons learned in Picardy were to be equally applicable during the 1917 battles in the Salient – and for trench raids which had been regularly carried out by both sides since positional warfare had begun. The purposes of a raid were to bomb shafts and inclines, gather intelligence (and for many, souvenirs), and hopefully capture an enemy soldier or two.

DEEP DUGOUT.

Showing Bomb Catches and Entrance and method of
blocking entrance of last Dugout of a Series.

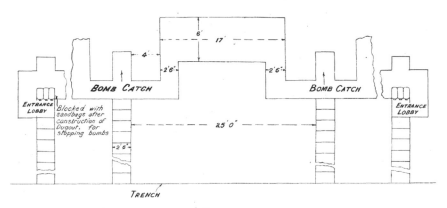

PLAN
Scale 8' to 1'

GERMAN MOBILE CHARGES
30 lbs.

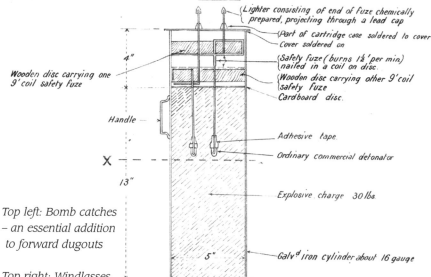

PORTABLE CHARGES.
Fig.1. 25-lb. Ammonal Tin.

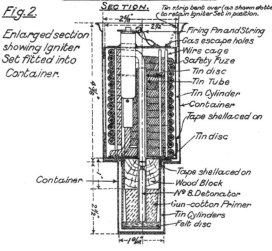

*Top left: Bomb catches
– an essential addition
to forward dugouts*

*Top right: Windlasses
were useful for more than
just hoisting spoil. German
prisoners assist British
soldiers in lifting an injured
man up an incline*

*Above left: German mobile
charge for use in destroying
dugouts and shafts during
trench raids*

*Above right: British portable
charge*

Bombing of dugouts was especially feared.
Attacking a shaft was simple – one just tossed the
charge over the lip and retired to a safe distance,
but inclines were a different matter. Fitting solid
protective doors of any kind was clearly out of
the question because of the need for continuous
ventilation and immediate and constant access
and egress, so in most British dugouts a 'bomb
catch' was installed at the foot of each incline.
This was a small recess in the gallery opposite

the foot of the stairs; the idea was that any bomb
thrown down the stairs might roll across the
gallery and into the trap; when it exploded the
force of the blast was diverted back up the incline
rather than through the galleries. It was in fact
the only form of passive defence available. The
Germans sometimes employed a simple and
ingenious device against grenades. By fixing a
sheet of chicken wire like a portcullis just inside
entrances, a bomb tossed into the orifice would

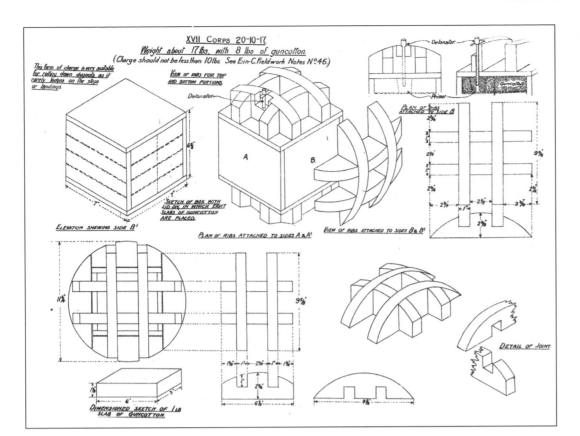

A British Ferret Bomb,
specifically designed to roll to
the bottom of inclines of all
kinds without 'catching' on
steps. The effect was like an
oversized Mills grenade.
The Mills was known to the
troops as the 'co-op bomb'
– everybody gets a bit

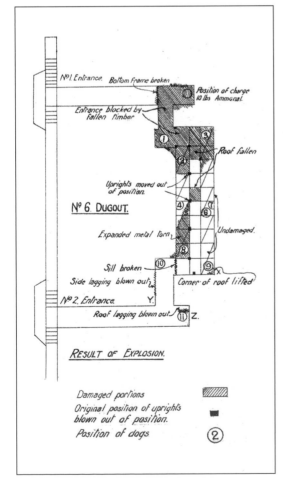

rebound and explode at the feet of the thrower. In chutes or flues a similar method was employed whereby the bomb sat on the wire and blew outwards. The effectiveness was limited – the ruse was immediately obvious to the attacking party, but at least it bought a little time for those below.

In true RE fashion the effects of bombs and mobile charges on dugouts was made a serious area of study, and extensive tests were carried

Left: Results of an explosive
tests in a dugout. All the
animals were killed

Above: German troops at rest
underground with man's
best friend

out to determine what size of charge was required to kill the occupants or destroy the construction. Every form of grenade, including German varieties, were tested for 'rollability' down stairways, and their destructive effect. Both grenades and Ammonal-based mobile charges were tested on a variety of dugouts which had been deliberately built to German dimensions, using enemy construction methods and materials. Whereas a thirty-pound (13.5-kg) charge was found to be unreliable in destroying the fabric of the dugout by bringing the roof down, a twenty-pound (9-kg) charge was sufficient to kill the occupants either through obliteration or concussion. The demands of warfare were such that experiments were even made using dogs tethered at various points in a system. The constrictive nature of underground workings meant that even at fifteen metres from the explosion the poor beasts were torn to pieces.

THE FINAL PHASE

By September 1917 the forward zone of the Ypres Salient had become a wasteland of tortured fields filled with the chaotic detritus of two years of static warfare; a month later the autumn rains turned parts of the battlefield into a swamp. The Battle of Passchendaele was grinding to a halt in the Flanders mud.

Then we were at Langemarck on the Pilckem Ridge, overlooking Houthulst Forest. As the weeks slipped by, and one looked at the mass of shell craters filled with poisonous coloured liquid, the narrow trench board tracks straggling eastwards, and considered the astounding loss of life in this most barren region of the world, a feeling of futility lurked in the background. For the first time I heard open expressions of doubt. Was it worth it? Human nature was being strained to the limit. Divisions came, and half or less divisions returned. The endless tide of men went on. Looking over that vast plain of mud, I heard one man say:

'If they want it, why don't we let them have it?'

A corporal of mine started a discussion amongst the men as to why we were fighting and what for. No one seemed to know. If they ever did know it was all so long ago, and they had forgotten. To most men who look back through their war years there are many bright lights, shining out through the darkness. It may be some lucky billet they had, the charms of one or more pretty faces, a good dinner with their 'pals', or even some trivial incidents which they cherish to themselves alone. But the Salient. Here was nothing, except abomination and desolation.

Lieutenant F Howkins, 253 TC, RE

A front-line entrance to a British dugout on the crest of the Broodseinde Ridge. Probably part of 'Cemetery South' dugout

Natural shelter was now almost non-existent on the surface, and if anyone was going to survive to hold the meagre gains and tell the tale, secure accommodation for yet more thousands of men was going to be critical when the lines completed their expansion into the post-Passchendaele Salient. Between mid-August and Christmas 1917 an extra 12,000 British troops were safely housed deep beneath the battlefield. Between January and April 1918 at least another fifty-nine new or extended dugout systems – it is difficult to give an exact number as ongoing research throws up fresh information all the time – were installed. Throughout both periods German dugouts had also been occupied, improved and extended, and many hundreds of pillboxes, those which were still habitable after the battle, were cleaned out, made gas-proof, named and numbered, and altered for British use by blocking the original German entrances (now facing the enemy of course) and blowing fresh ones on the new leeward side.

Two of the best known pillboxes in the Salient, 'The Barnacle' (on the right) and no.15 'Irksome' (left) at the front of Tyne Cot Cemetery, horrific charnel houses during the battle, were converted into aid posts until the fighting subsided in November 1917. Afterwards the RE moved in, fitted stoves and flues, and made

kitchens to feed the troops in the front lines and dugouts a few hundred metres ahead on the Passchendaele Ridge: from charnel house to cookhouse. Larger concrete strongpoints like these had small mined dugouts installed underneath – a neat and economical use of labour and materials by the Sappers.

After Passchendaele the German artillery mercilessly harried and harassed the British supply and communication routes, which they knew were being expanded and extended

British officers outside a captured and well camouflaged German dressing station

Flandern Stellung concrete defences. 'The Barnacle', one of five pillboxes within Tyne Cot Cemetery. After Passchendaele it was converted into a cookhouse

towards the new front lines. Activity along the newly-won ridge at this time was frantic. The old British system of an unbroken entrenched front line was discarded in favour of forward posts with elephant shelter dugouts situated about fifty metres in front of the main line of defence on the crest of the ridge.

Along the heights between Passchendaele village and Clapham Junction on the Menin Road, the British constructed dugouts with multiple observation posts. These were installed wherever the drier sandy soils overlying the Kemmel Sands were deep enough to give adequate protection. Here, the dugouts were only six metres beneath the surface. In normal conditions this was an unacceptable depth for safety, but the 'arresting power' of sand held the key. Sand not only stopped a shell's progress much more swiftly than clay or chalk, but the softness of the medium meant that fewer actually exploded on impact. These ridge dugouts, although often damp, were therefore generally safe from all but the 'heavies'. Here were installed brigade and battalion headquarters, corps signals, flash-spotters posts, and photographic positions. Around Broodseinde isolated forward machine gun positions were also connected to the safe 'lee' side of the ridge by access tunnels, whilst in the old positions now safe behind the lines, aid posts were extended,

dressing stations installed, and underground accommodation space doubled for infantry, artillery and HQ personnel.

With the threat of a German offensive looming as the spring of 1918 approached, large numbers of further mined shelters for smaller groups were also begun in the rear areas behind Ypres and along defence lines through Dickebusch, Westoutre, Kemmel, Mont Noir and Mont Kokereele, towards Bailleul. When the British withdrew from Passchendaele in April 1918, voluntarily giving up all of the hallowed ground so hard won the previous year, this work was found to be invaluable – the rear areas had suddenly become front-line positions.

The German breakthrough during the Kaiserschlacht, the Kaiser's battle, on the Somme in March 1918 ushered in one of the most critical periods of the war for the Allies. Five tunnelling companies were furiously installing deep dugouts – and now also building concrete pillboxes – along the full length of the defence lines behind the old Salient; the most unlikely of units were given picks and spades and taught the basics of underground construction. Although tuition in dugout work had long been underway in camps throughout the UK for members of RE Tunnelling and Field Companies, and infantry Pioneer Battalions, specialist teaching under qualified RE personnel had also begun in the field

Officers of 255 TC, responsible for many dugout schemes, roads and bridges in the Salient

during the winter of 1917–18, for the benefit particularly of artillery personnel. It was at this time that the knowledge gained from a recently introduced specialist dugout course came into its own.

Run by Captain H Standish Ball, the course had been devised in April 1918 to train officers and other ranks from non RE or pioneer units in the mysteries of mined dugouts. In two intensive weeks men were given a telescoped period of tuition in techniques developed during the previous two and a half years, including construction of inclines, galleries and chambers, strutting and lagging, as well as survey, planning and design. The course also covered the detection and defusing of enemy booby-traps in captured workings, and was to prove invaluable throughout the uneasy summer of 1918 – and in the advance to victory.

Yes, we had to dig dugouts. I forget where exactly, but somewhere near Yeepree, and under the instruction of a sapper NCO. I don't know if he was a tunneller. It wasn't a difficult job, but it took a bit of getting used to for a driver not used to spade work. The sapper was very keen on our not wasting energy, not digging more than was necessary, and using the tools properly. After two years in France I thought I knew how to use a pick and spade – I'd watched others doing it often enough – but I was wrong! He taught us how to make these dugouts about 20 or 30 feet down I suppose, with staircases which led to dormitories and rooms. I remember the wood arriving mucky and wet, but it soon dried out once we got it in. They also had us make false saps that looked like dugout entries, about 200 yards from the guns. There were no dugouts there but we had to make it look as though there were; they had us marching about Indian fashion, dragging our feet making these fake paths – fake paths to fake dugouts! Typical army nonsense. Then they brought up some wooden affairs that looked like something a kid might knock up if he was given a load of wood and a few nails. We were told that Jerry would see them as 18-Pounders from the air, but it was hard to believe. They had to be camouflaged a bit too – but not too much. As far as I remember the Jerries never fell for it – they always shelled the real ones! The dugouts were marvellous. Our gunners would fire a series and then dive down into the

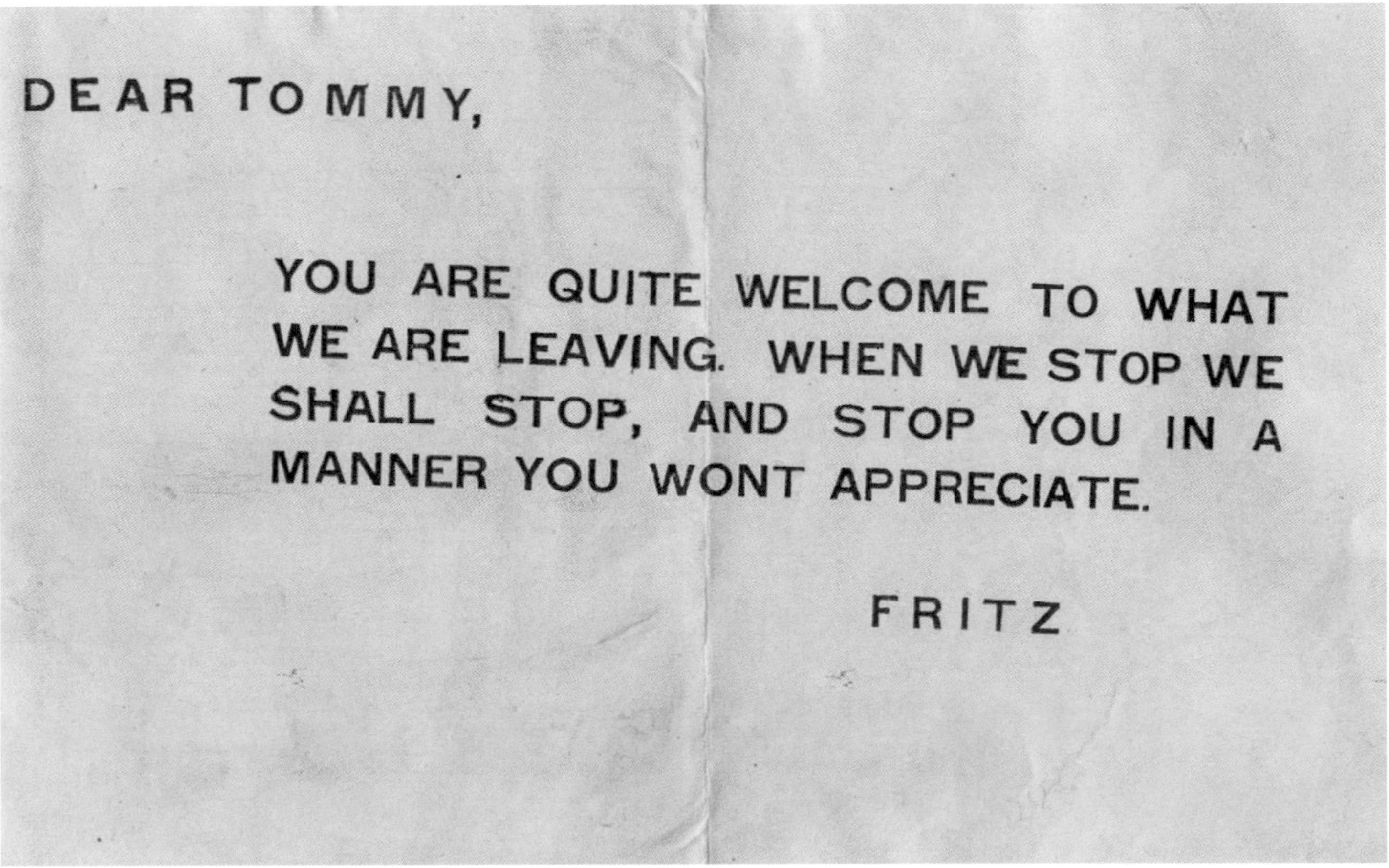

Propaganda message left in a dugout for British soldiers by retreating German forces in 1918

DEAR TOMMY,

YOU ARE QUITE WELCOME TO WHAT WE ARE LEAVING. WHEN WE STOP WE SHALL STOP, AND STOP YOU IN A MANNER YOU WONT APPRECIATE.

FRITZ

THE YPRES TIMES

229

Collapse of Dug-outs in the Ypres Salient.

SOME five years ago considerable subsidences took place in the pathways along the ramparts of Ypres owing to the decay of the timbering of British dug-outs underneath. At the same time the canal bank between the basin and Essex Farm

[Reproduced by kind permission of " The Daily Mail."]

THE UNDERGROUND DRESSING STATION ON THE YPRES—MENIN ROAD
which has just been revealed owing to the recent heavy rains causing the roof to give way and the road to subside.

dugout ready for when Jerry came back with his counter-batteries. As a driver, I had to dig the bloody things, but never got to use them [the dugouts] – my job was to get my horses back out of the way. We drivers had umbrellas for cover!

Driver Leo McCormack, Royal Field Artillery

Although courses for gunners gave excellent results in training, it seems that their apparently extreme keenness for digging had to be forcibly curbed when in the field, as lateral galleries driven from the foot of inclines too often failed to meet underground!

As 1918 wore on, the need for safe accommodation became so acute that even the Chinese Labour Corps were pressed into service. After a shaky start – they were at first uncomfortable working underground – the men quickly became adept, and constructed many dugouts, tunnelled machine gun positions and magazines.

Left: The collapse of Birr Crossroads after the war. Belgian workmen removing the dugout structure prior to filling the void

Below: The Birr Crossroads dugout and dressing station beneath the Menin Road, built by 177 TC

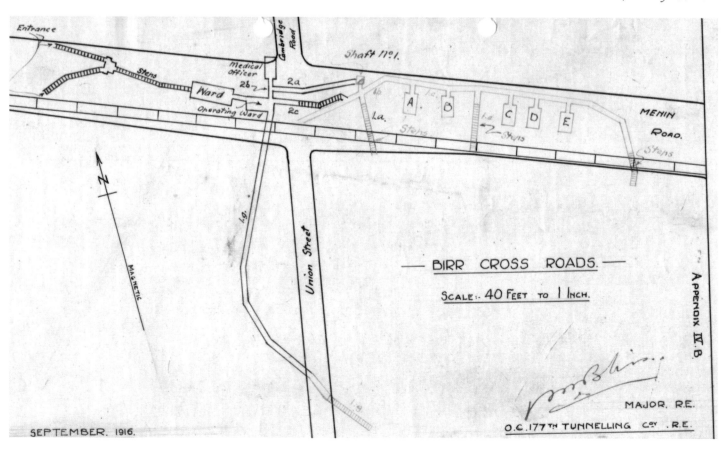

Employed mainly on back line works, the fine quality of the workmanship and the enthusiasm of the labour force so impressed their tunneller mentors that it was suggested that an important dugout scheme – no less than the Headquarters for the Fifth Army – should be entrusted to the Chinese. The war was to take a more mobile turn before it could be fully commissioned. By the end of September 1918, when the German advance had run out of steam, the Allies once more began to push forward, and once more found themselves back in their old dugouts in the Salient. But the advance to victory was soon to sweep rapidly through Flanders towards the German border, and the sojourn in the old homes was brief. Engineer troops were now required to lead the way clearing land mines, defusing booby traps, finding water supplies, enabling communications, and building and repairing bridges. The Salient had suddenly become redundant. Dugout maintenance ceased, and one by one the pumps fell idle. Hundreds of subterranean sanctuaries silently filled with water and slipped gently into hibernation. Today, these are the *Titanics* of the Great War; time capsules, dark and cold, many preserved as if in aspic deep in the clay awaiting the scientists and historians of the future to reveal their secrets.

And so began a new kind of trouble for the peoples of the Immortal Salient: the legacy of the tunnellers and *Pioniere* of the Great War.

Prophetic words in a 1923 Flemish newspaper

Zonnebeke – De frontstreek is waarachtig een land van tooverachtige verrassingen. In landerijen nabij de Polygone en de Zandberg hebben er, in velden sedert bijna twee jaar vereffend, zich grondinzakkingen voorgedaan en ontstonden er putten van 4 tot 5 meters diepte. Zulks was veroorzaakt door het instorten van Duitsche onderaardsche gangen waarvan het hout der gewelven gerot was. Nu zijn er duidelijk nog einden van zulke holen te zien wel tien meters diep en wiens geheimen niemand durft onderzoeken. Waarachtig men staat verstomd over de reuzenwerken welke de Duitschers alhier verricht hebben. Al de heuvels rond de Polygone en den Zandberg zijn letterlijk doornaaid van ondergangen. Men vreest en niet zonder reden dat er huizen mochten gebouwd worden boven zulke holen waarvan het instorten ongelukken zou teweeg brengen.

Zonnebeke – the front area is truly a land of magical surprise. In the acres around Polygone and the Zandberg, in fields that were levelled almost 2 years ago, subsidence has occurred, causing craters 4 or 5 meters deep. This is caused by the collapse of German underground galleries the timber shoring of which is rotting. Now there are entrances appearing to shafts, 10 or more metres deep and no-one dares to explore them and discover their secrets. Truly people are struck dumb by the sheer magnitude of the works built by the Germans. All of the hills around Polygone and the Zandberg are riddled with tunnels. People fear, and not without reason, that the building of houses above such diggings and the further collapse of which would result in accidents.

Chapter XIII

BACK TO THE FRONT: THE LEGACY

People at home would tell you without hesitation the whereabouts of Belgium, and the geography of it generally. I was never very sure. I only know that my chief impression now is that Belgium is in sandbags. I ought to know something about it, for I feel quite certain that this company has put a tidy chunk of the country in bags, all nicely tied up, with the corners well tucked in. On looking at the map one notes that Belgium's rivers are marked in a definite manner. One could almost say that this is fairly correct in a dry summer, but after a few days rain that map is a delusion – the country is all rivers, except perhaps where there are ponds. Writing of ponds reminds me: Here is a useful rule. When looking for a farmhouse when it is dark, mind the pond. Some people might dignify it by the name of 'moat'. Moat or pond, they are not good to walk in.

From an officer of 89 Field Company RE,
The Sapper, November 1915

Repairs to the battlefields of the Salient started before the Armistice. During the final offensive of the war, the 'Advance to Victory' or 'Liberation Offensive', the Royal Engineers began reconstruction of the roads, the Ypres–Roulers railway, and telephone communications. A part of their work was also the filling in of tunnels beneath roads and railways; other underground workings away from these routes were ignored, and then forgotten. During the first winter of peace road transport was still unavailable for local use, and families who wished to return to the farms and villages to view the desolation, and calculate whether the task of reconstruction they now faced warranted

the effort, could either walk or come by train. 101,332 were eventually to return from Holland, 162,676 from England, and 325,293 from France. Those who had spent the war in Holland or behind German lines in Flanders came from Roulers – the only line which was open from the north, whilst others, who had been living behind Allied lines or refugeed to France and Britain, arrived via the Poperinghe–Ypres line.

When the first of these early 'pioneers' began to drift back in early 1919 they gazed upon a grim panorama. The landscape was unrecognisable. Not a house and hardly a tree was left standing. In the wreckage of the small village of St Jean (Sint Jan) one young couple were unable even to locate the site where their terraced cottage had stood five years earlier. Amongst the rubble a few shards of broken porcelain glinted amongst the pulverised bricks; they recognised the pattern as that of a dinner service received as a wedding present before the war. The fragments were gathered up and stuck on a small stone pillar – it would mark the place where life would begin afresh. This curious little memorial still stands on the same spot today.

Contrary to popular belief, the extent of devastation in the Salient was restricted to a narrow ribbon of severe destruction barely six kilometres wide, outside of which by comparison, damage was limited. Within this band, however, the contamination of static trench warfare and years of relentless shelling was so intense that today the physical remnants have actually been laid down as a distinct geological feature. Just under the surface between the clay subsoil and the surface loams lies a stratum of metalliferous debris, a ruddy and rusting callous made up of shells and shell fragments, cables, rifles, shrapnel, sheeting, rails, expanded metal, wire, all kinds of weaponry, pickets, timber – and men.

The returning peoples, surrounded by a mass of jumbled detritus, viewed a wasteland of craters filled with foetid water and obscured by rank undergrowth as far as the eye could see. It seemed that the rats, not the Allies, were to be the final conquerors of the Salient. Many families arrived, looked, wept, and left, returning to France and other parts of Belgium; for them, the land seemed beyond repair.

Those who chose to stay built the first dwellings from battlefield 'debris' using timber from 'plank roads', expanded metal from trenches, and sheets of corrugated iron – there was no shortage of materiel. Nissen huts became instant homes whilst elephant sections turned into excellent roofing and shelter for animals; screw pickets made simple and easy fence posts, and barbed wire was hardly in short supply. Millions of tons of timber of all kinds meant that fuel for burning would be plentiful for years. At the end of 1919, the village of Zonnebeke, totally obliterated as the epicentre of the Third Battle of Ypres, had a meagre 217 inhabitants; a year later the number had risen to 2,200. The people were coming back; they needed to make a living – and find somewhere to live.

At a subsidised cost of three thousand Belgian francs a prefabricated wooden house

was made available by the Belgian Government; a sort of 'flat-pack' kit known as a *Drieduister* (*drieduizend* meaning three thousand in the native Flemish), resembling a large shed. Whole conurbations of *Drieduisters* appeared where once the old villages and towns had stood. Applications for compensation for war damage, which was to be paid by the German nation, required a description and sketch of the property which had been destroyed to be lodged with the 'Court of First Instance' in Ypres. Claims were paid out in full, but the process was a slow one; it could be up to two years before funds arrived. In the meantime, the ubiquitous British Army

Above: A common example of ingenious recycling: British rumjar top used as an insulator for an electric fence at Railway Wood

Left: Some of the first 'pilgrims'; Captain H L Morton, 255 TC and friends near St Julien, 1919

Far left: Screw pickets. Hundreds of thousands are still in use on the Western Front today

Below: One of the first estaminets to re-open in the Salient, 1919

Nissen huts were put to a new use to serve a new purpose: they were decorated and furnished as tea rooms catering for the first trickle of battlefield pilgrims. In Ypres market places were re-established, and trade resumed. Hotels opened. Within a few short years the trickle of foreign visitors to the Salient had become a torrent.

From Zillebeke the road leads up to Hill 60, one of the most exploited places in the Salient. Even as you reach the few squalid homes of Zwarteleen you meet huge signs telling you of this or that canteen, advertising the sale of souvenirs, postcards and what not. Wooden canteens are there, and then one meets a fenced in area. Inside, the proprietor is very cordial and gentlemanly and really has something to show you. He has cleaned out all the trenches on the British side of the hill. The old corrugated iron sides hold position, and duck-mats are there. Strewn about is all the debris of war he uncovered in his work – countless steel helmets, gas masks, cartridge clips, rifles, bayonets, a gas alarm, a fixed rifle.

W J Bird, 1932

THE DETRITUS OF WAR

Battlefield clearance and reconstitution was carried out by a variety of personnel. The British Army were involved and local workers were brought in daily by train to tear down the thousands of timber, steel and concrete shelters across the battlefields, fill hundreds of kilometres of trenches and millions of craters. In the process five unexploded shells per square metre were uncovered. For a while, the local populace was assisted in the reconstruction by German prisoners of war, who were finally repatriated in November 1919, and Labour Companies consisting largely of Chinese, who left in September of that year.

There were also Exhumation Companies, special units formed to locate and remove the remains of tens of thousands of missing soldiers of nations from five continents. To carry out this sad task the terrain was divided into 500 square metre blocks by Survey Companies, then thoroughly searched by groups of four men. Tell-tale signs that the remains of one of 'the Missing' might lie beneath included obvious battlefield grave remains like the wooden cross – or perhaps fragments of equipment, an unusually thick growth of grasses, localised discolouration of the soil, and groups of holes made by vermin. Exhumation was supervised by Army Burial Officers, who also gathered together personal items to help with identification. Many bodies were, and still are, found by the local people; for some, these too were considered a source of

A member of an exhumation squad with the remains of a British soldier in 1919

extra income, being stripped of valuables. A large percentage of British soldiers found on the battlefields after the war now lie buried in concentration cemeteries like Tyne Cot, near Passchendaele. Many of the neat and pretty German burial grounds which had appeared throughout the Salient between April 1915 and July 1917 were obliterated during Messines and Third Ypres; after the war all the residual remains were repatriated to Germany or concentrated at the great burial ground at Langemarck.

I never wanted to go back until much later in life. You're back there in the trenches every day anyway: there's not a day gone by in 75 years that pictures of people and places from those two years haven't been in my mind half a dozen times. It wakes you up at night and you can't go off again, your thoughts are full of irrational guilt, and images you don't want to recall. Smells are one of the big things. I can often still smell gas today, and that musty dampness of men and mud at Yeepree comes back when I'm doing the garden. That's all it takes: a sniff and you're back there again. HP sauce does it; hot sweet tea outside on a cold day; misty autumn mornings. Walking past a butchers brings back 9 October 1917; the blood was in the air after the shrapnel exploded, in the mist. We could taste it; we were breathing it – and the sight…I froze, even with the bullets and shells everywhere, I just stood there. I'd seen enough war by then and been on raids and that, but nothing prepares you for sights like that. Torn to shreds they were. Something like that never leaves you. How can you get rid of it when every sense is involved. I can see it crystal clear now, and I'm blind. I don't know how I survived those days. I went back once – and didn't recognise a thing at all. Nothing. Apart from the cemeteries you wouldn't know anything had ever happened there. I'm surprised the war office didn't ask to keep something preserved, like a park, you know. Shameful really. I can't describe that battlefield, but it's hard to believe they ever cleaned it up.

Private Bert Fearns
2/6 Battalion, Lancashire Fusiliers, June 1996

A substantial contingent of British engineers stayed behind to assist with reconstruction, salvage, and ordnance disposal work. With the departure of the Germans and Chinese, the influx of locals increased and re-building work began in earnest. Without the regular housekeeping skills of tens of thousands of troops, sandbag parapets and revetments soon rotted and slumped, partly filling in the old trenches, but the visible and accessible residue of warfare was enormous, and became a vast resource of essential raw materials for the Flemish people. Apart from timber for building and burning, metal for roofing, and pumps for draining, there was much else of value to local people to be found amongst the craters, including tools by the hundreds of thousands. Huge quantities of brass shell cases and copper driving bands, and much other booty was uncovered. Although it had been declared illegal to gather and sell such material, the capacity to earn extra money (often two or three times the daily wage of a labourer) ensured that it was hoarded and surreptitiously sold to scrap merchants. To clear away all the debris would have taken decades, so having salvaged the most useful material the remaining 'junk' was pushed into the nearest and deepest trench or shell hole and covered over; lying well beneath the plough's blades it would pose no problems for future cultivation.

HEALING THE LAND

After clearing the original *beeks*, restoring roadside ditches and installing hundreds of kilometres of earthenware land drains, ploughing began. Afterwards, 400 kilograms of lime per hectare was spread and harrowed into the ground in an attempt to 'sweeten' the earth. The people had also made impressive progress in blowing up or pulling down by hand the heavyweight legacy of the Great War: the pillboxes. A trip to the site of the Salient today cannot begin to give the visitor an idea of the thousands of these concrete MEBU blockhouses which once carpeted the fields like blind sentinels. There were pillboxes everywhere, so many in fact that in places cultivation was practically impossible. Some of those adjacent to new farm buildings were preserved for animal use or storage, but over the years most have been wiped forever from the face of the battlefield.

At Wieltje I took the old plank road to Passchendaele, past Bridge House to Spree farm. There I stopped and looked around. A land of pillboxes. There were 38 in the vicinity of Fortuin on my left, and three long concrete fortresses near Pond Farm. In the Fortuin district, pillboxes used as tool sheds and

Dismantling pillboxes in Passchendaele several years after the war

The slow and arduous task of removing a monolithic pillbox

chicken pens. Elephant iron forms roofs, sheds, and corrugated iron serves as fences. Barbed wire is strung from the old wire stakes – screw ones – we used. At one spot I could count 58 pillboxes, and, viewing them, one cannot understand how the enemy was ever routed from his holdings. Most of the men one meets in the Salient seem averse to conversation, are not friendly. They hate all things connected with the war. One spoke bitterly in his rough-throated fashion, as he told me how his son had been killed in '21 through the explosion of a shell. 'These English made poor shells' he finished angrily, 'They should have exploded at the time.' I pointed out that it was quite possible his son had uncovered a German shell, but he would not have that side of it. No, he was sure it was the English who caused all the deaths.

W J Bird, 1932

Slowly the killing fields were returned to agriculture. But yields remained low with plagues of copper worms and mice adding to crop destruction. It was suggested that after four years of churning and re-churning by high explosive, much of the topsoil had perhaps been trapped at a level lower than the blades of an average plough could reach. A deep ploughing scheme was instigated. This helped more than just the fertility of the soil – it lifted another huge hoard of valuable war debris to the surface.

Yet in places the land stubbornly refused to

grow crops; the problem sometimes turned out to be sheets of infertile soil from tunnels and dugouts which had been spread on the surface, and was completely useless for arable farming; the area was covered with topsoil and put down to pasture. In Zonnebeke the villagers returned to find small mountains of blue clay which had been dragged from workings beneath the village and left uncamouflaged. Some still also speak of permanent pollution by poisonous gas.

By 1930 the majority of the land had been returned to farming. Since then time and the enveloping nature of the Flanders geology has healed practically all visible wounds, except the great craters of Messines and those very few sites deliberately kept open by the hand of man as landscape memorials. There are still war-related problems: the continuing discovery of the bodies of the missing – an estimated 200,000 still await detection, and the annual harvest of dangerous unexploded ordnance. These may eventually be solved one way or another by the passing of time. However, research over recent years suggests that the final legacy of warfare in the Salient appears perhaps not to lie just beneath the plough blades but much deeper, and in a most insidious and awkward form – the slow but sure degradation and collapse of the old dugout and tunnel systems.

During the summer season tables are put up around Hill 60, and the canteens have competition from vendors of postcards, fruit etc.,

Below: Collapsed dugout under repair on the St Eloi–Wytschaete Road, 1931

Right: Martha House dugout; unexploded ordnance found with a metal detector. Excavation works are beginning in the background.

and drinks – tea, coffee and chocolate. All the Hill is a festering sore on the landscape. There is an immense crater next to the railroad that is water-filled in the wet season. When I saw it in December '18, it was then a slough with the cross of a French soldier leaning over the slimy water. The Hill was so shelled, tunnelled and mined that it is a morass. All over you find traces of old shafts and cuttings and dugouts, and ruins of pillboxes. All the German ones are sunken beneath the surface and only pieces serve to show you where they lie.

Down by the trenches the enterprising proprietor has cleaned the tunnels he located there. One goes down a flight of steps into the evil-smelling workings where tunnels branch off in all directions. Supports and braces have been fixed in many places, but the whole seems a risky passage. There one can see where meals were cooked, the charred beams giving mute evidence; and remnants of old gas curtains are still in place. Spades and tools are there. I went along two turnings and into a very small gallery, low and narrow. It had water a foot deep and would daunt almost anyone.

Up at 'Whitesheet', a priest's house was recently built. One day his housekeeper seemed an unreasonably long time bringing his dinner, so he went to the kitchen. It was a huge gaping hole. The floor, stove, cook and all had fallen 30 feet into a huge German dugout.

Hellfire Corner is a nice spot with a pleasant cafe close by, the road itself smooth and hard, and the traffic does not wait until nightfall. Down in the hollow, beyond Birr Cross Roads cemetery, the Menin Road has caved in. All traffic detours, and even the tramway has been shifted. A huge opening is there, and scores of men are working to fill it in. The road dropped into a huge tunnel, strongly timbered. Rotted tunics and kilts and caps and trousers, all kinds of equipment and uniforms, have been brought up from the dark cavities below, and the tunnel stretches away a seemingly endless distance.

W J Bird, 1932

THE 'SILENT CITIES'

Even had they known of the labyrinths of galleries that lay beneath their feet, the last thing the returning Flemish population of 1919 had the interest or energy for was excavating small waterlogged holes in filthy trenches. Yet these were, and still are, the doorways to a vast hidden world: the silent cities carved by the military troglodytes of the Salient – the tunnellers.

Unlike many dry tunnels in Picardy and Artois which were blown up by the French army for safety after the war, almost all those in the Salient are believed to have survived. There were exceptions of course. A few workings collapsed, demanding immediate remedial work, whilst some which were known or believed to undermine roads or buildings were revealed and made safe, such as the great Menin Road tunnel that stretched back from Hooge to Clapham Junction and beyond the crest of the ridge. It was by this route that prostitutes were reputed to visit the German front-line trenches and dugouts. A few dry systems were preserved as tourist attractions: at Hill 60, the now demolished Redan at Nieuport on the Belgian Coast, and also the famous Bremen Redoubt near Zonnebeke found during the 1980s, but which has tragically been recently lost to decay. The vast majority were impossible to explore, however; apart from being deep – up to forty metres beneath the ground – and often huge rambling structures, they were not just damp but completely waterlogged, filled to within a metre of the surface.

Alexander Barrie, whilst researching his book *War Underground*, recalled some of the Hill 60 tunnels still being open to the public. Even these shallow workings, driven in a relatively dry sandy ridge, looked so perilous he dared not venture inside. The Flemish farmer of 1919 had neither Sandy Barrie's inquisitiveness, interest, nor a publisher's commission; all he wished to do

Mr Maurice Baerts examining a dry dugout in the late 1920s

Above: Post-war salvage of dugout timbers for firewood

Right: Plaque made and fixed in Gordon House under-ground machine gun post by 227 Field Company RE

BUILT BY Nᵒ 3 SECTION 227ᵀᴴ Fᴰ Cᵒʸ R.E MARCH 1917

The names of the Sappers of 227 FCRE who built Gordon House – all survived the war. Note also markings of later occupants, members of 117 and 118 Machine Gun Companies

SAP. W. SPALDING . 227. RE
W. ANDREWS
D. ERWIN
F. LAMBE
F. McLAUGHAN

was return the land to agriculture as soon as possible and start life afresh. Many of the 'water-logged holes' were therefore put to the most logical of uses – as a water supply for animals.

In the 1950s the price of steel made it worthwhile to blow up more of the remaining concrete blockhouses of the Salient for their valuable metal content, and in the same way as they had been doing since 1919, some hardy Flemish families were still exposing and stripping the abundant timber of old trench systems on the ridges for use as winter fuel; the upper elements of many dugout systems – the stairways, inclines and shallow chambers – were found during this process, and the timbers removed – but only as far as the water table allowed. To go farther would entail the employment of costly pumps. They also often made the mistake of dismantling the timber from the surface downwards instead of from the inside out, and many a lucky escape was made from collapsing roofs. In one shallow dugout at Mount Sorrel a whole chamber full of folded British uniforms was discovered. After drying in the sun on the surrounding fences they were taken to Ypres – and sold in the marketplace.

EXPLORING A FORGOTTEN WORLD

For exploration purposes military mines and dugouts must be separated. Two and a half years of mining by tens of thousands of tunnellers and attached infantry had created a colossal network of defensive and offensive galleries of various sizes. After the Battle of Messines Ridge, however, the overwhelming majority instantly became redundant. Too deep, too small, too poorly located, or too wet to warrant conversion into dugout accommodation, and in some cases – more than we shall probably ever know – still charged with various quantities of explosive, their useful life was over. Being so short the timbers of mine setts were useless for dugout work or indeed any other practical use, and therefore were not salvaged. The legacy of the several phases of deep dugout construction between August 1915 and September 1918 in the Salient has been to leave a vast array of small, medium, large, and a few simply huge systems, predominantly British built, still lurking in the subterranean gloom of the Salient.

Battlefield archaeology is a developing science, a multidisciplinary study that draws from many avenues of academic endeavour. In recent years some tentative approaches have been made to explore in a systematic and thorough manner the relics of the Great War. Small zones of surface battlefield have been examined: at Arras, under the auspices of the city authorities; at Auchonvillers on the Somme; and most recently, at Pilckem in the Ypres Salient – where the Flemish archaeological institute, the IAP, is examining in much detail the site of a proposed extension to the A19 motorway, and the scene of much endeavour between 1915 and 1919. The archaeology of the underground war is also gathering momentum, built upon the efforts of pioneers whose aim is to understand more of what it was like to live below ground as battle raged overhead, and to consider more deeply the construction, constraints and conditions of this most peculiar and secret of wars. Many of these investigations are a reaction to the ongoing degradation of the structures themselves; in a significant percentage of cases there is no doubt that we are witnessing the final phase of existence of these carefully and finely engineered structures; they were built to withstand months of wartime occupation not years of neglect – yet many have survived for over eighty-five years in extraordinary condition.

Top left: Preservation in deep dugouts. A British water bottle on a bunk

Left middle above: A preserved broom in Martha House dugout

Left middle below: British bayonet in South Lane dugout near Hellfire Corner

Bottom left: Articles of clothing perfectly preserved by the water

Top right: A pair of thigh boots made by the British Rubber Company, Edinburgh

Middle right: Webbing and other articles from South Lane dugout

Bottom right: A pair of British .303 Lee Enfield Rifles left on a bunk in South Lane dugout

WATER, WATER EVERYWHERE
PRACTICAL POINTS FOR PIONEERS
By No. 50403, Sapper Weary William
PUMPS AND THEIR USE

Never take a pump to pieces. Most makers of repute insert the necessary quantity of works before issue. Valves and washers are domesticated little fellows, and resent intrusion into the privacy of their home.

Use the pump for water only. If required to remove equipment, bully beef tins, bottom boards, corpses, etc., special fittings may be obtained from the makers at six months' notice.

Economise labour. When hygiene need not be subordinated to tactics, it is better for one bloke to bale with a bucket than for several to dismantle the pump with a bike spanner.

Keep all spare parts. The obstruction at the lower end of a stove pipe pump is the foot valve. When cleared out with a pick, it should be retained as a memento. Only the upper part of the central rod should be used as firewood. The lower part contains some of the works.

Place the delivery hose outside the parapet. If this hose is retained for convenience in the trench, do not send for RE to deal with a 'spring'. The RE have lost all sense of humour, and never understand springs, in which the water appears to run uphill.

When the pump refuses to work. Dig out the end of the suction hose. (Tools required: 2 shovels, 1 pick). Pour a bucketful of water containing not more than 99% of mud into any hole you can find in the pump, and wiggle the handle. N.B. – This is called 'priming the pump.'

The Sapper, 1915

The continued existence of many Great War tunnels and dugouts can be credited to one major factor: the tunnellers' old enemy, water. This marvellous medium has a double benefit for battlefield archaeology in both preserving the timber and giving it the necessary hydrostatic support, i.e. the pressure of water inside the flooded galleries helps to hold the structure in position. Experience has shown that most of the deep dugouts on the plain and in the valleys, all entirely flooded, are probably still in good condition today.

There are variations: dugouts where steel has been used in the construction process, during the war a very common and necessary addition where clay pressure was intense, can today be considerably less stable than exclusively timber structures; metal generally faring much worse than wood in water. Another aspect is whether hardwood or softwood was used in construction.

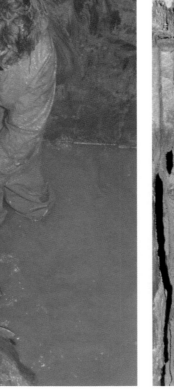

Left: Keeping the pump clear of blockages. Dugout exploration is not a pursuit for the faint-hearted or vain

Right: Colours in Ravine Wood dugout. On first opening all the internal structure is black; the orange hues gradually increase on exposure to air

Martha House, a deep British dugout near Zonnebeke for instance, was found to be constructed almost entirely in oak; as it was also in the stable Paniselian 'bastard blue clay' stratum no steel was considered necessary, and as a consequence the fabric of the dugout and its contents are in an extraordinary state of preservation.

Water is therefore key. Most of the workings built in the dry upper contours of the ridges are air filled and subject to a generally constant dampness with only an occasional incursion of water – the worst possible conditions for preservation – and are now in various states of decay. They have been collapsing for many years, and soon will require more work, risk and archaeological effort to explore than is perhaps wise or worthwhile. Local fluctuations in the water table over time have also adversely affected some structures. In the summer of 1916 Lieutenant John Westacott gave today's battlefield archaeologists some valuable information about the nature of the Observatory Ridge sector.

After considerable difficulty we found what was left of the sap heads at Mount Sorrel. It was an unrecognisable mess. The sapheads were smashed to pieces and they were full of water and choked up with dead. I think some had been taking cover in there and had been

caught by shellfire. We pumped them out and got the bodies out and got the mines working again. And then I found where I lost my officers. I never did find the body of one. Another was back in my headquarters – Lt May – it had then been nearly a month since the attack. I found him in what was left of the dugout, it was all smashed. I tried to get him out the first night – he had got a beam caught across his body; I couldn't get near him because of the rats. I'd never seen such things, they would bite, come right up to you. The next night I went back; he was decomposed a bit; I only got half his body away and I buried him with the others at the back of the hill where there was a graveyard for the British Brigade of Guards – hundreds of them.

Lieutenant John Westacott,
2nd Canadian TC

In the mid-1950s these very same trenches were being stripped of timber for firewood. Several dugout entrances were exposed and all were found to be explorable to a shallow level – around four metres; beyond, the workings were flooded. In 1998 during the filming for a British television documentary on tunnelling, exactly the same systems were explored and found to be totally dry to a depth of nine metres. All the galleries were in a very poor and dangerous

A superbly built gallery in Yorkshire Trench dugouts and a 1917 equivalent

condition of advanced decay, and evidence of collapse in the form of sunken pits stretched across the fields. Indeed, a gallery system could be traced by the line of recent collapses. Discounting seasonal variation in water table (the filming was in February), this is still a massive alteration over a period of eight decades.

Wet dugouts, however, although perhaps well preserved and more stable, are still dangerous to survey once the water providing hydrostatic support has been pumped out. In the same way that during the war the clay swelled when moisture was added, so it contracts when moisture is removed, causing movement in the sediments surrounding the gallery which are transferred to the timbers. Dugouts and tunnels were built by skilful craftsmen without the need for screws, nails and other items to hold the construction together. By using 'spreaders', 'cleats' and steel I-beams, the overall stability of the dugout actually relied upon the swelling action of the geology itself to compress all the structural elements firmly and safely together. When water is removed and drying out commences, a shift of just a few centimetres will be enough to move a leg or cap slightly out of true, and potentially bring down the roof. Indeed, the failure of a single spreader can start a chain reaction of natural destruction.

When underground therefore it is critical that careful measurements and records are regularly made of changes in joint widths in walls and roofs throughout the workings whilst they remain empty. Any excess movement over a short period will necessitate the internal propping of the entire structure. Dugout exploration is not an activity for amateurs. Large systems, apart from needing many pumps and a great deal of time to drain, are especially dangerous. Often built on two or even three levels like a multi-storey car park, there is always the possibility of millions of gallons of water being unknowingly trapped by a roof collapse deep within the dugout system. The blockage acts like a dam – a dam which could potentially break at any time releasing a tidal wave throughout the workings. For this reason it is always smaller dugouts – and certainly ones unconnected to mine systems – which have been explored. Identifying plans of these small systems in archives is straightforward enough. However, on no account should plans be entirely trusted as later alterations and extensions may well have been made by other units, and even by the enemy, leaving the dugout a much more substantial size than might be thought.

Another problem, remote collapse, applies to every dugout, large or small. As all systems had multiple entrances, it is often the case that the removal of water from one entrance brings about a 'slide' of earth in another; in some dugouts these may be 50 or 100 metres away from the original entry point – and may lie beneath houses, roads, farm buildings or, following 172 TC's experience at St Eloi in 1915, cesspits. Again at Martha

A remote collapse at a misty Martha House caused by earth sliding down a second incline during pumping. The entrance under excavation is next to the tractor

House, it was gauged from incomplete war diary details (there are no known surviving plans) that the dugout was around company size, accommodating approximately 250 soldiers. When excavation work had cleared the entrance, and pumps had been installed in the stairway and switched on, the system appeared much more extensive than suggested by the records, due to the much slower than anticipated rate at which the water level was dropping. After many hours pumping, it was noticed that water from the outlet pipe, which had been flowing across a field towards a ditch, was actually disappearing into another entrance to the same dugout which had appeared due to a 'slide'. It later transpired that Martha House dugout was in fact an unfinished system, smaller than expected; the British engineers having had to leave the workings during the withdrawal of Allied troops in spring 1918.

TRACING A DUGOUT

Although the precise locations of most British dugouts can be easily uncovered through archival research, the same cannot be said of German workings. Indeed, the opposite is the case. During the Second World War records were destroyed by Allied bombing, and the partition of Germany led to regional archives being separated between east and west. During the period of separation little effort was made to catalogue war archives by the authorities on either side of the Berlin Wall. Only recently

reunited, the task of sorting and cataloguing records from two World Wars is now gargantuan. At best the German records from the Great War are thought to be substantially incomplete, and it may be many years before a comprehensive database is compiled.

The Royal Engineers and German *Pioniere* produced and worked from finely detailed trench maps throughout the war. Huge numbers of these masterpieces of survey have thankfully survived both in archives and private collections, and they are an essential adjunct to research. Having established and plotted the position of a dugout on a trench map from war diary references, an overlay onto a modern map of the same scale can give the exact present location. To know that one is standing directly above a particular system can therefore be straightforward. Today the advent of GIS (Geographical Information System) has made the process more technical, but nevertheless no more accurate. It should be noted that the map reference of a dugout in a war diary always refers to the location of the first entrance that was sunk. Having a copy of the plan is obviously a great advantage: as long as the north arrow is marked the original starting point, orientation and precise plot of the system can be simply established and plotted on the surface. As dugouts were built into rear-facing slopes wherever possible, with galleries lying parallel to the contours and the majority of entrances driven perpendicular to it, the 'lie of the land' offers the most obvious clue to both location and orientation.

For systems without plans the ancient method of dowsing appears to give remarkable – if inexplicable – results. In 'blind' dowsing, where the dowser pegs out a system on the

Left: Entrance to a kilometre-long German tunnelled subway connecting rear areas to the forward trench systems

Right: Abandoned house in Nieuport on the Belgian coast, condemned due to subsidence from Great War cut-and-cover tunnels

surface without having seen a plan, the results seem to be uncannily accurate. A good dowser can apparently tell the depth of a system no matter what the overlying strata, and even the depth of water lying in the galleries should they not be totally flooded. The technique has been used in the clays of the Salient, and in the sands of the Belgian coast where large areas of the town of Nieuport are affected by subsidence, along with potentially hundreds of buildings in the recently developed dune belt. Other more scientifically understood techniques exist such as Ground Penetrating Radar (GPR), but to the converted dowsing has been a key tool in plotting not only the waterlogged tunnels of Flanders, but dry chalk tunnels up to thirty metres beneath the surface at Vimy Ridge in northern France, and less deep workings on the Somme battlefields.

Geophysical techniques such as GPR are now being widely used in archaeology, but there is no doubt that most of them struggle for success in Flanders, due to the churned surface deposits, the massive callous of metallic debris, and reflection from water saturation in the Flemish soils. Other techniques such as magnetometry may be employed where steel was used in underground systems, and this has given good results in dry conditions on the Passchendaele Ridge top and in the sand dunes of the Belgian Coast. Here the geophysics clearly identifies the precise locations of steel shafts, trench lines revetted with metal elements, and the remnants of rail and tramway

Geophysics at the site of Primus dugout. The large red anomaly in the centre is believed to be a steel shaft

networks, but when used to find deeper objects, and despite having built in 'filter' systems, it is confused by the sheer density of the ferrous-based detritus that still litters the subsurface. Experienced operators, however, are able to distinguish potential caches of hazardous ordnance – clearly an important aspect of any professional investigation of the battlefields. Several other types of geophysics – resistivity, for example – are also in the process of being tested on the battlefield 'architecture' of the Great War.

Eventually, when the results of all these investigations are correlated against archive details, it will be possible to create a series of colour-coded engineering maps showing areas of projected risk for the benefit of planners, builders and engineers – a peacetime echo of Edgeworth David's pioneering dugout suitability maps.

THE DANGER BELOW

How are dugouts known to be failing? The simple answer is by the physical evidence – collapses. The most common sign is the 'crownhole', a subcircular depression caused by failure of the supporting timbers. However, the sudden appearance of one does not necessarily mean that a dugout roof has given way through decay; it may be the result of an incline slide, or a shaft head platform collapse. Only excavation can fully answer the question. The appearance of crownholes is very common in the Salient and the average motorist on a battlefield tour will unknowingly drive past many an example during a day's outing – a considerable percentage may well be caused by earth sliding into shallow wartime features, and convey little danger – but that last sudden dip in the road may well have been a failing dugout. Farmers too are at risk from more than unexploded shells; the fields may seem peaceful and fertile to us, but many which could be growing crops are deliberately left as permanent pastureland – to venture across them too often by tractor would be inviting disaster. Livestock too are not immune to risk. The appearance of a crownhole cannot be predicted even if a dugout or tunnel is known to be present as the failure can take time to reach the surface from the deeps. The collapse first forms a bell shaped chamber above the initial point of failure, the roof of which gradually collapses over time until the final crownhole at the surface appears.

Sections of offensive and defensive tunnels systems were very often used for the safe storage and easy access of mining explosives. Records of

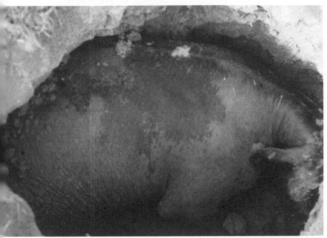

these stores are seldom noted in diaries, and it is likely that large amounts of explosive, cut off by enemy action, geological troubles, movement of the lines, or simple abandonment, still exist beneath the fields of Flanders. In this respect dugouts, as opposed to mine tunnels, pose far less of a problem.

Shells were not stored in deep dugouts simply because they would be inaccessible. The majority of dangerous materiel comprises just two easily transported and retrieved articles: bullets and hand grenades. Whereas bullets present a small threat, grenades are a different kettle of fish altogether and are treated with great care before being passed into the capable hands of the DOVO, the Belgian Bomb Disposal Service. Visitors touring the Salient on Fridays during the summer months may be glad to know that sounds of distant explosions emanate from the DOVO base in Houthulst Forest where an average of 150 tonnes of ordnance per year is blown up. A special facility for dealing with gas shells of all kinds has also been erected at Houthulst.

Like high explosive and shrapnel shells, projectiles containing poison gas have also not yet been encountered during underground exploration. However, one gas can be a serious problem in dugouts – methane. On breaking into dry tunnel systems this gas, produced not by evil scientists but as a natural product of decaying timber, is often found trapped in quantity in the galleries. Although methane clears quickly once exposed to air, an initial lungful can cause headache, nausea and occasionally, momentary unconsciousness. A more common though much less dramatic problem is the decrease in oxygen levels inside a dugout due to only one entrance being opened for exploration. To cover most eventualities a small electronic multi-sensor is carried which detects and audibly warns against

Top left: It wasn't there yesterday! A crownhole near Zonnebeke which opened up overnight

Top right: The most common evidence of tunnelling. A crownhole in a field at Mt Sorrel

Middle left: A cow which died as a result of failing ground at Tor Top

Middle right: Fields known to be undermined are often left fallow. This tanker has had a lucky escape

Bottom left: A typical problem in the Ypres Salient. An earth slide on a roadside verge. The dugout inclines had been driven beneath the road for extra protection from artillery. Polygon Wood

Top left: Exploration. The entrance appears

Top right: Fully excavated and consolidated entrance

Middle left: A nest of British Mills bombs in a chamber

Middle right: German stick grenades from a dugout near Merckem

Bottom: British .303 rifle bullets on an incline

the presence of all common dangerous gases, and decreasing oxygen levels – a far cry from the feathered wartime 'tunnellers' friends'. It is believed that small quantities of wartime carbon monoxide has also been encountered during excavation work, but so far this has been a feature of tunnels in the shattered chalk geology of Vimy Ridge and the Somme.

How many systems exist? Disregarding the very many miles of mine galleries and associated workings, the latest dugout count carried out within the confines of the old Ypres Salient from Boesinghe in the north to Ploegsteert in the south shows 284 separate British systems of various sizes and at various depths. How many of these pose a threat to surface structures is yet to be determined, but it is likely to be more than might be realised. And the number and location of German workings is likely to take a great many years to determine. Many are located beneath farmland, but wherever the 'new' post-war farm, house or road was built close to or on the same site as the devastated original structure, problems of undermining and subsidence can arise. To date, only one such 'rogue' dugout has been fully investigated, documented and saved for posterity: Beecham Dugout near Tyne Cot Cemetery is a textbook example of the potential future risk to people and property along the old Western Front.

BEECHAM FARM – A CASE STUDY

The Beecham dugout was discovered in 1999 when a crownhole opened close to the external wall of a farm near S'Gravenstafel at the foot of the Passchendaele Ridge. The circumstances of its discovery were both unusual and perilous. One morning retired farmer's wife Mrs Simonne Callens was cleaning the windows when the earth gave way beneath her feet. A few moments later she found herself trapped in a two-metre deep funnel-shaped pit – a crownhole. Escape was impossible. Her husband André was attending a funeral in Zonnebeke, and Mrs Callens was to remain trapped until his return at lunchtime. When he arrived back at the farm the soup was simmering gently on the stove as usual, and everything was prepared for the meal – but there was no sign of his wife. She was soon

found, and apart from a little shock and a few scratches, she was thankfully unhurt. Andre's next move was to call the local council.

Initial archival investigations identified the wartime name of the property as Beecham Farm. It was clear that the present farmhouse had not been reconstructed on the ruins of the former buildings but some sixty-five metres to the south, unwittingly placing it over the dugout, the roof of which lay just a metre or so beneath the foundation base. Enquiries were made with older residents of the area about previous troubles, but they could only recall odd holes opening here and there throughout the area. In the same way that the Flemish people accept uncovering hand grenades and a great deal worse in their vegetable patches, the appearance of unexpected holes has simply become a part of everyday life in the Salient. So it was at Beecham.

Bottom left: Local news report of the collapse at Beecham Farm near Tyne Cot cemetery

Below: The offending hole at Beecham in which Mrs Simonne Callens was trapped

Bottom right: A German dugout entrance beneath a Flemish farmhouse

Boerin Simonne Deleu uit de Schipstraat 57 in Passendale had er geen benul van wat er gebeurde toen zaterdag kort voor de middag de grond onder haar voeten verdween. De vrouw bleef een uur in de grote put van twee meter diep zitten. Na een zoektocht van een kwartier kon haar man haar met een ladder uit haar hachelijke situatie bevrijden. Zie p. 2. (MAD-foto SB)

Apart from Mr Callens occasionally having to fill one or two small hollows which opened up along his garden fence, and finding a few lengths of old timber whilst installing a new slurry tank, no more detailed information was forthcoming. Initial archive research uncovered no plans of underground workings on the site, but this too is far from unusual as so many diverse units were involved in dugout construction and a great deal of time is required to comb all the paper records.

During the first physical investigation of the collapse, both garden and buildings were immediately found to be undermined, and every sign was that the mysterious structure had not been touched since 1918. Inside the farmhouse itself there was also evidence of internal structural failure caused by subsidence beneath one of the main rooms. Two maps found in 2002, one British and one German, revealed the existence of tunnelled dugouts at or near Beecham. The British example shows a simple deep dugout symbol without any further detail; the German maps show a complex of five further dugouts nearby, clustered around the site of the original farm.

The dugout was clearly a threat to the house and an investigation with a view to remediation was the highest priority for the householders, as apart from having fears for their own safety they were regularly invaded by large numbers of grandchildren who loved to play in and around the farm. The crisis offered a unique opportunity for a detailed study of an original dugout.

An investigation was planned which would encompass five phases: 1, stabilisation of the crownhole and initial underground investigation; 2, survey of the dugout and mapping of artefacts; 3, removal and recording of dugout timbers and artefacts for preservation; 4, remediation of the dugout complex undermining the house; and 5, archival and historical contextualisation. Together these would provide a valuable insight into a forgotten world.

STABILISING THE HOLE

The first task for the team was to stabilise the crownhole. Expanding the hole a little for ease of working, a timber shaft was sunk to create a safe working environment. Built according to Great War patterns as laid down in the contemporary Royal Engineer Mining Notes, Fieldwork Notes and Fieldwork Designs, the shaft was 1.5 metres square, framed with supporting timbers or sets, with at 1.5 metres depth a timber decking work stage for lifting and lowering.

Top right: Construction of timber shaft to consolidate collapse before pumping

Right: Recording the excavation

Middle right: First view of a Beecham gallery after two hours pumping

Bottom right: The main gallery drained and ready for clearing and stabilisation

Preliminary examinations showed that the crown hole had been caused by a failure in the timber roof of a wide gallery, which was completely filled with ground water. The gallery was pumped out, slowly at first to ascertain whether further collapses might result from removal of the hydrostatic support, before draining the dugout to a useable level. Drainage took only ten hours, which offered clues (but no proof) about the potential scale of the workings: they were thankfully not extensive. Further investigation demonstrated that the supporting wall timbers or 'legs' near the failure were sound, and that the roof timbers or caps elsewhere in the structure were also in good condition.

However, the failed roof timbers showed signs of degradation. This may have been due to leakage from a brick-built underground manure pit directly adjacent to the crownhole coming into contact with timbers and possibly accelerating natural decay. Mr Callens' reported failures in other parts of the garden demonstrated the need for care during the survey. Evidence of at least three earlier surface failures was consistent with the history of crownhole development over the last decade. It was later found that they corresponded with the locations of entrances rather than structural failures – a 'slide' of earth down a stairway as opposed to a structural collapse; such slides are very common throughout the Salient, particularly after heavy rainfall. When the initial gallery had been fully accessed, drained, and the original fall of earth cleared, the roof timbers, although sound, were found to have a substantial 'sag' and additional propping was put in using longitudinal timber baulks on floor and ceiling supported by modified Acrow props at 1.75 metre centres.

Top: A stairway uncovered and partly removed. Note shallow depth of dugout and decay of the tops of timber uprights due to fluctuation in water level. The blueness under the steps is the original colour of the earth; the brown soil is oxidised – a result of the tunnelling process

Middle: The main gallery cleared of artefacts and bunking, and ready for Acrow propping

Bottom right: The foot of the north entrance

Bottom left: A typical roof failure at Beecham

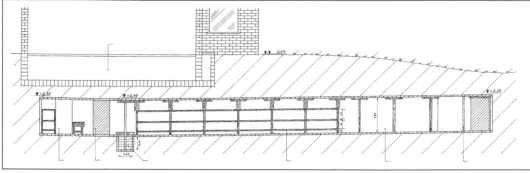

Right: Section showing undermining of the farmhouse

Below: Plan of the Beecham dugout by Johan Vandewalle

Bottom: Geological map of the Beecham area illustrating why the dugout had to be built at such shallow depth

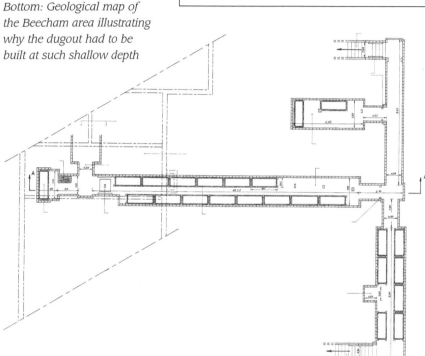

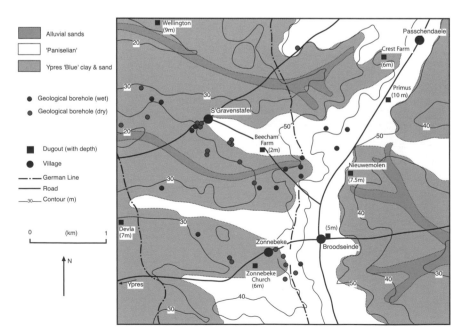

Alluvial sands	
'Paniselian'	
Ypres 'Blue' clay & sand	
● Geological borehole (wet)	
● Geological borehole (dry)	
■ Dugout (with depth)	
● Village	
—·—· German Line	
—— Road	
—30— Contour (m)	

0   (km)   1

N

SURVEY AND MAPPING

The documentation phase included an accurate survey of the dugout, its construction and geological context, systematic film and still photography, and the drawing and listing of the *in situ* artefacts and timber architecture of the system. Particular emphasis was paid to the construction techniques used by the military engineers, as these would provide clues to Beecham's provenance. By the time the British had reached this location in October 1917, they were building most dugouts to regulated depths, dimensions and designs, and with standardised timber components, so careful examination of timber elements would provide evidence of origin. Attention was also paid to the nature and arrangement of the supporting timbers in the galleries, entrances and smaller rooms, together with the arrangement of bunking and the storage of equipment.

The structure only had between 1.2 and 2.0 metres of headcover, varying according to slight variations in slope, with an average total depth including the gallery of four metres. The possibility of the dugout being of the cut-and-cover type was disproved by finding undisturbed strata above the roof timbers. Beecham was undoubtedly therefore a mined dugout, but a very shallow and unsafe one. However, the dugout is located on the flank of a spur that preserves a thin silty-sand layer between wet sands beneath and the overlying and treacherous Kemmel Sands. Relatively dry geology could only be provided by the silty-sand layer in which Beecham was built. The dugout had to be built at this level to avoid the water-bearing sands beneath. It appears far too shallow for a late 1917 British design of which there are many others in the immediate vicinity. Undoubtedly the British would have attempted to pierce the wet sands to find dry clay. Broken masonry was identified at a depth of 0.25 metres, but it is likely that this represents part of the debris of the original farm rather than a protective burster course.

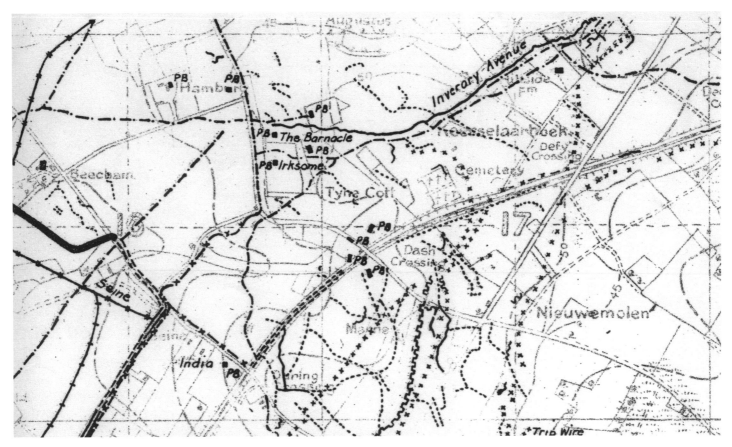

There had apparently been three entrances. Two of these, stepped inclines at either end of the 'T', corresponded with the earlier ground failures in 1991 and 1992. The rubble which Mr Callens had used to fill earlier slides was found in both. A third entrance was suspected to be directly beneath the present-day farmhouse adjacent to the sump. In this small dugout there needed only to be one sump, 0.75 metres deeper than the floor level, which was evidently adequate for draining this size of system.

No steelwork had been used in the construction. This was a piece of evidence which pointed to German origin – if the British had decided to build a dugout of such shallow depth at this time (Beecham was not captured until late September 1917 and no dugout work would have taken place in this sector until November), they surely would have made the structure far stronger and better able to withstand shelling by doubling or even trebling the timber thickness, using steel I-beam caps and legs and by constructing burster and deflection courses above with logs, steel girders, etc.

The average height of the galleries was 1.8 metres and the timber used was all softwood. The main structural timbers – the sills, legs and caps – were found to be irregular in dimensions except for length, so that plank widths and thicknesses varied. The galleries were close-cased throughout with the majority of timber being roughly 22 centimetres wide by 7.5 centimetres thick.

Duckboards with non-slip protection consisting of a single strand of heavy plain wire stapled along the slats were found covering the floor of the complete construction. Both are clues to the provenance – the British produced duckboards designed and built to a standard pattern with rolls of special width heavy mesh 'trench mat wire' for protection against slipping. The Beecham duckboards were irregularly made, suggesting that they had been constructed specifically for the dugout from whatever timber was available locally. Stepped inclined entrances, gallery junctions and doorways were fitted with inclined timber frames for gas blankets. Remnants of the blankets were still evident. These may have been fitted by the many RE Field Companies who spent weeks gas-proofing dugouts and pillboxes in this way during the winter of 1917/1918.

The main gallery was fitted with three-tiered bunks on each side comprising timber frames and chicken-wire bed supports. Previous excavations have suggested that the quality of preservation of ferrous artefacts seems to improve with

Section of VIII Corps Defence Scheme map of January 1918 showing wire defences, duckboard tracks, tramways, and plank roads, and marking the captured German dugouts and pillboxes (PB) in use at that time by British troops. Beecham dugout can be seen at far centre left. Another dugout at Hillside Farm is shown top right

Top: Bunks retaining the marks of chicken-wire supports

Bottom left: Main gallery propped

Bottom right: A similar view for the tunnellers of 1917

the increasing depth of the dugout; in Beecham it was noticeable that the nails holding bunks and duckboards together were in a poor state, and that the wire for the bunks had all but disappeared. This may also have been due to the long-term acidic leakage from the cess pit.

The gallery contained forty-two separate bunks, the remainder of the space being for the storage of materials, tools and weaponry. The south-eastern end of the gallery terminated in a small room, again bunked with accommodation space for three men, probably non-commissioned officers, adjacent to a supposed third entrance, blocked by an earlier collapse. It was a typical arrangement for dugouts to have troops in authority close to an exit. The transverse gallery was found to contain three-tier bunking for twenty-one men in its north-eastern arm, together with a small area for storage, a feature known to the British as a 'cuddy'. The south-western arm was not bunked, but instead provided a single room that was considered to be officers' quarters. Inside there was a two-tier bunk and a simple bed constructed in the same manner as the bunks. Unlike the other galleries the officers' room was roofed with corrugated iron to catch water – a task which was also performed in captured German dugouts by the RE and Pioneers. There was also a small table in this room, and on cleaning the duckboards beneath the table ink stains were found. In total the dugout offered sleeping accommodation for sixty-six men and three officers.

Beecham was not electrically lit, but there was ample evidence of candle light from *in situ* stumps, smears of wax, and burn marks on the walls. No electrical wiring other than small-gauge telephone wire was found.

ARTEFACTS, DUGOUT REMOVAL, PRESERVATION AND RECORDING

The numerous artefacts confirmed British occupancy if not British construction. It is known that Commonwealth forces occupied this ground between October 1917 and April 1918, and then from October 1918 until the Armistice. The majority of artefacts corresponded to artillery use, and these included: personal equipment – artillery pattern high boots, an ammunition bandolier with field artillery markings, mounted pattern mess kit and waterbottle cradles; British 18-pounder shell cases; fuse protection covers, and a primer key for the British 13- and 18-pounder shells. In common with other dugouts explored in the Ypres region many of the artefacts were clothing and blankets, and the condition of these was good to fair due to the

Top: Separate chamber for officers with bunks

Middle: A contemporary underground scene in a similar location

Left: British 'Bulldog' spades in a 'cuddy'. The same company still makes the identical tool today

Top left: Artillerymen's boots and bandolier under a collapsed bunk

Bottom left: British artefacts (not to scale): Boots, 18-pounder key, 18-pounder shellcase, bandolier, fuse-cap covers, tin box

Top right: British greatcoat found at Beecham

Bottom right: British Small Box Respirator

permanently flooded, lightless environment. Typical items included rolled puttees, a short, mounted pattern greatcoat, and a scarf. All were of British origin. Small artefacts were recovered from the dugout floor during deconstruction using hoses and sieves. These mainly consisted of buttons – mostly British, but including one Canadian example – and buckles. The only evidence of potential German occupancy came from a single Mauser rifle round.

Before and during deconstruction of the dugout all the timber elements including the bunks and stairways were systematically marked using numbered lead tags to facilitate exact future reconstruction. Each artefact was recorded relative to its original position and removed to storage. The first stage of deconstruction began with the removal of the bunks.

The resulting void was cleaned out with pressure hoses, the large amount of mud being lifted out in buckets and sieved. Removal of the dugout structure was completed by hand with the assistance of a tracked earthmover with extendable arm with a two-metre wide draining bucket.

The roof of the dugout was first exposed, relieving the pressure, and the cap timbers removed before the installation of horizontal Acrow props which prevented inward collapse of the now unsupported gallery legs. The legs were then systematically removed, working back from the 'T' towards the farm with each 'set' being lifted in sequence. All the timber including the duckboards, bunks and tables was cleaned with pressure hoses immediately after removal and open-stacked in a Dutch barn to encourage a slow drying process, in preparation for chemical

preservation. The duckboards and roughly made tables suffered during removal but were reconstructed after cleaning.

The dugout structure beneath the garden was completely removed and the resulting void backfilled with compacted earth, leaving the remaining portion of the dugout still *in situ* beneath the farm. This section was shuttered with timber before expanding foam concrete was pumped in to make good the cavity and perma-

nently support the farm. After this work was completed the excavation team top-soiled, graded and seeded the external area, and completed the remediation by extending the existing granite cobbled driveway over the site of the original crownhole. A new boundary fence was also erected.

ARCHIVES AND HISTORICAL CONTEXT

Despite being a 'mined' construction, Beecham cannot be described as a deep dugout in the accepted use of the term. Given the vulnerability due to its shallowness, and the concentration of artillery bombardment in this locality over prolonged periods in late 1917 and early 1918, it is most surprising that the dugout survived in the state in which it was found in 1999. It is possible – indeed likely – that the structure may have been damaged during the various battles and later repaired by occupying troops. The British VIII Corps map mentioned earlier is dated 27 January 1918. It was produced to show all the serviceable enemy surface and sub-surface structures in the sector. Beecham is clearly marked as a dugout, as opposed to the surface structures which had been inscribed 'pb' – pillboxes. No British constructions, of which there were a great many under construction at this time, are marked at all on the map. This, combined with the unusually shallow depth, also suggests that the dugout was originally German.

The shallow depth of headcover suggests that the dugout may date from 1916 or even earlier. From mid-April 1915 until August 1917 Beecham lay over three miles behind the front line in what was then a very quiet sector. The German manual *Stellungsbau*, dated June 1916, states that about four metres of 'earth' (making no distinction as to soil type) was then considered shell proof. Beecham had only two metres. In 1917 and 1918 when British engineers were constructing large numbers of dugouts in newly captured territory in this region, around thirty feet (ten metres) of headcover was recommended as a minimum; only the dugouts of the Passchendaele and Broodseinde Ridge were less deep but were considered safe simply because of the sandy nature of the soil, the most 'arresting' material for shells.

Beecham is only the second German dugout known to have been entered in an archaeological context, and is certainly the first to have been comprehensively examined. The other example was of a different nature, being a deep (nine-

Top: The roof of the main gallery exposed prior to removal of the structure

Middle: Repairing duck-boards

Bottom: André and Simonne Callens gaze upon their own personal battlefield

metre) dugout in the north of the Salient at Bixschote. As for ascertaining the design of the construction and whether it fits a particular pattern, the maximum number of sixty-six other ranks and NCOs plus four officers housed at Beecham suggests that the dugout was not built for infantry use as the accommodation would have been too limited. The design also precludes it being a headquarters. It would also have been simple to extend the structure to hold a Company – about 250 men – but this was not done. However, it is known that until September 1917 the German forces had an artillery battery on the low ridge marked as 'Abraham Heights' on British trench maps, which lies immediately adjacent to the north-west. The accommodation at Beecham corresponds with the strength of a field artillery unit. After October 1917 British field artillery used these same battery positions; they

also used Beecham dugout, as demonstrated by the artefacts, particularly the bandolier stamped '15[8?] Royal Field Artillery'. Unfortunately, unit records appear to offer no further information. Research continues on Beecham, and a great many other dugouts await serious study.

Beecham dugout is a perfect example of the lack of certainty regarding the scale of these structures. In January 2004 further subsidence took place beneath the farm – indeed, beneath the farmers' bedroom floor, causing it to drop eighteen centimetres in places. The fault lies directly above that portion of the dugout which the team were unable to reach and fill during the 1999 repair works, due to a long established collapse. Further difficult remedial work will now be necessary. It is only during such works that the full extent of the dugout may – and only may – become apparent.

Royal Field Artillery number stamped into a bandolier

EPILOGUE

When I went to London University I broke up, I went to pieces. I was in a dark room for three months. I had two years of it after the war but I'm alright now. I've had some shocking nightmares. You didn't always know that you were going to get away with it. We were wet – drip, drip, drip from the saps all the time. We had rum, as much as any man wanted to drink. I'd send the batman for a mug of rum before I got out of bed in the morning. All the tension all the time – the strain underground and the darkness. It was terrible. It was no war, it was murder.

Lieutenant John Westacott, 2nd Canadian TC

After the Great War the achievements, comradeship and spirit of the tunnellers were perpetuated through the private publication by Ralph Stokes, ex-Assistant Inspector of Mines, and later Controller of Mines for the Third Army, of the *Register of Tunnelling Company Officers*. The register gave a brief history of the tunnellers and the actions of each company, and informed old comrades as to the whereabouts of ex-moles all around the world (two-thirds lived outside Britain). It also contained the first Roll of Honour of tunnelling officers killed in action. A dedicated organisation for all ranks was also formed: The Tunnellers Old Comrades Association (TOCA), which brought together groups all over the British Commonwealth for dinners, speeches, and simply a good natter. A little newsletter, the *Tunnellers Old Comrades Association Bulletin*, published reminiscences, news of members' activities, births and deaths.

In these various ways the camaraderie of the tunnellers was kept alive for twenty years. The very last TOCA Dinner in London was held in June 1939, as the world once more teetered upon the precipice of armed conflict; Harvey was there, and many others, but Sir John Norton-Griffiths, the

The last ever Tunnellers Old Comrades Association Dinner, held on the eve of the Second World War. General Harvey is seated in the centre of the right hand table

TUNNELLING COYS, ROYAL ENGINEERS.
Operation Orders No.1.

Reference   Ordnance Map, No. T. 101225   10·12·25.

General Scheme.

Trencher attack, followed by smoke barrage and small concentrations of gas.
A list of successive objectives is attached under the code name "MENU."

SPECIAL OPERATIONS: TUNNELLERS.

The Tunnellers are required to undermine the resources of the enemy commissariat. Every unit will be allotted a definite sector, and will endeavour to paralyse enemy movement by removing, or otherwise disposing of, all dumps of material encountered.

Rendezvous. — ENGINEERS' CLUB. — Map Ref. C. 741998-10·12·25. Troops will assemble at 7 p.m., when a rum ration or its equivalent will be issued.
Zero. — Time will be issued. separately.
Dress and Equipment. — Troops will be properly dressed for night operations, Regulation footwear is compulsory; sandbags must not be worn. A complete set of tools will be issued to each unit, the prevalent method of acquiring anything handy (scrounging), and making it do is forbidden.
Demolitions. — Units will make their own arrangements as to the method of dealing with each objective. Where possible, a mine will be fired and the debris shovelled into the crater in an orderly fashion.
      Damage done by filling up with liquid supplies will be charged to the Unit.
Smoke Barrage. — This will be organised after the final objective is reached and Tunnellers will cooperate.
      Smoke bombs will be issued to each unit and the barrage will be continued at the discretion of Officers commanding each unit, until troops or supplies are exhausted. O.C. Units will make their own arrangements for stretchers for C.O. poisoning.
Casualties. — VINE STREET. — Map Ref. C.737997 will receive Tunnellers, the use of other stations is forbidden.

—— || —— || ——

Above: Menu for the TOCA dinner, 10 December 1925

Right: Emblem of 172 Tunnelling Company RE: 'We'll see you blowed first'

being told so in no uncertain terms, the old mole still attempted to enlist – as a subaltern. He was to get in – retaining his higher rank. Although tunnelling was certainly carried out, it was not of the same nature as that of 1914–1918, and no military mining involving British forces was to take place during the Second World War.

Throughout this book there has been little mention of high military honours and medals for gallantry. A number were won by the tunnellers, but far fewer than might be expected in a conflict where the selfless saving of life was as much a part of the routine as its taking, under conditions of solitary terror and psychological strain which most would never comprehend. The ordeal and stoicism of Sapper Bedson for instance, the single survivor of the thirteen tunnellers trapped at Petit Bois in June 1916, was not recognised by any form of decoration. It has been suggested that chief amongst the reasons for the lack of 'gongs' was the overwhelming need for secrecy in the tunnelling game – that too many medals might give too much of the game away. Whatever the reason, amongst the multitude of daring, dangerous, ridiculous, valiant, foolhardy, and heartbreaking escapades that tunnellers were mixed up in, one in particular stands out as being markedly distinct. It is the story of the moles' only recipient of the Victoria Cross: 136414 Sapper William Hackett, of 254 Tunnelling Company RE – a true 'everyman' of the tunnelling companies if ever there was one.

A miner from Manvers Main Colliery at Mexborough near Rotherham, married to Alice, and with two children, Mary and Arthur, William Hackett was determined to serve his country

mercurial tormentor of the German Army – and his own – was absent; sadly, he had died in 1931.

But the story of the moles was not quite finished yet. Game to the last, on the outbreak of the Second World War some ex-tunnellers saw the possibility of more subterranean adventures and tried to join the re-formed 170 Tunnelling Company at RE HQ in Chatham. R S G Stokes, now a Brigadier, was more than keen to serve again. Although well past military age for active service (he was a tunneller after all) and after

despite being able to remain at home thanks to his age and reserved occupation. Rejected four times by the York and Lancaster Regiment on account of his forty-two years, at the fifth attempt he tried the sappers – who were more than happy to take on a steady, skilled and experienced miner. In October 1915 after less than a month in uniform, he was already on active service with 254 TC at Givenchy.

In May 1916 tragedy struck the family; Arthur, fourteen, who had begun work in the coal mines himself to augment the family purse, was struck by a wayward mine truck. The injuries were severe; Arthur's right leg had to be amputated. His father, having been lucky enough to survive two roof falls during his own civilian mining career, was unable to visit his son. In common with thousands of other British soldiers, William Hackett could neither read nor write, and his letters home were composed by a pal, Sapper J R Evans.

I hope Mrs Hackett that the letters I write for your husband is alright, because he never tells me anything to put in. I know it is not like writing one himself and I know it must be very hard lines that he can't write…

February 1916. It is very hard to have his leg off but God knows best…its very hard for me to be in this foreign land and have a lad placed in hospital…I cannot help him but I know you will do all you can.

March 1916. We shall have to look on the bright side of things and pray for the best you know because all our lives are full of troubles and I wish to God they was all over with and the war is only just starting since I have been

out here but the young fellow that writes for me says it is only just the same as it was last year but dear Wife there is going to be some bloodshed before so very long they don't intend it going on so very much longer and they all seem to think so too and I don't care how soon because we are all fed up.

Sapper William Hackett was to die a few weeks after this last letter was received. This tragedy occurred on 23 June 1916 at the Shaftesbury shaft near the Red Dragon Crater, part of the Givenchy mine system in French Flanders. The Shaftesbury mine was a fresh project for 254 Tunnelling Company. The lateral tunnels were still unfinished but the main drive had made

MRS. HACKETT and Family, Widow and Children of the late Sapper W. Hackett, V.C.

Old tunnellers never die… Officers of the re-formed 170 TC at Chatham in January 1940, in the early months of a new war. R S G Stokes is seated fourth left on the front row. In this same group are five other ex-Great War moles who could not resist the call of the camouflet

The Hackett family: Arthur, Alice and Mary

good progress to a point almost two-thirds of the way across no man's land before a German mine explosion shook the gallery. Four of the five men working below at the time headed back to their shaft to find it badly damaged, with earth and clay sliding through the broken timbers; the fifth, Private Thomas Collins, also a coal miner, attached to 254 TC from the 14th Battalion, The Welsh Regiment, had been seriously hurt by the blow and was unable to move. With no laterals yet in place to provide auxiliary exits, the single Shaftesbury shaft was their only route to the surface and safety.

254 Tunnelling Company. June 22nd / 23rd 1916. After the enemy had blown a mine, he and four others were buried. A rescue party was soon on the spot, and, regardless of their own safety, succeeded in reaching the unfortunate miners. Three of them were withdrawn, but Hackett refused to leave the mine until his comrade who was badly injured, was removed, saying, 'I am a tunneller, I must look after the others first'. Unfortunately, owing to the activity of the enemy on this particular spot, the rescue party were forced to withdraw, and the CO was reluctantly compelled to discontinue the good work, and, alas, we have lost the hero and his comrade.

The Sapper, 1917

William Hackett was dead. The following week Sapper Evans again wrote to Alice, but this time the letter was penned as a very personal message from himself.

146205 Sapper J R Evans
2 Section, 254 Tunnelling Company R E
B E F
July 3rd

Dear Mrs Hackett,
I am most sorry to have to write to you under such circumstances that is to inform you that your Husband Sapper Hackett was Killed in Action on 22nd June but I can tell you that he died a heroes death as brave as any man as died in this war which I hope before long you will hear more about it. And I can tell you your Husbands death is sadly felt as he was respected by all the officers and men of the 254 Company and as for myself I miss him so much as if he was my own Father as you know I used to write his letters for him. And all the

Spr. W. Hackett, V.C., R.E.

The sole tunneller VC of the Great War, Sapper William Hackett of Mexborough, Nottinghamshire

boys of his section wish me to send you their best wishes and hope that you and the children will have the best of health and good luck and hope you will try and bear the sad news and they ask me to tell you that you can be proud of the way your husband died as he was a hero if ever there was one. I only wish I could tell it the way it happen but as you know we are not allowed to but if I am spared to come over this lot I will come and see you and let you know all about it. Well Mrs Hackett I must draw to a close by wishing you and the children the best of health and good luck.
    I beg to remain
    Yours truly
    J R Evans

The rescue team had returned to the shaft site after the shelling had subsided, and worked for four days to reach the two trapped men. All attempts failed. On 29 November 1916 Alice Hackett silently received her husband's posthumous VC from George V at Buckingham Palace. Sapper Hackett continued to be remembered in many quiet ways by his comrades for refusing to leave an injured mate to die alone in the dark.

17.3.17 St. Francis Barracks, Malta.
Dear Sir,
Will you please be good enough to forward the enclosed cheque for £19. 12s. 6d. to the widow of the late Sapper Hackett VC. This amount was realised at a football match played between a team selected by Sapper Phillips RE, and Sliema Wanderers...

Letter to the Editor,
The Sapper,1917

31.3.17 Brompton Barracks, Chatham
Dear Madam, It gives me much pleasure to forward you herewith a letter and cheque for £19 12s. 6d, which have been received from Malta. Will you kindly let me know if you receive it safely. I am also very glad to tell you that your husband's company have forwarded the sum of £100 6s 8d for the erection of a panel to his memory in the Union Jack Club in London.
    Trusting that your children and yourself are keeping well,
        H F De Carteret, Editor, *The Sapper*

May 1917
Dear Sir, I received your letter and the money this morning and I don't know how to thank my kind friends that God has raised up for me

in my trouble. He has taken with one hand and given with the other. I am very grateful both to Him and to all my friends. Will you kindly know how deeply I appreciate their goodness to me and my children?

I am glad to be able to tell you that I have not had to use the £67 that my husbands comrades sent me, but I banked it to use for my children's education, so that if anything should happen to me they would be able to keep themselves. They are going to the secondary school here, and my boy is also learning shorthand to fit him for an office. I put him to it as soon as he came out of hospital, and his Dad was so pleased to know that he would not have to go to the pit again. But he knew I should do my best for my chicks, and I trust they will grow up a credit to their brave father.

They unite with me in forwarding our heartfelt thanks to Sapper Phillips and Lance-Corporal Woolgar and all those interested in my welfare, and I also have to thank you very much for the trouble you have taken on my behalf, and I sign myself

Yours ever gratefully,
Alice Hackett

In 1966 William Hackett's daughter, Mrs Mary Hopkins, donated her father's Victoria Cross to the Royal Engineers' Museum at Chatham. *The Sapper* reported on a deliberately subdued event.

Mrs Hopkins was insistent that there should be no ceremony when she entrusted her father's Victoria Cross to the Corps. She declined suggestions that the hand-over should take place either at the local T.A. Drill Hall or at the colliery at which her father once worked and is still remembered. As she placed the small bronze cross in Brigadier Inglis' hand she remarked: 'It seems such a little thing in exchange for a life.'

The Sapper, May 1966

William Hackett had been forty-three years old when he died. His body, and that of Thomas Collins, who was only twenty-two, was never recovered, and both still lie in their 'ever silent tunnels' at Givenchy. Hackett is remembered in perpetuity on Panel 1 of the Ploegsteert Memorial to the Missing near Armentières, and Collins on the Thiepval Memorial on the Somme. Why two men who died together are not commemorated together is unknown.

It is fitting that some of the last words in this book should be those of Sir John Norton-Griffiths whose vision and indefatigability formed the tunnellers into the remarkable and unsung band of comrades that they became. In a cable to Ralph Stokes in 1921 supporting the idea of the Tunnellers' Register, he wrote:

> Co-operation and register a splendid idea. For the clay-kickers, no record in the world ever touched the footage, yield per ounce of pluck, endurance and devotion to duty, and no forces endured more. One silent toast to those who memorise a glorious record in their ever silent tunnels.
>
> Sir John Norton-Griffiths

John Norton-Griffiths' toast was in honour of all the 1,516 'moles' who gave their lives during the war. It was really a toast to heroes of obscurity, men whose names feature only marginally on the great lists of dead, wounded and missing, but whose contribution was critical. Few have spoken or written of their ways in the last eight decades, few monuments have been erected to their memory, and yet fewer poets have immortalised their hidden and selfless endeavours in the most secret, personal and savage battlefield of the Great War.

1915   1918

The simple 'T' of the tunnellers' badge

SOURCES

The primary sources for this book are archive materials (particularly personal testimony, maps, plans and unit war diaries) held principally by the Royal Engineers' Library and Museum, the Imperial War Museum, and the National Archives. These, and important published accounts, are listed in the Bibliography. The following notes record the location of quotations used in each chapter, and provide some guidance for further reading or follow-up; the full range of sources consulted is given in the Bibliography.

PREFACE
E. Synton, *Tunnellers All*, 1918

INTRODUCTION
Lieutenant Billy Congreve, *Armageddon Road*

I: FLANDERS FIELDS: THE YPRES SALIENT
Major S H Cowan, RE, Diary,
　　Royal Engineers' Museum
Oberstleutnant Otto Füsslein, in *Im Felde Unbesiegt*,
　　1921
Major H W R Hamilton, Indian Sappers & Miners,
　　RE Journal
C J Macgrath, *The Pilgrim's Guide to the Ypres Salient*,
　　1920
Captain Hugh Pollard, *The Pilgrim's Guide to the Ypres
　　Salient*, 1920
Lieutenant B K Young, RE, *RE Journal*
War Diary 49th Division CRE Papers, spring 1915,
　　Royal Engineers' Library

A general account of the geography of the Salient is given by Johnson (1921), with aspects of the geological conditions outlined by Doyle (1999). The background to the development of the Salient is developed by many works, particularly the Official Histories of the British and German armies, and is discussed in several one-volume histories, such as that by Falls (1960). Details of the opening campaigns, the Yser and the inundations are given by O'Meara (1915), Thys (1922) and Deguent (1928); First Ypres is discussed by Farrar-Hockley (1967). The 'meaning' of the Salient is expressed in the post-war guides, such as *the Immortal Salient* (1926) and *The Pilgrim's Guide to the Ypres Salient* (1920).

II: FROM SIEGE WAR TO WORLD WAR
Captain A Genez, H*istoire de la Guerre Souterraine*,
　　1914, subsequently reprinted in parts, *RE Journal*
Colonel C V Hume, *report on Japanese Mining
Operations at Kokura, Japan, 10th to 26th October 1906*,
　　1907, Royal Engineers' Library
Professor I Landmann, *Treatise on Mines*, 1815,
　　Royal Engineers' Library
Henry Manningham, *Manningham on Mines*, 1756,
　　Royal Engineers' Library
*Military Engineering: Mining and Demolitions,
　　Part IV*, 1910

Many texts deal with the history of fortification, and the development of mining as a method of prosecuting siege operations, particularly Genez (1914), Hogg (1975, 1981) and Toy (1966). Wiggins (2002) gives a good overview in his slim volume. Historical texts include Vauban (1748) Manningham (1756), Muller (1757), Landmann (1815) and Pasley (1852). Numerous articles discussing siege warfare and fortification have been published in the *Royal Engineers' Journal*; of these, Thackeray (1914–15) and Clifford (1977) are worthy of note. The impact of the Russo–Japanese war is described by von Donat (1910), Genez (1914), and in Hume's War Office Report (1907). The use of mining at the Siege of Petersburg in the American Civil War is usefully discussed by Gary Gallagher and others (2003). The technical 'textbook' development of mining and demolitions can be seen in the appropriate editions of the Royal Engineers' *Manual of Mining and Demolitions*.

III: SAPPERS AND MINERS
Anon., in Treves, Sir Frederick and Goodchild, G,
　　Made in the Trenches, 1916
Captain T W J Connolly, in Head, F B,
　　The Royal Engineer, 1869
History of the Corps of Royal Engineers, Volume V
　　General the Hon. Sir N G Lyttelton, in *Report of a
　　Preliminary Siege Staff Ride held at Chatham,
　　6th – 10th May, 1907, and subsequent Siege
　　Operations held at Chatham, July and August,
　　1907*
Professor John Muller, in Clifford, N D,
　　RE Journal, 1977
Captain Matthew Roach, Diary,
　　Royal Engineers' Library
The Royal Engineers at Work and Play.
　　Recruitment booklet, 1915
The Sapper, 1914
Lieutenant Colonel B R Ward, in *Report of a
　　Preliminary Siege Staff Ride held at Chatham,
　　6th – 10th May, 1907, and subsequent Siege
　　Operations held at Chatham, July and August,
　　1907*
Wellington to Lord Liverpool, in Clifford, N D,
　　RE Journal, 1977

The development of the Royal Engineers is dealt with in full in the volumes of the Corps History, a single, short abstracted volume having been produced in 1993. Several other accounts provide background, including Head (1869), Smithers (1991) and Napier (1998), as well as numerous articles in the *Royal Engineers' Journal*. The organisation of the Corps at the outbreak of war is dealt with in Volume V of the history, and for their German counterparts, in Heinrici (1931) and Anon. (2002). Good published examples of the diaries of Field Company officers are Eberle (1973) and Glubb (1978). Discussion of the work of the British Pioneer Battalions is given by Mitchinson (1997).

IV: MINE WARFARE, TUNNELLERS AND *PIONIERE*, 1915
Anon, Barrie Papers, IWM
[Empire Jack] Barrie papers, IWM
Lieutenant Brian Frayling, *Back to Front*,
　　unpublished memoir, Royal Engineers' Library
Oberstleutnant Otto Füsslein,
　　in *Im Felde Unbesiegt*, 1921
Lieutenant Walter Gardner [WG], *One Mole Rampant*,
　　unpublished memoir, Royal Engineers' Library
Captain A Genez, *Histoire de la Guerre Souterraine*,
　　1914, subsequently reprinted in parts, RE Journal
Manual of Field Engineering 1911 (reprinted 1913)
Major-General R N Harvey, *RE Journal*, 1929, and
　　unpublished lecture transcript *Military Mining in
　　the Great War*, National Archives
Major-General F Gordon Hyland, Barrie Papers,
　　Royal Engineers' Museum
Sapper Hubert Leather, Barrie Papers,
　　Royal Engineers' Museum
Lance Corporal Harry Mosely, Barrie Papers,
　　Royal Engineers' Museum
Major John Norton-Griffiths, War Diary,
　　National Archive
Drill Corporal Frank Parsons, interview,
　　Parapet Productions
Report to Major-General Bulfin, Commanding
　　28th Division, 2nd Army HQ Papers, National
　　Archives
Leutnant Otto Riebicke, in *Unsere Pioniere in
　　Weltkriege*, 1920
Lieutenant Matthew Roach, diary, RE Library

The development of John Norton-Griffiths' career has been discussed in print in *Tunnel Master and Arsonist of the Great War*, co-written by Norton-Griffiths' grand-daughter, Anne Morgan (Bridgland and Morgan, 2003); his own account is highly coloured (Norton-Griffiths, 1921). Archive sources in the National Archives, the Imperial War Museum and private hands provide invaluable background material. Grieve and Newman (1936) and Barrie (1962) are important, as are a number of German accounts, including Anon (1917) and Heinrici (1931) and several translations to be found in the *RE Journal* and the *Professional Memoirs, US Army Corps of Engineers*. Numerous articles dealing with individual experiences provide useful background to the subject. Some contemporary colour about the tunnellers' life is provided by the accounts by Synton (1918), Trounce (1918) and Walter Gardner's privately circulated account, *One Mole Rampant*. An interesting tunnelling company miscellany is the possibility that a female journalist, Dorothy Lawrence, posed as a male tunneller and served briefly with 179 TC (Lawrence, 1919). This has yet to be fully substantiated.

V: *KRIEGSGEOLOGIE*: GOING UNDER-GROUND
Captain H R Dixon, *The Lighter Side of a Tunneller's
　　Life*, unpublished memoir,
　　Royal Engineers' Library
Lieutenant Oscar Earnshaw, The Merivale Collection,

Imperial War Museum
Lieutenant Arthur Eaton, Barrie Papers,
    Royal Engineers' Museum
Private Bert Fearns, interview, Parapet Productions
Oberstleutnant Otto Füsslein, in Heinrici, Paul,
    Das Ehrenbuch der deutschen Pioniere, 1931
Lieutenant B C Hall, Barrie Papers,
    Royal Engineers' Museum
Brigadier-General Harvey, discussion to W B R King,
    Geological work on the Western Front,
    Geographical Journal 1919
Private Donald Hodge, interview, Parapet Productions
Walter Kranz, *Vierteljahreshefte für Pioniere*, 1935
Sapper Hubert Leather, Barrie Papers,
    Royal Engineers' Museum
Company Sergeant Major J Lyhane,
    unpublished memoir, Royal Engineers' Library
Trooper Albert 'Smiler' Marshall, interview,
    Parapet Productions
Captain William J McBride, Barrie Papers,
    Royal Engineers' Museum
Lieutenant R R Murray, *Annual Journal of the United
    Services Institute of Nova Scotia*, 1929
Sapper Frank O'Callaghan, Barrie Papers,
    Royal Engineers' Museum
Lieutenant Matthew Roach, diary,
    Royal Engineers' Library
Lieutenant Alan Reid, Barrie Papers,
    Royal Engineers' Museum
Captain Basil Sawers, 177 TC, RE, Barrie Papers,
    Royal Engineers' Museum

Geological work by Walter Kranz, Bill King and Edgeworth David has been discussed by King himself (King 1919); and anonymously in the Royal Engineer volume *Geological Work on the Western Front* (RE, 1922). Kranz's (1935) own account, and that of the 4th Army Commander Otto Füsslein (1921) give the German side. Recent reviews of military geologists include Macleod (1995), Rose and Rosenbaum (1998) and Rose and others (2002). David's (1937) biography of his uncle, Edgeworth David is valuable. The application of geology in war is discussed by Brooks (1920) and Rose (1978), and the geology of the Western Front itself by Doyle (1998). Leriche's (1920) account is a study of the geology exposed in the shellholes and mine craters. The Royal Engineer volume on *Military Mining* (1922) provides important detail, as do the relevant contemporary RE handbooks. As with all other aspects of the underground war, numerous articles by the participants published in the immediate post-war period provide background and detail, including Ball (1919), Woodward (1920) and Harvey (1929). A recent overview of the subject was given by Hammond (1992).

VI: THE SILENT WAR

Lieutenant Kenneth Anns, Barrie Papers,
    Royal Engineers' Museum
Anonymous 250 TC officer, TOCA *Bulletin*, 1927
Captain G R Cassels, diary, Royal Engineers' Library
Major H S Cowan, diary, Royal Engineers' Museum
Lieutenant Brian Frayling, *Back to Front*,
    unpublished memoir, Royal Engineers' Library
Lieutenant Walter Gardner [WG], *One Mole Rampant*,
    privately published memoir,
    Royal Engineers' Library
Oberstleutnant Otto Füsslein, in Heinrici, Paul,
    Das Ehrenbuch der Deutschen Pioniere, 1931
Lieutenant Colonel A Hacking
Lieutenant B C Hall, Barrie Papers,
    Royal Engineers' Museum

Sapper H Mawson, Barrie Papers,
    Royal Engineers' Museum
Captain William J McBride, Barrie Papers,
    Royal Engineers' Museum
Captain R S Mackilligan, Barrie Papers,
    Royal Engineers' Museum
Lieutenant F J Mulqueen, unpublished memoirs,
    Royal Engineers' Library
Captain Matthew Roach, diary,
    Royal Engineers' Library
Captain Basil Sawers, Barrie Papers,
    Royal Engineers' Museum
Major R S G Stokes, War Diary, National Archives
Lieutenant John Westacott, Barrie Papers,
    Royal Engineers' Museum

The listening war has been discussed in general in the appropriate *Work of the RE in the European war 1914–19* volume, *Military Mining*, the official mining handbooks, issued after the war, and the standard sources of Grieve and Newman (1936) and Barrie (1962). Other accounts are valuable, such as Ball (1919), Walker (1930), and *Professional Memoirs* of the US Corps of Engineers. As with other chapters, valuable source material has been gathered from numerous published articles by the participants, and the many technical reports and handbooks produced by the War Office for the Royal Engineers, both before and after the war. Further more comprehensive technical details of listening instruments can be found in the above publications.

VII: ENEMIES BELOW

Captain G R Cassels, diary, Royal Engineers' Library
Major H S Cowan, diary, Royal Engineers' Museum
Captain Cecil Cropper, letter to his mother,
    Barrie Papers, Royal Engineers' Museum
Sapper Hubert Leather, Barrie Papers,
    Royal Engineers' Museum
Colonel David Dale Logan (1919)
Memorandum on Gas Poisoning, *Military Engineering
    Volume IV, Mining and Demolitions*, 1923 and
    1935
Lieutenant F J Mulqueen, unpublished memoirs,
    Royal Engineers' Library
Lieutenant Matthew Roach, diary,
    Royal Engineers' Library
The Sapper, 1915
Captain Basil Sawers, Barrie Papers,
    Royal Engineers' Museum
Private James Taylor, Barrie Papers,
    Royal Engineers' Museum
The Times, 15 October 1915
Lieutenant John Westacott, Barrie Papers,
    Royal Engineers' Museum

Mine rescue and the dangers of CO gas have been the subject of a few detailed post-war accounts, including, specifically, Ball (1919), Logan (1919) and Eagar (1919–20). The most recent account is that of Jones (1995 and 2000). The post-war RE technical manuals on *Mining and Demolitions* give insights into the lessons learned during the war, as does the work of Smart (1921). Other details are provided in the *Military Mining* volume of *The Work of the RE in the European War, 1914–1918* (Anon., 1922). Accounts of fighting below ground are given by Barrie (1962) – the presumed inspiration for Sebastian Faulks' much acclaimed novel *Birdsong* – and were explored in the Channel 4 documentary *The Underground War* (1998).

VIII: THE MINE WAR DEEPENS, 1915–1917

Captain G R Cassels, diary, Royal Engineers' Library

Sapper George Clayton, interview,
    IWM Sound Archive
Major H S Cowan, diary, Royal Engineers' Museum
Oberstleutnant Otto Füsslein, in Heinrici, Paul,
    Das Ehrenbuch der deutschen Pioniere, 1931
Major Clay Hepburn, Barrie Papers,
    Royal Engineers' Museum
Lieutenant F J Mulqueen, unpublished memoirs,
    Royal Engineers' Library
Major John Norton-Griffiths, war diary,
    National Archives
Captain Alan Reid, Barrie Papers,
    Royal Engineers' Museum
Captain Basil Sawers, Barrie Papers,
    Royal Engineers' Museum
Captain H D Trounce, *Fighting the Boche
    Underground*, 1918
German Official History,
    (6 Kompagnie, 126 Infanterie Regiment)

The chronological development of military mining on the Western Front has been touched upon by Harvey (1929), and in the narratives of Grieve and Newman (1936) and Barrie (1962). Füsslein (1921, 1931) and Kranz (1935) present the view from the other side of no man's land.

IX: 'EARTHQUAKING' THE RIDGE: MESSINES, JUNE 1917

Anonymous 250 TC officer, TOCA *Bulletin*, 1927
Captain Cecil Cropper, Barrie Papers,
    Royal Engineers' Museum
Oberstleutnant Otto Füsslein, in *Im Felde Unbesiegt*,
    1921
Oberstleutnant Otto Füsslein, in Heinrici, Paul,
    Das Ehrenbuch der Deutschen Pioniere, 1931
Lieutenant B C Hall, Barrie Papers,
    Royal Engineers' Museum
Captain H M Hudspeth, Barrie Papers,
    Royal Engineers' Museum
Major General F Gordon Hyland, Barrie Papers,
    Royal Engineers' Museum
Captain William J McBride, Barrie Papers,
    Royal Engineers' Museum
Major John Norton-Griffiths, war diary,
    National Archives
Lieutenant Haydn Rees, Barrie Papers,
    Royal Engineers' Museum
Captain Alan Reid, Barrie Papers,
    Royal Engineers' Museum
Major R S G Stokes, war diary, National Archives
Captain Harry R Urie, Barrie Papers,
    Royal Engineers' Museum
    Lieutenant O H Woodward, *The War Story of
    Oliver Holmes Woodward, Captain*. Private
    circulation.

The prelude to Messines and the Third Battle of Ypres in 1917 has been discussed in numerous accounts. Passingham (1998) is the only full account of Messines itself. The topography of Messines is considered by Doyle and others (2002). *The Official History* (Edmonds, 1948) provides important background, and a concise account of the planning process is described by Prior and Wilson (1996). Numerous accounts by tunnellers exist, published in the *RE Journal* and the *Tunnellers' Old Comrades Association Bulletin*. Other aspects of planning and technical aspects of the subsequent Third Battle of Ypres are discussed in Liddle (1998).

X: MOUNTAINS IN THE SKY: MESSINES AND AFTER

Anonymous Australian tunneller [possibly
    Captain J Bowry], *Melbourne Argus*, 7 June 1926
Anonymous 250 TC officer, TOCA *Bulletin*, 1927
Gunner Charles H Brett, Barrie Papers, RE Museum
Der Weltkrieg 1914–1918, Official German history, 1939
Lieutenant Guy Chapman, *A Passionate Prodigality*,
    1933
Captain H R Dixon, *The Lighter Side of a Tunneller's Life*,
    unpublished memoir, Royal Engineers' Library
Captain Frank Hurley, private diary,
    Australian War Memorial
Captain H R Dixon, War Diary,
    IWM Department of Documents
Brigadier Sir James Edmonds, *Official History of the
    Great War, Military Operations, France and
    Belgium. 1917, Volume II, Messines and Third
    Ypres (Passchendaele)*, 1948.
Lieutenant Brian Frayling, *Back to Front*, unpublished
    memoir, Royal Engineers' Library
Oberstleutnant Otto Füsslein, in *Im Felde Unbesiegt*,
    1921
Lieutenant Martin Greener, interview,
    IWM Sound Archive
Lieutenant B C Hall, Barrie Papers,
    Royal Engineers' Museum
Major-General R N Harvey, *Royal Engineers' Journal*,
    1929, and unpublished lecture transcript *Military
    Mining in the Great War*, National Archives
Private John Rea Laister, interview,
    Parapet Productions
Sapper Thomas Lloyd, Barrie Papers,
    Royal Engineers' Museum
Captain Marvin Maxwell, Barrie Papers,
    Royal Engineers' Museum
Lieutenant J MacD Royle, transcript of radio
    presentation *'An Explosion like an Earthquake'*,
    1934
Major R S G Stokes, War Diary, National Archives
General Sixt von Arnim, captured document,
    War Diary, 49th Division CRE, RE Library
Lieutenant O H Woodward. *The War Story of Oliver
    Holmes Woodward, Captain*. Private circulation.

The experiences of the Messines tunnellers is
recounted by Barrie (1962), and the outcome of the
battle by Edmonds in the Official History (1948), and
more recently, by Passingham (1998). The story of the
Messines mines is recounted in many articles, in the
TOCA Bulletin (Anon 1936) and *RE Journal* (Anon.,
1940, Pennycuick, 1966) and elsewhere (Mullins, 1965;
Robinson, 1999).

XI: 'A HOLE IN THE GROUND WITH A LID ON'

Anon., in Treves, Sir Frederick and Goodchild, G, *ade
    in the Trenches*, 1916
Captain G R Cassels, diary, Royal Engineers' Library
Lieutenant Guy Chapman, *A Passionate Prodigality*,
    1933
Major H S Cowan, diary, Royal Engineers' Museum
Private Bert Fearns, interview, Parapet Productions
Lieutenant Brian Frayling, *Memoirs of Bryan Frayling*,
    unpublished, Royal Engineers' Library
Private Walter Gardner [WG], *One Mole Rampant*
Captain H W Graham, *The Life of a Tunnelling
    Company*, 1927
Lieutenant Colonel C H Harington, War Diary, CRE
    49th Division, Royal Engineers' Library
Second Lieutenant B J Marden, Barrie Papers,
    Royal Engineers' Museum

John Masefield, *The Old Front Line*, 1917
Lieutenant Colonel John Norton-Griffths, War Diary,
    National Archives
Second Lieutenant Robin Skeggs papers,
    Parapet Archive Trust
Corporal Frank Williams, Private Archive,
    courtesy of Giles Guthrie
War Diary, CRE 39th Division,
    Royal Engineers' Library

The construction of dugouts has received less attention
than offensive mining, although numerous post-war
accounts of the work of the Tunnelling Companies
dwell on these aspects. John Masefield's classic *The Old
Front Line* describes the German dugouts on the
Somme; while life undergound in the arras sector of
Artois is touched upon by Girardet and others (2003).
Considerations of artillery in trench warfare are outlined
in Ashworth (2000) and Saunders (2000). The technical
volumes produced by the War Office for the RE are also
of value. The development of MEBU blockhouses or
'pillboxes' in Flanders is discussed in detail by Oldham
(1995).

XII: DEGREES OF PROTECTION, 1917–1918

W J Bird, *Thirteen Years after*, 1932 (reprint)
Lieutenant Edmund Blunden, *Undertones of War*, 1929
Sapper James Colly, Barrie Papers,
    Royal Engineers' Museum
Captain H R Dixon, unpublished memoir, *The Lighter
    Side of a Tunneller's Life* (1932),
    Royal Engineers' Library
Captain Frank Hurley, private diary,
    Australian War Memorial
Lieutenant F Howkins, unpublished memoir,
    Under No Man's Land (1929),
    Royal Engineers' Museum
Driver Leo McCormack, interview,
    Parapet Productions
*Military Engineering, Part IV. Military Mining and
    Demolitions*, 1923
Private Ted Rimmer, interview, Parapet Productions
Private Wilf Walworth, interview, Parapet Productions
War Diary, CRE 49th Division, RE Library
Private Harry Wells, interview, Parapet Productions

The development and construction of dugouts is dealt
with in the numerous technical volumes of the RE.
Discussion of Edgeworth David's dugout suitability
maps is given in *Geological work on the Western Front*
(1922) and David (1937). Consideration of the artillery
war is given by Wade (1933), Liddle (1998), Prior and
Wilson (1998), Ashworth (2000) and Saunders (2000).
Discussion of depth of protection is given in Brooks
(1920), Doyle and Bennett (1997) and Doyle and others
(2001). Numerous archive sources provide technical
details. Many memoirs touch upon dugout life;
notables include Guy Chapman and Edmund Blunden.

XIII: BACK TO THE FRONT: THE LEGACY

W J Bird, *Thirteen Years after*, 1932 (reprint)
Private Bert Fearns, interview, Parapet Productions
The Sapper, November 1915
Lieutenant John Westacott, Barrie Papers,
    Royal Engineers' Museum

Background to the post-war Salient is provided by Bird
(1932), and in the guides produced by Talbot House
(1920) and the Ypres League (Pulteney and Brice,
1925). The archaeological legacy of the underground

war has not been fully discussed, although important
recent work includes that of ABAF (1999) and Doyle
and others (2002, and in preparation), who describe
the Beecham Dugout. General considerations of the
archaeology of Great War battle sites are given in
Desfossés and Jacques (1999) and Saunders (2002).
The environmental legacy of tunnels and dugouts has
been the subject of a number of articles, notable being
those of Doyle and others (2001, 2002), and research
continues.

EPILOGUE

Cable, John Norton-Griffiths to Ralph Stokes,
    Barrie Papers, Royal Engineers' Museum
The Sapper, 1917
The Sapper, 1966
Sapper J R Evans, Letters to Alice Hackett,
    Royal Engineers' Museum
Lieutenant John Westacott, Barrie Papers,
    Royal Engineers' Museum
Captain Matthew Roach, diary,
    Royal Engineers' Library

BIBLIOGRAPHY

UNPUBLISHED SOURCES

1. Royal Engineers' Museum, Chatham
   Barrie Papers

2. Royal Engineers' Library, Chatham
   War Diaries and papers:
       Army, Corps and Divisional Engineer
       papers
       Field Company RE War Diaries
       Signals Company War Diaries
       Tunnelling Company RE War Diaries
       Engineer Papers on Miscellaneous Subjects,
       Documents from Brigadier Sir James
       Edmonds
       49th Division CRE papers
   Manuscript memoirs:
       Memoirs of G R Cassels
       The Lighter Side of a Tunneller's Life,
       H R Dixon, 1932
       Memoirs of Bryan Frayling CBE, RE
       Biographical papers of Captain
       F D Gurrey RE
       Memoirs of F Howkins
       Memoirs of J Lyhane
       Memoirs of F J Mulqueen
       Just a Small One, 172 TC
   Diaries
       Matthew Roach
       W H Sansom
       Sapper H W Taylor RE

3. National Archives (formerly Public Record Office),
WO series, including numerous consulted Tunnelling
Company war diaries, maps and plans

4. Imperial War Museum, Department of Documents
   Barrie Papers
   Merivale Collection, Letters of Lieutenant Oscar
   Earnshaw, 17.4.16
   Mining Warfare, Captain D Ivor Evans MC

5. Imperial War Museum, Sound Archive
   George Clayton 10012
   Mark Dillon 9752
   Brian Frayling 4105
   Martin Greener 8945

6. Australian War Memorial.
   *Extracts from the Old Mining Regulations, issued by
   the General of Pioneers, Army Headquarters, Laon,
   April 1915*. Translation of captured German
   document, AWM 25[985/9]
   *Papers of Captain F Hurley, Official Photographer
   for the AIF*. Australian War Memorial AWM
   419/71/45

7. Parapet Archive Trust, documents, film and sound
archives
   Thomas Colepepper's Engineer Pocket book, c.1680
   A Mining Engineer on the Western Front, Captain F
   D Gurrey DSO, MC, Croix de Guerre

8. Anne Morgan, unpublished *Memoirs of Gwladys,
Lady Norton-Griffiths*

9. Vandewalle archive

10. ABAC archive

PRINTED BOOKS

ABAF, *Beecham Dugout, Passchendaele 1914–1918*,
   Studies 1, Association for Battlefield Archaeology
   in Flanders, Zonnebeke, 1999
Anon., *Atlas zur Abhandlung uber die Kriegsminen*,
   Anstalt von L Forster, Wien, 1852
Anon., *Rules for Military Mining according to the
   Practice of the Royal Engineer Establishment at
   Chatham*, Windeyer & Cackett, Chatham, 1853
Anon., *Mineur Exercir und Dienst Reglement*, Berlin,
   Verlag von M Bath, 1866.
Anon., *Index to the Professional Papers of the Corps of
   Royal Engineers 1837–1892*. W & J Mackay and Co.,
   Chatham, 1893
Anon., *The Royal Engineers at Work and Play*, recruit-
   ment booklet, RE, Chatham, 1915
Anon., *The work of the Royal Engineers in the
   European War, 1914-19*. Various volumes
   including, *Geological Work on the Western Front;
   Military Mining; Miscellaneous; Supply of Engineer
   Stores and Equipment*, Institution of Royal
   Engineers, Chatham, 1922
Anon., *Der Mineur in Flandern*, von Gerhard Stalling,
   Oldenburg, 1917
Anon., *Der Weltkrieg 1914–1918* [official German
   history], Mittler, Berlin, 1939
Anon., *History of the Corps of Royal Engineers*, The
   Institution of Royal Engineers, Chatham, various
   volumes and dates
Anon., *History of the Corps of Royal Engineers, Volume
   V, The Home Front, France, Flanders and Italy in the
   First World War*, The Institution of Royal Engineers,
   Chatham, 1952
Anon., *Index to the Professional Papers of the Corps of
   Royal Engineers 1893-1956*, RSME, 1961
Anon., *A Short History, The Royal Engineers*, Institution
   of Royal Engineers, Chatham, 1993
Anon., *Handbook of the German Army 1918*, IWM and
   Battery Press, 1996
Anon., *Handbook of the German Army 1914*, IWM and
   Battery Press, 2002
Anon., *Standing Orders of the School of Military
   Engineering*, RSME, Chatham, various years
Ashworth, T, *Trench Warfare 1914–1918: The Live and
   Let Live System*, Pan, London, 2000
Baldey, Donna and Thomas, Ross, *1st Australian
   Tunnelling Company*, The Formation, Unpublished
   research, Queensland, 2003
Barrie, Alexander, *War Underground; The Tunnellers of
   the Great War*, London, 1962
Bean, C E W, *Official History of Australia in the War of
   1914–1918*. Angus & Robertson, Sydney, 1933
Bird, W J, *Thirteen Years After*, Maclean Publishing,
   Toronto, 1932 (reprinted IMCC, Hampton, n.d.)
Blunden, Edmund, *Undertones of War*, Cobden-

Sanderson, London, 1930
Bradford, Ernle, *The Great Siege*, Hodder & Stoughton,
   London, 1961
Bridgland, T and Morgan, A, *Tunnel-Master and
   Arsonist of the Great War*, Pen & Sword, Barnsley,
   2003
Brown, G I, *The Big Bang: A History of Explosives*,
   Sutton Publishing, Stroud, 1998
Chapman, Guy, *A Passionate Prodigality, Fragments of
   an Autobiography*, London, 1933
Committee of the Corps of Royal Engineers, *Aide-
   Memoire to the Military Sciences*, Lockwood,
   London, 1860
Congreve, Billy, *Armageddon Road, a VC's Diary,
   1914-16*, William Kimber, London, 1982
Coutele, M, *Memoire de la Guerre Souterraine*, Felix
   Rossi, Paris 1812
David, M E, *Professor David*, Edward Arnold, London,
   1937
Doyle, Peter, *Geology of the Western Front, 1914–18*,
   Geologists' Association, London, 1998
Eberle, V F, *My Sapper Venture*, Pitman, London, 1973
Edmonds, James [and others], *Official History of the
   Great War, Military Operations, France and Belgium*.
   HMSO and Macmillan, London, 1925–1948
Edmonds, James, *Official History of the Great War,
   Military Operations, France and Belgium: 1917,
   Volume II, Messines and Third Ypres (Passchendaele)*,
   HMSO, London, 1948
Falls, Cyril, *The First World War*, Longman, London,
   1960
Farrar-Hockley, Anthony, *Death of an Army*, Batsford,
   London, 1967
Gallagher, Gary W, Engle, Stephen D, Krick, Robert W
   and Glatthaar, Joseph T, *The American Civil War:
   The Mighty Scourge of War*, Osprey, Oxford, 2003
Genez, Captain A, *Histoire de la Guerre Souterraine*,
   Librairie Militaire Berger Levrault, Paris, 1914
Geuss, M J M, Dufour, Jean-Edme and Roux, Philippe,
   Théorie de L'Art du Mineur, Maestricht, 1778
Girardet, J-M, Jaques, A and Duclos, J-L, D,
   Somewhere on the Western Front, Documents
   d'Archéologie et d'Histoire du XXe siècle No. 8,
   Arras, 2003
Glubb, John, *Into Battle, a Soldier's Diary of the Great
   War*, Cassell, London, 1978
Graham, H W, *The Life of a Tunnelling Company*, J
   Catherall, Hexham, 1927
Grieve, Captain W Grant and Newman, Bernard,
   Tunnellers, Herbert Jenkins, London, 1936
Harrison, G H, *Index of Extracts from the Proceedings
   of the R.E. Committee 1871–1927*, Chatham 1905
   (1905–1927 added in MS)
Head, Francis B, *The Royal Engineer*, John Murray,
   London, 1869
Heinrici, Paul, *Das Ehrenbuch der Deutschen Pioniere*,
   Verlag Tradition Wilhelm Kolt, Berlin, 1931
Historical Section of the Committee of Imperial
   Defence, *Official History of the Russo–Japanese War*,
   HMSO, 1912
Hogg, Ian, *Fortress*, Purnell Book Services, London,
   1975

Hogg, Ian, *The History of Fortification*, Orbis, London, 1981

Johnson, D W, *The Battlefields of the World War: Western and Southern Fronts*, Oxford University Press, New York, 1921

Klijnsma, S J, *Handleiding tot de Minerkunst*, Te's Gravenhage, 1842

Landmann, I F A S, *A Treatise on Mines for the use of the Royal Military Academy at Woolwich*, T Bensley, 1815

Lawrence, Dorothy, *The Only English Woman Soldier, Late 51st Division, 179 Tunnelling Company, BEF*, John Lane, London, 1919

Liddle, Peter (ed.), *Passchendaele in Perspective, The Third Battle of Ypres*, Leo Cooper, London, 1997

Macdonald, Lyn, *They Called it Passchendaele*, Penguin, London, 1978

Mangold, Tom and Penycate, John, *The Tunnels of Cu Chi*, Guild, London, 1985

Manningham, Henry, *Manningham on Mines*, A Millar, London, 1756

Masefield, John, *The Old Front Line*, Heinemann, London, 1917

Mercur, James, *The Attack of Fortified Places*, John Wiley, New York, 1904

Mitchinson, K W, *Pioneer Battalions in the Great War, Organized and Intelligent Labour*, Leo Cooper, Barnsley, 1997

Muller, John, *The Attack and Defence of Fortified Places*, J Millan, London, 1757

Napier, Gerald, *The Sapper VCs*, The Stationery Office, London, 1998

Neillands, Robin, *The Great War Generals on the Western Front*, Robinson, London, 1999

Oldham, Peter, *Pillboxes on the Western Front*, Leo Cooper, London, 1995

Pasley, C W, *Pasley on Sieges*, John Weale, London, 1852

Passingham, Ian, *Pillars of Fire, The Battle of Messines Ridge 1917*, Sutton, Stroud, 1998

Prior, Robin and Wilson, Trevor, *Passchendaele, the Untold Story*, Yale University Press, New Haven and London, 1996

Pulteney, William and Brice, Beatrix, *The Immortal Salient*, John Murray, London, 1925

Sandes, E W C, *The Military Engineer in India*, Institution of Royal Engineers, Chatham, 1933

Saunders, A, *Weapons of the Trench War*, Sutton, Stroud, 2000

Schwarte, M, *Die Technik im Weltkriege*, Ernst Siegfried Mittler and Son, Berlin, 1920

Smart, Rex C, *Recent Practice in the Use of Self-Contained Breathing Apparatus*, Griffin & Co, London, 1921

Smithers, A J, *Honourable Conquests – An Account of the Enduring Work of the Royal Engineers throughout the Empire*, Leo Cooper, London, 1991

Steel, N and Hart, Peter, *Passchendaele, the Sacrificial Ground*, Cassell, London, 2000

Striffler, Robert, *Der Minenkrieg in den Dolomiten. Schriftenreihe zur Zietgeschichte Tirols*, Band 9, 1993

Synton, E, *Tunnellers All*, London, 1918

Talbot House, *The Pilgrim's Guide to the Ypres Salient*, Herbert Reiach, London, 1920

Thys, Robert, *Nieuport 1914-1918*, Constable, London, 1922

Toy, Sidney, *A History of Fortification*, Heinemann, London, 1966

Treves, Frederick, and Goodchild, George (eds), *Made in the Trenches*, George Allen & Unwin, London, 1916

Trounce, H D, *Fighting the Boche Underground*, New York, 1918

Vauban, M, *The New Method of Fortification*, Paris, 1748

von Donat, Karl, *German Official Account of the Russo–Japanese War*, Hugh Rees, London, 1910

von Hauser, Georg Freyhern, *Die Minen und der Untererdische Krieg*, K K Hof und Staats-Ararial-Druckerey, Wien, 1817

Wade, Aubrey, *The War of the Guns*, Batsford, London, 1936

'WG' [Walter Gardner], *One Mole Rampant*, Printed for private circulation, Richards Keans, London, n.d [c. 1930]

Wiggins, Kenneth, *Siege Mines and Underground Warfare*, Shire, Princes Risborough, 2003

Wolfe, Leon, *In Flanders' Fields*, Longman, London, 1959

Woodward, O H, *The War Story of Oliver Holmes Woodward*, Captain, private circulation, n.d.

ARTICLES, *ROYAL ENGINEERS' JOURNAL*

Addison, G H, The German Engineer and Pioneer Corps (*Ingenieur und Pionier Korps*), RE Journal, September 1930

'Anagapa', Science and war, *RE Journal*, May 1916

Anon., The Royal Engineers and the Battle of Waterloo, *RE Journal*, February–March 1917

Anon., The Messines Ridge mines, 7th June, 1917 – German Accounts, *RE Journal*, September 1940

Berthaut, Henri, The future of forts, *RE Journal*, January 1917

Bond, R L, History of the 23rd (Field) Company RE in the Great War, 1914–18. *RE Journal*, 1928–29

'Buccaneer', Notes on the history and employment of Army Troops Companies, RE, *RE Journal*, June 1920.

Clifford, N D, Early history of sapper tunnelling, *RE Journal*, December 1977

Craster, J E E, The organization of engineers, *RE Journal*, January 1915

Grant, P G, Control of engineer work in war, *RE Journal*, December 1920

Grimsdale, G E, Shell fire versus permanent fortification, Liège and Namur, 1914, *RE Journal*, June 1927

Hamilton, H W R, History of the 20th Field Company, Royal Bombay Sappers and Miners, Great War 1914–1918, *RE Journal*, 1926

Harvey, R N, Some notes on fieldworks, *RE Journal*, August 1913

Harvey, R N, The organisation and duties of Field Companies RE in peace and war, *RE Journal*, October 1913.

Harvey, R N, Permanent fortification, *RE Journal*, December 1913

Harvey, R N, Military mining in the Great War. *RE Journal*, 1929

Harvey, R N, Lt.-Colonel Sir Tannatt William Edgeworth David, KBE, CMG, DSO, DSc, FRS. *RE Journal*, December 1934

'H B', The siting of trenches, RE Journal, June 1919

Jones, S R, A Mine Rescue Officer on the Western Front, *RE Journal*, December 1995

Martin, J K, Some Notes on the organisation and equipment of the engineers of foreign armies as compared with our own, *RE Journal*, October 1914

Norton-Griffiths, J, The origin of the Tunnelling Companies, *RE Journal*, March 1928

O'Meara, W A J, Review of the operations of the Belgian Army, 31st July to 31st December 1914, *RE Journal*, November, 1915

Pennycuick, J A C, Hill 60 and the mines at Messines,

RE Journal, July 1966

Pressey, H A S, Notes on trench war, *RE Journal*, March 1919

Rose, E P F, Geology in war, *RE Journal*, 1978

Sim, G E H, The Employment of Divisional Engineers in conjunction with other arms in war, *RE Journal*, December 1922

Skey, F E G, The tactics of Divisional Engineers, *RE Journal*, February 1914

Thackeray, E T, Sieges and the defence of fortified places by British and Indian armies in the XIX century, *RE Journal*, December 1914 and January 1915

Thomas, G I, Fortifications in 1914–18, *RE Journal*, March 1930

Thuillier, H F, Organization and employment of engineers in war, *RE Journal*, May 1920

Young, B K, The diary of an RE subaltern with the BEF in 1914, *RE Journal*, 1933-1934

Young, J, Military explosives of today. Lectures delivered to the Royal Society of Arts April 8, 15 and 22 1918, *RE Journal*, July 1918

PROFESSIONAL MEMOIRS, US ARMY CORPS OF ENGINEERS

Anon., *Consolidation of Trenches, Localities and Craters after Assault and Capture*, Professional Memoir 9, 1917

Bond, S, and Leisk, R D, *Deep Gallery Shelters; a Lecture*, Professional Memoir 10, 1918

Gay, A, *Sapping Operations, especially for Infantry*, Professional Memoir 10, 1918

Livermore, W H, *Mining Operations, especially for Infantry*, Professional Memoir 10, 1918

Livermore, W R, *Tunnels and Galleries*, Professional Memoir 10, 1918

Munroe, Charles E, *Zones of Silence in Sound Areas from Explosions*, Professional Memoir 10, 1918

Swift, H, *Use of Corrugated Iron for Construction of Shelters*, Professional Memoir 10, 1918

Trounce, H D, *Mine Rescue Work*, Professional Memoir 10, 1918

OTHER PUBLISHED ARTICLES

Anon., La Guerre Souterraine, *Gazette Des Armes* No. 68, Fevrier 1979

Anon., Some notes on surveying for the deep offensive mine galleries in front of the Messines–Wytchaete Ridge, *Tunnellers' Old Comrades Association Bulletin*, 11, 1936

Ball, H Standish The Work of the Miner on the Western Front, 1915–1918, *Transactions of the Institution of Mining and Metallurgy*, 28, 1919

Branagan, David, The Australian Mining Corps in World War 1, *Transactions of the Australian Institute of Mining and Metallurgy*, 292, 1987

Brooks, A H, The use of geology on the Western Front. *United States Geological Survey Professional Paper*, 128-D, 1920

Couthard, R W, Tunnelling at the Front, *Transactions of the Canadian Mining Institute*, 22, 1919

Davis, A W, Tunnelling reminiscences, *Transactions of the Canadian Mining Institute*, 22, 1919

Desfossés, Y, & Jacques, A, Vers une definition et une reconnaissance de l'archéologie de la Première Guerre mondiale, *14-18 Aujourd'hui*,1999

Deguent, R, Les Inondations sur le Front Belge, *Revue du Genie Militaire*, August, 1928

Doyle, P, Battlefield conservation: conserving the heritage of the underground war in Flanders, *Battlefields Review*, 12, 2001

Doyle, P and Bennett, M R, Military geography:

terrain evaluation and the British Western Front, 1914-18, *Geographical Journal*, 163, 1997

Doyle, P, Barton, P and Rosenbaum, M S, Geohazards: last legacy of warfare? *Geoscientist*, 11, 2001.

Doyle, P, Barton, P and Rosenbaum, M R, Archives and field observation as the basis for geohazard assessment of the legacy from warfare: the impact of military tunnels on the town of Nieuwpoort, Belgium, in Nathanail, C P, Rosenbaum, M S, and Turner, A K (eds), *Characterisation of the shallow subsurface: Implications for urban infrastructure and environmental assessment.* TUD Publishers, Delft, 2001

Doyle, P, Barton, P, Rosenbaum, M S, Vandewalle, J and Jacobs, K, Geoenvironmental implications of the underground war in Flanders, 1914–1918, *Environmental Geology*, 2002

Doyle, P, Barton, P, Saunders, N and Vandewalle, J, Archaeology of a Great War dugout: Beecham Farm, Passchendaele, Belgium, *Cambridge Archaeological Journal*, in preparation

Doyle, P, Bennett, M R, Macleod, R and Mackay, L, Terrain and the Battle of Messines, 1917, in Doyle, P and Bennett, M R (eds), *Fields of Battle: Terrain in Military History*, Kluwer, Rotterdam, 2002

Doyle, P, Bostyn, F, Barton, P and Vandewalle, J, The underground war 1914-18: the geology of the Beecham dugout, Passchendaele, Belgium, *Proceedings of the Geologists' Association*, 112, 2001.

Eagar, G F F, The training of officers and men of the Tunnelling Companies of the Royal Engineers in mine-rescue work on active service in France, *Transactions of the Institution of Mining Engineers*, 58, 1919–20

Füsslein, Otto, Der Mineur in Flandern, in *Im Felde Unbesiegt*, 1921

Griffiths, P, The effects of weather conditions on the third Battle of Ypres, 1917, *University of Birmingham School of Geography, Working Paper Series*, 51, 1989

Hammond, Bryn, Professionals and specialists: Military mining on the Western Front, *Imperial War Museum Review*, No. 6, 1992

King, W B R, Geological work on the Western Front, *Geographical Journal*, 54, 1919

Kranz, W, Militärgeologie, *Kriegstechnische Zeitschift*, 16, 1913

Kranz, W, Minierkampf und Kriegsgeologie im Wytschaetebogen, *Vierteljahreshefte für Pioniere*, 1935

Leriche, Maurice, Observations sur la constitution géologique des colines belges des environs de Bailleul de d'Ypres, *Bulletin de la Société belge de Géologie*, 30, 1920

Logan, D Dale, The difficulties and dangers of mine-rescue work on the Western Front; and mining operations carried out by men wearing rescue-appartatus, *Transactions of the Institution of Mining Engineers*, 57, 1919

Macleod, Roy, Phantom soldiers, Australian tunnellers on the Western Front 1916-1918, *Journal of the Australian War Memorial*, 13, 1988

Macleod, Roy, 'Kriegsgeologen and practical men': military geology and modern memory, *British Journal of the History of Science*, 28, 1995

Mullins, Lawrence E, The mines at Messines, *Military Review, Professional Journal of the United States Army*, April 1965

Murray, R R, Tunnelling in the Ypres Salient, *Annual Journal of the United Services Institute of Nova Scotia*, 1929

Reynolds, L B, Mining in chalk on the Western Front, *Transactions of the Canadian Mining Institute*, 22, 1919

Riebecke, O, Der Kreig in der Erde, in *Unsere Pioniere in Weltkreige*, 1920

Robinson, Phillip, The abandoned Messines mines. *Battlefields Review*, 3, 1999

Rose, E P F, Häusler, H and Willig, D, Comparison of British and German applications of geology in world war, in Rose, E P F and Nathanail, E (eds), *Geology and Warfare*, Geological Society, London, 2001

Rose, E P F and Rosenbaum, M S, British military geologists: the formative years to the end of the First World War, *Proceedings of the Geologists' Association*, 104, 1993.

Rosenbaum, M S, Lu, P, Doyle, P, and Barton, P, The impact of old military tunnels on buildings at the town of Nieuwpoort, Belgium, *Proceedings of the 7th International Conference on Inspection, Appraisal, Repairs and Maintenance of Buildings and Structures*, Nottingham, 2001

Rosenbaum, M S and Rose, E P F, Geology and military tunnels, *Geology Today*, 1992

The Sapper, bound volumes, Royal Engineers' Library, 1914–1919

Saunders, N J, Excavating memories: archaeology and the Great War, *Antiquity*, 76, 2002

Tatham, H, Tunnelling in the sand dunes of the Belgian Coast, *Transactions of the Institution of Mining and Metallurgy*, 28, 1919

Trounce, H D, Notes on military mining, *Occasional Paper Number 57*, Engineer School US Army, Washington Barracks, DC, 1918

'Tunneller', Messines, *Tunnellers' Old Comrades Association Bulletin*, 5, 1930

Tunnellers Old Comrades Association Bulletin, 1–14, 1926–1939

Varley, Paul M, British Tunnelling Machines in the First World War, *Newcomen Society*, October 1993

Walker, J W, Mining on the Western Front, *Land and Mineral Surveying*, 6, 1988 [Reprinted from Institute of Mine Surveyors, 1920]

Weatherbe, K, Blind Man's Bluff, *Canadian Defence Quarterly*

Woodward, O H, Notes on the work of an Australian Tunnelling Company in France, *Proceedings of the Australian Institute of Mining and Metallurgy*, 37, 1920

MILITARY MANUALS

Field Works for Royal Artillery, General Staff, May 1918

Field Works for Pioneer Battalions, General Staff, 1918

Military Engineering: Mining and Demolitions Part IV, 1910

Military Engineering: Mining and Demolitions Part IV, 1910 (reprinted 1915)

Military Engineering Part IV – Mining and Demolitions, 1915

Military Engineering (Vol. IV): Demolitions and Mining, 1923

Military Engineering (Vol. IV): Demolitions and Mining, 1934

Manual of Military Engineering, 1905

Manual of Field Engineering, 1911

Manual of Field Works (All Arms), 1921

Manual of Field Works (All Arms), 1925

OFFICIAL PAPERS AND REPORTS

Instruction in Military Engineering, Volume I Part IV, Military Mining, HMSO, 1883

Instruction in Military Engineering, Part I, Mining and Demolitions, HMSO, 1892

Military Mines and Blasting Under Water, C W Pasley BC Colonel, RE, FRS, Royal Engineer Establishment, 1836

Mining Operations at Chatham in 1868, The Royal Engineers, Chatham, 1868

Notes on Field Defences, Number 13 – Employment of Tunnelling Companies RE, General Staff, June 1915.

Notes on Field Fortifications, Anon., Royal Engineers, Chatham, c.1824

Practical Operations on Mining 1844, Anon, Royal Engineers, Chatham, 1844

Proceedings of the Royal Engineer Committee, various extracts, 1910–1920

Register of Tunnelling Company Officers, 1925

Reports on Military Operations by The Royal Engineer Establishment of Chatham on Friday 11th August 1848, Anon., Royal Engineers, Chatham, 1848

Report of the Siege Operations and Mining Practice carried out at the S.M.E. Chatham, 1877. Lt. Col. J P Maquay RE, Instructor in Field Fortification. Royal Engineers, 1877

Report of a Preliminary Siege Staff Ride held at Chatham, 6th–10th May, 1907, and subsequent Siege Operations held at Chatham, July and August, 1907. School of Military Engineering, 1907

Report on Japanese Mining Operations at Kokura, Japan, 10th to 26th October 1906. Brevet Colonel C V Hume MVO, DSO, RA, War Office, February 1907

Rules for Military Mining according to the Royal Engineer Establishment at Chatham, Chatham, 1853

Siege Operations carried out by the 20th and 42nd Companies, Royal Engineers, June 1913. Major G R Pridham, RE, War Office, 1913

Statistics of the Military Effort of the British Empire, HMSO, 1922

Training of the RE, During the Last Three Years of the War, Reports by Inspector of RE, Brigadier A W Roper RE, 1918

MISCELLANEOUS

Transcript of *'An Explosion like an Earthquake'*, by J MacD Royle (1st Australian TC) 2BL Australia Radio Children's Session, 1934

The Underground War, Parapet Productions and Foxy Films for Channel 4, 1998

PICTURE AND ILLUSTRATION REFERENCES

IWM – Imperial War Museum
AWM – Australian War Memorial
JV – Johan Vandewalle
NA – National Archives, Kew
(Formerly Public Record Office)
PA – Parapet Archives
REL – Royal Engineers Library
REM – Royal Engineers Museum

6, Dedication photographs. Courtesy of the Fearns family
7, Preface drawing from *The Sapper* magazine, 1916

Chapter I
17, Henri Geeraerts. From *Nieuport* by Captain Robert Thys. See bibliography
18/19, Panorama, inundations; IWM, Panorama no. 72
18, French troops; JV
19/20, Panorama, Ypres from Passchendaele, April 1915; IWM Q47784
22, JV
23, Top: REC Extracts 1916; bottom, JV
24, Menin Gate 1917; IWM, E 3102

Chapter II
34, Captain Fulton, REL
35, 36, Russo–Japanese War, REL
38, 39, Japanese mining exercises, REL

Chapter III
42, Sgt Major Hanson, PA
43, Mine blow, REL
44, Mining Exercises, Chatham, REL
48, New Expeditionary Force, REL
49, Volunteers, Peter Doyle collection
51, German *Pioniere*, JV

Chapter IV
54, Broodseinde Crater, JV
55, Mine shaft, PA; mine plan, REL
57, John Norton Griffiths, courtesy of Anne Morgan
58, 2nd King Edward's Horse, courtesy of Anne Morgan
59, Manchester sewermen, courtesy of Manchester Museum and Art Galleries
62, Tunnelling Officer Class, REL
67, Tunnellers' camp and hut, courtesy of Patience Hilton
68, Top, 172 TC officers, courtesy of Patience Hilton; bottom, German officers, courtesy of Ross Thomas
69, *Pioniere* Group, courtesy of Ross Thomas
70, Otto Füsslein, courtesy of Simon Jones

Chapter V
72, Lt W B R King, courtesy of Dr Ted Rose
73, Edgeworth David, courtesy of Ross Thomas; Brigadier-General Harvey, REL
75, Top and bottom left, REL; bottom right, IWM HU87951
76, Vimy tunnels, PA
77, RE Boring Team, IWM, Q 31681
78, Test Bore map, NA, WO 153 / 915

Chapter VI
80, German miners, courtesy of Ross Thomas
82, Tubbed Shaft, JV
85, Listening gallery, JV
86, Merckem dugout, JV
87, German miners picking, courtesy of Spellmount Publishers
88 and 89, JV
90, JV

91, Timber store, IWM, CO 3068; bottom JV
92, Miner's Dial, Parapet Archive; bottom, courtesy of Ross Thomas
93, German miners, courtesy of Ross Thomas
94, Courtesy of the National Museums, Liverpool N2004.0027
96, left German tramway, JV; right, Monorail, REL
98, Listening stick IWM, FLM198
101, Geophone operator, REL
103, German listeners, PA
106, Listening Station, REL; Hawthorn Ridge mine chamber, IWM, HU 87950
107, RSG Stokes, REL
109, Hollandscheschuur plan, NA, WO 153/221
110, Air supply, REL
111, French miners, JV; captured mining gear, courtesy of Patience Hilton
112, Ammonal charge at Vimy, PA
117, German gallery, JV
119, Mine plan, fuses and test blows, REL
120, Practice mines, REL
121, Wisques crater, IWM, Q 4163
122, Cuinchy crater, PA
122/123, Bluff panorama section, IWM, Q 44434–44437
123, Aerial photo, REL
124, Fortified crater, IWM, Q 41761

Chapter VII
127, Rescue kit, REL
128, Whitwick rescue team, NA WO 158/129
129, Proto dugout, IWM, E 1683
130, RE Rescue team, REL, Proto-man, IWM FLM 1983
131, Tunnellers Friends Memorial, Peter Doyle collection
133, Bratticing, REL
137, Knuckle-knife, REM; .303 Rifle, NA, WO 158/137
139, JV

Chapter VIII
142, IWM, FLM 1981
143, 175 Group, courtesy Spellmount Publishers
145, Norton-Griffiths' Rolls-Royce, courtesy of Anne Morgan
146, Norton-Griffiths in trench, courtesy of Anne Morgan
149, Captain G R Cassels, courtesy of David Cassels; Hooge, PA
150, Hooge, PA; 177 plan, REL
151, Push-pick, PA
153, PA
154, Top left, PA; others courtesy of Ross Thomas
155, All photographs courtesy of Patience Hilton
156, All pictures courtesy of Patience Hilton
157, Diary page, REL; Mine blow, courtesy of Patience Hilton
158, Shaft, courtesy of Patience Hilton; message page, REL
159, St Eloi crater, courtesy of Ross Thomas; St Eloi crater panorama, IWM
160, Norton-Griffiths, courtesy of Anne Morgan
161, cartoon, REL

Chapter IX
161/162, Hill 60 panorama, IWM, Q44172
163, Trench on Hill 60, IWM, Q 45382
165, German Mining officers, courtesy of Ross Thomas
166, Top and bottom left, courtesy of Ross Thomas, bottom right, JV

167, Mining plan, NA WO 153 / 449
168, Excavation, JV; Canadian mine plan NA WO 158/153; Hill 60 plan, NA, WO 153 / 909
169, Hill 60 plan, courtesy of Col. Phillip Robinson
170, Australian Mining battalion, courtesy of Mrs Barbara Woodward
171, Hill 60 firing party, courtesy of Mrs Barbara Woodward
173, Factory Farm mines, NA, WO 153/909
174, Bois Quarante Shaft, JV
175, JV
176, Petite Douve plan, NA WO 153/909
177, Peckham mines, NA WO 153/909
178, Spanbroekmolen mine, NA WO 153/909
179, Clay-cutting machine courtesy of AWM
180, plans, top, NA, WO 158/205 ; bottom, NA, WO 158/153
181, Top secret map, REL

Chapter X
185, IWM, FLM 1986
187, Cartoon, REL; Exploder, JV
188, Kruistraat plan, NA, WO 153/909; Peckham crater, JV
189, German sections, German Official History
190, IWM, E 1269
191, IWM, Q 100633
192, Birdcage mines, NA, WO 153 / 909
193, Caterpillar Crater, JV; Hollandscheschuur mine plan, NA WO 153/909
194, Petit Bois plan, NA, WO 153/909; Petit Bois craters, JV
197, courtesy of Ross Thomas
198, JV
201, Peter Doyle

Chapter XI
203, top IWM Q 1384; bottom left, IWM, Q 51533; bottom right, JV
204, JV
205, REL
206, Dugout frame, IWM, Q 48949; plan and section, REL
207, Skeggs photographs, PA
208, bottom, REL
208/209, top, IWM, E 1400; bottom, REL
211, JV
212, JV
213, JV
214/215, Panorama, PA
216, Lt Hickling, courtesy of Patience Hilton; Front Line Post, REL
217, Lille Gate, JV; Ramparts dugouts, IWM, Q 2894; dugout plans, REL
218, Top and middle, REL; bottom left IWM, Q 3892; bottom right, IWM, Q 55317
219, Top, REL; bottom, JV
221, Top, JV; bottom IWM

Chapter XII
224, IWM, E 1504
225, Top IWM; Q 44621 bottom left, IWM, E 1661; bottom right, JV
226, Top, JV; bottom, Peter Doyle
227, Diagrams, REL; Cut-and-cover, IWM, Q 4598
228/229, Canal dugout plan, REL
228, Canal dugouts, IWM, Q 45947
230, Dugouts and geology, NA, WO 158/163; Wieltje plan, REL
230, REL
232, Drawings, REL; dugout interior, REM

233, Photo, IWM E 1712; drawing and plans, REL
234, Incline and chamber, JV; 'Catacombs', IWM, E 4487; plan, REL
236, Larch Wood, courtesy of Col. Phillip Robinson; bunking, IWM E 4622
237, JV; drawing, REL
238, REL
239, Panorama, PA; drawings, REL
240, Drawings, REL; dugout interior, IWM, E 690
241, REL
242, Drawings, REL; Martha House, JV
243, Cookhouse, REL; photos, JV
244, Indian foresters, IWM, Q 849; women forestry workers IWM, Q 3070
245, Diagrams, REL; photos, JV
246, Boyaux Couvert, IWM E 4631; drawings, REL
247, Top, IWM, E 1396; middle left, IWM, E 4621; middle right, IWM, E 1513; Hooge plan, PA
251, JV; drawings, REL
252, Top, IWM Q 15; bottom two photos, JV
253, Westacott drawing, REM
254, Ventilator, IWM CO 3036; drawings, REL
255, Wombat borer, IWM, E 1687
256, Drawings, REL; Winching out wounded, JV
257, Drawings PA; Germans with dog, JV
258, PA
259, Top, IWM, CO 3801; bottom, Peter Doyle collection
260, 255 TC Officers, courtesy of Mr Martin Morton
261, Peter Doyle collection
262, Top, JV; bottom, Birr Cross Roads plan, REL

Chapter XIII
265, Top and bottom left, Peter Doyle; Estaminet, IWM, Q 100381; pilgrims with tank, courtesy of Mr Martin Morton
266, IWM, Q 100915
267, JV
268, Left, courtesy of the In Flanders Fields Documentation Centre, Ieper; right, JV
269, courtesy of the In Flanders Fields Documentation Centre
270, JV
271, JV
272, JV
273, Left, JV, right, REL
274, JV
275, Left, IWM, Q 51039; right, Peter Doyle
276, courtesy of Bactec International
277, JV
278, JV
279, JV
280, JV
281, JV
282, JV
283, Map section, REL
284, JV; dugout construction, IWM
285, JV
286, JV
287, JV
288, JV

Epilogue
289, Courtesy of Mr Martin Morton
291, REL
292, Sapper William Hackett, REL

INDEX

CHAMBER OF St. ELOI MINE

BLOWN JUNE 7th, 1917.

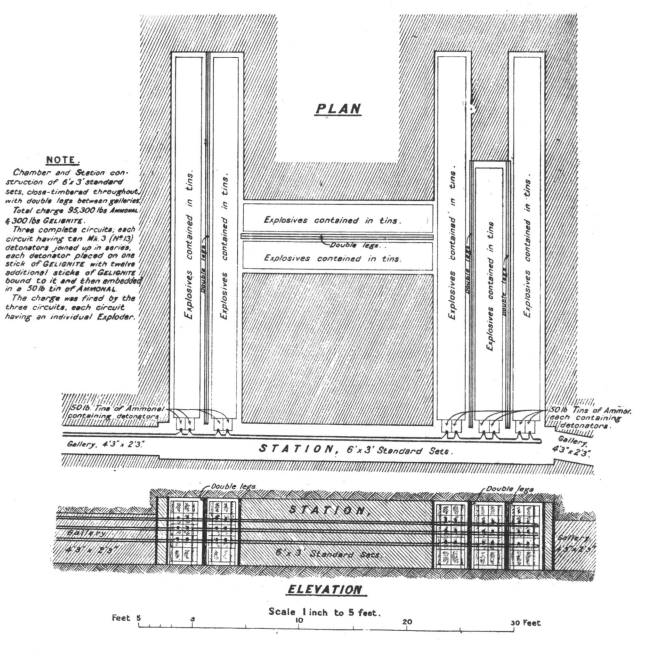

PLAN

NOTE.

Chamber and Station construction of 6'x 3' standard sets, close-timbered throughout, with double legs between galleries.

Total charge 95,300 lbs Ammonal & 300 lbs Gelignite.

Three complete circuits; each circuit having ten Mk. 3 (Nº 13) detonators joined up in series, each detonator placed on one stick of Gelignite with twelve additional sticks of Gelignite bound to it and then embedded in a 50 lb tin of Ammonal.

The charge was fired by the three circuits, each circuit having an individual Exploder.

Explosives contained in tins.

Explosives contained in tins.
Double legs.
Explosives contained in tins.

50 lb. Tins of Ammonal containing detonators.

50 lb Tins of Ammonal each containing detonators.

Gallery, 4'3"x 2'3".

STATION, 6'x3' Standard Sets.

Gallery, 4'3"x2'3".

STATION

Gallery 4'3"x 2'3".

6'x 3' Standard Sets.

Gallery 4'3"x 2'3".

Double legs.

Double legs.

ELEVATION

Scale 1 inch to 5 feet.

Feet 5   5   10   20   30 Feet